ELEMENTS

OF

ART CRITICISM

COMPRISING A TREATISE ON

THE PRINCIPLES OF MAN'S NATURE

AS ADDRESSED BY ART

TOGETHER WITH A HISTORIC SURVEY OF

THE METHODS OF ART EXECUTION

IN THE DEPARTMENTS OF

DRAWING, SCULPTURE, ARCHITECTURE, PAINTING, LANDSCAPE GARDENING, AND THE DECORATIVE ARTS.

DESIGNED AS

A Text Book for Schools and Colleges,

AND AS

A HAND-BOOK FOR AMATEURS AND ARTISTS.

ABRIDGED EDITION.

BY G. W. SAMSON, D.D.,

PRESIDENT OF COLUMBIAN COLLEGE, WASHINGTON, D. C.

PHILADELPHIA

J. B. LIPPINCOTT & CO.

1874

INTRODUCTION.

THE following treatise on Art Criticism, an abridged edition of the larger work published one year ago, is specially designed to meet a demand whose existence has now been called forth. The aim of both is to awaken, to foster and to aid the growing aspiration of American students and amateurs in art.

The Introduction to the larger work indicates the lack in American education which creates this demand, the methods by which teachers in other lands and ages have supplied this common æsthetic need, and the nature and ground of the author's attempt.

The conviction is general that a compendious elementary treatise on the principles of design and the methods of execution in the fine arts is a special desideratum in American literature. The general education of American youth, male and female, the aspiration of men in every pursuit to fit themselves for cultured society, the growing fondness for foreign travel, have awakened a desire for compendious information as to the great world of art. The limited time given to general education, and the brief leisure of business men, have created in the United States a demand for text-books in science rudimentary in principle and elementary in illustration; while in Europe, alike in England, Germany and France, there has been a corresponding call for condensed descriptive hand-books adapted to the traveling community. To supply both these needs, akin to each other as they are, has been the author's aim.

The larger work presents the comprehensive statement of principles and the compendious abstract of history essential to the teacher and artist; while it adds citations from authorities ancient and modern for the purpose of confirmation and illustration. The abridged edition omits no important principle and passes by no important field of history; but it leaves to the teacher, with the aid of the fuller work and his own collateral study, to fill up the outline.

To the abridged edition a few pages of outline illustrations, especially in architecture, are added for pupils. Teachers will naturally provide themselves with large drawings taken from numerous works at command. The thorough student can now obtain also stereoscopic views of every important work in sculpture and architecture, and photographic copies of the gems of every European gallery of paintings; which, with suitable magnifying lenses, will introduce him to the subjects of almost every section in the treatise now offered to the public.

CONTENTS.

BOOK I.

MAN'S NATURE AND RELATIONS TO THE WORLD AS AFFECTED BY ART.

CHAPTER I.

GENERAL VIEW OF THE CONSTITUTION OF MAN AS DESIGNED TO BE ADDRESSED BY ART.

CHAPTER II.

THE LOWER SENSES INDIRECTLY CONTRIBUTING TO THE IMPRESSIONS MADE BY ART.

CHAPTER III.

THE IMPRESSIONS OF THE HIGHER SENSE OF HEARING AS ADDRESSED BY ART.

CHAPTER VII.

THE INFLUENCE OF NATURAL CHARACTERISTICS AND OF DEGREES OF CULTURE IN MODIFYING THE IMPRESSIONS PRODUCED BY ART.

BOOK II.

DRAWING; THE REPRESENTING OF FORMS ON A PLANE SURFACE.

CHAPTER I.

PLANE DRAWING; THE REPRESENTING OF FORMS AS LOCATED IN A SINGLE PLANE.

CHAPTER V.

DESIGN IN DRAWING.

BOOK III.

SCULPTURE; THE EXECUTING OF FORMS IN ALL THEIR DIMENSIONS.

CHAPTER I.

GENERAL PRINCIPLES RELATING TO THE EXECUTION AND CLASSIFICATION OF WORKS OF SCULPTURE.

CHAPTER II.

PRIMITIVE SCULPTURE; ILLUSTRATED IN THE EGYPTIAN.

CHAPTER III.

CLASSIC SCULPTURE EMBODIED IN THE GRECIAN.

CHAPTER IV.

MODERN SCULPTURE; PLASTIC ART AS AFFECTED BY CHRISTIAN CIVILIZATION.

BOOK IV.

ARCHITECTURE; OR THE COMBINING OF FORMS, WITH THE UNITED ENDS OF UTILITY AND BEAUTY.

CHAPTER I.

ORIGIN OF ARCHITECTURE AS AN ART; AND THE PRINCIPLES CONTROLLING ITS FORMS.

CHAPTER II.

EGYPTIAN, THE TYPE OF ASIATIC ARCHITECTURE; IN WHICH MASSIVENESS IS THE AIM.

CHAPTER III.

GRECIAN ARCHITECTURE; CHARACTERIZED BY MATHEMATICAL EXACTNESS IN FORMS AND DELICATE GRACE IN ADORNMENT.

CHAPTER IV.

ROMAN ARCHITECTURE; CHARACTERIZED BY STATELINESS IN DIMENSIONS AND PROFUSE ELEGANCE IN ORNAMENTATION.

CHAPTER V.

SACRED ARCHITECTURE, AS CONTROLLED BY THE SPIRITUAL WORSHIP AND THE PRACTICAL CHARITY OF THE CHRISTIAN FAITH.

CHAPTER VI.

SECULAR ARCHITECTURE AS INFLUENCED BY THE SOCIAL AND INTELLECTUAL, THE CIVIL AND DOMESTIC WANTS INDUCED BY CHRISTIAN CIVILIZATION.

BOOK V.

PAINTING; THE ADDING OF COLOR TO FORM.

CHAPTER I.

THE ANALYSIS AND COMPOSITION OF COLORS.

CHAPTER II.

GENERAL PRINCIPLES AS TO THE EMPLOY OF COLORS IN PAINTING.

CHAPTER III.

MATERIALS AND SPECIAL METHODS OF USING THEM IN COLORING; AND CONSEQUENT CLASSIFICATION OF AGES, STYLES AND SCHOOLS IN PAINTING.

CHAPTER IV.

ASIATIC PAINTING; RUDIMENTARY COLORING DEVOID OF TRUE ART IN FORM AND SHADING.

CHAPTER V.

GRECIAN PAINTING; NATURAL COLOR UNITED TO IDEAL FORM.

CHAPTER VI.

ROMAN AND MEDIÆVAL PAINTING; CHARACTERIZED BY ARTIFICIAL COLOR AS AN ADJUNCT AND ORNAMENT OF ARCHITECTURAL FORMS.

CHAPTER VII.

THE RISE OF MODERN PAINTING IN SOUTHERN EUROPE, INCLUDING ITALY AND SPAIN; PRE-EMINENTLY RELIGIOUS IN ITS THEMES, CLASSIC IN FORMS, AND SPECIALLY CHARACTERIZED BY PERFECTION OF LIGHTS IN COLORING.

CHAPTER VIII.

THE ADVANCE OF MODERN PAINTING IN CENTRAL EUROPE; INCLUDING GERMANY, THE NETHERLANDS, HOLLAND AND FRANCE; EMINENTLY SECULAR IN SUBJECTS, NATURAL IN STYLE AND CHARACTERIZED BY PERFECTION OF SHADES IN COLORING.

CHAPTER IX.

THE LATE DEVELOPMENT OF MODERN PAINTING IN ENGLAND AND AMERICA; COMPREHENSIVE IN SUBJECT AND AIM, AS WELL AS IN THE NATIONALITY OF ITS ARTISTS; NATIVE IN CONCEPTION, BUT CULTURED IN STYLE.

BOOK VI.

LANDSCAPE-GARDENING; THE GROUPING OF NATURAL OBJECTS TO SECURE ARTISTIC EFFECTS OF FORM, COLOR, RELATION AND MOTION.

CHAPTER I.

THE EFFECTS TO BE SOUGHT IN LANDSCAPE-GARDENING.

CHAPTER II.

THE MATERIALS BY WHICH THE EFFECTS OF LANDSCAPE-GARDENING ARE SECURED.

CHAPTER III.

ANCIENT AND ASIATIC STYLES OF LANDSCAPE-GARDENING.

CHAPTER IV.

MODERN EUROPEAN LANDSCAPE-GARDENING.

BOOK VII.

THE DECORATIVE ARTS; ARTIFICIAL ACCESSORIES AND ORNAMENTS OF OBJECTS IN NATURE AND OF WORKS IN ART.

CHAPTER I.

THE FIELD OF DECORATIVE ART; COEXTENSIVE WITH HUMAN WANTS; AND VARIED ACCORDING TO MATERIAL EMPLOYED AND TASTE EXERCISED.

CHAPTER II.

ASIATIC DECORATIVE ART; RUDIMENTARY IN STYLE, DEFECTIVE IN FORM, EXCESSIVE IN ORNAMENT, BUT ELABORATE IN FINISH.

CHAPTER III.

EUROPEAN DECORATIVE ART; CONTROLLED BY THE ALTERNATING PROGRESS AND DECLINE OF SCIENCE AND ART, OF SOCIAL, INTELLECTUAL, MORAL AND RELIGIOUS IMPROVEMENT.

ART CRITICISM.

BOOK I.

MAN'S NATURE AND RELATIONS TO THE WORLD AS AFFECTED BY ART.

ART addresses the mind through some one of the bodily organs. Its appeals, unlike mere corporeal impressions, affect the mind as well as the body with pleasurable emotions; while too, unlike purely intellectual or spiritual impressions, such as the delight of Newton in mathematical calculations and the rapture of Descartes in metaphysical inquiries, they are always accompanied by and are produced through a sensation on the bodily organs.

The eye is the chief organ through which art addresses men; yet the other organs of sense, especially the ear, have their own classes of art to appeal to them; while it is the combination and co-operation of all these that give the highest delight possible. When, for instance, in a ride through a beautiful country in spring, the fanning of the warm breeze is a soothing luxury to the touch, the exhilaration of gentle motion gives a delightful play to every muscle, the fragrance of the flowers refreshes the sense of smell, the flavor of the first ripe fruits feasts the palate, the singing of the birds makes melody for the ear, and the ever-varied forms and hues of hill and vale, mountain and meadow, leaf and flower, insect and bird, beasts and passing human beings, give a never-ending variety in their address to the eye, we are satisfied, that while all our senses were given for our pleasure, the organ of vision is the one to which the broader field has been assigned. These suggestions hint the appropriate order to be followed, and the proportionate consideration to be given in treating of the powers in us to which art makes its appeal.

CHAPTER I.

GENERAL VIEW OF THE CONSTITUTION OF MAN AS DESIGNED TO BE ADDRESSED BY ART.

THERE is in us by creation an *admiration* of art. By implanting this capacity the "Father of Spirits" has declared his design that it should be cultured as a source of happiness and a means of virtue. There is also created within us a fondness for the *imitation* of art. By endowing us with this faculty our Creator intimates that it should be exercised as a power for promoting the happiness and virtue of others.

SECT. 1. THE WORLD WITHOUT US AS MADE FOR THE ENJOYMENT AND THE EMPLOYMENT OF ART SENSIBILITY.

When God made man in his own image, and he was perfect in all his powers, we read that he made every tree *first* "pleasant to the eyes," *then* "good for food." The eye saw the *beauty* of the fruit *before* the palate tasted its sweets; the intellect was addressed more than the mere bodily sense; the delights of the mind were made both to precede and to exceed those of the flesh. The *love of art*, and the power it exerts to promote man's happiness and welfare, was the first made to bless and govern us. The infant is stilled as readily by a pretty toy, or by the nurse's song, as it is by the luxury of its mother's milk. This is the first element entering into our love of art and our impulse to make it our study.

We read again that man was placed in Eden, where every tree was *already* "pleasant to the eye," "to *dress* and to keep it." There were additional forms of beauty and grandeur that man was made to conceive and execute, which, even amid the Creator's perfect works, might be studied and put into shape. In all Adam's posterity the love of *doing* and of *making* is a natural impulse.

The child loves to draw and to make letters before he cares to learn their names and their connections in words. The first impulse of even the maturest mind on taking up any volume is to examine the artistic illustrations; for the artist speaks quicker to the eye than the pages of the author can speak to the mind.

SECT. 2. THE NATURE WITHIN US TO WHICH ART APPEALS.

Philosophers have divided the elementary principles entering into our impressions of things and beings into three distinct classes: "The True, the Beautiful, and the Good." To this analysis ethical philosophy adds "the Right." The love of the true, the beautiful, the good, and the right, with the aspiration to attain them as a personal possession, forms the ideal of a complete man. Truth speaks to the intellect, beauty to the sensibilities, goodness to the instincts, and righteousness to the conscience of man.

Under the idea of the beautiful is included an extended class of emotions; as the admiration of the delicate and the graceful, of the melodious and the harmonious, of the grand and the sublime. These emotions, when produced by objects appealing either to the eye or to the ear, or to the conception of the mind, make up what is properly termed "the love of art;" and the objects of perception and conception, which man has created in order to awaken these emotions, come under the designation of "The Fine Arts."

The fine arts, as distinguished from the useful arts, are those that appeal to the love of beauty in distinction from the love of utility. *Art* is properly human skill in constructing. When the end sought and the result secured in the employ of human skill is an article for man's *use*, without regard to its beauty, that skill in constructing belongs to the class of useful arts. When the end sought and the result secured by this skill is an object that awakens pleasurable emotions, without reference to the idea of utility, that work of skill belongs to the fine arts.

SECT. 3. THE BODILY ORGANS THROUGH WHICH ART ADDRESSES THE HUMAN MIND.

Man has five organs of sense, smell and taste; touch, to which some add the muscular sense; and hearing and sight. These the practical and discriminating Grecian philosopher Aristotle grouped in two classes; those which receive impressions from objects by immediate bodily contact with them, as taste, touch, and the muscular impressions associated with touch; and those which receive knowledge of objects at a distance, as sight, hearing and smell.

Regarding the pleasures attending their exercise, the senses are appropriately arranged in three classes; *first*, smell and taste; *second*, touch and muscular pressure; *third*, hearing and sight.

To the first of these, smell and taste, belong the grosser and purely material pleasures. It is only by a direct meeting and mingling of the material bodies not belonging to our organism with the organs that taste can address us; while smell is made chiefly to be a servant to taste. Yet even these lower senses become dignified when made associates of the higher impressions of art.

Next to these lower and material pleasures come those of touch, including the whole range of muscular and nervous sensation common to the entire bodily frame; which, as Hobbes suggested, may be called *physical*. The delight of the fanning breeze and of the laving bath, the gambols of the lamb and of the child, the luxury of action and toil in every stage and department of human life, minister indirectly to the mind's pleasant as well as successful employ.

The directly *intellectual* impressions and pleasures are those derived from the eye and the ear. In smell, taste and touch, as Lord Kames suggests, we are conscious of contact with the object producing the impression; hence we naturally refer the pleasures derived from these sensations to the organs themselves; and therefore we properly as well as naturally regard these pleasures as corporeal. In pleasures derived through the eye and ear, however, we do not at all think of the eye and the ear as the seat of the sensation experienced; we refer the delights of sight and hearing immediately to the mind itself. Hence Kames ranked these as intermediate between purely intellectual and corporeal impressions and pleasures.

It is important to note that the ancient Greek writers on art laid great stress on the media which, as they supposed, intervene first between the external object and the higher organs of sense, and second between those bodily organs and the mind dwelling within. Impressions are made, they imagined, on the eye, the ear, and also on the organs of smell, through subtle fluids, air and ether, whose vibrations extend from the objects to the organs; and one of the nice distinctions between the theories of Plato and Aris totle as to the source of human knowledge was the question whether, as Plato averred, these vibrations originated in the organ, or, as Aristotle argued, they proceeded from the object. The same ancient writers believed that a yet more subtle fluid intervenes between the organ and the spirit; an agent intermediate between matter and spirit. This agent Plato regarded as the medium through which higher intelligence inspires the poet and artist. Modern science finds important truth in these ancient theories, and art learns much from antiquity while mindful of them.

SECT. 4. THE METHODS BY WHICH ARTISTS MAKE THEIR ADDRESSES TO HUMAN SENSIBILITIES.

The power of art to sway men may be traced in every age and clime. Its exuberant early aspiring is seen in the Assyrian tower which was to reach heaven with its top, and in Egyptian statues cut out of mountains and Egyptian pyramids reared as new mountains in their place. It is observed in its humbler form in the nicely-carved articles of ebony and ivory brought now from the centre of Africa, in the coral and shell ornaments of the simple islanders of Polynesia, and in the hideously-adorned pipes and tomahawks of the rude natives of America.

The Greeks spoke of the origin of art and of its power over their ancestors under the legend of Orpheus, who charmed the forest trees and wild beasts with the music of his lyre. The idea cloaked under this imagery is the power of mental culture, beginning with the attractive instruction that comes through the fine arts, to influence men for good. In that early era all arts were united in one; but afterward philosophers began to classify the arts. The Muses, the spirits presiding over art, were divided first into three: *Melete*, Thought; *Mneme*, Memory; and *Aœde*, Expression. At a later day, when the analysis of art, and of the sensibilities to which it appeals, became more elaborate, nine subdivisions of the third, *Aœde*, were made. Their names and symbols were these: *Clio*, History, pictured with an open scroll in her hand; *Melpomene*, Tragedy, veiled, leaning on a pillar, and holding in her left hand a tragic mask; *Thalia*, Comedy, holding in one hand a comic mask, in the other an augur's wand; *Euterpe*, Music, holding two flutes; *Terpsichore*, the Dance, in a dancing attitude, playing upon a seven-stringed lyre; *Erato*, Amatory Poetry, holding a nine-stringed lyre; *Calliope*, Epic Poetry, with a roll of parchment in one hand, and a straight trumpet sometimes in the other; *Urania*, Astronomy, holding a globe in her left hand and a pointing rod in her right; *Polyhymnia*, Histrionic Art or Eloquence, with the forefinger of her right hand on her lips or a scroll in her hand.

At a very early day the Muses were inaugurated as chief teachers in the schools of Greece. Pythagoras, about B. C. 500, learned in Egyptian methods of instruction, introduced *music* into his school; that term including the whole range of philosophic and artistic studies. As a figure of the harmony of the universe, he taught the "music of the spheres;" that the heavenly bodies in their steady sweep through space produce, as on an Æolian harp, a beautiful and sublime harmony. Nearly one hundred years before Plato, Eumolpus of Sicyon, near Corinth, introduced into the common schools of Greece instruction both in the principles and the execution of art; so that all the boys thus trained could not only appreciate and justly criticise the works of their artists, but could even themselves execute works of plastic art. Athens was not long in copying such a suggestion. Plato speaks of education in his time as "first for the body gymnastic, then for the soul *musical.*" Pericles and cultured men generally, as Plutarch mentions, were trained to the highest degree of skill in art.

The influence of this training in chastening the sensibilities and moulding the character was most powerful and most happy. The religion of the Greek was love of art; their deities were embodiments of art ideas; and the common property of the state, the *res publica*, consisted of collections of art in temples and statutes, to whose increasing fund the Athenian people willingly devoted half their time and labor, while their own private houses were of the plainest style. Art education raised the Greek people to the highest rank in intellectual advancement and in moral refinement. Most of all, it begat in them that exalted religious yearning which made them the first people to appreciate and embrace the truth and beauty taught and exemplified in the Christian system.

The early Romans cultivated the arts because of their moral influence. Sterner, however, than the Greeks in their maxims and habits of external morality, they rejected some branches of Grecian art. The Romans in their better days made a wide distinction between the nine Muses. "Melpomene" and "Thalia," the

Drama, both tragic and comic, they rejected as cultivating a fictitious and unpractical virtue; and "Terpsichore," the Dance, they utterly expelled as an open enemy to healthful physical development and as a secret foe to moral purity. When, however, the Republic, with its sages and moralists was gone, and the first days of the Empire, with its bright lights of literature, had set in twilight, and when Roman artists became even more licentious than Roman historians and poets, then the choice relics of ancient and true Grecian art were buried beneath the ashes of Vesuvius in Southern Italy and by the ravages of the Goths in Northern Italy, until a people breathing the spirit of a purer faith exhumed the hidden treasures and made them models for modern artists.

Since the days of the Romans the love of art has lingered in the south of Europe, especially in Italy. At times the spirit of error and of evil has triumphed over man's better impulses so much as to corrupt even art itself. Such, however, is the inherent and native power of art to purify man's desires that its permanent perversion is impossible. As their name indicates, the fine arts are and must be agencies for human refinement. In Italy they still exert a chief moulding influence. The French as a people have received a new intellectual and moral impulse amid the galleries of art gathered by Napoleon. In England the growing power of art to refine her rising people may be traced; while in the American republic, specially requiring this influence as a social bond and as a moral refiner, the importance of art study is just beginning to be realized.

SECT. 5. THE CLASSIFICATION OF THE FINE ARTS IN ACCORDANCE WITH THEIR MODES OF APPEAL.

As we have seen, art makes its appeal to the human mind for good through all the avenues of sensation, but chiefly through the two organs highest in their nature and mission, the ear and the eye.

Cousin remarks that "all classification presupposes a principle" on which classes are arranged, "which principle serves as a common measure." In the fine arts, he says, "this common measure is nothing else than expression;" a word which he compares with the Greek "*logos.*" "Expression," he adds, "being the supreme and, the art which most approaches this is the first of all arts."

He makes sculpture and music the extremes; the former the least, the latter the most expressive, of the arts proper. Painting he ranks as intermediate, being the art "nearly as precise as sculpture, and nearly as touching as music." Poetry he regards the highest of all, though not strictly a fine art proper.

The fine arts which address human emotions through the ear are, in their elementary forms, music, eloquence and poetry. Music proper addresses the ear with pleasant sounds disconnected from sentiment; eloquence, in sounds that may be indifferent or agreeable, addresses the reason by sentiment alone; poetry appeals to our emotional nature by the combined influence of the sentiment it embodies, and of the grace of its diction and the melody of its rhythm. Each of these has its own divisions and subdivisions, as well as its combinations with one or more of its own or of different classes. Music is melody when one voice alone is heard or one part alone is performed; and it is harmony when different but concordant parts unite. Instrumental music is simple music, and vocal music is music and poetry combined. So eloquence and poetry have their classifications and combinations. The histrionic art is eloquence combined with acting and scenery. The opera, again, is music added to the histrionic art.

Music seems to have been developed earlier than the arts which address the eye. Jubal, "the father of all such as handle the harp and organ," lived before Tubal-Cain, the "instructor of every artificer in brass and iron;" as also Orpheus, the leader in Grecian musical art, preceded Dædalus, the father of Grecian sculpture. In rank, too, the arts addressed to the ear are superior. Poetry, associated with music, is made the chief of the fine arts by Plato in ancient, and by Cousin in modern times. Socrates, as Plato relates, in early life heard a voice which said to him, "Socrates, cultivate the Muses;" a mandate which in his youth he sought to obey as a sculptor, in his mature manhood as a philosopher, and in the last hours of his life as a poet. Cousin says, "The art *par excellence*, that which surpasses all others, since it is incomparably the most *expressive*, is poetry."

The fine arts addressing emotions through the eye are more numerous. *Drawing* is the first and simplest, and has its classes of outline and shaded, plane and perspective; to which are to be added engraving in its varied branches and photographing. *Sculp-*

ture presents single figures or composite designs as decorations of architectural structures; and its finished works are reliefs or complete statuary. *Painting* has its subdivisions according to material, as pastelle, water and oil colors; according to subject, as animal, portrait and landscape painting; and according to design, as miniature and life-size, scenic and finished. *Architecture* is the moulding and grouping of forms of plastic art, as ornaments of structures called forth by the useful arts. *Landscape Gardening* is the union of the architect's with the painter's arts, the arranging of varied forms of nature into one vast whole, and the shading and harmonizing of the tints of nature as the painter arranges and blends them on his canvas. The *Decorative Arts* embrace fragmentary details associated with all the fine arts.

CHAPTER II.

THE LOWER SENSES INDIRECTLY CONTRIBUTING TO THE IMPRESSIONS MADE BY ART.

THE general division of the senses into five, and the recognition of the distinct sources of knowledge and of pleasure furnished by each of these senses, may be observed in the opinions of men at every stage of philosophic advancement, among all nations and in all ages. There has, moreover, been a virtual division of one of these five, touch, into two orders of impressions, indicating a recognition of six distinct sources of knowledge arising from impressions on the body.

SECT. 1. THE GENERAL RELATION OF THE LOWER SENSES TO THE APPEALS OF ART.

The Egyptian artists, while addressing the eye by the massiveness of their architecture and sculpture and by the gorgeousness of their painting, sought to heighten their impression by adding an appeal to the lower senses. The walls of their tombs, made to be the home of departed spirits still united to sentient bodies, covered with scenes of all forms of sensual delight, are witnesses that the true artist must be master of the whole range of human sensibilities, and must make his work appeal to the lower as well as the higher of the human senses.

There is a general relation between the different senses in their laws of producing pleasure. Cicero, illustrating the charm of a voice well modulated in the orator, says: "How much more lively in beauty and variety of colors are many parts in new than in old pictures! which nevertheless, although they arrest us at first sight, do not delight us for any length of time, while we are permanently attracted by the very uncouthness and old-fashioned look which belong to ancient paintings! How much softer and more delicate in song the minor key and falsetto tones than the sharp and shrill notes; against which not only critics, but the multitude itself, exclaim if they are oft repeated! The same may be seen in the other senses; that we are not so long pleased with ointments prepared with the strongest and most pungent odor as with those of a medium character, and that what seems to smell of wax is more praised than that which smells of saffron; that in touch itself there is a limit both as regards lightness and softness. Yes, even the taste, which is the sense most voluptuary, and the one which is moved more than the other senses are by sweetness, how quickly it spurns and spits out that which is excessively sweet!" The poet Young, though a stern moralist, teaches that all the senses should be gratified, since "Our *senses* as our *reason* are divine." The laws controlling the pleasures of the lower and higher senses are thus parallel because they are a family together; and the power of the fine arts over human sensibilities can never be appreciated, as Burke intimates, unless this relation be observed.

In considering each of the senses in its relation to art, the general distinction between the useful and the fine arts must be kept in mind; that the former are designed to secure utility, the latter to promote pleasure. The pleasures of taste and smell, designed chiefly for utility, when combined with the higher pleasures, are always subsidiary; and when their sole gratification is sought, it is a mark of the degradation, not of the elevation, of the mind. It is only when these pleasures are associated with those higher in rank that they become dignified, and then they may even aspire to be courtly refinements.

SECT. 2. THE IMPRESSIONS OF THE SENSE OF SMELL IN ITS RELATION TO ART.

The sense of smell seems to be restricted to the higher orders of the animate creation: while as a power for *cultivated* delight it belongs only to man. Its office is twofold. As a source of simple pain when affected by nauseous effluvia its office is manifestly that of utility. In the peculiar delight given by the odors of flowers, when the honeysuckle and the orange blossom load the air with fragrance, we must regard this sense as mainly, if not wholly, designed to minister to pleasure.

The classes of sensibilities which pleasant odors address are, as in the higher arts, mainly three. They minister to social luxury and refinement; they arouse religious incitement and devotion; and they serve as tributes of affection and as counter-reliefs amid the struggle of attachment which clings to, and the disgust which puts away, the corrupting form once loved. When Mary poured over the head of Jesus the "box of precious ointment of spikenard," and even "anointed his feet" with it till "the house was filled with the odor of the ointment," it was the natural expression of the conviction that agreeable odors minister to social refinement. When God directed for the service of his sanctuary "spices for anointing oil and for sweet incense," we are assured that the agreeable impression produced by pleasant odors may aid in bringing man's spirit into a fit temper for devotional service. Yet again, when not only women, moved by the impulse of feeling, but senators in their wisdom, "brought a mixture of myrrh and aloes," and "wound the spices in the linen cloths about the body of Jesus,' we have a confirmation of the fact that we are made as rational beings to be addressed for the highest spiritual ends through the lowest of the bodily senses.

The appeal to this sense is distinct though associated; for the rose is admired more than the peony, the dahlia or the camellia, which have equal beauty, but no fragrance. Even the "lily of the valley" mentioned by Hebrew poets loses to our imagination half its loveliness when the rules of strict biblical interpretation compel us to renounce the idea of the fragrant delight of our childhood, and oblige us to think of it as a gem of the sod equally fair indeed, but without spicy odor.

As a study in art the power of this humbler sense has called forth genius to a remarkable degree. Among Egyptians and Hebrews, Persians and Arabians, Indians and Chinese, the "art of the apothecary" has been celebrated by such men as Moses and Solomon as a worthy one; while among Greeks and Romans and nations of modern Europe, just in proportion to the general advancement and culture of a people has always been the dignity given to this same art.

Probably, however, this appeal is best made not by the artifically extracted and concentrated essences of natural odors; but, according to the suggestion of Cicero, in the moderate and unconcentrated perfume of flowers. So far as the sense of smell is concerned, art must rather employ than copy nature to produce its impression. The poet has struck the chord that vibrates in universal human nature in the call, "Bring flowers;" "flowers" for the joyous, and "flowers" for the sad; "flowers for the bridal wreath," and "flowers for the early dead." At the ancient Egyptian feast servants held flowers to the nostrils of the guests; in Turkish cities the corpse of the dead is borne through the streets uncoffined, but loaded with flowers; the simplest shrine of the Madonna at an Italian cross-road is festooned with flowers; and modern advancement in refinement has found no method of improving the simple custom suggested alike by refined philosophy and by rustic intuition. The artist in still-life will ever study fragrant flowers as a mode of appeal.

SECT. 3. THE IMPRESSIONS OF THE SENSE OF TASTE IN ITS RELATION TO ART.

The sense of taste in man, as that of smell, performs a double mission, the first office being that of *utility*. The craving of hunger is opposed to, rather than identical with, the pleasure of the palate, since we reject unsubstantial delicacies, however tempting at other times, and choose the simplest beverage, water, and the plainest aliment, bread, till hunger and thirst are sated. The pleasures of taste proper seem to begin, rather than to end, when hunger is sated.

It is doubtful whether taste in its stricter signification is applicable to any creature but man. As the necessities of the lower animals are only corporeal, and not spiritual, we can see no end to be accomplished by the gift of a source of gratification designed for an intellectual and a moral being. Certainly the Creator has given them no capacity to culture the higher gift like man. They do not go over the sea to seek new luxuries, nor have they any scientific cooks, or convivial banquets, with viands studiously compounded, for an increased appeal to the sense of taste. Taste, in its higher signification, belongs to the attributes of man, as designed for a higher than corporeal delight, and indirectly at least it is an art sensibility.

The ends sought by an appeal to this sense are the same three already alluded to; individual gratification, social culture and religious refinement. That is in any age or land a happy home where skill and industry spread every day a tastefully prepared though frugal meal; as that household is always a cheerful one among whom a fondness for flowers or music reigns. From the days of Job birth-day feasts have been scenes of pleasure, filling up the whole year with bright anticipations and pleasant recollections. As a social bond, from the days of simple shepherd-princes no substitute has been found for the banquet as a power to heal old grudges and bring to a point pending negotiations either of personal or of national importance. As a religious obligation. the Divine Being enjoined on His ancient people the attendance of every man at the three annual feasts. The Great Teacher himself also set the example of attending not only on established public feasts, but also of partaking private banquets; while, too, the chief expounder of his system taught Greek and Roman Christians that they should still attend upon the national and religious festivals of their fellow-countrymen.

The dignity to which this sense may be made to rise is seen in the fact that its culture has been most advanced by men most devoted to philosophy, to literature, to oratory, and to the pursuits nearest allied to true art. Socrates and Plato, though so different in temperament, were drawn out in highest discourse at the banquet-table: and Aristotle, whose genius embraced the whole range of science and philosophy in his day, cultivated his taste to the nicest delicacy in judging of the flavor of a fish. Around the honored board of Mæcenas gathered in the Augustan age not only poets and artists, but also sages and orators of the greatest name; and even Cicero was never happier when retired for his philosophical studies than amid the dinner-table disputations which have made the name "Tusculanum" for ever famous. Not only such men as Garrick, Curran and Sheridan, but also the scholarly Johnson and Burke, gathered their inspiration amid the tempered convivialities of the club-room supper. No one can doubt that there has been often an excess in the resort to the pleasures of the palate, and that this excess has tended to render its voluptuousness a means of degrading instead of refining man's nature. The abuse of the banquet, however, like the adulteration of coin, is a concession to the real value of that which it counterfeits.

The close association of this sense with the intellectual has in part, perhaps, led to its employ as the expressive designation of that power by which the mind forms a judgment of beauty in art. The word "taste," borrowed from the corporeal sense allied so strongly to art, has been the almost universally chosen figure of speech by which to designate that power of the mind which judges of the beautiful. The artist should study the manifestation of this corporeal sense, that he may in his works appeal to it in itself, and more especially that he may appreciate its high relationship to that purely intellectual nature in man which he must strive to address in his works.

Sect. 4. The impressions of the sense of touch, and its relation to art.

Dr. Reid begins his chapter upon "Touch" thus: "The senses which we have hitherto considered are very simple and uniform; each of them exhibiting only one kind of sensation, and thereby indicating only one quality of bodies. By the ear we perceive sound, and nothing else; by the palate, tastes; and by the nose, odors. These qualities are all likewise of one order, being all secondary qualities; whereas, by touch we perceive not one quality only, but many, and those of very different kinds. The chief of them are heat and cold, hardness and softness, roughness and smoothness, figure, solidity, motion and extension."

The complex character of this general sense suggests a classification of effects very different, as well as of their causes distinct in the human organism; the germ of which Sir Wm. Hamilton has traced back to Aristotle and his predecessor Democritus. This analysis is founded upon the manifest distinction between the mere tactual impression made upon the skin by heat and by contact with external bodies, and that entirely distinct impression produced by pressure upon and tension of the muscles. The nature and extent of this analysis become more apparent when this sense called "touch," with its multiform elements, is viewed in its relation to art.

There are most manifestly three classes of agreeable sensations made upon the human organism, aside from the local senses of taste and smell, of hearing and sight. The first of these is the pleasing impression made upon the *surface*, on the *skin*, by gentle heat or the slight stroke of a soft body, solid, liquid, or gaseous, as of smooth fur, of lukewarm water or of a spring zephyr; and these are the pleasures of touch proper. The second is the agreeable sensation of *pressure* more or less gentle on the muscles, as in embracing, and of action in them as called forth by the gambols of animals and children and by gymnastics and the dance in youth; and these are the pleasures of what may be called muscular tension, or, for brevity's sake, simply "tension." The third is the exhilarating excitement arising from any *stimulus* acting upon the nerves, and thence upon the brain; the seat of this impression being neither the superficial skin nor the muscles underlying the skin, but the nervous fibres imbedded within the muscular system, centring in the brain; its producing cause being either a material stimulant acting through the digestive organs, or mental excitement operating through the brain on the nervous system: while its distinctive character may be perhaps appropriately designated by the term "nervous stimulation," or simply "stimulation." It is the first of these three classes of pleasurable sensations, the sense of touch proper, whose relation to art is in this section to be considered.

The sense of touch, Aristotle argues, is the discriminating test by which plants and animals are separated one from the other; its most perfect development being found in man. While superior to any animal in the power of touch as a source of utility, man is not only superior to, but distinct from, animals in the pleasures derived from this sense.

Touch proper is but a surface impression, whether ministering to utility or pleasure. Its impressions are of two classes; the pleasant impressions of temperature, and those arising from gentle *contact* of a material agent, gaseous, liquid or solid, upon the surface of the body. The soft brushing or "kissing" of the zephyr, the gentle fanning of the light breeze, or, as Dr. Franklin said, the rude yet exhilarating friction of the sweeping gale, is one of the luxuries of life. Of the same nature is the luxury of the water-bath, the laving of the wash, the dripping of the shower, the coursing past or cutting through of the river current in swimming. So, too, in the soft or smooth rubbing of the sponge or towel, of the brush or comb and of the hand, the pleasure of this sense is more or less exquisite.

The exquisiteness of the pleasure which may be derived from this sense when that of any other is denied is the true indication of its value. Children deprived of sight alone, show this in their inclination to feel any soft substance, such as velvet or fur, glass or ivory; while to those destitute of both sight and hearing, this only source of gratification left, mediate as it is between the highest and the lowest senses, appears to be a never-exhausted source of varied delight. The blind deaf-mutes will sit or stand for hours holding a piece of fur, rubbing it with apparent ecstasy over every portion of the body that they can lay bare; the Creator having opened to them a universe of delight in a field never entered by those absorbed in the pleasures of the other senses. Were the emotions awakened by the fine arts limited to the impressions of sight and sound, then this most intelligent class, deprived of the two higher senses, could have no art sensibility.

The relation of "touch" proper to art is perhaps the least intimate and important of any of the lower senses; though that of its attendant sense, the muscular, is the closest and broadest. The true artist, however, like the poet who studies nature, will often appeal to this form of delight. Lightness of touch, and its exquisite effect on marble or canvas, as well as on the viol string or the organ key, will be constantly suggesting to the painter, the sculptor, the musician, the relation, by analogy at least, which the sense of touch has to his art. Most of all the gentle impulses of the soul that fall pleasantly on kindred spirits, of which those of the zephyr, the stream, the hand are the types, must always be present to control the mind and the heart of the artist in conceiving as well as in executing his works; and if he has studied thoroughly the theory of the sense of touch and of its pleasure, the chastening influence of a right mental bent early received will prove a habit in his art that will give the charm of a subdued tone to everything he touches.

SECT. 5. THE IMPRESSIONS OF MUSCULAR TENSION IN THEIR RELATION TO ART.

The seat of the sense of tension is in the muscles underlying the skin. The track of the impressions made upon this sense is not, therefore, as in touch, superficial upon the extremities of the nervous fibres, whose minute and delicate terminations in the skin are so peculiarly sensitive; but it is a dull pressure felt on the body of the nerves imbedded in the mass of the muscles. These impressions arise from two classes of muscular action; the pressure of an external object from without, and the tension of self-action from within.

The knowledge obtained through muscular tension is of two kinds; knowledge of qualities of material objects communicated to the mind by the pressure of those objects on our muscular and bony framework; and knowledge of the position, actual and relative, of different portions of our bodies by their angular separation, their gravity and other muscular impressions. The blind man learns the form of a body by clasping it; he ascertains its composition as hard or soft by pressing upon it, and he judges of its weight by lifting it. From the amount of pressure exercised by the will on the muscles which move the eye, the tongue, the shoulders, the elbow, the thigh, or the knee, we know so perfectly how to adjust the direction and amount of their angular motion that not only the skill of the engineer, of the pianist, and of the gymnast, but the ordinary powers of a child in directing his eye and his hand and of preserving his balance, are a wonder to us. As Sir Wm. Hamilton has shown from the treatises of Aristotle, Galen, and a line of acute thinkers succeeding them, this source of knowledge has ever been recognized in metaphysical analysis; Aristotle designating it "motion;" the Germans, following him, "the muscular sense;" while Hamilton unites both designations in the characteristic expressions "locomotive energy" and "muscular tension,"

The pleasures derived from muscular impressions are of two classes. The first of these is that produced by pressure from without. It is seen in the manifest enjoyment of the infant, who has as yet attained no power of muscular self-action, when it coos with satisfaction at the scrubbing of the bath and crows with delight at the fondling hug of its nurse. The pleasure of the kiss and the embrace in youth and mature years, dignified in Asiatic more than in European custom as the natural accompaniment of the joy of meeting and the sorrow of parting, the pressure of the hand, of the lip, and of the breast is a pure and noble gratification.

The second class of agreeable muscular impressions is that resulting from the tension of the muscles in the exercise which forms their healthful play; a development of delight in the child somewhat later than that just mentioned. Goldsmith pictures this in the gambols of "The playful children just let loose from school;" Cowper graphically sketches it in the gleesome race of "the bounding fawn," the frisking gallop of "the wanton horse," and in the romp and "dance" of "the very kine that gambol at high noon."

In youth, sports of the turf, such as cricket and the foot-ball, racing and leaping, wrestling and boxing, are a more studied and less unmeaning employ of this same delight. With this class of sports, at first rude, art allied itself more and more until a system of artificial exercises became in vogue, which among the Greeks took the name of *gymnastics;* the "education for the body" commended by Plato. The fascination of this class of sports led to an excess and abuse. Aristotle, the teacher of Alexander, carefully noticed their effects thus: "Those accustomed to gymnastic exercises bear the cold with more difficulty than those not conversant with them." "The same habit is not advantageous to both health and strength." The practical Romans also observed what Diodorus in the Augustan age records of the Egyptian educators: "They think that by the exercise of daily wrestling youth improve in their strength but for a little time, and that with a great deal of hazard, while they gain no advantage at all as to the health of their bodies." This, however, as an abuse from over-straining, is no more an objection to the enjoyment rightly employed than over-eating is an objection to eating at all.

Among these last-mentioned exercises the dance finds place; to whose excess and abuse a double objection exists. Among the Hebrews it was a natural diversion for "children" and "virgins" to "dance;" and the wisest of men declares "There is a time to dance." As expressing patriotic exultation, Jephthah's daughter "came out to meet him with timbrels and dances;" and after

David's victory "the women went forth singing and dancing with tabrets." As an hallowed act of devotion, the prophetess Miriam, and the women with her, worshiped "with timbrels and with dances;" and David made dancing a religious act.

Among the Greeks in their early days the dance held an elevated position. One of the nine Muses was its presiding genius. Homer speaks of the dances of the illustrious suitors for the hand of Penelope as a manly accomplishment; and represents even sage Ulysses as an admirer of the skill of dancers. Xenophon mentions Socrates as present at a dance; and Plato argues in his "Laws" that the dance should be among the Greeks, as it was among the Egyptians, founded on religious ideas. The Greek dances proper, introduced by Theseus, were very simple in their movement and expression. A different view was taken by the best Greeks when the frantic war-dance of the Corybantes superseded the hardy training of their warriors; when, too, the Bacchanalian dance became but a representation of a drunken debauch; and when again the licentious dance of the Hetaræ was practised by harlots. From this time Aristotle among the Greeks, and Diodorus and Cicero among the Romans, objected to the dance, first, because it induced physical weakness from the over-exertion to which its exciting influence tended; second, and especially, because of the lascivious associations of which it was regarded the direct expression. During the better times of the Roman republic it was deemed disgraceful for grave men or even ingenuous youth to engage in any form of the dance. Julius Cæsar introduced the Pyrrhic or war-dance from Asia Minor into the games of the Roman theatre; after which the tendency was so rapidly downward that Nero degraded the imperial purple by dancing publicly on the stage. The uncovered walls of private houses in Pompeii now reveal to what an extent not only the manly war-dance, but the licentious waltz of the courtesan, had been carried. The Great Teacher appearing near this crisis to call back Greeks and Romans to the true as well as the good in every relation, seems to have himself made, and to have inspired his apostles to make, a just discrimination between the simple home expression of delight at a son's return and the depraved dance of the adulterous woman's daughter.

The *chase*, again, in rude and polished ages, has been an exhilarating pleasure of muscular action, associated with the higher delight in successful skill. The poets have ascribed to it an ennobling and refining influence. Moses quotes a couplet dating back to a period long before his day, extolling "Nimrod, mighty in hunting before the Lord." The Greeks and Romans installed Diana as the special patron of the chase; and their poets made it one of the marks of a hero that he excelled in this art. William Somerville, in his poem, "The Chase," traces the history of hunting from Nimrod, mentions its introduction into England by William the Conqueror, and shows its influence in refining the before rude manners of the British nobility.

To this class of pleasures must probably be attributed, to some extent, the fascinating charm of *war* itself. The measured tread of files of men in marching, with all the studied evolutions of the military drill, are directly pleasures of muscular action; and the hold upon the human mind which military exercises gain, the tenacity of their power even in old age upon the veteran soldier, are witness to the fascination attending this delight. Partisan warfare, the scout, the raid, the ambush, and even the dashing charge of the pitched battle and the slow approach of the regular siege, are but the hunt and the chase of a higher order of beings. The conflict taxes to the intensest energy the exercise of the mind indeed; but the exhilarating play of the muscular frame is the coveted pleasure that outweighs the pain of wounds and even of mutilation.

As already intimated, the association of art with the pleasures of muscular action was so apparent to the ancient Greeks that one of the Muses, Terpsichore, was appointed to preside as its head. Among modern critics "beauty of motion," as treated by Lord Kames, Sir Wm. Hamilton, and others, should find place here. The study of attitudes and of every variety of muscular effort, represented in such sculptured forms as the Dancing Fawns, the Boxer, the Wrestler, the Huntsman, the Warrior, and Hercules in his varied labors, all have their origin in this impulse of human nature; while in this too dwells the fascination coming from the painter's grouping of children playing, of men and women toiling, of men and beasts bounding in the chase, of horse and footmen struggling in bloody conflict, and even of angels soaring in clouds or ether.

SECT. 6. THE IMPRESSIONS OF NERVOUS STIMULATION IN THEIR RELATION TO ART.

Beneath the skin and within the muscles, acting in part as their ministers, lie the two classes of nerves; the one called afferent or nerves of sensation, terminating in the skin, the other called efferent or nerves of motion, having their attachments to the muscular fibres. In addition to the two kinds of impressions on these, distinguished as those of touch and of muscular tension, there is another class of impressions quite distinct in both nature and source from the two previously considered.

The impression distinctively called *nervous* is a feverish flutter of the whole nervous organism, the brain included, which no one thinks of referring to an action upon them through either one of the bodily senses, and which it would be absurd to call the impressions of smell, taste, touch, tension, sight or hearing. They are produced in part by external stimulants introduced into the body in a solid, liquid or gaseous form, such as tobacco, opium, tea, coffee, alcohol, ether, exhilarating gas, or some other kindred agent which acts upon the nervous system. They more generally originate from a cause within, familiarly known as self-excitement, whose abuse is characterized as "working one's self into a frenzy;" a state of mind exemplified in devotees of every religious system, in public speakers of every class and country, and even in the wild enthusiasm of a whole people lost in the whirl of a show or carnival. Animals below man seem destitute of this nervous excitability. They have no inward power of mind to act as an exciting cause, and they shun narcotic plants such as tobacco and the poppy, as well as the alcoholic stimulus of fermenting fruits. It is man, the intellectual being alone, whose intelligence prompts him to resort to nervous stimulation as a source of pleasure.

The pleasurable sensation of nervous stimulation becomes a resistless spell over the youth or the man who gives himself up to its indulgence. The child soon discriminates between the momentary gratification of the palate coming from the sweetened draught and the intoxicating sensation that follows from it; and very soon he prefers the latter separate from the former. Very soon, too, even the nauseous taste of tobacco ceases to be disagreeable, because of the exciting influence produced by it. When, too, the almost delirium of nervous excitement arising from hilarious society where wit and humor kindle and sparkle, when the first fresh glow of personal success in speaking under the complete possession of body and soul which absorption by one's subject of discourse produces, when the entrancing thrill of imaginative composition in prose or verse, or even the reading of poetry or romance, history or the drama, philosophy or science, comes to be tasted, when either of these forms of nervous stimulation arising from the ecstatic play of one's mental faculties is first experienced, a new world of surpassing delight breaks on the young student. It is a source of pleasing exhilaration to which mature manhood fondly resorts, and which even in old age still holds its devotee spell-bound.

The resort to this source of pleasure is seen in the earliest and latest history of mankind. Noah "planted a vineyard," and "drank of the wine thereof" until "he was drunken;" and among all nations, rude or refined, the use of fermented liquors and the smoking of some narcotic have been found. In sacred history we are told that God "giveth wine to make glad the heart of man;" and even that Jesus, the perfect man, "drank of the fruit of the vine." In every age, too, men have sought this same excitement coming from the mind's own imaginative employ. Both true and false prophets like Samuel and Saul, as well as bards and seers like Chalcas, orators and poets in every age and land, have spoken and written under a nervous stimulus which has seemed to be the working of a supernatural power.

As with the other pleasures of sense, the end sought through nervous stimulus has been threefold. As an individual gratification, and to gain the ear and take possession of the mind and heart of men for good or evil, public speakers have sought to attain this power of self-excitement. The wonderful energy of the double stimulus of the wine cup and of imaginative enthusiasm in the speaker, who sways at will the throng of even stolid men, has been a theme of admiration and an attainment most coveted in all ages of man's history. As a means of religious determination, the power of self-excitement peculiar to great leaders like John Knox, Martin Luther and George Whitefield has been, though peculiarly liable to abuse, a mighty instrument for good, akin as it is to that fervor of the great apostle, whom many philosophic hearers regarded "beside himself" and "mad."

It is a perversion of this source of pleasure and of power when the means is made but an end, and the mere ecstasy of nervous excitement is sought for its own sake or for any inferior end. Noah and the sons of Aaron are set forth as a warning by the Jewish lawgiver in the command, "Do not drink wine nor strong drink when ye go into the tabernacle of the congregation, that ye may teach the children of Israel." Elijah and John, the greatest of preachers, abstained entirely from artificial stimulants; while Timothy, the select model of a Christian pastor, was so abstemious that only an apostle's express direction could persuade him to use a stimulant even as a medicinal restorative.

It is an excess of the same worthy stimulus when the genuine equable excitement flowing from the fervor awakened by a great theme degenerates into a mere *rant*, the offspring of a forced, strained and unnerving excitement; a fault in many American speakers, both political and religious, often noticed by English and French critics. The wearing and deranging self-excitement witnessed in the phenomena called clairvoyance, spirit-rappings and the like, is a careless experimenting with the most delicate of all the parts of our organism, made to be in its healthful excitement the source of a genial and ennobling delight.

This abuse, however, is no argument against the proper use of any power for good or of any source of pleasure which our Creator has implanted within us. The ecstasy of nervous stimulus, as felt by an orator like Demosthenes declaiming on the sea-shore thrilled by the tones of his own voice, or by a poet like Schiller writing all night when the inspiration was on him with a wet towel about his head to cool his fevered brain, or even by a mathematician like Sir Isaac Newton toiling for weeks to reach his result, and, when so near as to be sure of its nature, completely unmanned by nervous excitement and obliged to transfer his work for completion to another hand,—this is a source of superior pleasure which always has controlled and always will sway the truest genius.

The artist, above all men, needs this delight, so inexpressibly fascinating, to cheer, to prompt, to sustain him in his long years of unrequited toil; years most drear were it not for this constant and exquisite delight. If Coleridge had occasion to say, "Poetry has been to me its own exceeding great reward," much more may the sculptor or painter utter it of his art. More than this, the artist must be able to infuse this same, his own fervor of spirit, into the beholder, otherwise he carves and paints in vain. As the speaker in prose or verse that carries away his audience with him has learned the almost magnetic power of an imparted nervous stimulus, so the artist who succeeds must learn to possess it at his work, since it will then be readily imparted to those who come within the sphere of his influence as beholders.

CHAPTER III.

THE IMPRESSIONS OF THE HIGHER SENSE OF HEARING AS ADDRESSED BY ART.

THE arts which address the ear belong rather to the sphere of *rhetorical* than of art criticism, For two reasons, however, the analysis of the laws of musical sounds, one department of these arts, may be made to occupy a brief space in a treatise on art criticism. The departments of poetry, oratory and the histrionic arts from the days of Aristotle have been abundantly treated in works on rhetorical criticism. The special field of music and musical sounds, like that of the other fine arts proper, as painting and sculpture, has been mainly the subject of professional teaching; partly from the fact that its teachers instruct by the voice instead of the pen, and address only practical pupils, who do not need written treatises; partly also from the necessary technicality of all professional study which makes its text-books unsuited to the general student. Hence a brief cursory view of this field of art is essential for the general student.

SECT. 1. MELODY; THE NATURE OF SOUNDS CALLED MUSICAL, AND THE MODES IN WHICH BY THE VOICE AND BY INSTRUMENTS THEY ARE PRODUCED.

Sound, as the ancients before Aristotle understood, is caused by vibrations in the air; the jar produced by a blow on a wall causing the wall to vibrate, which vibrations are communicated to the air and through the air to the ear; the human voice producing vibrations in the air, first within and then without the lungs, which in a similar manner are transmitted to the ear. Sounds called musical are caused by vibrations of the air so rapid and regular that they produce a continued and agreeable impression on the ear.

A wheel made to revolve with increasing rapidity comes at a certain velocity to give forth a low musical tone, which tone takes a higher pitch as the speed increases. All musical tones are characterized by a clear and smooth ring when prolonged; and as distinguished from each other they are classified, first, according to length, as long and short; second, according to pitch, as high and low; and third, according to force, as loud and soft.

The human voice is the natural first instrument for producing musical sounds. A child very soon catches the idea of their nature; and instinctively gives his vocal organs the conformation to produce them. In sounding the seven distinct notes of the scale called "natural," both the increased size and length of the vocal organs in mature life make the natural notes deeper than in the child's voice; while to produce the next succeeding seven higher notes, or the octaves in the scale, the air-passage is narrowed and the breath is forced through it with greater velocity.

The transition from the voice to *wind* instruments was simple and natural. At first, seven pipes of the same size, but of different lengths, were bound together, side by side, so that the lips could pass readily from one to the other: a form represented on the monuments of ancient Egypt, and used now by the Sandwich Islanders. Afterward a single reed or pipe, with holes cut at the proportionate lengths, was found to give the same alternation of seven notes; while a double force of voice was seen to produce the octaves. The next transition seems to have been to *beaten* instruments: elastic substances, as a hide drawn over a hoop, or a circular plate of metal, the drum and cymbals, giving tones in accord with those of the pipes. Next *stringed* instruments were added; a readily vibrating cord tightly stretched giving the same smooth, clear, ringing sounds produced by the pipe and drum. From the days of Jubal and Job, rude in Egypt but finished in Greece, the three kinds of musical instruments already mentioned have been found; indicating that they originated in a principle "in the nature of things" instinctively suggested to man, upon which, in no stage of advancement, can he make any material advance.

The word *melody*, in the ancient Greek, expressed the general effect of musical sounds. As a technical term of art, it refers to an arrangement of a single musical strain for a single voice or instrument. All musical performances, of children and rude tribes, naturally take this character; and the earlier and simplest popular songs, seldom committed to a written form, are pure melodies, having only one strain, in which all classes of voices join.

SECT. 2. SYMPHONY; THE CONSONANCE OF MUSICAL SOUNDS, THE LAWS OF ACCORD DEVELOPED BY PYTHAGORAS, AND THE CONCERT OF DIFFERING VOICES IN PRODUCING ACCORDANT TONES.

In music, as in other arts, practice precedes theory; and even in its advanced stages the ablest performer may be unaware of the science which underlies his art. In very early times, however, the ablest minds began to investigate the philosophic principles of this everywhere-admired art.

Pythagoras having studied music as an art in Egypt, and having introduced it into his school at Crotona, in Eastern Italy, set himself to the effort to reach the laws of nature on which its subduing and moulding power is to be explained. His mind was led to the scientific principle of the musical scale by this incident. Going into a smith's shop one day, he noticed that as several smiths were striking the same piece of iron with hammers of different sizes, all the sounds were harmonious except one. Reflecting upon the cause of this difference, he could refer it to nothing but the different sizes of the hammers. Having weighed the hammers on returning home, he suspended by cords of equal length and size pieces of iron having the same proportionate weights as the hammers of the smiths. On striking these cords, he observed that they gave forth notes corresponding to the ring of the iron. The discovery led him to the *cause* of the distinctions in musical sounds produced by musical instruments; and thence he obtained a law of proportions in the size of musical strings and pipes, which enabled the Greeks greatly to improve musical science.

The rapidity of vibrations in cords depends upon length, size or weight, and tension. The number of vibrations in a given period is inversely as the length of the cord, inversely as the square root of its weight, and directly as the square root of its tension. Hence in a guitar, harp or violin, one-half the length of any string vibrates twice while the whole vibrates once; in two strings of the same length, one must be one-fourth the weight of the other in order to vibrate twice as rapidly; and the same string must have four pounds of tension put upon it in order to vibrate twice as quick as when stretched by the tension of one pound.[1]

When two cords vibrate with the same rapidity the waves of air vibrating with them strike together on the ear, producing "unison;" called by the Greeks "homophony," or the same voice. When again the proportions between the vibrations are such that the slower vibrations chime in with, instead of breaking against the quicker vibrations, an effect is produced pleasant to the ear, called by the Greeks "symphony," but in modern times "accord." Vibrations of disproportionate numbers clash with each other, and thus produce the unpleasant impression called "discord."

The division of the cord as it vibrates into two, three, four and other proportionate parts or nodes is natural, not arbitrary. Thus, if a long tightly-stretched cord be placed in the crack of a window, forming what is popularly called an Æolian harp, it will be observed that according to the strength of the air-current it is vibrating first as a whole; then in two equal parts, each half giving forth the octave above the note first heard; and then again if the wind strengthens sufficiently it is vibrating in three separate parts, each giving the fifth of the second octave. The cause of this division is thus illustrated. If a long cord be fastened at one end, while the other is made to vibrate up and down, at first slowly, then more rapidly, its capacity to move as a whole will be soon reached; when its oscillations will break first into two, then into three, then into more equal nodes. So if a pebble be thrown into a smooth lake, the first circling ripple necessarily creates by its oscillation a second, and that a third, of the same size as the first, be that larger or smaller.

The main principles, indeed, in the science and art of music

[1] *Formulæ.*—If T = time of one vibration, L = length of cord in inches, W = weight of one inch, t = tension in pounds, g = force of gravity, or 386 inches the distance a body falls in one second of time, and N = number of vibrations in a second, then $T = L \frac{\sqrt{w}}{\sqrt{gt}}$, and $N = \frac{\sqrt{gt}}{\sqrt{w}}$.

were recognized by early Grecian philosophers and artists to such an extent, that the very terms used in musical science, as the Roman Vitruvius confessed of the Latin tongue, are borrowed from the mother-tongue of the arts. The word tone from "*teino*," to stretch: and the division of the natural musical scale into two parts called "tetrachords," recalls the fact that the Greeks constructed their first rude lyres with four "chords," or strings, so adjusted as to size, length, or tension, that when struck successively their tones were those of the human voice in rising through the first half of the natural scale. This result they found to be secured by making a difference of what they called a whole tone, or stretch, between the first and second and the second and third cords, and between the third and the fourth cords half a tone or stretch.

With this practical science, already attained, Pythagoras proceeded by experiment to ascertain the proportions in cords giving out musical tones. Taking two strings of equal size, length and tension, dividing one by a rest in the middle and sounding the whole of the undivided cord and the half of the divided one together, the note called the octave was obtained, and the chord which the Greeks called "*diapason*," because it was necessary to go through all the notes of the scale to reach it. Again removing the rest so as to cut off one-third, and sounding the two-thirds of the divided together with the whole of the undivided cord, they obtained the fifth note and the chord which they styled "*diapente*," because it was necessary to go through five notes to reach it. Yet again, placing the rest so as to cut off one-fourth of the string, and sounding together the whole and the three-fourths, they obtained the fourth note, and the chord which they named "*diatesseron*," because it was necessary to go through four notes to reach it. Two notes were thus reached following each other in the order of the natural scale, and one tone apart. Here, too, by striking two-thirds and three-fourths of the string at the same time the first discord was encountered.

The ratio of three-fourths to two-thirds of the cord, which produced the alternation of a natural tone and the discord, was observed to be as eight to nine. This latter difference in sound was called a "tone;" and the ratio of the length of strings, which gave this first distinction of tone, they made the proportion for the division of the others among the seven tones not yet fixed, namely, the second and third, the sixth and seventh. Dividing off, then, one-ninth of the whole string by a rest, the eight-ninths gave the first whole tone, and the second note in the scale; while eight-ninths of that eight-ninths gave the third note. The ratio between the length giving the third note now reached, and that giving the fourth before fixed, was only as about fifteen to sixteen,[1] or about one-half of the ratio proposed as the measure of a whole tone. Taking eight-ninths of the two-thirds, another whole tone and the sixth note was obtained; while again eight-ninths of the remainder of the string gave another whole tone and the seventh note. The remaining portion of the string, compared with the one-half which gave the octave, was only a half ratio, about fifteen to sixteen, giving the second half tone in the scale.

The first note of the scale or *do* was called by the Greeks *hypate*, the low; the second, *parhypate*, next the low; the third, *luchnos*, light or guide; the fourth, *mese*, or middle; the fifth, *paramese*, or next the middle; the sixth, *trite*, or third from the highest; the seventh, *paranete*, or next the highest; and the eighth, *nete*, or highest. The modern Indian musicians designate the seven notes by the Sanscrit words *sa*, *ri*, *ga*, *ma*, *pa*, *dha*, *ni;* their origin showing their antiquity. The modern names are attributed to Guido, a monk of Arezzo, in Italy; an eminent musician, who lived about A. D. 1022 and who derived the first six from the Latin hymn to St. John the Baptist;

"*Ut* queant laxis *Re*sonare fibris, *Mi*ra gestorum, *Fa*muli tŭorum, *Sol*ve polluti *La*bii reatum."

The seventh syllable *si* was afterward added by Le Maire, a French musician. In modern times the notes of the scale have been indicated by the first seven letters of the alphabet.

The notes thus obtained by vibrations of the *longer* portion of the divided string are all included in the natural scale, whose chords were called simple chords. Of the shorter portions the one-third gives the fifth of the second octave; and the chord called by the

[1] The ratio was between $\frac{8}{9}$ of $\frac{8}{9}$ of the string which gave *mi* and $\frac{3}{4}$ of the string which gave *fa*. The fractions reduced are $\frac{256}{324}$ and $\frac{243}{324}$; or about as 16 to 15.

5 C

Greeks "diapason-diapente," now called the twelfth, one of the sweetest of all chords. The fourth of the chord gives the octave of the second scale, and the chord called by the Greeks "bisdiapason," now named the fifteenth. These five, three simple and two composite, all included within two octaves, were the principal chords as developed by the Greeks.

Modern improvements have introduced three or four octaves into the range of musical instruments. The proportion of strings which give the first octave are $1 - \frac{8}{9} - \frac{4}{5} - \frac{3}{4} - \frac{2}{3} - \frac{3}{5} - \frac{8}{15} - \frac{1}{2}$. In each successive octave the proportionate lengths required are respectively one-half those in the previous octave. The number of vibrations in each cord in a given time is found by inverting the same fractions. The proportionate number of vibrations in the first octave will be $1 - \frac{9}{8} - \frac{5}{4} - \frac{4}{3} - \frac{3}{2} - \frac{5}{3} - \frac{15}{8} - 2$. If reduced to a common denominator, the numerators of these fractions will be 24 : 27 : 30 : 32 : 36 : 40 : 45 : 48; in which there are three sets of proportions. The ratios between the 1st and 2d, 4th and 5th, 6th and 7th, are as 8 to 9; those between the 2d and 3d, and the 5th and 6th, are as 9 to 10; and those between the 3d and 4th, and the 7th and 8th, are as 15 to 16. It should be carefully observed, therefore, that of the five intervals called whole tones in the scale, three are of a larger ratio than the other two; while the intervals called half tones are not precisely the halves of those marking the whole tones.

The Greek word "symphony" refers immediately to the consonance of associated voices of different tone singing the same melody. Even savages, however, notice the change of voice in youth, and the different pitch of male and female voices; and in their simple melodies the male voice after change sings the same common strain a fifth below. Besides this first variation yet a third, a fifth below the ordinary male voice, is heard from men of deeper-toned voices; a fact noticed among the native tribes of Africa, and also among the negroes of the American continent. In the earliest stage of improvement the study of symphonies, or accords, leads to the independent strains which make up the different parts in music. First, male voices, differing more than female, are trained according to their pitch to sing strains different, though in accord; then female voices, including those of boys of half growth, are separated into two classes. The Brahmins of India have three parts in their music; which were studied by Pythagoras, and are mentioned by Plato in his beautiful figure picturing the triple virtues of a good magistrate, "he should attune them like the three musical chords, bass, tenor and treble." To those three ancient divisions, "bass" or low, "tenor" or medium, "and "treble," that is, triple or high part, modern refinement has added subdivisions of each; "soprano" or high, "mezzo-soprano" or midhigh in female voices, "alto" a high tenor in medium male voices, and "barytone," or deep-toned, in lower male voices. In the practical business of teaching music, it is found that while the voice may sound with ease notes both higher and lower, the range of tones to be specially cultured by those singing different parts is as follows: for the soprano or treble from B below to A above the staff; for the alto or second treble from G below to B or C; for the tenor from E to G; for the bass from F below to D above; and for the barytone from F below to F above.

SECT. 3. HARMONY; THE THREE SCALES OF MUSICAL TONES ON WHICH IT IS FOUNDED; THE DELICATE SHADES OF TONE AND THE TEMPERING OF MUSICAL INSTRUMENTS BY WHICH ITS HIGHEST EFFECTS ARE SECURED.

In the "natural scale" which men by nature, without culture, employ, the half tones occur between the third and fourth, the seventh and eighth notes of the octave. This was called "diatonic" by the Greeks, because the voice or instrument passes in it through all the natural divisions of tones.

The suggestion was a natural one that half tones might be introduced between all the whole tones. For, if the rest were made to slide gradually along from the whole to the half length, the cord, vibrating meanwhile, would give forth an unbroken succession of varied tones. The stereotyped, unprogressive spirit of the Asiatic race in art is strikingly illustrated in this, that while the Chinese had, centuries before Christ, both the natural scale and a division of it into twelve half tones, yet they have never secured the higher effects of music. The superior Brahminic race in India and the Persian in China have been from the earliest ages masters in higher musical performances. The perfection of the division in musical tones attained by the Greeks, realized what they designated by the word "harmony."

The introduction of half tones between each of the five whole tones made twelve instead of seven different notes to the octave, thus giving greater variety in the same compass. A slight contracting of the vocal organs sharpening a note gave half a tone higher in pitch, called a sharp; and a slight relaxing of the organs gave a note half a tone lower, called a flat. Thus a new scale was formed, which, because of the overlapping of its tones like colors in painting, producing an adorned style of music, the Greeks called the "chromatic scale," from "*chroma*," color.

In constructing the chromatic scale of sharps and flats by transposition, the fixed law of the movement of the human voice in tones and half tones becomes more apparent. Taking three octaves of the natural scale, one above and the other below that of the ordinary pitch, and making G, the fifth note, the first note of a new scale, the two whole tones and a half tone from G to C give the same succession as from C to F. From E to F, however, where the new scale demands a whole tone, there is but a half tone; and hence F must be raised in pitch or sharpened a half tone. Thus one new note is secured. Making the fifth of this second scale, or D, the first of a third scale we find between D, F sharp and G, the two tones and a half tone required in the third scale; but, to obtain three whole tones succeeding, C must be made sharp; which secures one more new note. In a third transposition beginning with A, G must be sharpened; in a fourth transposition beginning with E, D must be sharpened; a process by which all the possible divisions of tones are exhausted.

Taking now the second, instead of the first of the notes, by which the Greeks fixed the interval of a tone, namely, the fourth instead of the fifth of the scale, the transposition by flats gives another set of scales. Making the fourth note, or F, the first of a new scale, B must be flattened, introducing a half tone where there was a whole tone in the natural scale. Beginning again with the fourth of this new scale, or B already flattened, E must also be flattened; beginning with E flattened A must be flattened; and beginning, finally, with A flattened D must be flattened; the process here exhausting itself, as in the scale of sharps.

The construction of the "chromatic scale" led the Greeks naturally to the "enharmonic scale;" the practical application of whose principles belongs to the highest order of musical composition. As the intervals fixed as whole tones are not uniform, the ratio of some being 8 : 9 and of others 9 : 10, the semitones, brought in by transposition of the scale between whole tones having these differing ratios, must be also of different ratios. Dividing all these varied intervals by the least common measure, and calling the subdivisions "*commas*" or segments, the Greeks found that nine commas are the measure of the larger intervals and eight of the smaller intervals forming whole tones; while the measure of the diatonic or natural half tone was five commas, and that of the chromatic semitone either three or four commas. In the enharmonic scale two chromatic half-tones and a quarter of a half-tone, sometimes called a "vibration," were made the interval given to a tone.

In employing the chromatic and enharmonic scales, the human voice can readily strike the nice shades of variation in half and quarter tones. The violinist by a slide of the finger, and the flutist by a slight turn of his lip, accomplish the same. Modern art, however, has embodied all stringed instruments in the piano and all wind instruments in the organ; which are called keyed instruments. In the piano the length of the string, and in the organ the angle of the wind's pressure and the size of the orifice, are fixed in the mechanism; and no fingering can vary them. To secure in keyed instruments the nice distinctions of quarter-tones is therefore impossible; and the resort is to what is called "tempering." For example, the 6th note of the natural scale may be fixed not precisely at an interval of 8 to 9, nor of 9 to 10 from the 5th, but intermediate between them; so that the fraction, reducing both to a common denominator, shall not be $\frac{8}{9}$ or $\frac{160}{180}$, nor $\frac{9}{10}$ or $\frac{162}{180}$, but $\frac{161}{180}$.

SECT. 4. MUSICAL COMPOSITION; THE IMPRESSIONS ON THE SENSIBILITIES SOUGHT BY MUSIC; THE MODES OF WRITING MUSIC; THE MAJOR AND MINOR CHORDS AND THEIR ÆSTHETIC EFFECTS; THE KEYS AND RULING NOTES IN MUSICAL COMPOSITION.

When the mere unconnected hum of the child at its play becomes a connected strain, the subject of musical composition requires consideration. This relates directly to the musical strain alone; the words connected with the strain belonging to the subject of musical expression. The ends of musical composition, as of other arts, are the promoting of individual gratification, incitement to worthy public deeds, and the awakening of religious enthusiasm. The dance is made artistic and pleasurable chiefly from the musical accompaniment. The march of armed men would be a toil intolerable but for the nerving impulse of martial music; and every form of religious worship, Asiatic idol adoration, Grecian philosophic idealism, alike with the most formal and most spiritual devotion of Jewish and Christian assemblies, would be soulless without the aid of both instrumental and vocal music.

In order to meet the ends thus sought, music must take a composite form. Even the child's lay of the nursery, and the rude song of most savage people, are so perfectly conformed to law that scientific travelers have been able to put them into the form of a written composition. The early Greeks understood the art of written musical composition, though their methods of notation are lost. In the modern writing of music five parallel lines, with four intervening spaces, called the "staff," furnish a scale upon which the notes indicating the pitch and succession of tones are inscribed. The four ordinary parts are usually written on four, though sometimes on two separate staffs. The place of the first note of each part is indicated by a character called a clef or key; of which there are usually three. The first called the G "clef," or key, has G on the second line from the bottom arranged for the treble or highest part. The second or C clef has C on the first line for the *soprano*, on the second line for the *mezzo-soprano*, on the third line for the *alto*, and on the fourth line for the *tenor*. The third called the F clef has F on the third line for the barytone, and on the fourth line for the bass.

In the practical business of musical composition the principles of "accord" and of "harmony" are brought into requisition. To become master of these demands a comprehensiveness of study, an acuteness of critical skill, and a grasp of genius equal to that requisite in the higher fields of plastic art; Haydn and Mozart being the Lionardo and Angelo of musical composition; and Beethoven the Raphael. The "common chord" consists of three notes sounded together, and is called "perfect" when the first, third, and fifth are thus united. Chords are called "close" when the three notes in accord are within the compass of a single octave; of which there may be three, the chords of the first, third, and fifth, of the third, fifth, and octave, and of the first, the fifth, and the octave. Chords are called "dispersed" when the three notes in accord are not all in the same octave; of which there may be also three, the chord of the first and fifth with the third of the octave above: of the third and octave with the fifth in an octave above; and the fifth in the octave below with the third and octave in the fundamental scale. In all cases a proper chord includes three notes; the leading note of which is called the fundamental. As the same chords are found in each of the scales in music, natural and chromatic, any one of the notes from first to seventh may be selected as the fundamental note.

The class of chords which furnish the sweetest harmonies are the "major and minor chords;" the character of these chords being dependent on the intervals between the notes by which they are formed. Thus the interval between *do* and *mi* is two whole tones, and is called a "major third;" while that between *re* and *fa* is but one tone and a half-tone, and is called a "minor third." In each common chord, made up of the first, third and fifth, there will necessarily be one major and one minor interval; and the designation of chords as "major" or "minor" is derived from the lower of the two intervals. As the minor chords are sounded, the ear recognizes a slight clashing of the vibrations, occasioning a partial dissonance, whose effect is to soften the sharp ring of perfectly chiming vibrations, and thus give a subdued tone to the strain in which they predominate. Minor chords therefore are adapted to produce pathos, while the major chords are more elevating and grand.

The human voice does not naturally pass from one chord to another of extremely different character; but there are rules in nature for the succession of notes and chords which men without art have adopted. The principal laws of that succession of chords which constitutes harmony are the following. *First*, any chord may be followed by another chord having the fifth of the preceding as its fundamental, which is called the *dominant* or "leading" chord. *Second*, any common chord may be succeeded by one whose fundamental is a fourth above or a fifth below that of the preceding chord: and this is called the "relative-major" or *sub-dominant* chord. *Third*, any common chord may be followed by a chord having the sixth of the preceding chord as its fundamental note; and this is called the "relative-minor" chord. Certain intermediate tones as passing notes may be interposed between the chords mentioned; and some of the finest effects are produced by the introduction in one of the three parts of the chord of a short dissonant, leading the way to the principal note which is in consonance.

The *tonic*, or key note, is the chief sound on which a melody is constructed; the note which is repeated oftenest in the progress of the song, and with which it ends. The *dominant*, or *ruling* note, the fifth above the key note, whenever repeated before the key note, indicates that a fall of the voice or cadence closing a strain is to follow: and it is always heard in the final cadence in the bass. The *sub-dominant*, the fifth below the key note, requires that the key note follow it in some cadences. The *mediant* is the middle note between the *tonic* and *dominant*, and the *sub-mediant* is the middle note between the tonic and sub-dominant. These notes are specially to be observed, in music of major and minor keys constructed upon the chromatic and enharmonic scales. So manifestly is music, like human language, founded on law, that in the songs of the rudest tribes in ancient and modern times these principles are observed. In the early Grecian and the yet earlier Indian art a similar designation of the tonic, mediant and dominant notes in their musical compositions has been found.

SECT. 5. MUSICAL EXPRESSION; THE ADAPTATION OF MUSICAL STRAINS TO THE EXPRESSION OF POETIC COMPOSITION, AND THE CLASSES OF SENTIMENT TO WHOSE EXPRESSION MUSIC IS ADEQUATE.

Music, like the other fine arts, never assumes its high character, so as to be esteemed noble, unless it is made the vehicle of important sentiment and the awakener of practical emotion. When language is thus made to keep company with song, it is observed that, as there are notes long and short and tones high and low in music, so there are long and short syllables in words and a rising and falling of the voice in the utterance of sentences. The rudest song requires alternation of sentences of similar length, and the rise and fall of voice in successive portions of each strain; both parallelism and cadence being the first elements of poetry. Increased refinement in verse demanded again that clauses, words and syllables should be arranged into feet of fixed measure, so that in the union of musical strains with poetry the two should keep step with each other; and thus rhythm was introduced as an element of poetic expression. Still again, as in strains of music of fixed length the key note is the natural terminator of the cadences, so song soon came to add rhyme to rhythm, or the recurrence at fixed intervals of syllables similar in sound. Hebrew poetry, both in structure and in its chanting, illustrates the *parallelism* and *cadence* which are the first essentials of words adapted to musical expression. Greek and Latin poetry excel in perfection of *rhythm;* every syllable in each successive foot being as nicely adjusted to its associates as are the parts in the human body. Modern European verse again excels in the attribute of *rhyme.* The modern Italian, the language at once of music and poetry, is so constructed, its five vowel sounds being always pure and unvarying and its syllables consisting almost without exception of a single consonant and vowel, that one can hardly help speaking in both rhythm and rhyme: a characteristic which makes the business of the Italian "*improvisatore*" a very easy task.

The subject of expression in music naturally suggests two points for consideration; the character of the poetic feet employed to express different emotions of the mind; and the style of music as to key, range of pitch and stress of voice in harmony with different emotions represented. In each of these the Greek led the way to the true science of this art; while modern German composers have in this latter respect reached a perfection which the ancients never attained.

The Greeks had no less than twenty-eight feet, simple and compound, made up by different arrangements of long and short syllables in combinations of two, three, or four members each. The adaptation of these classes of feet to different sentiments is often indicated in their names, as in the four feet of two syllables; the "spondee" or *votive*, two long, used in the solemnly-slow, prayer-like dirges accompanying offerings presented to the gods; the "pyrrhic" or *warlike*, two short, breaking forth amid the furious darting of the war dance and song; the "trochee," or *running*, a long and a short, falling on the ear like a horse's gallop, and tripping in sportive roundelay; and the "iambic" or *sportive*, the flippant trolling upon the tongue of satirical song, intensified in the choliambus or halting iambic. The nice gradation of proportion entering into the movement of syllables, called in general long and short, though of varied proportion in length, is indicated in such names as "dactyl" and "anapæst;" the former like the fingers, having its three parts sesquialteral, each one and a half of its successors, while the "anapæst," or *rebounding*, was the reverse or counterpart of the dactyl, a short, medium, and long syllable.

In Hebrew poetry there was an evident adaptation between the poetic and musical strains made to accompany each other; as is manifest in the exultant Song of Moses and in the lyrics of David, Ethan and Asaph, now sweet and plaintive, and now thrilling and majestic. Among the Greeks the triumphs of heroes took the stately tramp of the heroic or epic metre, made up in Greek and Latin verse of spondees and dactyls; the hymn of reverential adoration to the gods assumed the slow and solemn movement called spondaic; the endearments of love could find no expression but in the lively trochaic or graceful iambic; and the fierce and furious war song ran instinctively into the jerking pyrrhic. The epic, lyric and pyrrhic styles in poetry were thus directly associated with *expression* in music; while the tragic muse again sought a combination of the more elevated styles; mingling the stately heroic, the solemn dirge, and in the chorus the lightest and gayest of metre in verse and of accompaniment in music; the germ of the combinations of modern times having found expression in the critical writings of the Grecian sages Plato, Plutarch and Ptolemy.

There is no art whose adaptations to the production of moral influence has been so studied and guarded as has that of music. The Chinese moral teacher, Confucïus, wrote: "Wouldst thou know if a people be well governed; if their manners be good or bad. Examine the music they perform!" In his Model Republic Plato dwells on the necessity for governmental control over the music of the common people; discussing in detail the nature and special influence of the iambic, trochaic, dactylic and spondaic measures, as also the laws which should regulate music.

Lord Kames, in common with many able critics, has argued that music cannot be made expressive of sentiment inspiring dread; since in its very nature it is designed to please and soothe. Without doubt both hymns and songs denunciatory in sentiment and severe in expression are opposed to the true idea alike or art and of religion. The attempts, however, of great musical composers to produce the impression of grandeur and of awe in their sublimest oratorios, may be parallel to the appeal of the dying gladiator and the Laocoön in sculpture. As in nature the ear is addressed by sounds that awe, by the rolling thunder, the howl of the gale at sea, and the crash of dashing air, water, and earth, so to a certain extent music may be made to imitate these and kindred sounds, and thus art produce the impression of nature.

SECT. 6. MUSICAL MODULATION; THE GENERAL RELATION OF MUSIC TO PITCH AND CADENCE OF VOICE; AND ITS SPECIAL RELATION TO THE ENUNCIATION OF DRAMATIC COMPOSITION IN HISTRIONIC ART AND OF DIDACTIC COMPOSITION IN ORATORY.

In music as in oratory the subjects of expression and modulation are closely associated. The change of sentiment in a poetic composition set to music demands often a change of the musical key to secure a more perfect adaptation of one to the other. Modulation is properly the passing of the voice from one key to another. Associated as it is with expression, modulation has an important relation to all the musical scales; but especially to those called the "minor scales." In the scales thus far considered, called "major scales," the half-tones have come between three and four and between seven and eight. In the minor scales, however, the half-tones in ascending the scale are made to come between the second and third, and the seventh and eighth; and in descending between the sixth and fifth, and the third and second. As the minor chords have a peculiar sweetness and gentleness of tone, so strains written in minor keys have a subdued and plaintive succession of sounds in themselves charming to the ear, when the voice in passing from strain to strain is skillfully modulated.

With the subject of modulation is associated that of "dynamics;" or varying energy and force of voice. When common conversation becomes animated, when at different distances or for different purposes men address each other, a correspondent tone is assumed. We soon distinguish the tone of a master or captain giving command. When a public speaker is addressing a large audience in order to please by the ease and smoothness of the tones of his voice as well as to instruct and move by the sentiment uttered, a tone and pitch are required which shall be distinctly audible to the most distant while it is not disagreeable to those near. As his mind warms with the progress of thought, as new classes of conceptions arise and sudden emotions awake and break forth, fresh and changing modulations of voice are of course demanded. The universal resort of uncultured speakers to musical or ringing tones, as those in which transitions of the voice are most easily made, shows that there is a natural origin for what is popularly called "sing-song." What was thus *naturally* introduced became an art; for in a speaker of genuine genius that becomes a wondrous power which in one without animation is a humdrum and lullaby. This musical modulation fallen into by rude orators in uncultivated nations, as also by the first uneducated and earnest heralds of every new religious reformation, is continued as a religious practice revered for its sanctity even where the highest literary culture prevails. It is, however, an art founded on true science when men like Demosthenes have trained the modulations of their voice to the accompanying notes of the flute; a practice commended by Cicero in his treatises upon oratory.

This association of music with oratory was most marked in the chorus or interlude of the drama as constructed by Æschylus, Sophocles and Euripides. The vocation of the chorus or choir, chanting between the acts of the drama accompanied by instrumental music the history which connected and illustrated the scenes preceding and succeeding, took naturally the designation, "histrionic art."

It was a natural suggestion of later times that music joined with the histrionic art only in the interlude by the Greeks should be united with speaking and acting throughout the whole play. When the musical accompaniment was set to the words of a drama, and the recitation was an unexcited chant much like a dramatic reading without special acting on the part of the performers, it took the appropriate name of an "oratorio;" because it was a quiet address like that of a suppliant in prayer to his God, or of a preacher addressing his auditory. When there were added in the oratorio the accompaniments of stage representation, scenery, dresses, and the gestures and action of the stage, the performance took the name of "opera;" the opera being as the name implies the gathered treasures of all arts addressing the ear, and their skillful union into one complete whole.

CHAPTER IV.

THE SENSE OF SIGHT, THE HIGHEST OF THE SENSES, AS ADDRESSED BY ART.

THE eye is the special organ by which art addresses the mind. The range of the pleasures of the ear is limited; for the music that falls with such mellowness at a slight remove from its source is soon lost by increasing distance. On the other hand, the stretch of vision is into regions without bound. Again, the variety in objects of beauty occupying but a small space around, seems perfectly limitless; while there are, in comparison, but few varieties in the natural tones, even of music, that address the ear. Most of all, while the addresses of sound are essentially one in kind, there are several separate sources of delight in objects of sight, such as form, color, relation, which make their own distinct and peculiar appeal to our æsthetic nature. A classification of the elements of visual impressions pleasant to the mind is essential in the criticism of works of art.

SECT. 1. FORM; ITS PRINCIPLES AND THEIR CONCURRENCE AS THE GROUNDWORK OF ART.

In forms which delight us varied characteristics are to be observed. Some are minutely apprehended by the eye near at hand, as the parts of flowers and the features of the human countenance; others are but dimly comprehended in the distance, as the sweep of towering mountains, the swell of the ocean in the horizon and the blue arch of the sky. Some are of fixed form, as plants and animals, the sun and separate stars; others are of figure unfixed, as rocks and star-clusters; while others still are of undefined and indefinable outline, as waves and clouds. Of fixed forms again there are mineral, vegetable, animal, and human; the first having only regularity of structure, the second adding also life, the third self-motion, and the fourth intelligence, to give to them their special attraction.

The *outline* of all forms is composed of lines straight or curved. The lines of crystallization, of a beam of light, of upward growth in plants, and of motion in falling bodies are straight lines. In plants and animals there is a union of curved with straight lines; the trunk of every tree and the limb of every animal having its length in straight lines and its circumference in curved lines. Straight lines meet at angles forming broken lines or polygons; and curves may be regular, as circular, elliptical, parabolic and spiral; or irregular, as waving, serpentine and convoluted.

An outline is but a combination of lines enclosing a space. Form is conceived as possessed of three dimensions; though but two are apparent to the eye. Figure is properly the conception of the designing mind as distinct from the embodied object; while form is the actually executed object of which figure was the conception. We speak, therefore, of figures in rhetoric, but of forms in art. The word figure is also applied to representations or modifications by art of natural objects; as when we speak of mathematical figures, or of the figure of a man or woman whose form is modified by dress. Form, therefore, is the generic term expressing the elements of extension in objects of sight giving pleasant impressions to the eye.

Several distinct elements of forms in nature furnish each its respective delight. The mind seems to observe these in the following order.

First: Outline in substance.—Substance alone may arrest attention and give pleasure; as when we gaze in admiration on the green sea or blue sky, on the black thunder-cloud or the rosy dawn. When, however, the eye traces the outline of a billow, a cloud, a horizon line, or a rock, however indistinct, indefinite and fragmentary the form, the mere *outline in substance* gives us pleasure.

Second: Unity in Multiplicity.—The mind has an oppressive sense of discomfort when confused objects are passing before it, and it can give no unity to their forms. Dim glimpses through the fog of an occasional headland along the coast give uneasiness to the mind; but a thrill of delight is felt when the mist is lifted and the multiplied forms along the shore are taken in as a whole. Crowds of people without order thronging the streets have little attraction; but columns of men in military *uniform* arrest the gaze.

Third: Regularity in Complexity.—Lines made by one rule, as circles or parabolas, are called regular. Figures made up of straight lines of either *uniform* parts, as squares or hexagons, or of *uniformly recurring* parts, as rectangles, are *regular* figures. The five *regular* bodies, the cube bounded by six squares, the dodecahedron by twelve equal rhombs, and the pyramid, octohedron and eikosihedron respectively by four, eight and twenty equilateral triangles, were regarded by Plato as the forms of the ultimate elements making up the great "Cosmos" or "Universe of Beauty." The four regular curves formed by cutting sections through a cone, the circle, the ellipse, the parabola, and hyperbola, were known to the early Greeks, and the admirable law of their formation was calculated: their beautiful sweep entered as an element into Pythagoras' conception of the harmony of the universe; and Galileo and Sir Isaac Newton saw in them a principle of truth and beauty which led them to the secret of the mechanism of the universe.

Fourth: Simplicity in Variety.—The principle of simplicity rejects every adjunct which disguises the form of the simple object to which it is attached. The head-dress in fashion a century ago is hideous to modern eyes; but the simple central parting of the hair in front, its straight combing to the form of the head, and its collection in a plain knot behind, won the admiration of the Greek artist as a perfect ideal, and drew forth the encomiums of Roman poets, because of its inherent beauty. There is a grandeur in the majestic dome of St. Peter's at Rome; there is sublimity in the sky-piercing pinnacles of the Gothic cathedral at Strasburg; but the inimitable simplicity of the plain Grecian gable won from Cicero the comment "that it was worthy to be the model for temples in heaven." That adjustment of drapery or dress which makes the form seem to round out in all its own loveliness as through a transparent veil, is one of the chief charms of beauty in form.

Fifth: Order in the collocation of parts.—*Order* relates not like the preceding principles to an object as a whole; but it expresses the relation which parts considered as making up a whole have to each other. Order, as to furniture in a room, requires that each piece be in a place peculiarly its own; in a company of men it may depend on age, or size, or likeness of pursuits. In the grouping of a picture or of a landscape order relates to the collocation of parts which make the whole conspire to one effect.

Sixth: Proportion in dimensions.—Proportion is not the relation of parts to a whole, but parts not of the same class to each other. Thus the three portions of the human finger are proportional; the ratio of each to its successor as to length being sesquialteral, or that of one to one and a half. The arms considered with relation to each other are *uniform;* but, when regarded as of different classes, the arms and legs are *proportionate* in length. The parts of a building are well proportioned when any two parts of the structure seem to be in keeping as to their dimensions. The columns of a portico compared with each other are uniform; but when the foot, shaft, and capital are compared with each other, or the whole column with the entablature above, they are said to be well or ill proportioned.

Seventh: Symmetry in the connection of parts.—The literal meaning of the Greek word "*summetron*" is, an *inter-measure;* and implies that one part of a whole is taken as a standard of common measurement for all the other parts. While order relates to the collocation of parts in the whole, and proportion to the respective dimensions of each part in its relation to each other part, symmetry relates to the graduation in measurement of all the parts connected in a whole to the dimensions of one taken as the standard. When we say of two limbs of a statue that they are in proportion, we think of them mainly in but one dimension. We could not say that two limbs were in symmetry; we must take in the entire figure, if we use at all that specific word, and say "the whole body is symmetrical;" and in so saying, we should regard rotundity, the thickness and plumpness of muscle, as well as length of bony framework, and also the interlockings and blendings of each limb. The idea of symmetry led the Greek artist to the simplest of common measures, the nail, finger, foot, cubit, pace, fathom, in studying the proportions of the child, the youth, the maiden, the matron and of the mature man; by following which they made their works true ideals, the models for all future time.

Eighth: Congruity in the adaptation of parts.—Congruity relates to physical adaptation, propriety to moral appropriateness. Congruity requires that all the parts of an object have an office, and that in size and position they be adapted to that office. It is an incongruity in Egyptian sculpture that a flaring head-dress should be cut in solid stone whose weight is enough to cause the wearer to sink under the burden; and that in Roman art a Mercury should have miniature wings projecting from his ankles and head, which could serve no purpose because they could have no muscular attachments. Congruity requires that in taking a portrait the posture, dress, insignia of an office or implements of a trade should be in keeping with the character of the subject represented.

Ancient and modern writers as Plato and Aristotle, Kames and Alison, discuss at length the elements of beauty thus considered. To commit them to memory in the order of nature is of practical utility in the criticism of art.

SECT. 2. COLOR; ITS ELEMENTS, AND THEIR CO-OPERATION AS THE ACCESSORIES OF ART.

In color as in form there is a natural order in which the elements which pleasurably impress the mind present themselves to our thought. When an object breaks first on our view, we seek to trace its outline; we consider whether it be one, and if one whether it be simple; if made up of parts, we notice their order, then their proportion as to each other, and then the symmetry of the whole; and finally we judge of the congruity or fitness of all the parts, so far as their form is concerned, to accomplish some design. In the observation of color as pleasantly affecting the mind, the order of thought may perhaps be resolved into the following.

First: Determinateness of Hue.—When we gaze by day into the heavens and see nothing but the light azure produced by the direct sunlight, or at night study the dark blue black of the faintest diffused light still present even at midnight, simple color has its pleasing charm. In the rich gold and purple of evening twilight, which has no background to make it stand out, and no form from which it is reflected, it is the determinateness of the varying yet positive hue which, like outline in substance, is the source of pleasure to the eye.

Second: Purity of Colors in themselves considered.—When color so far develops itself as to take a perceptible hue, the eye and the mind of the savage or cultured man desire that, whatever be the color of an object, it be clear, unmixed and unspotted. It demands, first, that it show nothing but its own hue; second, that it be not muddied with the tinge of foreign hues; and third, that it be not soiled by scattered spots and irregular lines of another color. The savage is as much dissatisfied with a dull or a faded color, or by a stain on his mantle, as is the most fastidious belle in polished society. When increased culture leads to a preference for the graver hues, the artist calls the pure clear tint resulting from the admixture of colors in their regular proportions "lively" hues; while disproportionate mixtures he designates as "dirty" colors. Whatever be the hue which taste selects, it demands purity in color as it does unity in form.

Third: Evenness of body.—Viewed alone, color must be pure in order to please. Color, however, is an attribute of substance; its richness depends on the substances it adorns; and evenness of color is a feature akin to regularity of form. A grove with foliage alike green and lively, a house whose paint is either all fresh or all sobered by age, are types in common observation of what the eye demands in higher art.

Fourth: Distinctiveness in Character.—As simplicity in form so distinctiveness in color impresses, because it brings out the special character of the object painted. The sky is recognized as clear, or cold, or sunlit, when its hue is blue, or gray, or rosy; the sea is known to be calm, or ruffled, or raging, according as it mirrors the varied colors of objects above it, or reflects its own green from its thin and half transparent wave crests, or absorbs all light at the black base of its swollen billows and transmits all light from the white transparence of their attenuated tops. Among the varied flowers and fruits and leaves that cover the earth as a carpet, and even throughout all the varieties of beasts and birds and of human beings, fur and hair, and even flesh tint, has, in each class, if not in each individual, its own peculiar characteristic. Art must catch these precise hues or fail in its aim.

Fifth: Accordance in juxtaposition.—As notes sounded together and as lines taken in at the same angle of vision, so colors viewed in immediate juxtaposition must have due proportion in order to produce accord. A house painted red, glowing amid the shade of the country, does violence to an instinctively recognized law of accord in colors. On the other hand, nothing can excel the charm of the rainbow, in whose arch the red, orange, yellow, green, blue, indigo and violet succeed each other in an order that is pleasing, not simply because it is common or natural, but because we are made for it, and it for us.

Sixth: Harmoniousness as a whole in the association of colors.—Though two notes struck together make discord, the same two struck separately but successively may produce harmony. So two lines or colors which, meeting the eye together, produce a disagreeable impression of jarring on the vision, may, when distributed at fit intervals, and of proportionate breadths, give harmony to the whole. In the rainbow it is not simply the order in which the colors succeed each other, but their grouping as a whole, the proportionate breadth, the adjusted place, the graduated vividness of each which produce the pleasant impression. In the varied hues of flowers, not overloading but simply studding the background of green, and in the distribution upon the light flesh color of the human face, of the ruby of the lips, of the ivory white of eyeballs and teeth, and of the dark lines of eyebrows and eyelash, there is just that amount of contrast which gives greatest completeness to the whole.

Seventh: Blending in conjunction.—As modulation of voice in music is the easy transition by which tones melt and flow into one another, and as symmetry in form is the similar tapering and mortising and dovetailing of parts into the one statue, so blending in colors is the imperceptibly varying shade, the nicely graduated scale of modified admixture by which one color flows into and loses its own hue in that of its fellow. No possible line of distinct demarcation can be traced between the distinct colors of the rainbow; no flower has any point of separation between the white foot and the crimson or purple tip of its petal; no single hair on an animal, or feather upon a bird, has at any part of its length a sudden transition in the varying shade, that, from its root outward, grows darker to its tip. When the artist in his effort at copying nature imitates her perfect work in this respect, every eye is conscious that the imperceptible blending of hues and shades into each other is one of the elements of the pleasure derived from beholding color.

Eighth: Appropriateness to the subject.—As in music expression gives soul to harmony, and in form congruity makes things to be real, not made up, so appropriateness of color gives its subject the chief attribute of living beings, which is life itself. This principle even in sculpture and architecture controls the selection of color in the material used; and in landscape-gardening it guides as to the amount and character of foliage introduced. In painting it seeks the power of giving to each object its own specific tinge, so that the eye without thought sees the thing itself through the deception of accurate coloring. In decorative art it decides between the claims of material and subject; demanding, for instance, that an iron cemetery gate representing a lamb under a willow shall all be bronze or black, and not allowing that the tree be colored green and the lamb white.

The classification here suggested may intimate to the student of art the value of analysis in his own impressions as to color.

Sect. 3. Fixed relation; the association of objects presented as at rest.

The impressions of beauty produced by form and color relate to a single object. The statue, however, with its exquisite form must stand on something resting upon the earth; the water lily with its attractive color floats on a liquid bed; the fleecy cloud flits and rocks in an airy cradle; and even the moon, rolling so far off, is held in its place by some power. In considering the beauty of any conceivable object its relations will force themselves into thought and give character to our æsthetic impressions.

When the relations of an object begin to come into review the mind resolves them into natural classes. Considered as at rest, objects have certain fixed relations; and regarded as acted upon by forces within or without, physical or spiritual in their nature, the same objects have changing relations; which relations, fixed or changing, enter as elements into our estimate of beauty. The principal relations, so far as art is concerned, of objects considered as at rest are comprehended under the ideas of place, time, quantity, and number; while those of objects regarded as changing are motion, life, action and emotion.

The idea of *space* suggests that of place; for when two objects are considered, each has its position in relation to the other. Next arises the idea of *balance.* When a single object is dimly seen in the mist, we look for the foot on which it rests; as the ancient Arabian inquired after the "balancing of the clouds." As no beauty of form can overcome our unpleasant nervousness when a noble man or fair woman is seen in a position exposing them to a fall, so a building, a statue, or even a figure painted upon canvas produces an unpleasant impression, destructive of the idea of beauty, when it seems insecure because unbalanced; of which the leaning tower of Pisa is an illustration.

As balance in one object, so *relative position* in two or more objects is to be observed. In painting the law of perspective makes the central figure foremost and prominent, because nearer the beholder. The Greeks in ranging a group of statuary in the pediment of a temple, placed the central figure under the roof-peak on a throne; while the remaining figures, as the diminishing height allowed, were represented, first standing, then seated, and finally reclining. This law led Hogarth to contend that all groups in both sculpture and painting should be pyramidal in shape; the central figure having the larger proportions, especially in historical composition.

Next to the relation of place comes that of *quantity*. As proportion and symmetry should be regarded in a single object, so there is a due comparison in the size of objects grouped as a whole. The interior of St. Peter's, like Niagara, seems at first dwarfed because every part is alike colossal; but when each feature is separately comprehended the stupendous whole assumes its just grandeur, because of the due proportion in each part. On the other hand, when Phidias made his colossal statue of Minerva hold her spear in one hand and a statue of Victory in the other, it was true art to swell the spear shaft till it seemed a beam, and to dwarf the statue to the natural proportions of about six feet in stature. In an historical painting the central figure may occupy too much space, as in some of Rubens', or too little as in Trumbull's; while again the effort to give breadth to two distinct and distant scenes in one group may mar the effect of even such a masterpiece as Raphael's Transfiguration.

Last among fixed relations is that of *number*. In art, as in nature, a small range limits the view; and when the number of objects contemplated becomes indefinite and without limit, the emotion of beauty is lost in confusion of mind. The ancient observers clustered the stars in groups of "seven," "eleven" and "twelve." The scene of all others on earth most tragic, the crucifixion, may have too many figures introduced, as in that of Titian, who was seeking the effects of color; or it may have too few, as in masterpieces of Florentine artists who were striving after the higher effect of form.

The relations of objects as fixed, or at rest, have been observed by writers of every age. Aristotle asks, "Why the bodies of deformed men look larger proportionally than those that have symmetry:" and his reply is, "That symmetrical forms are naturally viewed as one, while the limbs of the deformed man seem parts of different bodies, and hence appear to occupy more space." Lord Kames mentions a like effect in the divisions of a flower garden, or of fields in a level country.

SECT. 4. CHANGING RELATION; THE DISPOSITION OF OBJECTS REPRESENTED AS IN MOTION.

There is motion in inanimate objects, or those without life; the rain falling, the rivers flowing, the tides rolling, the clouds flying, the mountain rocks tumbling, and the volcano heaving; while beyond the earth, moons, planets, and starry suns, all seem coursing in their circles through the heavens. It is because "all things are full of labor" that poets and artists have believed that all things are "beautiful in their time."

Motion in unorganized matter is produced from without. The plant builds itself up; animals have the power of physical locomotion; while man, gifted with intellect, sensibility and will, has self-action both of body and of mind.

Motion is produced by *power;* which is either *physical* or *moral;* and the idea of power leads to that of *cause.* Causation implies intelligent *purpose;* which always must originate with a *personal being.* The subject of changing relation, therefore, in its bearing upon art leads to the different classes of motion and emotion which may be represented, to the methods of art by which they may be presented to the eye, and to the study of design by which works of art are adapted to awaken any desired impression.

Change, produced by motion, suggests the idea of *time;* embracing considerations relating to day and night, to summer and winter, to ages of man's life and of the world's history. If the time chosen by a painter be noon, he must give appropriate length and direction to his shadows; and if it be winter the deciduous trees must be bare and the pines clothed with foliage. If the scene be the visit of Eastern Magi to the babe Jesus, the stable must not be of modern carpentry and the costumes mediæval.

Motion, which in nature is real, can only be *represented* in art; except in landscape gardening. Mere motion in any solid body gives delight; the infant being pleased with a stick shaken before it, the boy with the skipping of a stone or the bounding of a ball, and mature men with the whirl of machinery, the rush of a railway train, the coursing of a vessel at sea, or even with the lazy drag of a cart or a plough. The delight we take in such movements is proportioned to the regularity of their speed, and to their line of direction whether straight or curved.

In the motion of a *fluid* the perfect ease with which the particles move upon each other, as well as the gentle curving of its lines of movement, gives delight. The swift rush of the mountain torrent, the gentle meandering of a river in low lands, the glistening spheres of falling rain, the parabolic curves of the fountain-jet and water-fall present a beauty of motion which solid bodies cannot equal. Even the air moving in columns, the ever-changing forms of clouds flying and of trees waving before the breeze, have an inspiring charm.

The representation by the artist of any form of motion awakens delight, as trees bending or smoke wreathing before the wind. The picturing of the attitudes of motion in animate beings has a yet higher charm. Indeed a mere implement of motion, suggestive of the idea, a boat-oar lying on a sandy beach as truly as a bear in a forest, a sheep on a lawn, or Adam surrounded by groups of animals as he is naming them, by its implying a more studied design and holding the position of superiority among subordinates, becomes a centre of attraction. In Grecian sculpture, the representation of corporeal action is the very perfection of art; as is seen in the visible shrinking of modesty in the Venus de Medici, and in the advancing attitude and strain of limb in the Apollo Belvidere hurling his arrow. The great success of the German painters, as compared with those of Southern Europe, is the amount of motion, of life, of changing relation, they crowd upon their canvas.

SECT. 5. PHYSICAL COINCIDENCE; THE LAW OF HARMONIOUS PROPORTION BETWEEN TONES PLEASING TO THE EAR AND FORMS AND COLORS AGREEABLE TO THE EYE.

Though in some respects speculative, the study of physical coincidence between the impressions made by sight and sound has commended itself to the ablest minds of every age; many of whom have believed that the laws of beauty like those of truth may be so reached that the artist may attain to a science in the former as in the latter field. Philosophers as well as poets have believed in an age of human advancement of which it might be said:

> "There thou shalt learn the secret power
> Of harmony in tones, and numbers hit
> By voice or hand."

Ancient philosophy suggested, and modern science has established, that the impressions of sight coming from form and color are produced by vibratory waves in ether; as sound is the result of similar waves in the air. Common taste among men has recognized that the proportions of a door or window are pleasing when the length is to the breadth as two to one, or as three to two; while if they be as nine to eight it is specially displeasing. Since these are the same proportions which in the length of vibrating cords produce accordant or discordant impressions, it is natural to infer that the vibrating waves in ether, coming from lines that subtend different angles of vision having different breadths, may harmonize or clash like air-waves with one another. Again, the investigations of Sir David Brewster and others have established that the waves of light producing different color impressions are of different breadths. When in a crack made by a blow upon ice the narrowest part of the aperture is black, while bands of violet, indigo, blue, green, yellow, orange and red succeed each other till the white transparence appears, it is a natural inference that the waves of ether producing these colors are of the breadth of the aperture from whose space these special colors are reflected. These waves producing colors pleasing in juxtaposition are found to be of a breadth kindred in their proportions to air-waves pleasantly affecting the ear. There is then a coincidence between the impressions of sight and sound.

Pythagoras, who discovered the law of inter-measurement in the length of cords producing harmonious sounds, believed he had reached a similar measure for harmonious proportions of length and breadth in objects addressing the eye; and hence he named the highest note of the scale *neate* after the moon, the body bound to the centre by the shortest cord, and the lowest note he called *hypate*, after Saturn, as the planet bound to the centre by the longest cord. Plato in his Republic says that "as the eyes seem to be fitted for the harmonious proportions of the celestial orbits, so the ears seem to be fitted for the harmony of musical intervals;

and these seem to be sister sciences; as the Pythagoreans indeed affirm, and we must accord with them." Aristotle, when speaking of colors produced by admixture, says: "These may subsist in the same manner as musical symphonies; for, like musical symphonies, colors which correspond most nearly to their proportionate numbers are those which appear to be the most delightful colors." "It is for want of this skillfully adjusted proportion that, as there are but few delightful symphonies, so there are but few delightful colors."

In modern times Galileo revived this idea. Fond from childhood of music and drawing, a remark of his father that "drawing and music had their principles in the relations of numbers as taught in the mathematics," gave a new bent to all his life's labor. Sir Isaac Newton had his attention turned to this analogy; and wrote, "I am inclined to believe some general laws of the Creator prevailed with respect to the agreeable or unpleasing affections of all our senses; at least the suggestion does not derogate from the wisdom or power of God, and seems highly consonant to the simplicity of the microcosm in general."

Taking up the principles of these great philosophers, Hay, an English artist, has drawn out an elaborate system of harmonies in form; while Unger, a German critic, has applied them to color. Mr. Hay's first position is, "That the eye is influenced in its estimation of spaces by a simplicity of proportion similar to that which guides the ear in its appreciation of sounds." His second position is, "That the eye is guided in its estimate of dimensions by direction rather than distance, by angular rather than linear proportion; just as the ear is guided by number rather than magnitude of sounds." The substance of his theory therefore is, "That a figure is pleasing to the eye in the same degree as its fundamental angles bear to each other the same proportions that the vibrations bear to one another in the common chords of music." The conclusion at which he thus arrives is stated in the following emphasized sentence: "Thus the eye is capable of appreciating the exact subdivision of *space* just as the ear is capable of appreciating the exact subdivision of intervals of *time;* so that the division of space into an exact number of equal parts will æsthetically affect the mind through the medium of the eye, in the same way that the division of the time of vibrations in music into an exact number of equal parts æsthetically affects the mind through the medium of the ear." Following out these principles, Hay has with most elaborate comparison and collation of numerous measurements of the human frame, drawn up scales of established angles of harmony; showing also their analogy to those ruling in musical harmony. In like manner, Unger of Göttingen, tracing through the exhaustive deductions of Frauenhofer as to the breadth of waves in ether producing the impressions of the different colors, has drawn out a similar scale of harmonious proportions; showing also a kindred analogy to the proportions giving the sweetest of musical harmonies.

From these historical facts Winckelmann, the eminent German art-critic, argues; "It is probable that the Grecian, like the Egyptian artists had rules by which not only the greater but the smaller proportions of the body were accurately determined; and that the length, breadth, and circumference of parts suitable to each age and station were laid down with precision and taught in the writings of those artists who treated of symmetry." It is an interesting confirmation of this view that while the two arts representative of these two departments, drawing and music, are naturally admired by the same class of minds, when the one cannot be enjoyed the other takes its place. Deaf-mutes have as instinctive a fondness for drawing as the blind have for music; a hint of great importance in the education of the former.

Sect. 6. Moral correspondence; the harmony between objects presented and ideas represented in art.

Lord Kames states an important distinction between the ideas of congruity and propriety. Congruity relates to fitness and appropriateness of one material object to another. Thus when the naked African chief, donning the cast-off military coat of an English officer given to him, struts like a peacock in this single article of dress, we speak of the *incongruity* between the scarlet coat and the naked form of the black savage; but in speaking of the *nudity* of the savage we should use the word *impropriety.*

While the Greek philosophers, Socrates, Plato and Aristotle, dwelt with delight on the physical coincidences which made art a power to please, they urged that as its higher aim, art be made to correspond to true convictions of moral propriety, because of its power for good or evil on youth and men of mature age. The Roman critics, as Cicero the Eclectic, Cato and Seneca the Stoics, and even Horace and Juvenal who leaned to Epicurean notions, discussed especially the moral bearings of art, urging the demand of propriety more than of congruity in works of art. Horace, in his "Ars Poetica," makes a question of congruity in the Egyptian sphynx a key to his criticisms relating to the moral proprieties belonging to compositions in literature and art. As might be anticipated, the allusions to art which fill the Old and New Testament Scriptures relate to its moral proprieties as a power for good.

The applications of this principle of moral correspondence in art are varied and numerous. Moral propriety demands truth in position; requiring ease and security in the attitude of men represented as swaying to and fro under excited feeling; an attainment of gradual growth in the early stages of the revival of art in Italy. Moral propriety requires truth in respect to time; censuring anachronisms; a principle which the secluded lives, and especially the reverence for ecclesiastical precedents common to Italian artists of the best age, has led them to overlook in the dress, attendants and other accessories introduced into their representations of the life of Christ. Both congruity and propriety, not to mention other moral convictions, are opposed to that mutilation and transportation of works of ancient art which cause those exquisitely wrought gems to be viewed out of their proper position; a fact sensibly impressed upon the visitor to the detached and fragmentary specimens of bas-reliefs wrested from the cornices of Egyptian and Grecian temples, and gathered in the London and Paris collections of art; a principle which is still more deeply felt when the traveler's eye rests on the voids in the original structures, lonely and voiceless on their native soil, from whose walls have been cut and pried out the select portions of those masterpieces of ancient art. Congruity and propriety, too, are the essential elements of separate excellences, such as that of grace, in works of art. While, for instance, there is the rarest grace in a weary Hercules leaning on his club, in an exhausted dancing girl resting on her seat, and in a panting warrior reclining at full length on the ground, nothing could be more the opposite of true grace than the attitude of a belle or courtier lounging in ill-disguised ennui.

CHAPTER V.

THE FACULTIES OF THE HUMAN MIND AS AFFECTED BY ART.

In all human impressions two things are to be regarded; the mind on which the impression is made and the object without the mind which makes the impression. The external object and the senses through which it is perceived having been first considered, it is natural to bend back the mind's thought upon itself and to analyze its impressions as well as the thinking power which experiences these impressions.

Without this consideration of the power itself which he employs, the practical artist may use with a large share of success his mental faculties in designing and executing works of art. Without it, however, the student of art, not himself a practical artist, can gain no consistent knowledge; while moreover the artist himself may add indefinitely to the skill with which he can wield his powers, when, like the master in the mechanic arts he can from knowledge of its nature, mould and adapt the instrument with which he works. This Plato, ignorant of the practice but master of the theory of art, intimated in the inquiry, "Indeed then do those men seem to you to differ from blind men who in reality are destitute of theoretic knowledge; who, neither have in their own souls a distinct ideal, nor like painters looking above themselves to the true ideal, always referring their own conceptions to it and contemplating it with the greatest accuracy possible, are enabled, in this department as in those others, to establish just rules of the beautiful, as of the right and of the good?"

In this consideration these natural divisions will be observed. The general impression produced on the human mind by works of art is entitled "Beauty;" and the power of the mind both to appreciate and to create objects of beauty is styled "Taste." Each of these, the impression and the power, may be considered separate from its object, or in the *abstract;* and each in connection with its object, or in the *concrete;* while the comparative strength both of the power and of its impression in different beings and classes of men is naturally a concluding inquiry.

SECT. 1. BEAUTY IN THE ABSTRACT; OR THE NATURE OF OUR IDEA OF THE BEAUTIFUL.

As to the essential nature of our idea of the Beautiful there has been far greater unanimity than would be apparent to one failing to discriminate between beauty in the abstract and beauty in the concrete. Even upon the latter point of consideration, opinions discordant at first view assume a degree of harmony when principles maintained by differing theorists are put into their legitimate connections.

The distinction between the four elementary principles of human apprehension, the true, the beautiful, the good, the right, has been recognized by leading philosophers in all ages and of the most opposite schools. It may be illustrated by a simple example. If any one beholding an apple on a mantel should say, "That is a *true* apple," he would be understood as referring to the essence or substance of the apple; as the juicy pulp constituting the real fruit, in opposition to a fictitious representation of it in wax or marble. If he should say, "That is a beautiful apple," he would be supposed to refer to the form and color as conveying a pleasant impression; an idea, entirely aside from any consideration as to the material of which it is composed. If again he should say "That is a good apple," he would as manifestly refer to the *adaptation* of the real or fictitious fruit; the one as a *true* apple to afford by its substance gratification to the palate and health to the digestive organs, and the other to give pleasure as *beautiful* by its form and color addressing the eye, and through it the mind. If he should say, yet again, "That is a *right* apple," every hearer would feel that violence was done to the common meaning of language. The principle of right does not respect the essence of the apple as true, its form as beautiful, nor its adaptation as good; it can only be ascribed to an emotion, desire, or act which a human being may exercise in reference to the apple as possessing either of these qualities. This general distinction of these four elementary conceptions is of universal application; as when of a mental or moral quality or exercise, we say, "That was a true, a beautiful, a good act."

The questions, "What is beauty?" "Why is a thing beautiful?" Socrates argued are irrational. Abstract terms cannot be defined to a mind that has not already the idea which they express. If it be asked, "What is truth, beauty, goodness and right?" it can only be stated; truth is that which in the *essence* of a thing corresponds with the convictions of our understanding; beauty is that which in the *qualities* of an object affords pleasure to our sensibilities; goodness is that in the *relation* of one thing to another, which secures the welfare or promotes the interest of the latter; and right is that in the *act* of an intelligent being which corresponds with our conviction of the responsibility of one moral being to another. If these attempts at definition seem inadequate, it must be remembered that there is the same difficulty in defining by simpler language any abstract term; as the word white or round, equality or justice.

Thus Plato, after mentioning that right, goodness, honor, magnitude, strength, health, "are all abstract things," adds: "We speak of things as equal, or unequal. We not only see one stick as equal to another stick, and one stone as equal to another stone, but, besides, we think of equality in itself, as separate and real. Now where do we acquire this knowledge? Not from the sticks or stones; for these are strictly equal. Equality is not the same as equal things. But yet from seeing equal things we think of equality."

When asked why I believe that an object which I see exists, that two lines cannot enclose space, that every effect has an adequate cause, and why I regard certain lines and tints beautiful, I can only say that I am so made that I cannot but so regard them. As to the essential nature of beauty in the abstract, the thought of mankind has been remarkably coincident. Lucan, the Roman poet, says: "The idea of beauty is the same among nations in their decline and in their infancy." Augustine, the Christian philosopher, says: "If we both *see* that to be true which *you* say is true, and both see that to be true which *I* say is true, *where*, I ask, do we see it? Neither do I see it in you, nor you in me; but both in that which is above our minds, in the unchangeable verity itself." The reasoning of modern writers, such as Locke, Kames, Reid, Burke, Alison and others in England, of Kant in Germany, and of Cousin in France, might be quoted at length substantially to the same point. Thus Ruskin remarks, "Why some forms and colors are beautiful is as unknown as why sugar is sweet, and wormwood is bitter." Alluding then to the fact that our Creator has made men with a common impression of beauty, he adds, "We may, indeed, perceive as far as we are acquainted with His nature, that we have been so constructed as, when in a healthy and cultivated state of mind, to derive pleasure from whatever things are illustrative of that nature; but we do not receive pleasure from them because they are illustrative of it, but instinctively and necessarily; as we derive sensual pleasure from the scent of a rose."

SECT. 2. TASTE; OR THE POWER OF THE MIND WHICH GIVES ORIGIN TO THE IDEA OF THE BEAUTIFUL.

The four conceptions of the true, the beautiful, the good and the right are naturally referred to distinct powers of the mind. The power by which man recognizes abstract truth has in all ages been expressed by a word corresponding to the English term reason; while the faculty which discerns right has as uniformly been called by the name *conscience*. The good, or adaptation in things, may be referred to that power which in animals and man has, as distinct from reason, been called "instinct."

To the power by which the mind apprehends the second of these ideas, the *beautiful*, modern, popular language, as well as modern philosophy, has consecrated the word "Taste." It is a designation borrowed from the quickest and most controlling though most corporeal of the human senses. The ancient Asiatic patriarch employed it to express the instinctive power of the mind in discerning both the right and the true; asking at one time, "Is there iniquity in my tongue? Cannot my taste discern perverse things?" and again inquiring, "Doth not the ear try words, even as the mouth tastes its meat?" In the Greek and Latin tongues a similar tropical signification was given to the word by such writers as Sophocles and Pindar, Cicero and Quinctilian; Sophocles speaking of "testing a truth by the tongue;" Pindar of "tasting the sweets of song;" Cicero of "the taste for literary studies," and Quinctilian of the rhetorical "taste of the city." From those ancient tongues the same word used in the same figurative signification has passed to their modern successors, as the Italian and the French. About the middle of the eighteenth century, Reid, the Scotch metaphysician, followed by Kames, Burke and Alison, fixed the use of the English word "Taste" to designate the power by which the mind recognizes beauty; while

Kant, the German philosopher, brought into use the more classic name *æsthetic* sense or judgment.

As to the office of this power of the mind, Plato in his Republic reasons: "As to the beautiful and the good in existing objects, we say, indeed, that they are seen by the eye and are not objects of intellectual perception; but we also say that the ideas themselves of beauty and goodness are perceived by the intellect and are not seen by the eye." Of the two theories discussed in modern times Alison gives the following statement: "The first class is that which resolves the emotion of taste into an original law of our nature: which supposes a sense or senses, by which the qualities of beauty and sublimity are perceived and felt as their appropriate objects; and concludes therefore that the genuine object of the arts of taste is to discover and to imitate those qualities in every subject which the prescription of nature has thus made essentially either beautiful or sublime. To this first class of hypotheses belong almost all the theories of music, of architecture and of sculpture; the theory of Mr. Hogarth, of the Abbe Winckelmann, and perhaps, in its last result, also the theory of Sir Joshua Reynolds. It is the species of hypothesis which is naturally resorted to by all artists and amateurs; by those whose habits of thought lead them to attend more to the causes of their emotions than to the nature of the emotions themselves. The second class of hypotheses arises from the opposite view of the subject. It is that which resists the idea of any new or peculiar sense distinct from the common principles of our nature; which supposes some one known and common affection of mind to be the foundation of all the emotions we receive from the objects of taste, and which resolves, therefore, all the various phenomena into some more general law of our intellectual or moral constitution. Of this kind are the hypothesis of M. Diderot, who attributes all our emotions of this kind to the perception of relation; of Mr. Hume, who resolves them into our sense of utility; and of the venerable St. Austin, who, with nobler views, a thousand years ago resolved them into the pleasure which belongs to the perception of order and design. It is the species of hypothesis most natural to retired and philosophic minds; to those whose habits have led them to attend more to the nature of the emotions they felt than to the causes which produced them."

As to the nature of taste as an intuitive power of the mind re cognizing beauty, Reid says, "The sense of beauty is an agreeable feeling or emotion accompanied with an opinion or judgment of some excellence in the object which is fitted by nature to produce that feeling." Blair says, "Taste is ultimately founded on an internal sense of beauty, which is natural to men." Burke's statement is, "I mean by the word taste no more than the faculty or those faculties of the mind which are affected with, or which form a judgment of, the works of imagination and the elegant arts." Ruskin, after arguing that taste is a power of the mind, distinct from judgment which decides as to truth and that power unnamed which recognizes fitness, says of this power, "It is the instinctive and instant preferring of one material object to another without any obvious reason except that it is proper to human nature in its perfection to do so."

Sect. 3. Beauty in the concrete; or the elements in objects which give the impression of beauty.

It is in concrete objects that beauty is seen by the ordinary eye. All language for abstract ideas is primarily drawn from the field of the concrete; as words expressive of spiritual ideas are derived from material objects. It was natural when Socrates asked, "What is beauty?" that his interlocutors should constantly make the mistake in reply of citing some beautiful object, as a blooming girl, or a masterpiece of statuary to express their conception. We, for the same reason, use comparisons to illustrate our ideas; saying, "It was as beautiful as a rose; she was as fair as a lily; he is as graceful as a gazelle."

When any object gives us the impression of beauty, we instinctively think of the elements in the object which give this impression. If a boy's marble, a cornelian and a diamond were together held up before a company of men or of children, of savages or of refined scholars, all would refer the beauty in each respectively to its form, color and lustre. In a spirited saddle-horse by the side of a pack-mule, form and color would be quoted as elements of beauty, with the additional quality of grace in motion. In a lovely young female the three classes of qualities already mentioned would still be referred to, with the additional element of expression in the eye revealing traits of intellectual and moral character. Into each of these successive examples some new element enters to make up what in each instance we designate by the general name beauty; and abstracting the several elements in each case we can look for their counterpart elsewhere in nature, or seek to reproduce them in art.

Most of the ancient Greek writers on beauty, Plato excepted, satisfy themselves with referring to objects of beauty in the concrete. Pythagoras taught that beauty is "unity in variety, and harmony in opposite qualities." Later Greek critics recognize beauty as a quality in objects distinct from both truth and goodness; while, nevertheless, though truth and goodness are not themselves beauty, they are indispensable associate principles.

Thus Socrates having obtained two disconnected admissions that purple is the most beautiful color, and that the eye is the most beautiful part of the body, asks, "Why then do not painters add beauty to the eyes by painting them purple;" and having kept his weak antagonist perplexed a while he exclaims, "Wonderful critic! you do not imagine, do you, that in order to make the eyes more beautiful we should paint them so that they would not appear to be eyes?" The power of simple goodness to give the impression of beauty is admirably illustrated by a fancied or real conversation between Socrates, whose ugliness of form has passed into a proverb, and Alcibiades, who was a paragon of manly beauty. Alcibiades said to Socrates that in personal appearance he seemed to him like "the figures of Silenus," noted for his flabby and beast-like grossness, and, indeed, like "to the satyr Marsyas," the eminent flute-player, characterized by his grimaces in blowing his instrument, and added, "That in your outward appearance, Socrates, you resemble those beings, you yourself will not deny." Mentioning then that in spite of his ugly aspect, he was irresistibly drawn to him and even admired his features, Socrates recognizes this as illustrating his principle of beauty; and exclaims, "What is that matchless beauty you could see in me so vastly superior to your own fine form?"

The special qualities which united produce the impression of beauty are graphically pictured by Plato as meeting in Cupid. "Love is . . . the most blessed of the gods; at once the most beautiful and the best." "He is very young and very delicate; and in addition to these qualities, he is of a most flexible form; otherwise he would not be able to entwine himself around every form." "Another great proof that his form excels in symmetry and flexibility is found in its gracefulness; which excellence Love confessedly possesses in a manner superior to all beings." "His diet, too, on flowers points out the beauty of his color."

A surprising likeness in practical minds appears in their analysis of beauty. Hogarth on the title-page of his celebrated treatise, as the symbol of his theory, inscribed a triangle, within which he drew a serpent in the waving line which his body takes when moving. His idea, he says, is borrowed from Michel Angelo's maxim for his pupils, that figures should always be made "pyramidal, serpentine, and with a ratio of increase by one, two and three." This maxim, M. Angelo himself had borrowed from Aristotle's suggestion that "flame, pyramidal in form and serpent-like in its motion, is most indicative of life and symbolic of spirit." Hogarth finds these principles in the Grecian and Roman gables, and in the waving lines introduced into their architectural ornaments; while in the group of Laocoön the same idea is so controlling that the two sons at the side of the father are made of natural size, and the central figure colossal, so as to make the whole come within the triangle or pyramid.

The admirable critic Beattie, finds the chief elements of beauty to reside in form, color and expression; united with the moral idea of suitableness, or fitness. Thus he says, "Colors are beautiful, *first* when they convey to the mind a lively sensation, as white and red; *second*, when they cherish the organ of vision, as green; *third*, when they have that character which we term delicacy, and yield a sensation both lively and gentle, as pale red and light blue. But, *fourth*, the beauty of color depends chiefly on the agreeableness of the ideas it conveys to the mind. The verdure of the fields, for instance, is delightful because it leads us to think of fruitfulness, fragrance, and many other pleasant things; but greenness in the human face would be horrible because it would suggest the notion of pain, of disease, and of something unnatural." Again he says, "That which in the smallest compass exhibits the greatest variety of beauty is a fine human face. The features are of various sizes and forms; the corresponding ones are exactly uniform; and each has that shape, size, position, and proportion which is most convenient. Here, too, is the greatest beauty of colors, which are blended, varied and disposed with marvelous delicacy. But the chief beauty of the countenance arises from its expression."

Lord Kames, a critic of the greatest acuteness, divides beauty into two species, intrinsic and relative. Relative beauty depends not on what the thing is in itself, but on its relations to other things, its associations, its utility and its propriety. "Intrinsic beauty," he says, "must be analyzed into its constituent parts. If a tree be beautiful by means of its color, its figure, its size, its motion, it is in reality possessed of so many different beauties; which ought to be examined separately, in order to have a clear notion of them when combined. The beauty of color is too familiar to need explanation." "The beauty of figure, arising from various circumstances and different views, is more complex; for example, viewing any body as a whole, the beauty of its figure arises from regularity and simplicity; viewing the parts with relation to each other, uniformity, proportion and order contribute to its beauty. The beauty ot motion deserves a chapter by itself." The more elaborate Reid in presenting his analysis of beauty, says, "Our sense of beauty is resolvable into instinctive and rational, and beauty itself into original and derived." These he further analyzes thus: "The qualities of inanimate matter in which we perceive beauty are sound, color, form and motion; the first an object of hearing, the others of sight." "All that can be called beauty in the human species may be reduced to these four heads; color, form, expression and grace. The two former may be called the body, the two latter the soul of beauty."

Alison argues that the beauty both of color and form arises mainly from our associations connected with them. Thus three classes of colors are regarded beautiful; "*first*, such as arise from the nature of the objects thus permanently colored," as green in grass; "*second*, such as arise from some analogy between certain colors and dispositions of mind," as white for bridal dresses; "*third*, such as arise from accidental connections, whether national or particular," as purple in every land for a royal robe, and scarlet in England for a soldier's uniform. Forms, like colors, are dependent on the same law of association for their beauty. Thus foliage and flower are beautiful only when the material seems adequate; delicacy in marble, for instance, being a blemish unless cut in low relief, so that it seems firm as well as delicate; while also the serpentine curve, specially expressive of delicacy, is a blemish when, as in the rose stem, strength and erectness seem to be naturally requisite.

The modern French philosopher, Cousin, one of the ablest, as well as most comprehensive of critics, recognizes the distinction between abstract and concrete beauty; treating first of the "true, the beautiful and the good" in themselves, and second of "beaüty in things." He thinks the theory of Plato, in his Hippias, that beauty consists of the suitableness of means to an end, nearest to the true view. A condition. however, of *suitableness*, is proportion and order; unity and variety too are among its essential elements; while even the ideal, the fictitious, is in an important respect suited to our nature; and he concludes, "The great law of beauty, like that of truth, is unity as well as variety." Proceeding from material to spiritual elements, he refers to Winckelmann's masterly analysis of the Apollo Belvidere, especially of the face, as "expressing beauty of soul;" and using Plato's illustration that moral beauty may even make natural ugliness to appear beautiful, he adds, "The natural face of Socrates contrasts strongly with the type of Grecian beauty; but look upon him on his death-bed, at the moment of drinking the hemlock, conversing with his disciples on the immortality of the soul, and his face will appear to you sublime." A correct analysis of beauty in the concrete will lead us to fix upon the particulars already considered in the preceding chapter as its chief elements.

SECT. 4. ÆSTHETIC JUDGMENT; THE PROCESS OF THE MIND BY WHICH WE DECIDE THAT AN OBJECT IS BEAUTIFUL.

The process of mind by which we decide that a thing is true, good, or beautiful, or that an act is right, follows the same law of reasoning in either of these fields.

When a child first sees a cricket-ball neatly rounded and stitched, at rest or flying in the air, a process of syllogistic reasoning, with its two premises and its consequent conclusion, is instinctively suggested. He sees the ball, its elaborated form, its projectile motion; he has confidence in the testimony of his eyesight; and this axiom is his first premise. At the same moment he has the consciousness of an inward conviction that the ball could not possess such a form, or move in such a manner, unless the hand of some intelligent being had formed it and given it its impulse; he has confidence in this testimony of his consciousness; and this axiom is his second premise. He has thus arrived at absolute truth, by a process of metaphysical reasoning, upon which no philosopher can improve; for it is only superior skill in employing the powers of reasoning native to man, the power of observing facts, of marking the mind's suggestions as to their causes, and of referring the one to the other, that distinguishes a Newton from a child or a savage.

By a similar process the mind decides upon the goodness of a thing, or the right of an action; and also upon the *beauty* of objects. At the sound of a sweet-voiced singing bird, or of a well-trained musical band, at sight of a richly colored flower, a gracefully moving horse, or of a lovely female face, the eye of the child, of the savage, and of the philosopher would alike sparkle with delight; and were any one of this company of beholders, so diversified in character, asked the cause of his pleasure, he would present the same view and in the same order of thought. He has heard the peculiar melody from the single note of the warbler and the combined harmony of many-toned instruments; he has seen the peculiar color, form, movement, and expression; and this is his first premise. He has within him the common organism of ear, eye and associated soul, on which such sounds and sights are made to produce a pleasant impression; and this is his second premise. It is by the use of his judgment upon the facts, and of his taste upon a principle, that every beholder of an object decides upon its beauty as he does upon its truth.

This law of the mind, which enables the artist to forecast what will please men as certainly as the philosopher can predict what will convince them, has been set forth with great force by the ablest minds. Socrates employed his keenest power of analysis, his most comprehensive range of illustration and his closest logic, as well as his most admirable wit, in his reasoning upon beauty. Lord Bacon in his "Novum Organon" ascribes the same high office to *fantasy* in poetry and art as to *memory* in history, and to *reason* in science and philosophy. Kant places æsthetic judgment, which decides as to beauty, before the teleological which decides as to truth. Hume, replied to by Reid, in maintaining the position that the decisions of the mind as to beauty are not to be relied upon, had to contend that "beauty is not a quality of the circle"

Cousin's second course of Lectures presents an admirable outline of the exercise of the mind in this department. It is important for the pupil in art to be assured that there are certain elements in the form, color and relations of objects which will always please, and that the artist and his critic may attain positive knowledge of these.

SECT. 5. COMPARATIVE TASTE; THE VARIED DEVELOPMENT OF THE IDEA OF BEAUTY AMONG MEN; ITS PROBABLE ABSENCE IN BEINGS INFERIOR, AND ITS POSSIBLE PERFECTION IN BEINGS SUPERIOR TO MAN.

If the powers of the mind are employed in the same manner to decide upon the beauty as on the truth of an object, it is a legitimate inference that the natural and acquired power of correct decision on questions of beauty must differ in different persons, as does the power of logical reasoning upon questions of truth. Moreover as no being inferior to man is supposed to possess the power of arriving at principles of abstract truth, though all animals below man have an intelligence which gives them practical knowledge of truth in the concrete, so animals may be supposed to have no theoretical apprehension of principles of beauty, though subject in a measure to impressions from its objects. Yet again, as we are assured that there are beings higher than man in the gift of reason which apprehends truth, and as we ourselves may in another state of being possess this endowment in a higher degree, so may it be with the power of apprehending and judging of beauty.

The child is fond of pure unmixed colors and rudely carved forms, and is restricted by the limit of a child's development. The female sex, though quicker than the male in intuitive conceptions, seem as a rule, to which there are noble exceptions, to tire in the effort at higher execution in the field of beauty; since in the history of art eminent female sculptors and painters are as rare as eminent female sages and poets. The Asiatic, and especially the African race, quick to attain the elements of science and art, have stopped short, each at its own fixed limit, of the goal attained by the European race. The general fact that age, sex, race and grades of culture place limits to the development of power in art has been recognized by ancient and modern critics. Aristotle discusses the limits of development in the appreciation of truth and beauty reached by different ages and sexes. Reid says, "The most perfect works of art have a beauty that strikes even the rude and ignorant; but they see only a small part of that beauty which is seen in such works by those who understand them perfectly and can produce them." Blair maintains that there is among all mankind a common standard of taste; adding this explanation, "When we refer to the concurring sentiments of men as the ultimate standard of taste, or of what is to be accounted beautiful in the arts, this is to be always understood of men placed in such situations as are favorable to exertions of taste." Burke remarks, "There is rather less difference upon matters of taste among mankind than upon most of those matters which depend upon the naked reason." He adds this important fact, "As arts advance toward their perfection, the science of criticism advances with equal pace."

In considering the manner in which animals are affected by sights and sounds that are pleasing, ancient and modern critics have distinguished between the active power of forming conceptions of beauty in the abstract and the passive capacity of being affected by beauty in the concrete. The weary camel is inspirited by his rider's flute, and the horse seems to feel pride in a gay equipage; but they do not, like the young child, attempt to copy what thus gives them a passive delight. The nightingale sings sweetly, and the bee builds skillfully; but, if these were arts with them, they could vary and improve upon their performance. Beings inferior to man may not only be affected by art, but may even delight the ear and eye of man; yet they have no principles to guide them in their execution, and they operate not as men, but as machines, turning out ever the same work.

As there seems to have been in the history of art, as well as of science, in Greece, Rome, and modern Italy, a limit beyond which neither nations nor individuals can go in their advance, while nevertheless each stage of the new rise and progress of science and art in each nation has seemed in some respects to exceed any preceding, so philosophers have believed there may be a state of being where the soul of man untrammeled by the body's grossness will have clearer perception, and attain higher execution in the fields of truth and beauty than are possible to even the most gifted genius on earth. Thus Plato says, the soul on earth "recollects the reality of beauty it has seen in its celestial journeyings;" and he adds that "It is by having seen the truth that man resumes the human form in the second life." In illustration of both these ideas Reid says, "We see many beauties, both of human and divine art, which the brute animals are incapable of perceiving; and superior beings may exce. us as far in their discernment of true beauty as we excel the brutes."

CHAPTER VI

THE CLASSES OF IMPRESSIONS PRODUCED ON MAN BY WORKS OF ART.

THE word beauty, like the word truth, is a term of comprehensive import. As there are many orders of truths, so there are various classes of beauties. Truth addresses the intellect, beauty the sensibilities. A general notice of the mental sensibilities to which art appeals, and a classification of the leading impressions awakened by its varied addresses, naturally follow the consideration of the intellectual faculties as employed in the field of the beautiful.

SECT. 1. CLASSIFICATION OF MENTAL SENSIBILITIES; AND DESIGNATION OF IMPRESSIONS PROPERLY ÆSTHETIC, OR CAPABLE OF BEING ADDRESSED BY ART.

The sensibilities may be divided into three classes; *emotions*, which are simple passive impressions; *affections*, which are emotions with an impulse awakened by the object; and *desires*, which are affections with a craving to possess or to serve the object.

Emotions are subdivided into instinctive and deliberative; which latter are awakened only when the reasoning powers are employed on an object. Among deliberative or rational emotions, to which alone art is addressed, are those awakened by the negative feature the novel, by the positive quality the lively, by the æsthetic attribute the beautiful, by the intellectual characteristic the witty, and by the moral element the proper.

Affections, styled passions when inordinate, are designated as benevolent and malevolent. Among the benevolent are love of kindred, of congenial friends, of benefactors, of dependents, of our Creator and Redeemer, as intelligent objects; and of home, country and nature, as objects without intelligence.

Desires, called appetites when inordinate and unworthy, may be classed as physical and mental, and they relate to the present or the future. Desires may arise from individual needs seeking as their aim wealth, knowledge or moral integrity; from social connections having as objects companionship, power, esteem or usefulness; or from religious aspirations for divine approval or benefaction. As they relate to the future, desires are hopes and fears.

In art these three principles are to be observed; first, the impressions made by the fine arts are *emotions* only; second, the end sought by design in the fine arts is the awakening of *affections*, and third, an indirect result of works of art may be the stimulating of *desires*. This distinction was clearly recognized by the ancients, Plato and Aristotle, and is carefully observed by writers of the present age, such as Reid, Alison, Cousin, Wayland and Haven. Reid says, "The emotion produced by beautiful objects is gay and pleasant. It sweetens and humanizes the temper, is friendly to every benevolent affection, and tends to allay sullen and angry passions. It enlivens the mind and disposes it to other agreeable emotions, such as those of love, hope and joy." "Beauty naturally produces love." Cousin argues, "The idea of the beautiful is free from all desire;" "The artist sees only the beautiful where the sensual man sees only the alluring and the frightful." He cites Horace Vernet lashed to the mast of a vessel in a storm that he might enjoy and then paint the scene, as proof that, "when he knows fear the artist vanishes;" and urges with warmth that the admiration of beauty in the female form utterly excludes every sensuous impression.

In works of sculpture and painting a legitimate appeal may be made even to the lowest of all deliberative emotions, the impression of novelty; yet their more worthy address is by the beautiful proper. In his design the artist may make the awakening of either of the affections, love of home, of country, or of the Creator, his direct aim. As a final end, the nurturing of any one of the nobler desires, individual or national, as thirst for knowledge, fame, or moral excellence, may, as Plato in his Republic and in his

Laws argues, be a result indirectly sought by the statesman in his patronage of art.

SECT. 2. THE BEAUTIFUL PROPER AND IDEAS ALLIED; AS THE DELICATE, THE EXQUISITE, THE FAIR, THE BRILLIANT, THE GRACEFUL, THE PRETTY; IN WHICH BEAUTY OF SUBSTANCE, FORM, COLOR, LUSTRE, MOTION AND EXPRESSION SEVERALLY PREDOMINATE.

In discriminating the characteristics of the beautiful proper, regard must be had to the organ that perceives, to the size of the object and to the elements of substance, form, color, lustre, motion and expression which severally constitute its special charm. The Greeks most thoroughly entered into the spirit of the beautiful proper, making its creations their special field of art execution.

Lord Kames observes as to the first point named: "Beauty in its native signification is appropriated to objects of sight." "An agreeable impression is made by the musical sounds of a bugle by the soft texture of velvet, by the delicious flavor of a peach, and the spicy fragrance of the honeysuckle." "The designation beautiful is given to each of these impressions probably at first, from the fact, that because of the pleasure they give to other senses, objects which otherwise would make no pleasant impression on the eye, come to be so agreeable to it, that we call the bugle, the velvet, the peach, the honeysuckle, beautiful. Going farther, we speak of a beautiful thought, metaphor, theorem, discovery; applying the word to ideas or objects that address us through no one of the bodily senses, but appeal to the mind itself without the intervention of the bodily senses; in which case there is not as before a transfer of the language of one of the senses to that of another, but a transfer of the terms of the material to the spiritual."

A second consideration, one fixing the limits of the beautiful proper, is thus suggested by Burke: "Attending to their *quantity*, beautiful objects are comparatively small." "In most languages the objects of love are spoken of under diminutive epithets." The true idea in this respect, as careful reflection intimates, seems to be this: We seem naturally to apply the word beautiful to an object however small or large which the eye takes in at its ordinary angle of vision. Thus we speak of a single statue and of small easel paintings, as beautiful, because the eye takes in the entire work. So, too, we call a building at a distance and even a vista view in a landscape miles in extent "beautiful," when, however extended, the entire view comes into the range of the eye's single glance.

After quantity that of *substance* is an element of beauty. This the word *delicate* is appropriately employed to express. Kames alludes to "the slender make of a horse," as a chief charm. Burke devotes a section to delicacy, citing the myrtle as opposed to the oak, the greyhound as opposed to the mastiff, and the Arabian steed as opposed to the war-horse, in confirmation of his view. Alison with discrimination says, "It is not delicacy in itself, but delicacy in the appropriate material that constitutes beauty; since delicate foliage in marble and iron seems unnatural, and therefore inappropriate. Delicacy is properly an attribute of substance; it is that quality in *material*, from fineness of texture and tenacity of particles united, that admits of a prolonged and slender form." Lexicographers make "fineness of texture," the primary definition of "delicacy;" and hence our association of the word "fine" with "delicate," in metaphorical usage, as when we speak of a man of delicate sensibility, adding by way of explanation that he is a person of "refined nature," and therefore of "fine feelings."

Beauty in *form* naturally follows that of substance. When marked or separated for special consideration, the natural term to express its impression is the word "exquisite." The word refers properly to the exact nicety with which straight or regularly curved lines are drawn by a master in art. Hence we speak of "exquisite workmanship," and metaphorically of "a man of exquisite mould in taste and sensibility," the figure showing that the idea of form is prominent in the mind.

The beauty residing in *color*, next in thought, we designate by the term "fair." The Saxon word refers to the bringing out of original color in wood, stone, or metal, by polishing or burnishing. Asiatics, better critics in color than in form, boast of their own as "the fairest of women." It is not to form but to color we refer in the expression "fair weather."

Associated with color is beauty derived from *lustre;* an aspect imparted by perfect reflection of pure white light. The word "*brilliant*" is used to express this element; a word naturally originating among the French, whose sky is in such contrast with that of England. The beauty of the diamond is exclusively its lustre; a characteristic embodied in the name "brilliant," which the world have agreed in giving to it. Burke, under the head of "light," alludes to this element of beauty; as do also other critics.

Beauty of *motion* is the foundation of that peculiar aim of the Greek artist, "grace." The Greek sculptor sought to make his work appear a living, moving being; and the rudest Greek architects in their first temples made the gentle curve of platform, column and roof seem in grace like a bird poised for flight. Plato calls Cupid the "most graceful" of beings, because he is "flexible and capable of twining about every object." Virgil illustrates it in Venus; the mere grace in the bend of whose neck as she turned from Æneas betrayed her divinity. Burke, defining "grace," says, "it is an idea belonging to posture and motion." Reid more fully remarks, "There is no grace without motion; some genteel or pleasing motion either of the whole body, or of some limb, or at least of some feature. Hence, in the face, grace appears on those features that are movable and change with the varying emotions and sentiments of the mind; such as the eyes and eyebrows, the mouth and parts adjacent."

Beauty of *expression* is popularly designated by the word "pretty," allied to a Welsh term meaning *appropriate*. The statement, "She is a pretty woman," expresses a judgment formed after acquaintance; and refers to mental and moral traits revealed in the expression of the features. We speak of a pretty dress as one becoming the wearer; and of a pretty story or song as one appropriate to the age of those to whom it is addressed.

All these attributes, as objects taken in by a glance of the eye or a single effort of the mind, belong to the field of beauty proper.

SECT. 3. THE GRAND; BEAUTY UNITED TO MASSIVENESS; AND THE ASSOCIATED IDEAS, THE NOBLE, THE ELEGANT, THE SUPERB, THE MAGNIFICENT, THE SUBLIME, THE MAJESTIC; IN WHICH THE ELEMENTS OF SUBSTANCE, FORM, COLOR, LUSTRE, MOTION AND MORAL DIGNITY ARE SEVERALLY PREDOMINANT.

As the beautiful is the general designation for the pleasing effects of smaller objects, so "the grand" is the appropriate designation of the general impression of pleasure produced by larger objects.

While the field of the beautiful proper was specially cultured by the Greeks, the wider domain of the grand is marked everywhere by the track of its Roman lords. Asiatic taste gloried in mere massiveness; but the Roman sought to combine the spreading breadth and towering height of the Egyptian with the finish of the Greeks. The words denoting special elements belonging to this general idea are chiefly Roman in their origin.

The grand, as it appears in *substance*, is designated by the word "noble." The Romans used the word in early times to designate a man noted for great qualities; though when Pliny wrote its modern degenerate signification prevailed. It suggests that in the very blood the noble is of superior nature. Hence the designation of mercury, silver, gold and platinum as the "noble metals." Applied to a monumental shaft or statue, the word "noble" properly used designates superiority of material.

Grandeur in *form* is properly designated by the Latin word "elegant." The Romans thus applied it first to their men, next to their edifices, and finally, in metaphor, they spoke of the "elegant arts." In modern acceptation an elegant mansion possesses mingled ampleness and finish; and an elegant scholar duly developed native faculties, cultured by proportionate study in varied fields.

The grand in *color* is naturally expressed by the term "superb." In early Roman times it designated splendor in personal achievements, in later times unworthy ostentation. Virgil alludes to the "superb purple robes" and "superb tapestry curtains of the early kings." In modern language a general superbly decorated is one parading gorgeous colors with great breadth of display. A man of superb imagination is one in whose imagery gorgeous coloring sets off boldness of conception.

The grand, lit up with *lustre*, is designated "magnificent." The Roman historian, Nepos, characterizes as "magnificent" a man fond of brilliant display, who nevertheless possesses true grandeur of character. Paris viewed in detail is brilliant; but the vast pile of the Hôpital des Invalides, with its gilded and glistening dome, cannot be called anything else than magnificent. Constantinople, with its numerous massive domes radiant with white paint in the morning sunbeams, is magnificent when seen as a whole from the Bosphorus; but it is far from brilliant when viewed near and in detail from the street.

The grand in *motion* is the "sublime." The Greeks in poetry often appealed to it; their word to express the sublime was an inadequate one. Native and congenial to the Oriental caste of mind, it is an impression specially sought by their artists; as is strikingly illustrated in the efforts of Hebrew poets and sculptors to give form to their conceptions of a living, moving Deity, unseen yet everywhere present; a spirit like the clouds floating above the earth, and like the clouds ever shifting yet brooding. The Roman use of their own word sublime is seen in Virgil's allusion to the "pole" of the heavens as "sublime;" and to Venus, graceful as she glides along the earth, but "sublime" when bounding upward to heaven. Theoretic critics, as Burke and Cousin, speak of the sublime as an impression of awe awakened by objects and ideas uncomprehended, because indefinite or infinite. Poets apply it to personified objects moving as self-acting agents. Mont Blanc, lifting its "bald awful front," and the "cross of Christ," "towering" with "light around its head," are declared by Coleridge and Bowring "*sublime.*" The jet of burning lava shooting from the crater of Vesuvius is sublime; the glowing stream overflowing at night is magnificent; the whole dark mountain with its sides and crest is grand. It is the elastic force of the upward motion that constitutes the sublime proper.

When the grand is accompanied by *moral dignity* the term "majestic" expresses its impression. The Latin poets and orators spoke of the *majesty* of their gods and of their state. In Christian theology "the majesty" of God is grouped with His "beauty and glory;" these three being the æsthetic impressions made on man by His relation to His physical, intellectual and moral creations. The proper discrimination of the subdivisions of the grand as well as of the beautiful will be found to give precision in thought and expression in the criticism of art.

SECT. 4. THE NOVEL, THE SURPRISE AT NEWNESS, AUXILIARY TO THE EMOTION OF BEAUTY; AND THE PICTURESQUE, AN EFFECT FROM GROUPING ALLIED TO GRANDEUR.

Lord Kames remarks, "Of all the circumstances that raise emotions, not excepting beauty nor even greatness, novelty has the most powerful influence." Though the lowest in dignity of all the impressions made by art, its power to arouse has been resorted to by artists in every department. The ancient Hebrews continually asked after new luxuries, new pleasures and even new gods. The Greeks, Plato said, were even in their best days fond "of novel things," and of "novel deities;" while Luke, the Greek Christian, attests that in the age of their degeneracy "the Athenians spent their time in nothing else than to tell or hear some new thing." Cicero in his day laments that the practical Romans were drawn after "new things." Yet Burke makes novelty the first element in the "sublime and beautiful," saying, "Some degree of novelty must be one of the materials in every instrument that works on the mind; and curiosity blends itself more or less with all our passions." The artist has the critic as his supporter in a due appeal to this impulse of human nature.

The "picturesque" derives its claim to consideration from its association with the modern advance of landscape painting and landscape gardening. It is a complex impression, coming from several objects, so grouped as to produce a pleasing impression; originating partly from mere novelty, and akin to the emotion of grandeur. The word picturesque, properly French, relates to that artificial grouping of objects which makes them seem parts of a picture. A picturesque costume is one so adjusted that every beholder at once says, "That is not natural; it is too studied: it is a dress for a picture." Alison quotes at length poets from Homer to Goldsmith who furnish a "grouping eminently picturesque;" and he characterizes its impression as that coming from "a variety of pleasing images passing with rapidity and awakening a sensibility beyond what the scene or description immediately before him can, of itself, excite, giving rise indeed to sublimity."

Modern landscape painting originated the style designated picturesque. The ancient painters did not work up the details of far-reaching background. When landscape proper was attempted, though nature was substantially the artist's standard, the landscape could not be truly, like a human being sitting for a portrait, an unchanging, ever present model to be copied. Sunlight and shade alternate; trees wave and animals move from their first observed positions; and even foliage and flowers change their forms and hues with every rolling hour. It was necessary, therefore, that the landscape painter should select some one definite position of each object, and some chosen grouping of the whole; and these chosen attitudes and preferred combinations, necessarily artificial to a certain extent, gave an ideal instead of a real character to the scene depicted, which took the name of picturesque.

In the same connection a style of landscape gardening arose, in which walks and trees were neither arranged in stiff, mathematically exact lines, nor yet left to the fortuitous grouping of nature; and, this artificial and yet artistic intrusion into nature's order, just far enough to add the charm of art to that of nature, was designated picturesque. Whether applied to personal adornment, to a painting, or to a landscape, the term picturesque relates mainly to the *grouping* of beauties.

SECT. 5. THE COMIC, GROTESQUE AND TRAGIC; EMOTIONS AWAKENED BY DISTORTED FORMS AND INCONGRUOUS RELATIONS, ALLIED TO BEAUTY AND GRANDEUR EITHER IN ANIMAL OR HUMAN EXPRESSION.

The *comic* is the combination of the ludicrous addressing the eye, and of wit addressing the ear; and as the expression of human passion and action it is accompanied by gestures and attitudes. It suggests ideas of smallness and meanness; as is seen in the *droll*, the semblance of the comic exhibited by animals like the monkey destitute of the intellectual element, wit.

The Hebrew poets as Job and Isaiah, Homer in his battle of the frogs and mice, Aristophanes in the Greek drama, as well as Grecian and Roman critics like Aristotle, Cicero, Quinctilian and Horace, show the law of the comic as employed by the poets. Aristotle's illustration of the ridiculous leads from the comic in poetry and song to the comic in forms addressing the eye in sculpture and painting. He says: "A countenance ugly or disfigured, but not occasioning pain, is ridiculous." As the actor by assuming a comic expression, or putting on a comic mask, accomplished his end more than by words, so the artist could embody comic expression in marble and on canvas. As there were artists to carve and paint Achilles and Agamemnon, so there were true masters in art who "recreated themselves," as Pliny says, "with comic subjects amid tragedy;" as Homer relieved painfully pleasing sympathy for Achilles and Briseis with the ludicrous appearance of the shallow-pated Thersites.

The *grotesque*, a name derived from the French grotte, is Oriental rather than Grecian; and as developed in Europe it belongs to the spirit of the Middle Ages. It is embodied in forms seen dimly as in a grotto; such as jagged rocks and shapeless stumps in a thicket, or sculptured bats clinging to the ceiling of a dark room, owls perched in jutting ledges, and toads squat in dark corners. The term is applied properly to objects at rest, not in action; and to individuals rather than to groups.

The grotesque pervades in excess Chinese sculpture, painting, architectural decoration and ornamental gardening; while the Egyptians, though fond of the comic, but rarely resorted to the grotesque. The Greeks had no sentiment in keeping with the grotesque; the universal spirit of animation and action pervading their art, their love of transparence, and their high-toned aspiring after the heroic forbidding it. To the Romans it was more congenial; as is witnessed in the decorations of baths and private sleeping-rooms now unburied at Pompeii. In the Middle Ages, throughout Central and Western Europe, the whole spirit of the people as well as of the rulers and the artists, seemed in keeping with this lower order of the art; as is seen in the old cathedrals of Paris and other French and German cities, perfectly overloaded with every species of grotesque and hideous figures sculptured in high relief. In the grotto proper the introduction of the grotesque is true art; but at the portal of a sanctuary for religious worship no propriety of art can justify the introduction of toads, lizards and other hideous devices.

The comic awakening mirth by diminutive or mean objects falls below the range of the grand; the grotesque rises as in the colossi of the Roman baths to its lower walks; while the *tragic* appealing to the intensest of human emotions towers to the loftiest heights of the sublime and majestic in its conceptions.

Plato used the words tragic and comic much as they are employed in modern times; calling Homer a "tragic poet," because he is highly dramatic in the mournful passages of his poems. Aristotle analyzes the principles of tragedy as one department of dramatic composition; indicating the connection between expression in the histrionic art, and in the arts of sculpture and painting. In early Grecian dramatic performances, as in modern Chinese theatricals, pantomime, or sign language, played an important part. As the living actor assumed attitudes and looks expressive of grief and anguish that spoke without uttered language, so the same attitudes and expressions cut in marble or pictured on the tablet gave to dead stone and wood an impressive voice.

The Laocoön and Niobe in Grecian sculpture, and the Iphigenia in Grecian painting, silent, yet eloquent in their "voiceless woe," are monuments of the power which art possesses to appeal to our impression of the tragic. The order in which these sensibilities, the beautiful, the grand, and their allied and subsidiary emotions, have been considered, will be found of value in tracing the history of plastic art.

CHAPTER VII.

THE INFLUENCE OF NATURAL CHARACTERISTICS AND OF DEGREES OF CULTURE IN MODIFYING THE IMPRESSIONS PRODUCED BY ART.

THE idea, common to mankind, that superior knowledge and skill in any department are above ordinary apprehension, and therefore beyond general attainment, seems to cling to the human mind when art is regarded; though increasing general intelligence has long since expelled this impression as to science. From time immemorial the superior race of India have been a caste bound by oaths never to divulge the secret principles of science on which their arts are practised; and as their science seems to the people supernatural, so their arts seem magical. Pythagoras having learned the science of this caste, thought to introduce it into Greece. But he mistook entirely the spirit of the Greek people, so different from the Asiatic. Among the Greeks the veil of pretentious mystery was torn off from all science and art; the common people demanded to know the secrets of both; and both alike they discussed, criticised and practised, regarding art no less than science the common heritage of man, just like the air they breathed and the water they drank. A principle was thus developed most important to be observed in the progress of every age or nation.

Another equally important principle, the necessary counterpart

of that just mentioned, was clearly recognized by the Greeks as leaders in true art. While among the thousands of intelligent and cultured youth in a nation all may be able to criticise art, and hundreds if devoted to the pursuit might succeed as artists, yet differing tastes and the varied and numerous wants of man in society call for only a limited class to make art the special business of life. Socrates taught that every man of the common people should think for himself, and learn for himself the true principles of religion, of morals, of political science, of letters and of art; but he by no means taught that every man should or could be a Phidias in sculpture, a Polygnotus in painting, a Pericles in statesmanship, a Plato in philosophy, or a Themistocles in generalship. There are inborn natural characteristics of national and individual mental capacity, and there are degrees of general and special culture, to be remarked in the history of art among men; without the observing of which it is vain to attempt a consideration of the varied tastes that have prevailed, and the wonderfully different success in execution that has marked the people and the artists of different lands and ages.

SECT. 1. THE INFLUENCE OF NATIONAL CHARACTER AND SOCIAL CUSTOMS ON THE SENSIBLE IMPRESSIONS PRODUCED BY ART.

He who "made of one blood all nations to dwell on the face of the earth," has allowed differing race and culture to separate "Greek and Jew, barbarian and Scythian." In art, palpable to the eye as its productions are, this distinction is perhaps more marked than in any other department of human attainment. One family of mankind have never passed the infancy of human development, and their art is that of a child; a second has never risen above mediocre talent and a style in art for ages stereotyped; while yet a third has soared at once to the very heights of human attainment.

Science in every department, especially ethnology and the history of language, join to confirm Guyot's analysis of the human family as suggested by the records of Moses and the testimony of universal Asiatic tradition. The Hamitic family, peopling Africa, are imitative but not originating in mental cast. The Shemitic, peopling Asia, are imaginative and ideal, but sluggish in action and tardy in improving. The Japhetic or Indo-European, quick and aspiring in conception and also energetic in execution, have from the earliest

annals of history been leaders in art, controlled often in their ideals by the people for whom they have designed, yet gradually elevating ruder races to a measure of their own superiority. The words referring to art used in Egypt transferred by Moses to his Hebrew records, the testimony of the sculptures everywhere on Egyptian monuments, and the declarations of Herodotus and later Grecian and Roman historians, all indicate that the noble Aryan stock of the Caucasus, the proud Brahminic caste of India, and the "beauty of the Chaldees' excellency" have been the moulding masters of all the ancient ages and nations in art.

In every land as we make our survey we shall trace the rude originals of a native art. That early uncultured native art, where barbarian and African rudeness has been unbroken by the intervention of a higher race, has been permanently dwarfed and remained in perpetual infancy. Wherever the proud and hoary Shemitic family has been undisturbed in its changeless ages of history, there stereotyped mediocrity has reigned. Where, however, as in Egypt, art has originated among a family whose popular spiritual notions were as low as the African's in fetish worship of reptiles, and as fixed as the Asiatics in blindness to the harmonies of nature in form and color, we shall find the rudest of all conceptions in art stimulated to their first step in progress by Indian resident artists, prompted to a higher advance by Persian intervention, refined to the farthest possible improvement of which its heavy massiveness was susceptible by the grace of succeeding Grecian genius, and finally ennobled into true grandeur by the all-absorbing and modifying spirit of the imperial Roman. Everywhere, in fact, where Ham has toiled alone we shall find art in its infancy; where Shem has dreamed secluded in petty tribes, or massed in colossal nations, art has advanced to youth's period of half-matured imagination; but wherever Japhet has both dreamed and toiled, whether domiciled alone in his native hills and plains, or "dwelling in the tents of Shem," or employing "Ham as his servant," there art has been marked with that progress which claimed for it a place in the analysis of history.

Sect. 2. The general influence of advancing civilization on critical appreciation of art.

The first marks of a nation's, as of an individual's progress, are not seen in the field of the true, or of the beautiful proper; but in that of the good.

The material advancement, however, of a people soon creates a taste for art proper; which demand foreign or native skill will seek to supply. That skill, once introduced, becomes an educating power, stimulating the zest and gradually refining and instructing the critical judgment of a people in their innate love of beauty and its creations. In Egypt, no less than four marked stages of progress are observable. Even the matchless art of Greece, culminating in Rome, had the same rude beginning; and it advanced by stages of progress to its climax of perfection. In the Saxon and German nations, all of whose steps in the progress of art are close down to our own era, this progress is specially manifest. Of the Germans at his day Tacitus says, "Among them silver vases, gifts to their ambassadors and princes, are held in the same low esteem as those which are wrought of clay." "The walls of some of their houses they smear with an earth so pure and glistening, that it imitates a painting and the lineaments of colors." And this is the comparatively modern history of art in a land that now boasts its Thorwaldsen in sculpture, and its Albert Durer, Vandyke and Rubens in painting.

The progress of art in a single nation, so like to its development in the individual artist, seems to promise a kindred advancement among mankind as a race. As the individual man leaves to his children his life-time accumulations as capital with which they can begin a new advance, so one generation of artists leaves to a succeeding age its perfected material and practice; and so, too, nations coming to their climax and decaying leave collected products of the chisel and brush and written treatises which enable a succeeding nation to take up the work where it had been left by other minds and hands.

Sect. 3. The special influence of forms of political organization on the patronage of art.

Artists like other men must secure a livelihood, if not wealth, by their profession. No private patron can meet the expense of higher works of art. Society in its civil organization must supply this need.

In the progress of civilization since the days of Herodotus and Aristotle, as before the ages whose record they give, civil governments by whatever name called have been virtually of two types; representative republics and hereditary monarchies. The question is an important one in the history of art criticism and art execution which of these two forms of government is most favorable to the patronage of art. The principle to which the mind might naturally be led seems conformed to fact. A government which fosters the free action of the intellect of the people, affording to genius, however obscure its origin, an open field for the indulgence of its aspirations, must be favorable to the development of a capacity for art. On the other hand, a stable government controlled by men of culture is essential to the intelligent and liberal patronage which art demands for its highest success.

In Greece the popular government of Athens called forth among its own citizens and attracted from distant provinces the rarest gifts and culture devoted to art; it culminated under Alexander, the first monarch of all Greece, whose ambition if not his taste led him to become the liberal patron of art; but its spirit declined rapidly under the successors of Alexander, who, with less nobleness of nature than the first monarch, were no less ambitious to make art subservient to their personal fame. At Rome, science, art and letters had their spring under the Republic; they attained their acme of advance under the first emperor; and steadily declined when the imperial ambition prostituted genius to low and selfish ends. In modern Italy the revival of art began under the cultured aristocracy of Tuscany, took wing during the brief reign of republican institutions, and went steadily on to its acme under emperors and cardinals who felt it an honor to be its patrons. The history of all ages and nations shows at least this; that popular institutions have been the early nursery of genius in art; but that despotism has blighted and withered every bud of promise in its most matured growth.

SECT. 4. SPECIAL INFLUENCE OF INTELLECTUAL PROGRESS IN SCIENCE AND LITERATURE ON THE STYLE OF ART.

In art as in literature, we speak of the style of an age, of a country, or of a school to designate the character of the conceptions embodied and the methods of execution employed. Intellectual progress, especially attained in the European races, has originated or modified styles; for the advance of a nation in metaphysical speculation gives form to *design*, and improvements in physical science add skill in execution. The philosophy of the Vedas of India, associated with practical energy among the people of Northern Africa, culminated in the wisdom of Egypt, in which the Hebrews Joseph and Moses became learned, and from which Pythagoras and Plato drew their inspiration. As a consequence all Greek and Roman writers trace back the origin of art in Greece to masters who drew their skill and their material from that earliest centre of intellectual development. Afterward Grecian philosophy so reacted upon Egypt that Alexandria under the Ptolemies became a chief centre of learning; and in nothing more than in the art of that age is the influence of this advancement to be remarked. The progress of the Greeks through the ages of the epic, the lyric and the drama, of philosophy and of oratory, and also the history of the Romans up to their Augustan era, all show that art is but the reflex of advancing culture. The appearance in modern Italy of Galileo and Columbus, Dante and Savonarola, at the same era with the great masters in revived sculpture and painting, demonstrates that the important element essential to a nation's progress in true art is the advancement of a people in science and culture.

SECT. 5. THE SPECIAL INFLUENCE OF MORAL REFINEMENT ON THE ACCESSORIES OF ART.

While principles growing out of intellectual development influence the style of art, moral considerations will control the accessories of sculptured and pictured forms. This has especially to do with the robing of the human figure. Climate and custom control fullness of dress and nudity. The portions of the person covered in the cold of winter are left bare in summer and in a heated winter parlor. The delicate maiden in Southern Italy, no less than in the mountains of Syria and in the African jungles, exposes her person without thought of impropriety when bathing in an open stream. Moral propriety in the climactic age of Greek ethics commended rather than censured the nude Apollo and Venus. The love of beauty is created in man to be the refiner of his moral nature. Among all the works of the Divine hand no form is so exquisite, no color so delicate, and no entire figure such a model of beauty, as that found in the human frame, both male and female; and that alike in childhood, youth and maturity. It cannot be conceived that the Divine mind designed that this form should be hidden from the eye made to admire beauty or that to copy its perfect outline can be opposed to His will. Hence everywhere that dress is most admired for its intrinsic beauty which most brings out and least hides the contour of the entire form. This principle early prompted the Greek artists to so general a study and representation of the nude in art as to call forth Pliny's remark, "Græca res est nihil velare;" the Grecian method is to drape no figure.

The most spiritual of poets, philosophers and artists have agreed that true and deep-seated morality is nurtured, instead of being vitiated, by ideals of the male and female form presenting the entire human figure in its nobleness and loveliness. This truth Milton earnestly argues when picturing Adam and Eve seen by angels and by Satan in their native perfection of form. The profound Cousin says, "It is the property of beauty not to irritate and inflame desire, but to purify and ennoble it. The more beautiful a woman is, the more, at the sight of this noble creature, is desire tempered by an exquisite and delicate sentiment; and is sometimes even displayed by a disinterested worship. If the Venus of the Capitol, or the St. Cecilia, excite in you sensual desires, you are not made to feel the beautiful." The most admired of all works of American sculpture is the Greek Slave of the modest, sensitively chaste and humbly devout Powers.

Truth, beauty and goodness always go hand in hand. The human frame must be studied, not only by the trained physician, but also by educated youth of both sexes, that the sacred obligation of care for a structure so delicate may be suitably felt. A kindred study of this masterpiece for its beauty's sake has realized the fact that the highest tone of morality always prevails where, under the influence of cultured taste in art, youth of both sexes can together admire such works as the Venus de Medici and the Apollo Belvidere, the Greek Slave of Powers and the Washington of Greenough.

Sect. 6. The special influence of religious culture on the subjects of art.

Pliny's statement that "the first statues made were images of the gods," suggests a principle of universal truth. Among rude African, Asiatic and American tribes, rude art is exhausted on images and shrines for deities; and in its progress through Western Asia till it culminated in Greece, its highest efforts in every department were consecrated to religion. Under Christianity, too, religion has given spring and guidance to the spirit of art.

The Old Testament forbade any graven image or likeness as an object of religious reverence. Yet the whole ceremonial service of the Old Testament required images wrought by art, and the Deity made His presence known by the flame of the Shekinah on the mercy-seat. The New Testament declares that God is a spirit to be worshiped in spirit; yet the Christian religion has its prescribed ordinances and forms of service addressing the eye and ear, and teaches that no man can approach unto God, except through the Mediator, the man Christ Jesus. It seems, therefore, a legitimate conclusion that art is necessarily associated with spiritual Christianity. The fact that by their art-culture the Greeks were prepared for a religion of such matchless harmony and beauty as the Christian system, while the Jews with the Old Testament prophecies were not thus prepared, is proof that art was allied to the spirit of the religion of Christ.

Under the Christian religion all other forms of art than the plastic have their most legitimate and necessary employ, and their very highest development in connection with Christian worship. Music was never so hallowed as when Jesus sang a hymn with his disciples; it was never so grand as in the pealing chorus of a thousand Christian voices shouting their enthusiastic hymns of praise to their Redeemer; and it was never so perfect in melody and harmony as in the sacred oratorios of Handel and Mozart. Poetry, too, never reached such a lofty strain as in the drama of Job, in the lyrics of David, and in the epic of Isaiah and Habakkuk; and if the true genius of ancient Poësy lingers yet on earth, it is in the souls of such men as Dante and Tasso, of Goethe and Schiller, of

Milton and Moore, when, stirred by the fervor of Christian devotion, they have poured forth those Christian melodies which will outlive even Homer's Muse. Most of all, the histrionic art, yet more akin to the plastic arts, never has had such masters as in sacred eloquence. Paul the Tarsian, according to Longinus, surpassed Demosthenes in effective eloquence; while the long line of pulpit orators from Chrysostom, the "golden-mouthed," have alone found a theme worthy the power of histrionic genius.

Moreover history shows that Christian culture has called forth the highest perfection of plastic art in all three of its departments. In Christian lands common utensils, dress and equipage have assumed a special elaborateness controlled by chasteness. There are no such aspirants for relics, for family portraits, and for adorned burial-grounds as a Christian people. Yet more, among the most scrupulous opposers of forms and rituals there is seen a demand, which no community can resist, that the house for Christian worship keep pace with, if it do not outstrip in symmetry and elegance, the private mansions that surround it. The singing of sacred hymns by an irresistible influence takes on more and more of artistic culture. The furniture and ornaments of the pulpit, the choir, the altar and the communion-table, assume a constantly increasing costliness of finish. And indeed the observing student that has visited the mosques of Oriental Mohammedism, the synagogues of ancient Judaism, and even the temples of the most formal and sensual heathenism, returns to observe the fact everywhere pressing itself on his notice in Christian lands, that plastic art never has been called forth in such profusion of subjects and in such chastened beauty and sublimity of conception and execution as in the accompaniments of Christian worship.

History too rightly interpreted settles the question as to the propriety of representations in sculpture and painting of the man Christ Jesus. The fact that no Grecian limner, sculptor or painter of Christ's age has left in marble or on canvas his form or features, and that no inspired historian of his life has even given the least hint by which a single lineament of either can be traced, is most instructive in many respects; but they manifestly err who take it as an indication that no ideal of his person may be legitimately conceived and executed with the pencil, the chisel, or the brush. It was not designed that Jesus should be the representative of one family, nation, age, sex, class, condition, or type of mankind; that he should be recognized as Asiatic or European, as Jew or Greek, Roman or Scythian, as a man of ancient or modern times, as of civic or rustic aspect, as of reflective or practical mental cast, as of mild or stern disposition, or as of sanguine or retiring temperament. Yet every Christian does and must form his own conception of Christ's human aspect; the preacher's glowing imagery is designed to aid this conception; and the artist's chisel and brush may serve, too, the same end, Augustine, living in the fourth century, a man whose religious experience after that of Paul the apostle is one of the most instructive in history, thus writes: "What was his personal appearance we are entirely ignorant. For the features of the Lord's fleshly nature are varied and sculptured according to the innumerable diversity of individual conceptions; which nevertheless were one, whatever they were." This statement, fully confirmed by early and later Christian writers, intimates first that very varied representations of Jesus' personal form and features had been conceived and executed by artists in the early days of Augustine; second, that the artist's ideal, like that of the private Christian, is for him and for all having kindred conceptions a *true*, because to such it is the real image of the perfect man; and, third, that these creations of high art were commended by the evangelical spirit of primitive Christian times.

It should be specially remembered, that true art always tends to spiritual conceptions. As Jarves has well remarked, "The works of Raphael, as those of Phidias, never have been worshiped . . . It is ugly and hideous associations that have always led to error and idolatry."

Sect. 7. The nature of art-study and the sources whence its lessons are to be drawn.

Education in art is needed for two classes of youth; first, for those of select genius who are to be artists; and second, for the general student who ought to be an art-critic. Some, like Giotto and West, are born to an intuitive power of conception and a suggestive skill in execution, which enable them without study to draw, mould, or color with surprising skill. Others as Socrates, Winckelmann and Kames, are gifted with critical judgment and logical power of thought and expression which make them surpass the artist in conception and suggestion, so as to be his instructors in design and his critics in execution; but who fail in every effort to put their own theories into practice. The studies requisite for these two classes are in theory, in elementary principle, the same; as the study of anatomy for youth designed for the legal, clerical and medical professions is the same. The consideration of these elementary principles of art belongs to the field of Art Criticism; the after study of the professional school fills volumes of detail and years of practice.

The three main sources of elementary Art Education are studies of nature, of works of art, and of text-books. The study of nature embraces three departments; *first*, material creations, inorganic as rocks, clouds and mountains, and organic as plant and animal forms; *second*, spiritual beings and their attributes, embracing man in all his variety of character and action; and *third*, since both the previous classes are but effects, the study of causes prior and superior to all finite material and spiritual existence, embracing especially the contemplation of the great First Cause, the Divine Author of all. The study of works of art, again, involves not only the employ of the eye on preserved works of antiquity and on present collections, but the reconstruction before the mind's eye of what history describes in words; in which study the art-critic may search only for principles, while the artist must scan and guess that he may attain methods of execution. The study of text-books, yet again, embraces the wise selection of books and the successful order of topics examined.

The study of nature is the study of the *true* or of actual existences. The transition from Egyptian to Grecian sculpture seemed an inspiration, because when Dædalus the early Greek sculptor wished to make a Hercules or a hero, he stripped a brawny peasant to his skin, and trained him to the bend of limb, the strain of muscle and the position of features which mark action and passion. Painting seemed in the revival of art in Italy to be angel touches, because Giotto as a shepherd-boy loved to draw his own sheep, because Lionardo would thread a crowd for weeks to select a face of miserly sordidness that might give him a Judas, and because Raphael drew his sweetest Mary with the babe Jesus on the head of a wine cask as he gazed on the unstudied attitude and unconscious expression of maternity seen in a simple peasant woman nursing her child. The truly admirable feature of Ruskin's popular works on art is embodied in this paragraph: "The chief aim and bent of my system is to obtain, first, a perfectly patient, and to the utmost of the pupil's power, a delicate method of work; such as may ensure his *seeing truly*. For I am nearly convinced that when once we see keenly enough there is very little difficulty in drawing what we see; but even supposing this difficulty to be still great, I believe that the sight is a more important thing than the drawing; and I would rather teach drawing that my pupils may learn to love Nature than to teach the looking at Nature that they may learn to draw. It is surely, also, a more important thing for young people and unprofessional students to know how to appreciate the art of others than to gain much power in art themselves."

The study of *human nature*, virtually the study of the *good* or of what is *adapted* to man *as he is*, is equally important. Mankind have intuitions that are right, and prejudices which may be wrong; and the artist, as truly as the lawyer, the physician, and the clergyman, will fail of satisfying his masters and patrons, the public, who does not study to harmonize popular convictions by guiding rather than insulting popular prejudices. Because Apelles paid just respect to the people's judgment when he placed his finished pictures in the window of his studio and put the extra stitch in the sandal suggested by the cobbler, he could make bold, when the cobbler criticised the ankle, to reply before an exacting Athenian populace, "Let the cobbler stick to his last." When Brahminic pride of consistency compelled Egyptian artists to cramp all promptings of improvement on the orthodox pattern of their statues and temples, it was the true spirit of art which prompted Grecian artists afterward to yield to this demand as to general form in the purely Egyptian temple at Philæ, in order that they might invest the structure with a charm of grace which to this day makes the rude Nubians call it "*Es-soor-el-Anas el-Wogood*," the palace of beautiful aspect. The artist who arrays himself against popular opinions, allowing himself to grow out of sympathy with those for whom as a servant he toils, is as truly opposing nature as he who should set at defiance the laws of gravity. The true master on the stormy ocean of human passions controls the inconstant and obstinate sea by humoring the gale; while at the same time he firmly breasts the billows and pursues his own chosen path.

The study of Nature, again, is the study of its *Author* and of *right* or duty to Him. The artist who thinks to copy the Divine works without any knowledge of the Divine workman, is like one who should attempt to copy a picture of Raphael without first studying the artist. Socrates and Plato laid the foundation of Grecian art by directing the contemplation of their pupils above His works to the great Author of all that is true, beautiful, good and right. The wondrous power of the great masters of Italy was the religious spirit that pervades their works. Human nature always has demanded, and, because man was made to adore and serve his Maker, it always will demand, that the artist, as truly as other public men, respect if he do not personally appreciate their religious opinions. Yet more as the experience of Cicero led him to declare, "That no man can be a successful orator unless he is a good man," so the history of art proves that no artist can be great who is not a religious man.

The study of the *works of art* produced by other nations has been auxiliary to the study of nature in giving spring successively to Grecian, Roman, Italian, German, French, and English art. The unburied statues gathered from ancient Greece and Italy, the collections of the masters in modern painting, are the necessary complement to the field of nature in the study of art. The one is the gallery of finished works to give the artist models in design; the other the studio to unfold to him methods of execution long tested.

BOOK II.

DRAWING; THE REPRESENTING OF FORMS ON A PLANE SURFACE.

DRAWING is the first of the plastic arts to be acquired; the earliest amusement of the child. In the tombs of Egypt, the artist's first work was the drawing in outline. The Book of Job, the earliest written record, alludes to inscriptions "graven with a pen of iron and lead in the rock."

Peale, in his "Graphics," calls writing with the pen a branch of drawing. The child prefers to try his originating skill in the pastime of drawing before he will consent to the slavish toil of copying letters of fixed shape and size.

In the practical execution of any single work in drawing the order of study in the art is hinted. The master first traces the outline of a principal figure; he next adds a background of subordinate figures, or of landscape; his sketch is next multiplied in engraved copies, or by the quick penciling of the sun's rays: while in all this work intelligent thought guides the true artist. Plane and Perspective Drawing, Engraving, Photographing and Design are, therefore, the leading studies in this department of art.

CHAPTER I.

PLANE DRAWING; THE REPRESENTING OF FORMS AS LOCATED IN A SINGLE PLANE.

PLANE drawing is the representing by lines of the form of an object upon a plane surface. It is sometimes called "Geometrical Drawing," because the figures are drawn as in Geometry in their actual proportions. As distinguished from drawing in perspective, plane drawing is the representing one instead of many objects; and it is the delineation of that one object as if all its parts lay in one plane at the same distance from the eye.

SECT. 1. LINES AS THE ELEMENTS OF DRAWING.

The elements of drawing are lines either straight or curved. The outline in all drawing is in straight or curved lines longer or shorter; and the shading, however executed, is made up of combinations of short straight lines or dots.

The first lessons in drawing are in straight lines. Three attainments are here requisite for the pupil; first, the practice essential to the making of a straight line; second, the combining of straight lines in parallels and in angles; third, the combining of these parallels and angles into figures of more or less sides. The shading of an unvaried surface, as the clear sky or a level country, is in parallel lines; while the varied configuration of clouds, mountains, and broken country is executed in broken lines. The drawing of geometrical figures, as regular polygons, in all conceivable attitudes and of all dimensions, until the slightest deviation in each figure from its correct shape and proportions can be detected, should follow. No amount of time spent in this attainment can be misemployed; as Lionardo da Vinci hints in his maxim, "Remember to acquire accuracy before attempting quickness."

The second lessons in drawing are in curves. First, all the regular curves in the conic sections, as circles, ellipses, parabolas and hyperbolas, should be copied till by a single sweep of the pencil any one of them can be accurately delineated; then every form of irregular or broken curves may be attempted. Finally, the combination of these different curves in every variety of form and figure which fancy may conceive should be executed with the pencil. The design of these preliminary lessons is to enable the pupil, first, to master all the combinations of lines possible; second, to comprehend the modifications to which the outline of an object is subjected by being viewed at every variety of angle and at different distances from the observer. It is in the nice discrimination of changes wrought by minute variations of position that character for truth and beauty in drawing consists; as a careful inspection of engravings after works of the best masters strikingly illustrates.

The next lessons are in figures of natural objects; in whose outline both straight and curved lines are united; such as, first ordinary utensils, cups and mechanics' tools; then houses, fences and other larger objects having regularly shaped figures. After these, the features of the human countenance and the parts of the human form are the most instructive study; first, the separate features and parts of the body, as the nose, the eye, the hand, the foot; then their combination in heads and entire human figures, at first nude, and afterward clothed in varied costume and drapery and in different postures. Sir Joshua Reynolds makes this the first and great study essential to success in the highest works of art; and he regards the secret of the grace and beauty seen in the finished works of the ancients their "attentive and well-compared study of the human form." In drawing the human features and figure, models in nature and plaster casts made from nature, as hands, feet, busts and complete statues, may be used. Leslie objects to pupils drawing the human form too long from antiques or plaster casts; and cites Sir Joshua Reynolds' suggestion that students begin very early to draw from life.

After the human figure those of animals, quadrupeds, birds, fishes, and insects may be drawn; while flowers, fruits, single shrubs and trees should be made the last essays in single objects. The executing of groups, as clumps of trees, ranges of buildings, herds of cattle, near views of single trees with foliage worked up, and finally of all the varied and extended combinations and complications of the landscape, will be the crowning effort of the pencil.

In vegetable forms, the complicated interior, which in man and in animals is hidden as in a case, is laid open to the eye, and must with its convolutions be copied by the pencil. It is this delineation, especially in landscape, in which Ruskin supposes the moderns have excelled the ancients. This, however, is to be remembered. The very exposure to the eye of the fixed forms and open workmanship of the vegetable creation makes it but a work of secondary skill to copy a flower; while to conceive the ever-changing and hidden swell and play of the human muscles is a profound study and its execution most difficult. This indicates that the ancients, who so highly excelled in the greater work, might have proved in the easier field still more in advance of the moderns had they turned their attention to landscape drawing.

SECT. 2. PROPORTION IN THE OUTLINE OF PLANE DRAWINGS.

Next to the executing of lines of a definite contour comes the study of just proportions in the different parts of figures. Here the work is two-fold; first, the preserving of the respective size of each part in a figure drawn in its natural dimensions; second, the securing of the proper enlargement or diminution in drawings made upon an increased or reduced scale. To assist in first essays at executing proportion, artificial aids may be for a time employed. The old masters recommended laying off the parts, as in plotting, by the dividers. Dr. Bell, the eminent writer on anatomy in its relation to art, recommends the drawing of a network of parallel lines over an engraving to be copied, or holding such a network of threads between the eye and the object in nature to be copied. As the astronomical observer measures the transit of a star by the network of spider's web in the field of his instrument, as the map drawer locates different sections of country by the parallels within which they lie, and as the embroiderer has a network pattern to follow, so the proportions of any object are most rapidly and distinctly learned by observing the squares in such a network in which the different parts naturally fall. This method, as is seen in the small ruined temple of Ombos near Syene, was employed by Egyptian artists; a network of fine lines being first traced over the field of their work. All artificial resorts, however, are to be laid aside when the pupil begins to draw; and the eye must be trained to be its own measurer.

In studying proportion the human figure most strikingly illustrates the extent to which the Creator has carried the law of inter-measurement in the forms of beauty given us as models. Lionardo makes the important remark: "In proportion the length of figures is to be regarded more than their breadth; for the *proportionate lengths* of the different parts of the human frame vary very slightly." The breadth and fullness of the human figure vary greatly in the changes of life; while the stature is fixed to the unvarying standard of the bony framework. In drawing all objects in nature, Lionardo teaches that altitude should first be regarded; then its main proportions should be fixed; after which the finish of details may commence.

A second study in proportion relates to the scale of dimnution in plane drawings made for different purposes, and of objects of varied sizes. The study of natural objects will soon give such a practical knowledge of the proportionate size of their parts that the artist's hand will possess an almost magical skill in preserving the scale of proportions he has adopted, whether the subject be a mountain compressed into a miniature, or the leg of an insect magnified by the microscope. The characteristic features, as well as the beauties of every object, consist in its main proportions and the distribution of its masses; not in its mere accessories and ornaments.

SECT. 3. ELEMENTARY SHADING; THE REPRESENTING OF THE THIRD DIMENSION IN PLANE DRAWING.

In drawing, the outline first sketched gives no idea of the rotundity of a figure. In nature the impression that a form observed is a solid body arises from the shadows on its surface. The sun's rays proceeding in parallel lines light up the parts of an object on which, because unobstructed, they directly fall; while the shaded parts are those on which the rays do not directly strike because they are interrupted by solid projections. The imitation of this law of nature in drawing gives the penciled outline the aspect of the real object. By Descriptive Geometry it may be determined aside from observation what portions of an object will be shaded in nature, and what parts of a drawing must therefore be shaded; but the habit of observation gives the artist the practical science that enters into this art.

Methods of shading have differed in different eras, and in the practice of different masters. Some ancient engravers covered the shaded parts with a regular network of straight lines crossing each other at angles of about eighty degrees. The method called "hatching," from the French *hacher*, to hack or notch, accomplished by lines jutting in from the outlines like the chippings of a hatchet upon the edge of a board, is appropriate in giving the slopes of mountains. Ruskin refers to the fact, that Raphael and Lionardo da Vinci shaded even rounded surfaces with short straight lines; and he regards this the mark of a great master. The old German masters differed much in their style of shading; employing lines straight or curved, dots or rubbings of India ink, of red or black crayon, as seemed best to suit their end; varying their method in works of different character: while, too, the same artist had different styles for the same work at different periods of life. Their great aim was to secure a resemblance to Nature by as few lines as possible.

SECT. 4. CHIAROSCURO; THE GRADATION OF LIGHT AND SHADE.

In nature no shadow is completely dark. Rays of light falling on objects, rough or polished, and having faces either perpendicular or oblique to the illuminating beams, are reflected with more or less completeness, according to the character of the surface, and in directions corresponding to the inclination on which they fall. Thus objects in nature have shades proportioned to the amount of light they receive. This effect is illustrated when two lamps in the same room cast each its own separate shadow of any form; a half shade being seen where the light of one only of the two lamps falls. In the sunlight the number of counter lights from reflection is without number, and the gradations are correspondingly numerous.

The Italian word *chiaroscuro*, or clear-obscure, designates this half shade in nature and in drawing. Lionardo who, in the revival of art in Italy, taught its principles, has the following suggestions: "Observe well among the lights, which, and how many hold the first rank in point of brightness; and so among the shadows darker than others. Observe, also, in what manner they blend together; compare the quantity and quality of one with the other; and observe to what part they are directed. Be careful also of your outlines, or divisions of the members. Remark well what quantity of parts are to be on one side, and what on the other; and then where they are more or less apparent, broad or slender. Lastly, take care that the shadows and lights be united, or lost in each other; without any hard strokes or lines. As smoke loses itself in the air, so are your lights and shadows to pass from one to the other without any apparent separation." Ruskin enlarges on light touches which give true shading in water and cloud; the former requiring delicate curves among the parallels to indicate shadows and ripples; while to attain skill in the latter, he recommends his pupil to draw a bunch of cotton placed in the rays of the sun.

SECT. 5. THE APPLICATIONS OF PLANE DRAWING.

The most important applications of plane drawing are found in the mechanical arts and in surveying. The manufacturer of a chair must first draw his pattern for a new fashion; of which work the patent agency furnishes an endless variety. The ordinary house-builder must have a ground-plot plan of each story; while the finished architect requires elaborated sketches of every section of interior and exterior details.

The business of the surveyor calls into requisition the same art. The humblest farmer needs a plot of his fields, and the country maiden of her flower-bed. To execute these skillfully requires the theory derived from geometrical study, and practice with the drawing-pencil. In the plotting of a field a mere outline is required. In the mapping of a town, the outline, including the great highways, is to be first laid down, as in the plot of a field; and then the varied delineation of roads, and water-courses, forests and open fields, houses and other buildings is to be artifically represented with the pencil. In ordinary maps the observer is regarded as looking from above; roads are represented by two parallel lines; railroads by two parallels with cross lines or bars; unfinished railroads by the absence of one of the side lines; water courses by two lines varying slightly from parallel with faint parallels between; plain land by dots sprinkled over the surface; sheets of water by faint parallels; forests by involved curves representing tree tops; rocky lands by broken dark lines forming irregular figures; dwelling-houses by small parallelograms; and public buildings by larger parallelograms with dots for front columns or spire. In maps of a more extended region, the parallels of latitude and the lines of longitude are first drawn; then the general outline of sea-coast, of mountains, rivers and state limits; and then the minuter delineations of towns, high-roads and lakes. The coast is marked by short horizontal parallels projecting from it; and mountains by a dark-ribbed delineation following the track which water-courses flowing from them would take.

In the representation of sections of railroad, and of the elevation of a country above the water level, a view of a perpendicular face is given. Upon a horizontal line perpendiculars of the proportionate height and distance from each other are raised, and the outline of the surface is drawn above in broken curves. Ledges of rock in such outlines are represented by oblique parallels, water-channels by fine horizontal parallels, sand by fine dots, and gravel by coarse dots.

The proportion as to size between the object and the drawing is in mechanical drawings from one-fourth to one-eighth of the natural object; in architectural drawings one-fourth of an inch to a foot; and in maps and plots, a given number of inches to a rod, a chain or a mile. In the U. S. Coast Survey, the proportions in mapping are expressed in fixed decimals; varying according to the size of the chart from the proportion of 1 to 5000, up to that of 1 to 400,000. In the engineer service, the proportion for plans of buildings is 1 to 120; of railroad sections 1 to 600; of maps of an extended country 1 to 2640, or two feet to a mile; the scale enlarging with the extent of surface. The rule for shading the slopes of hills and mountains is for a descent of 75°, nine of black to one of white, and thence decreasing to a slope of but 2° 30 m., where the proportion is one of black to ten of white.

CHAPTER II.

PERSPECTIVE DRAWING; THE REPRESENTING OF FORMS LOCATED IN PLANES MORE OR LESS REMOTE.

IN Plane Drawing the parts of an object are represented as they appear when the eye is equally distant from every part. In Perspective Drawing the parts of an object more distant from the eye are represented as diminished in size according to their remoteness.

SECT. 1. THE NATURE OF PERSPECTIVE, AND OF FORESHORTENING.

The term "perspective" means looking through. In a perspective drawing there is added to a plane drawing in the foreground a lengthened view of objects in the background. The law of perspective in nature is, that objects diminish in size as their distance from the eye increases. This arises from the law of optics, that the angle of vision filled by a small object near the eye takes in objects however large within its range in the distance; and also on the correspondent geometrical law. that in triangles the angle opposite to a side of fixed length diminishes in proportion as the length of the sides containing it are increased.

A simple method of illustrating to the eye perspective in nature is to look at a landscape through a network of lines crossing each other at equal distances; when the largest object in the distance will be seen to fill a square no larger than that occupied by a small object near the eye. A simple method of assuring the eye of the geometrical law of diminution is to look at any object, as a man, across the edge of a graduated ruler; when the form which covers ten inches near the eye will be seen to cover but five inches at double that distance. An easy method of accustoming the hand to trace correctly the proportions of objects in perspective, one recommended by the ablest masters and repeated by Ruskin, is to hold a pane of glass between the eye and the landscape, and to trace with the pencil upon the glass the outline of a row of trees, or other similar objects. As this diminution of the proportions of a retreating object exists in two dimensions, length and breadth, or in both the vertical and horizontal axes of the field of vision, the proportions of an object diminish as the square of the distance increases. The law of heat, light, electricity, and magnetism is the same, since their force issuing from a centre goes out in space enlarging in two dimensions.

Plane and Perspective Drawing are distinct in the end they propose, as well as in their method. Plane drawing is designed to represent only the face of an object, as a model of a machine or the front of a house, to be a guide to a workman. The eye in executing the drawing is supposed to move and to place itself at the same distance from each part of the figure; as the workman moves his position in executing each part of his work. In a plane drawing, therefore, all lines are parallel in the model of the draftsman which are parallel in the object itself; this representation being essential for the mechanic. Perspective drawing is designed to represent distant and near objects as they appear to the eye from one fixed point of view. Lines therefore which in nature are parallel, as the tops and bottoms of a row of trees, the eaves and sills of a house, or the side-walks of a street, are made to converge in the drawing toward a point where they meet each other in the picture as they apparently meet on the horizon in nature.

The drawing in perspective of the parts of an object near the eye but oblique to its line of vision, called "foreshortening," is the most difficult work in the art of drawing. The effect of oblique vision is illustrated by turning a pencil about from a perpendicular through an arc of 90°, and observing its aspect in changing from the long cylinder of its entire length to the mere circle of its end. To copy with the pencil these changes requires the highest skill in the art of drawing. Foreshortening is required in drawing the leg of a person seated, or an arm projecting obliquely; in sketching animals with their limbs or bodies advanced toward the beholder; also in a landscape drawing where trees or other objects are leaning in different directions.

SECT. 2. THE PRACTICAL EXECUTION OF DRAWING IN PERSPECTIVE; AND ARTIFICIAL METHODS OF ILLUSTRATING ITS PRINCIPLES.

Teachers of art suggest that the first lessons of the student in perspective be the copying of the best engravings to acquire the *method* of the engraver in the execution of perspective. Proceeding then to nature, the first attempts should be made in delineating the faces of objects with regular straight sides, as a cubic block, a house with its windows, or a door standing open at different angles; the eye looking at the more remote over the equal side nearer the observer. The drawing of the top of a cup or drinking glass, placed at different angles to the eye, gives practice in tracing curves in perspective. These lessons in single objects may be followed by drawing regular rows of trees and houses and chairs; then rows of animals and men. As a last study portions of landscape more and more extended may be attempted.

Pietro di Borgo, the earliest modern writer on the science, suggested the tracing of perspective on glass held between the eye and the landscape; a suggestion approved by Ruskin. Albert Durer constructed a machine which could be adjusted so as directly to measure the proportions of objects seen in perspective. Other teachers have suggested the holding of a thin paper on which the drawing is to be taken again and again before the eyes, and looking at the line of objects across the edge till their proportionate height and breadth compared with that of the drawing paper is fixed.

Yet others have recommended the use of a jointed ruler, opening with its hinge farthest from the eye, so that its sides sloping to an angle shall take in and range with the perspective lines of the objects to be copied; when, by placing the ruler on the drawing paper and tracing lines along the inside of the arms till they meet at the joint of the ruler, rows of houses, trees or other objects may be drawn of their altitude in perspective. The eye, however, should soon come to be its own measurer in fixing and following the perspective lines; as in plane drawing, the eye must learn to measure the proportions of objects drawn after a given scale.

Sect. 3. The lines and points to be first fixed in perspective drawing.

In perspective drawing the *horizontal line*, toward which all lines above and below the observer slope, is to be first fixed. In nature the line of the "horizon," a term derived from the Greek verb "*horizo*" to limit, is at the remotest point visible where the sky and earth seem to meet. In a long hall or street, as well as in the landscape and the canopy of sky, all lines above and below seem to slope downward and upward to this common line. The science of perspective teaches the method of copying in a drawing made with the pencil this law of vision.

To aid in fixing this line Lionardo gave this rule: "The point of sight must be taken on a level with the eyes of a common man, and be placed upon the horizon; which is the line formed by a flat country terminating with the sky." As that level is about five feet above the general surface, and as most objects, houses, trees, hills and mountains are above the artist's eye, the horizontal line in most perspective views is placed near the bottom of the picture. The bird, however, unlike man, soars above the earth; and there is more below than above his horizon. In taking a view from a mountain top, from a lofty rock, or from an elevated steeple, the artist occupies the position of the bird; and hence is said to take a "bird's-eye view." In general, the elevation, supposed or real, of the artist's stand-point while taking a view, determines the height on the picture of the horizontal line. In views of the interior of an elevated edifice, as a cathedral, the height of the horizontal line is about one-tenth of the distance from the bottom to the top of the picture; in architectural exterior views of houses, streets, one-sixth; in extended landscapes one-third or one-fourth; in domestic scenes one-half or one-third; and in historical paintings, where a limited view from an elevated position is taken, about three-fifths of the same distance.

In *landscape* the Flemish artists, accustomed to the lowlands of Holland, have fixed the line of their horizon very low; while Swiss, Scotch, and Italian painters in a mountain region have followed an opposite rule. In the period previous to Raphael, the horizontal line was often fixed at the extreme height of four-fifths, and even of nine-tenths of the altitude of the picture, thus giving to their works the aspect of bird's-eye views, and precluding the execution of landscape proper. The design of this method was to furnish a large field for the front view and action; thus leaving little for the background and the repose of the picture. In general the horizontal line in a perspective view is placed higher or lower on the picture according to the height of the artist's elevation, or to the extent of the field of action embraced in his design.

After the horizontal line, the point on that line called "the vanishing-point," is to be fixed. As lines above and below the eye seem in the distance to converge to a horizontal line, so lines on either side of the eye seem to converge from either hand to a perpendicular line; and these two combined effects make the seeming convergence tend to one point. This point, called the vanishing-point, is on the horizontal line at the point immediately before the eye of the artist, whence he can take in the whole of his picture without turning his head. In any drawing there may be subsidiary vanishing-points to which the lines of certain portions of the picture converge; points located within the picture, or without it, on either side; but all lying in the horizontal line prolonged. The principal vanishing-point is the one to which all lines parallel to the line of vision tend; as the walls of a hall, the sides of a street or valley within which the artist is located. It will be either at the centre of the picture, or, as the artist works with his right hand, a little to the left of his main standing-point. In the "Last Supper" of Lionardo, the principal vanishing-point is at the eye of Christ in the very centre of the group. In subsidiary parts of the picture, as in the *ends* of buildings whose *fronts* tend to the principal vanishing-point, and in all objects at either side of the line of vision, the convergence of parallels in the object is to points on the horizon toward which those parallels are directed. In a perspective view of a hall, the fronts of chairs and benches ranged on either side would converge to the principal, and their sides to a common subsidiary vanishing-point; but articles of furniture standing obliquely must have each its own separate vanishing-point. The same is true to a greater extent in a large field with many figures.

The *distance-point* or *eye-point* is the opposite of the vanishing-point; the point *without* and in *front of* the picture, to which the lines of light coming from each of its parts to the eye of the beholder also converge. The artist constructs his work with the design that it be viewed from his own fixed point of view in front of the picture, and at a certain distance. Its distance in front of the picture must be such that every part of the picture without the turning of the eye will fall within the angle of vision. Ruskin says to young artists: "*First* fix the *station-point*, or distance at which you will stand from your picture." Lionardo gives these directions: "Remember that objects diminish in size as distance increases. In calculating this diminution, stand at twice the length of your picture from it. Remember that if you vary your distance, you vary the rate of diminution. It must be *one point*, not only in distance, but also in elevation and laterally. It should be on a level with the eye of a man of ordinary stature." The practical effect of an error in this respect is seen in photographs when one part of the person, as a hand, is advanced in front of the other parts. Raphael's chosen distance for the eye of the beholder was one and one-half the breadth of his picture. Some objects, however, require three lengths of the picture as the distance of the eye-point; the larger dimension, whether height or breadth, being the one to regard. In all cases it should be the point where the field of vision takes in at a single glance, and without the *turning of the eye*, the entire picture; while at the same time the eye can be directed to each separate part of the picture without the *turning of the head.*

The skill of the artist in the selection of "eye-points" is magical in the illusion of frescoed walls and ceilings, which seem to open outward to the living landscape, and upward to the floating clouds, in which, however, the illusion fails and the enchantment is lost, unless viewed from the proper point.

SECT. 4. PRINCIPLES OF DESCRIPTIVE GEOMETRY AND PROJECTION ENTERING INTO PERSPECTIVE DRAWING.

Though genius for art may enable the pupil to become practically efficient in executing perspective, yet a knowledge of the science that enters into the art is *most* important to the artist, and *all* important to the amateur who has little or no time for practice. A brief reference to the leading applications of geometrical science to perspective is therefore requisite.

Descriptive Geometry presents the laws for representing with mathematical accuracy the visual appearance of objects having three dimensions on a plane having but two dimensions. This representation is called *the projection* of an object; and the plane on which it is executed is called *the plane of projection*, or the *perspective plane.* Every portion of the *thickness* of an object viewed in front of the eye lies in one of a series of *vertical* planes, or of planes perpendicular to the line of vision; and every portion of the *height* of the same object also lies in a series of horizontal planes, or of planes parallel to the line of vision. In projection, all the parts of an object are referred to two planes called the vertical and the horizontal; and the artist is obliged to transfer the representations upon both these planes to the one plane of projection or of perspective.

Descriptive Geometry treats *first* of the methods of projecting on the plane of the drawing single objects with straight or curved lines, as their contour; *second*, of drawing straight lines and plane surfaces as tangents to curved lines and curved surfaces, such as circles and spheres, ellipses and ellipsoids; and *third*, the method of representing the intersections of various bodies bounded by curved lines, as cylinders, cones, etc., which cut each other.

To illustrate the first principle, a book set upon its edge on a table may represent the vertical, while the table represents the horizontal plane. If a pencil be held between the eye and these two planes its trace will be straight or bent according as it falls in one or both planes. A coin thus held is but a line upon the vertical plane when viewed horizontally; it is a circle on the horizontal plane when viewed from above; and it is an ellipse of greater or less eccentricity when viewed from any point between the vertical and horizontal positions. The eye, trained to this observation with

11 *

the two planes, learns to trace any visual aspect of an object on the single plane of the drawing.

The *second* principle may be thus illustrated. On a sheet of tin the sun's rays are reflected from every point of the surface at the same angle. Upon a cylindrical tube, however, the observed reflection will be a single narrow line of light extending from top to bottom; while upon a globe it will be but a single circular bright spot; and upon an ellipsoid of a corresponding shape. Thus the bright spot called the white of the eye, indicates by its location the direction in which the eye is turned. The point on the sphere, and the line on the cylinder where the reflection is seen, is the portion of the curved surface which would be touched by a plane made tangent to that surface. Lionardo treats at length of the applications of this principle in drawing and in sculpture.

The third principle may be observed in the juncture of the stones in an arch, or in the joinings of mouldings in the ornamental carved work of doors; whose difficult attainment has made the name "joiner" the designation of a profession in the mechanic arts. The power to draw the *appearance* of such junctures, and that at every conceivable angle, is only acquired after long practice; while the method in theory can only be learned by careful study of Descriptive Geometry.

As the plotting of maps of a limited extent of country, supposed to be a plane surface, belongs to Plane Drawing, so the plotting of an extended region as of a hemisphere, in which the sphericity of the globe must be regarded, requires the application of the principles of Perspective and of Descriptive Geometry. The Greeks employed for this three methods. The first, called anciently *analemma*, but now *orthographic*, supposes the eye of the beholder, as in viewing the moon's surface, at a distance relatively infinite. In the second, styled *gnomonic*, the eye is located at the centre of the sphere whose opposite hemisphere is projected. In the third, invented by Hipparchus, and called by him *planisphere*, and used afterward by Ptolemy, the Roman, and by the Arabian geographers, the eye of the plotter is in the surface of the sphere at the upper pole of the globe whose lower half is copied. A fourth method. unknown to the ancients, places the eye on the axis of the hemisphere to be plotted, and at a distance above it such that lines from the eye to its surface shall cut the upper surface of the hemisphere, which is the plane of projection, half-way from its centre to its circumference, and at the same time cut the hemisphere to be projected half-way from its nadir to its horizon. To these four methods of projection that of Mercator has been more recently added.

SECT. 5. THE PRINCIPLES OF TRIGONOMETRY AND OF OPTICS AS THEY RELATE TO PERSPECTIVE DRAWING.

Trigonometry treats of the relation of sides and angles in triangles, by means of which the size and distance of remote objects are determined. Optics states the laws of the reflection and refraction of light as they relate to human vision.

The artist is called to observe especially three points; the diminution of objects in size according to distance, their different shadings as dependent on the laws of the reflection of light, and the distorted appearance of objects seen through a medium that refracts light. The first of these is associated with Plane Geometry, the second with Descriptive Geometry, and the third has a relation to color which connects it with painting.

The law of the diminution of objects is associated with that of the distance point. The angle of distinct vision covers about 30° in a vertical, and 45° in a horizontal direction; the chord of the former arc is about one-half, and of the latter about two-thirds of the radius; and hence an object having a breadth one-half greater than its height fills that angle at a distance of twice its height. A picture two feet in height, and three feet in breadth, fills the eye at a distance of six feet; and since a mountain three miles high, four and a-half miles broad at the base and at a distance of ten miles is seen through the frame of such a picture without the canvas, the mountain and all the intervening country can be brought into the field of that canvas.

By the law of reflection a ray of light is bent back at an angle equal to that at which it falls upon the reflecting surface. The form of Mont Blanc, rising four miles high, about forty miles south of Geneva, can be seen reflected on the bosom of Lake Leman, near that city, by a person on its northern bank. The student of perspective learns by observation that every object in nature, even a cloud, is a reflecting surface; that every body with several faces throws back light upon objects around it from each of its sides that the angle of each reflection is fixed; and that the intensity of the light reflected is always proportional to the smoothness or polish of the reflecting surface, and to the clearness of the atmosphere through which it passes.

The phenomena of refraction had been observed by the oldest painters. The early Egyptian and rude Chinese artists remarked that the rays of light are bent downward as they pierce a surface of water; so that the foot of a man or animal seen in water seems raised, and his leg shortened from the point where it enters the water. The Grecian sculptors understood that objects seen through vapor, especially white objects, appear colossal; chiefly, indeed, from dimness of outline, which makes them seem more distant and therefore larger; but partly also, as Lionardo has demonstrated, from the law of refraction.

The careful study of the laws of Trigonometry and of Optics is essential to the successful practice of the artist's profession; for though genius in art seems intuitively to catch from observation of nature the laws of perspective, it will fail in some of their applications if not master of their theory.

Sect. 6. The perspective of shadows.

Shadows in Perspective Drawing are to be distinguished from shades in Plane Drawing. A *shade* is the darkened portion of an object from which the light is cut off; a *shadow* is the indefinitely prolonged space behind an opaque object and in the line of rays of light intercepted by it. The west side of a house is shaded when the sun is rising; while the shadow of the house is cast, for miles even, westward on a line of objects from which it cuts off the sun's rays. The dark portion of the moon is shaded by its own body cutting off the sun's rays; while mountain peaks cast shadows on other peaks in their rear.

To represent shadows in perspective correctly three things must be observed; *first*, the position of the luminary; *second*, that of the object illuminated; and *third*, that of the observer. The position of the luminary may be in front of the observer and back of the object, and thus the shadow be cast toward him; or the luminary may be behind him and the shadow of the object be behind the object; or the luminary may be at the observer's right or left, and the shadow therefore fall at his opposite hand.

The important laws of shadows as they relate to perspective are the following. The *depth* or darkness of shadows is in proportion to the amount of light of which they are deprived compared with that which illuminates other objects; shadows in sunlight being really lighter than in moonlight, while nevertheless they are comparatively darker. The *shape* of a shadow is of the form of the object; either a cone converging to its apex, or a cone diverging toward its base, or a cylinder of equal dimensions throughout, according as the luminous centre compared with the object casting the shadow is of greater, less, or equal size. The *size* of a shadow at any given point will depend on the relative size of the luminous point as compared with the object casting the shadow, and also upon the distance between the object and the shaded spot as compared with the distance between the object and the luminous centre; the shadows from objects on the earth as men and trees being substantially of the same size as the objects themselves when cast on a wall near by, because though the size of the sun is immensely greater than that of a man on the earth, yet its distance from the man as compared with his distance from the wall is equally immense. The *length* of shadows is dependent on the same causes as its size; the shadow of the moon being shorter than that of the earth in eclipses; as may be illustrated by letting the shadow of a book larger or smaller, held before a window in bright sunlight, fall on a sheet of white paper. The *number* of shadows cast by an object depends upon the number of centres of light, whether of the sun or moon, or of one or more lamps added to the number of reflecting surfaces, as of mirrors, smooth waters and polished walls, from which light is reflected.

It is mainly by skillful copying of the contrasts of light and shade in nature that the pencil or brush can make an object seem to stand out from the canvas as real. The artist must, therefore, avail himself of a time when, and of a point of view where, the most advantage can be taken of the lights and shadows in nature. In portrait painting a position in which the light falls on the countenance at an angle of about 45° from above and at one side is most favorable. In landscape, noonday short shadows give the impression of languor, the morning and evening long shadows of delightful repose, while the medium shadows of midforenoon and afternoon furnish the strong contrasts of light and shade essential to the highest relief and action.

In tracing shadows in an enclosed room it must be observed that the lines of light are parallel to each other coming through a window from the sun, but diverge when the luminous centre is small, as a lamp's light or an aperture in a window. In shadows thrown upon a horizontal plane, as the floor of a room or the surface of the earth, an oblique section of the cylinder or cone of shadow is to be traced; prolonged in length but unchanged in breadth. When the shadow of an object falls on a broken surface and upon objects of greater or less height than itself, the nicest care is requisite that the cylinder of shade follow its true line in nature and cast a shade of truly *proportionate* height or length, or of the *precise* breadth of the object on every other object or part of an object behind it. Ruskin specially suggests that though the shading of water is in the main to be made by parallel lines, yet great skill is requisite in varying the depth of shade according to the shadows falling on the water, and also to insert the broken curves which indicate the outline of shadows on its face when smooth, or the ripples upon it where it is ruffled.

SECT. 7. AERIAL PERSPECTIVE, AND ITS RELATION TO CHIAROSCURO.

Distance not only diminishes the size but also obscures the distinctness of objects. Linear perspective relates to the due diminution of outline in drawing distant objects. The accurate gradation of distinctness in the shading of distant objects belongs to the province of aerial perspective. It is called "aerial" perspective because the air, whether clear or hazy, has even more influence than distance in rendering a remote object indistinct; as is witnessed in the clear atmosphere after a shower of rain.

The shading of a single object demands a practical acquaintance with the principles of chiaroscuro; otherwise the jutting corners and retiring indentations of an object with plane surfaces cannot be represented to the eye; and still less can the rounding of curved surfaces be so pictured that the alternate swell of the convex and depression of the concave will be made to stand out as in the object itself. In perspective a second end is to be attained. The known size of a man, a house, or a tree makes the proportion of their diminution in a background the measure of their distance. On the other hand, a cliff, a river, a mountain or a cloud has no fixed size; and therefore the space it is made to occupy in the drawing is not at all an indication of its distance. It requires a long training of the eye to determine the distance of such objects in the landscape by their peculiar tinge or shade; so that by the distant blue or the deep black, the beholder is able to judge rightly of the miles that intervene between the eye and the mountain, and to define the shape and the depth of the valleys on its side. It is only the practised huntsman on the prairie, or sailor on the ocean, that forms a just judgment of aerial perspective as it exists in nature. The artist has a double task; first, to learn by careful observation, and then to copy the aerial tinges of the landscape.

As aerial aspects vary with each alternate atmospheric change, so aerial perspective is a distinct and new study in every different country and climate. As in one's own clime the distant hills look nearer of a morning after a long storm, so the Englishman or Hollander, accustomed to a murky, hazy or foggy sky, has no standard for measuring distances in the clear atmosphere of the American prairie, of the desert about Egypt, or of the sunny plains of Italy. The artists of England and Holland who have never dreamed of the bright yellow preponderating in the green of a Southern clime, and of seeing the moon's dark side on a clear night, must be a school distinct from the Italian, the American, and even the French, in landscape sketching; since the "aerial perspective" they have studied is so different.

SECT. 8. CURVILINEAR PERSPECTIVE; AND THE RELATION WHICH THE ACTUAL CURVE OF PERSPECTIVE LINES IN NATURE HAS TO THEIR REPRESENTATION IN DRAWING.

In the Creator's handiwork, in flower, leaf, fruit, twig, branch, and even in the sloping height as well as the rounded sides of the tree trunk, in hill and vale, in mountain top and cloud, in the form of the round world and of the "grand o'erhanging canopy" of the vaulted sky, there is not, perhaps, a purely straight line to be met; while the human form, the masterpiece of beauty, has its myriad forms of grace wrought out in lines of varied curvature. The Greeks in their best works of architecture followed this hint of nature; for in the Parthenon there is not a single purely straight line.

In nature, too, all lines in themselves straight are in their perspective view curved. In the photograph, which copies the lines of a long building as we actually see them, we detect in the copy the fact which we overlook in nature. Careful attention indicates that the floor of an extended hall appears to rise in a slightly curved line; as every line in the landscape and the vaulted sky seems also curved. By the law of vision every point of each line in perspective is not only raised to a horizontal plane nearer the eye, but every point is by this very fact also drawn inward to a vertical plane nearer the eye; hence giving a curved appearance to the perspective line. This law is observed in all mountain and balloon views; from which elevated points the landscape appears as a hollow basin. In drawings upon a small scale, this curvature is so minute that it need not be taken into account; yet nature herself, the only perfect artist, does even in the smallest picture taken by her pencil of light, strictly regard her own law, that the curved line is the line of truth, if it be not the line of beauty.

The law of Curvilinear Perspective may be demonstrated by the principles of Geometry and of Optics; and the precise measure of this curvature may be fixed by the Calculus. Suppose the observer to be standing at a distance of 200 feet in front of the centre of a symmetrical building 100 feet long and 40 feet high. It is manifest while the centre of the front of the building is precisely 200 feet from his eye, each line in the remaining portions of that front, as he looks from the centre toward either end, is more than 200 feet from his eye; the ends of the building being about 206 feet distant. As now the space which an object occupies in the angle of vision is less in proportion to its distance from the eye, the apparent height of the building should be about one-thirtieth less at the ends than at the centre. In ordinary vision the knowledge that the building line is straight irresistibly overcomes the impression on the eye; but the photograph dissolves self-deception; and instead of a straight horizontal line it shows a curved line arching upward.

The same law applies to the horizontal lines in the building. The one five feet above the ground is at its centre 200 feet from the eye. The line, however, running along the top of the building, is about 203 feet at its centre from the eye; and must, therefore, be shorter in appearance than the lower line. Thus the vertical lines at either end of the building seem to slope inward as they rise; which slope the photograph makes a curve. It is equally manifest that every line or part of a line out of the centre of view, above or below, at the right or the left of the eye on the face of the building, will be correspondingly curved.

This general curvature makes the face of a broad surface seem to be a hollowed curve; the surface of a lake or plain, of a broad ceiling or of the heavens, appearing to be concave toward the beholder. The apparent cause of this aspect may be thus illustrated. When a company of men all known to be of equal stature, stand in a line, the observer unconsciously ascribes to the men at the extremes of the line the same size as to those at the centre; and hence regards them as at equal distance. The full effect of this illusion would bring the line into the form of an arc of a circle; whence the former designation of "circular perspective." The eye, however, does in part correct the illusion of the mind; and the name "curvilinear perspective" is truer to the fact.

By the simplest principles of geometry and of the calculus the law of this curve and the rate of its curvature are ascertained; and it can be laid off readily from the elements thus obtained. Suppose lines drawn from the eye to different points upon the horizontal line immediately before the eye on the front of the building above mentioned; the first line to the point immediately before the eye, the second ten feet to the left of this point, the third twenty feet, the fourth thirty feet, the fifth forty feet, and the sixth to the end of the building on the left, fifty feet of course from the centre. The first of these lines is now the altitude of a right-angled triangle; while the second, third, fourth, fifth and sixth lines will each be a hypothenuse of a series of right-angled triangles with bases severally of ten, twenty, thirty, forty and fifty feet. Each hypothenuse is the distance of the eye from the vertical line running from the top to the bottom of the building at its extremity; the length in perspective of each vertical line is proportional to the length of the corresponding hypothenuse; and the length of each hypothenuse is found by squaring the altitude and base, adding these squares, and extracting the square root of the sum. The curve may be drawn by laying off on an abscissa ordinates which shall be to each other inversely as the square root of the sum of the squares of two quantities, one of which is fixed, while the other increases at the same rate as that abscissa. The curve may be traced through the termini of these ordinates thus laid off.[1]

It is only in very recent times that the execution of perspective in extended landscape is giving practical value to these principles long observed. Tibaldi, a leading master in the Bolognese school, wrote three centuries ago, "The horizon of nature is a circular line; but this line drawn on a plane horizontally at the point of view is a straight line." Herdman, a recent and comprehensive writer, says of curvilinear perspective, "In views of large extent its use will give greater beauty and less distortion than rectilinear perspective;" and thus he adds, "Lateral extents and spaces hitherto totally unattainable in art may be wrought with *truth*, in accordance with what *is seen*."

SECT. 9. BINOCULAR VISION, IN ITS RELATION TO PERSPECTIVE.

The distance between the two eyes in ordinary persons is about two and one-half inches, which is termed "the visual base." When a small object is placed near the nose, as a thin book, one eye views one side, and the other the opposite side. At their focus, and beyond, the two eyes see more than half the circumference of a ball or other object. This *two-eyed* or "binocular" vision, which led Wheatstone to the idea of the stereoscope, has suggested methods in drawing for giving roundness, projection and life-like relief to objects in the foreground.

By binocular vision distant objects directly behind near ones are fully seen. If a book be held between the two eyes and in front of a wall, the right eye alone locates it on the wall far to the left of its central position, and the left eye alone far to the right; while both eyes see the entire wall behind it. From this effect two important principles are suggested in the execution of perspective. The object near the eye is *indistinctly* seen; while objects immediately behind it are completely observed. A careful attention to the impression on the eye will indicate that two separate images are recognized on the retina, and that two projections of these images are thrown upon the background.

---

[1] Taking a = altitude, x = base, y = hypothenuse, we have $y^2 = a^2 + x^2$; whence $y = \sqrt{a^2 + x^2}$. Differentiating, $dy = \frac{xdx}{\sqrt{a^2 + x^2}}$.

Lionardo, in his "Rules in Painting," describes the effects of binocular vision at length; and directs: "When a ball held before a wall is painted, the painted figure must cover the space behind it. Since, then, when seen with both eyes, the wall would appear behind the ball, the painter should place a mirror before the object, and paint it as it is seen reflected looking at the object with one eye only." This monocular or one-eyed method thus taught has required reconsideration in the age of landscape painting proper. In England Sir David Brewster has written upon the general theory of binocular vision. Professor Wheatstone has applied it to the construction of the stereoscope; and James Hall has discussed its relation specially to art execution. By its law "each line in perspective not parallel to the picture has two vanishing points," one corresponding to each eye. Hall's suggestions are these: *First*, all objects should first be constructed of life-size as they appear to *both* eyes when directed to the principal object, and on a vertical plane passing through the principal part of the chief object; and the "duplications and regulated obscurities" under which the very near objects are seen should be introduced. *Second*, this life-sized construction should be reduced to the miniature scale of the artist's design and be finished as seen by both eyes, with the "regulated obscurities" still retained. In support of this view, Hall cites the experience of the best artists; *first*, that the view of an object, drawn in perspective with one eye, has *less breadth* than if drawn with two eyes; and *second*, that a monocular view of an object gives no measure of its distance. Its adoption Hall thinks would realize Sir Joshua Reynolds' suggestion as to the overworking of minor details by able artists. The pre-Raphaelite theory was that the eyes of the artist be adjusted to every part of the picture separately; and that he delineate every part of the picture, whether in the foreground, middle ground, or distance, with the same distinctness with which he sees it when thus separately viewed. Sir Joshua advised against this method; remarking, "I have observed that an excessive labor of detail has, nine times in ten, been pernicious to the general effect, even when it has been the labor of great masters." Probably Turner has carried to an extreme this suggestion of Hall.

SECT. 10. THE HISTORY OF DRAWING IN PERSPECTIVE.

The artists of all rude and half-civilized nations have failed either in observing or in applying the laws of vision to drawing in perspective. In the sculptures and paintings on the monuments of Egypt the most distant in a line of soldiers, the farthest of four chariot horses abreast, is drawn of the same dimensions with the nearest in the line; and objects in more distant fields are put in compartments in corners of the main picture without any apparent connection with it. In Chinese paintings either everything is put in the foreground, or if there be a background and the figures in it are drawn smaller, the gradation of the intervening space is not preserved, and the geometrical law of convergence in the lines of the picture is not attempted.

Vitruvius, the Roman architect of the Augustan age, thus illustrates the Grecian knowledge of perspective: "Agatharsius, at the time when Æschylus taught at Athens the rules of tragic poetry, was the first who contrived scenery; upon which subject he wrote a treatise. After him Democritus and Anaxagoras went still further in that way, showing the power of imitating nature by making all the lines to vanish to one point as a centre, when viewed at a fixed distance; by which means they are enabled to represent in their scenery on the stage the image of real buildings as they usually appear to the eye, and that whether they were painted on horizontal or upright surfaces; and thus they exhibited objects near and remote." Pliny says of Pamphilus, a teacher of painting at Athens in the days of Demosthenes: "He was learned especially in arithmetic and geometry; without whose principles he declared that art could not be perfected."

The revival of the study in modern times has been allied chiefly to the department of landscape painting. The great masters, however, of Italy and of Germany, Lionardo and Durer, have especially developed its principles.

CHAPTER III.

ENGRAVING; THE TRANSFER OF DRAWINGS TO ENGRAVED PLATES FOR THE MULTIPLYING OF COPIES.

In the progress of art, its applications come often to overshadow the original; as printed books make us forget the day when the pen copied everything. Engraving, and its kindred arts, but copy that of which the drawing pencil has given an original; and photography, in its various branches, only compels nature to the imposed toil of penciling her own face.

Sect. 1. The nature and history of engraving.

In the study of an art proper we naturally consider the processes before tracing the history of its practice. It is the reverse in our consideration of an invention, or the application of the art. Engraving originated when drawing as an art was so perfected that men sought some method of multiplying its superior creations. An engraving is a drawing cut into wax, clay, wood, stone, metal, or other material; and it is executed for two purposes, first, to be itself a work of art; second, to be a mechanic's copy whose impressions are to be works of art. The first kind of engraving is alluded to by Job, and is preserved now in the monuments of Egypt and Assyria of the same age. The second kind of engraving existed in its germ in the signet rings of the ancients, worn even by the Pharaohs of Joseph's time, and also in the dies from which the earliest rude coins, marked with the image of a sheep, were struck, mentioned in Abraham's day, and found in the oldest tombs of Egypt. Engraving of the former class in its increasing perfection became the germ of the art of sculpture, while the exquisite specimens of the second kind executed in modern times have made engraving a master art.

To the first class belong the choice relics of Grecian engravings now among the richest treasures of art. Even the decorators of armor and rings, described by Homer, were advanced in the art. Herodotus mentions maps engraved on metal. In the days of Socrates engravers were numerous and skillful; and under Alexan-

12 *

der Pyrgoteles was so superior that the monarch forbade any other to engrave his portrait.

Plates from which to print pictured hieroglyphics are of very early date. In the oldest tombs of Egypt are found cones of clay stamped by engraved plates. In China the same art existed as early as B. C. 1120; and probably it was never lost in the East. The modern art seems to have been brought from Constantinople to Venice. It was first employed in the copying and multiplying of small pictured cards requiring very little art; as playing cards and pictures of saints executed in dark and colored figures.

Sect. 2. Xylography or engraving on wood.

The simplest material for engraving is wood; whence the Greek word *Xylography*. The best woods are box, beech and mahogany. The engraving is executed on a section cut across the fibre of the standing wood. The picture is first drawn with a pencil on thin or tissue paper, oiled so as to be transparent. A second paper, smeared upon one side with white, red, or black chalk, is laid with its chalked face downward upon the wood to be engraved; and over it is placed the first paper with the drawing upon it downward. With a hard pointed style the lines of the drawing are traced through the two thicknesses of paper upon the wood, so as to leave its lines in chalk upon the face of the wood. With a fine chisel a small groove is cut along both sides of each line in the drawing, so as to leave a thin raised edge corresponding to the lines of the drawing; and the intervening parts of the surface of the wood are scooped out with a gouge. The block thus prepared is used as a stereotype plate in printing; the raised lines only, like the type, being touched by the ink. As the drawing was reversed when traced on the wood, and as thus the engraved block is the reverse of the drawing, the print upon the paper is the reverse of the engraving on the block, or the original drawing restored again. The more experienced engravers will copy the drawing directly and in reverse upon the wood.

Wood engraving existed in China under the Emperor Ven Vang, about B. C. 1120; as this allusion in the "Book of Changes" then published shows: "As the ink which is used to blacken the engraved characters can never become white, so a heart blackened by vices will retain its blackness." The entire page is written carefully on thin paper through which the writing is seen; this page is then glued with the written face downward upon a block of wood of the apple or pear tree; when the engraver cuts the block in the manner already described.

The art was introduced into Europe from Asia in the twelfth century by Venetian merchants. At first the execution was extremely rude. Only the outside border lines were cut upon the wood; the printed outline being filled in by the colorist. Next inner lines, tracing limbs and features, were introduced; the shading, however, being left for the finishing touch of the artist. Still later, a species of shading by dots was added; until at length Wohlgemuth, a German, began to put in the cross-cuts and hatchings which formed the shading of the drawing.

It was, however, among the Flemish artists, between the eras of Van Eyck, A. D. 1395, and of Albert Durer, A. D. 1495, that engraving became truly a fine art. The difficulty of cutting the nice cross lines to a sufficient thinness, and the spaces between to a sufficient depth, to give at once fineness and clearness to the impression, was overcome by the skill of Albert Durer. The genius of Holbein gave its last perfection to the art. It is now superseded except in the very coarsest of work by plates of other material.

SECT. 3. CHALCOGRAPHY; OR ENGRAVING ON COPPER.

The maps engraved on copper mentioned by Herodotus were not, like those of our day, designed for printing copies. The word *chalcography* is modern, though the Greeks had similar compounds; as *chalcoergos*, to designate the coarser, and *chalchotypos*, the finer artificer in brass or copper.

The main distinction between wood and copper engraving is that the ink is transferred to the paper in the former from raised, and in the latter from depressed, lines. The ancients took impressions upon wax with signets; the soft wax being pressed into the depressions in the engraved seal. The idea, however, that ink might be made to fill the cavities of engraved plates, and that pressure on the plate might cause the fibres of the sheet to be so forced into its depressions as to receive the distinct lines of the engraving, seems not to have occurred to the minds of those accustomed to wood engraving. A happy accident revealed the fact.

Among the arts of adornment for chalices and sword-hilts, that called *niello* was extensively practised in Italy. It consisted in filling the depressed lines of the carved or embossed silver or gold with a fused compound of silver and lead, which turned black, thus giving the outline of the engraved figure. A servant woman in the studio of Tomaso Finiguerra, having accidentally laid a wet cloth on a piece of niello, the print left on the cloth suggested to that artist the idea of copper-plate printing. The art, though long restricted, like wood engraving, to mere outlines, grew in Italy, while in Germany it made slow progress; even Albert Durer, so skillful in wood engraving, failing to attain the grace of the Italian copper-plate engravers.

Copper-plate engraving embraces several varieties. The simplest method is first to cover the prepared copper-plate with a very thin layer of white wax; then to lay a copy of the drawing to be executed on the wax, and to subject it to a heavy pressure, so as to leave its outlines upon the plate; next, to remove the paper of the transferred drawing by moistening and gentle rubbing; afterward to expel the wax by heating the plate; and lastly, to cut the picture left upon its surface into the copper. The point of the graver by which the heavier lines are cut is triangular or pyramidal in shape; faint parallel lines for the shading of clouds are traced with a fine pointed instrument drawn along the edge of a ruler; while yet fainter shades are scratched in with a needle. The polish of the plate is completed by rubbing with olive oil. When prepared for printing the ink roller is passed heavily over the plate; after which the ink covering its entire face is removed by a rubbing of the hand so delicate as not to disturb that sunk in the engraved lines.

The method called *stippling*, from *stipula* or stubble, consists in puncturing the surface of the plate with dots, originally employed in certain portions of engravings, but a century ago made a special style of engraving. It gives a peculiarly soft appearance to human flesh and to the more delicate flowers. The best line engravers, however, are regarded the true masters in the art.

The delicate shading called *mezzo-tinto*, or half-tint, executed on copper-plate, is said to have owed its origin to Sir Christopher Wren. It is executed with a small steel wheel having a notched edge, which, when rolled over the plate, covers it with regular and superficial indentations which receive slight amounts of ink, and give to the print a delightful evenness and softness of aspect.

SECT. 4. ETCHING; ENGRAVING ON COPPER BY ACID REACTION.

Etching by acids was introduced about forty years later than copper-plate engraving. The plate is heated over a spirit lamp, and then covered with a varnish. Upon this varnish the copy is transferred, and then traced by the graver, only the varnish being cut. A solution of *aqua fortis*, or nitric acid, is then poured over the plate; which eats into the copper along the lines where the varnish is removed. When the acid has stood long enough to produce the light shading it is poured of; the plate is washed with water and dried; and the parts which are to remain of a light shade are covered again with varnish. The acid is then again poured upon the plate and allowed to stand until the shade next darker is secured; the deeper corrosion of the plate enabling it to take up a greater quantity of ink when used in printing. By repeating this process, any number of shades may be produced.

A double advantage over ordinary plate engraving was secured by acid reaction. The labor is diminished, and thus cheapness is secured; while the eating of the acid, forming a regular depression, secures a more uniform distribution of the ink. Etching has been specially in use for ordinary landscape engraving.

The *aqua-tinta*, or water-tint, a species of etching, is so called from its resemblance to drawing in water-colors with India ink. The light shade is first produced as in etching; when a solution of resin, or of Burgundy pitch, in alcohol, is poured over the plate. As the alcohol rapidly dries off, the resin is left in dots, or granulations, over the entire surface; and these dots remaining fixed during all the future process, preserve the light shade in dots. The portions of the plate to receive the darker shades are then covered with a gummy syrup called the bursting-ground; when the whole is again covered with varnish. Water is then poured on the plate; in about fifteen minutes the gum breaks and exposes the plate on all the portions which are to receive the deeper shade; when the acid is poured on the plate a second time. The granulated or dotted light spots amid the dark shade preserved by the resin gives a delightful softness to the aspect of backgrounds in portraits and night-scenes.

Sect. 5. Siderography; engraving on steel

Though early suggested as a material desirable for engraved plates, steel was little used until the process of alternately softening and hardening the metal was discovered. The great demand for costly engraving in bank-notes prompted the invention of Mr. Jacob Perkins, of Massachusetts, about 1808. The engraving is first executed on a hardened steel plate. A cylinder of soft steel is then rolled over the engraved plate under a heavy pressure until the soft steel has been forced into the indentations of the hard plate; forming thus on the soft cylinder a raised counterpart of the engraving. This cylinder is then hardened to serve as a punch in making engraved plates like the original. These copies are made on soft steel; which when hardened become each of them capable of furnishing from 50,000 to 100,000 impressions Plates of soft or uncarbonized steel are extensively employed for the illustration of works of popular literature having an extensive sale. While a copper-plate is worn out in printing 5000 or 6000 impressions, the soft steel will print nearly or quite 100,000 copies.

Sect. 6. Lithography; or engraving on stone.

Engraving on stone as a work of sculpture is one of the earliest, and its use as a plate for printing one of the latest arts. There are two methods of preparing stone for lithographing; the one corresponding to copper-plate engraving proper, and the other to etching proper.

As an engraved plate for printing a hard stone is employed; the lines are cut upon it as upon copper-plate, and the depressions receive the printer's ink,

The method of preparing the stone corresponding to etching is said to have originated with Senefelder, an actor of Munich in Bavaria. A calcareous limestone found in Bavaria and Hungary, as also the white lias of England, are specially adapted to this purpose. The drawing is executed with an oily or resinous paint; which from its chemical affinity adheres tenaciously to the stone. The design or copy is first traced upon paper with the paint; and is then transferred to the stone. By the action of vitriolic acid the stone is eaten away where it is not covered with the paint. Thus prepared, the stone, when about to be used, is kept wet with gum water. The ink is composed of an oily soap mixed with lamp-black; which when applied adheres only to the lines of paint, for which it has an affinity; while the portions soaked with water are left free from ink. The stone thus prepared is almost as durable as a steel plate.

A later suggestion has led to the employ of zinc plates, prepared as the stone by tracings with the oily ink, for which this metal has a strong affinity. When the drawing is completed this affinity for the ink is destroyed by dipping the plate in gallic acid, after which it is also washed with gum water. The zinc plate is said to be preferable to the stone, because the acid on the stone continues its action, and thus injures the finer lines, while upon the zinc the action of the acid is exhausted at its first application.

The chief advantage of lithography over any other kind of engraving is the rapidity and facility with which coarse prints may be obtained. Hastily prepared charts of marine and military surveys are printed from stone; but the finished work is engraved on copper-plates.

SECT. 7. PRINTING OF ENGRAVINGS; THE WEAR AND RENEWAL OF PLATES; PROOF IMPRESSIONS AND THEIR GRADUATED VALUE.

In printing from engraved plates the face is subjected to a heavy pressure; which has the effect gradually to wear and obliterate the outlines and make the impression indistinct. Two causes control this wear; the durability of the material of the plate, and the amount of pressure requisite to secure the impression. Relief surfaces, as wood, type-metal, and stone, which receive readily the ink from the roller passed over them, require far less weight of pressure in printing than do copper and steel plates.

The constantly growing wear of the plate produces a constant deterioration in the distinctness and value of the successive prints; which in higher works of art diminishes proportionately the value of successive copies. As the "press-proof" in book-printing is the first finished impression when all the author's and compositor's corrections are made, so in printing engravings, "press-proofs, first-proofs, engraver's proofs," have been used as terms indicating the earliest and most distinct impressions from engraved plates. Some of the more celebrated engravers, as Raphael Morghen, have made it a condition of subscription to their superior works that not more than one hundred impressions should be taken and that then the plate should be broken up, so that no inferior copies could detract from the privilege of the purchasers or from the merit of the artist. In all cases the wear of the plate compels its renewal either by retouching or reproducing.

Sect. 8. Renewal of plates; electrotyping, or the multiplying of engraved copper-plates.

The fact that a copper plate, whose engraving costs not less than ten years' labor, is soon worn out, calls for a cheap and expeditious method of renewing the plate. The electrotype has realized this demand.

In 1801 Wollaston observed that silver immersed in a solution of sulphate of copper at the negative pole of the galvanic battery is coated with copper. In 1805 an Italian chemist gilded silver by the same method. In 1837 Spencer observed that a drop of varnish upon the exposed coin prevented the uniting of the copper at the point thus covered. The idea of copying coins and medals in reverse, was thus suggested.

The suggestion that engraved copper plates might thus be multiplied was delayed by the difficulty of finding a material which, when spread on the plate, would allow the nicest lines of the engraver to be penetrated, while at the same time direct union of the deposit with the plate was prevented. Oil, first tried, failed to meet the demand. Mr. George Mathiot, of the U. S. Coast Survey, suggested iodine in solution with alcohol; a single grain of which may be spread so thin that 400,000,000,000 layers make but an inch in thickness.

Acting on the silver with which the plate is first coated a stratum of iodide of silver is formed so thin that the minutest line of the engraved plate is filled with the copper deposit in the battery, while a perfect cleavage is also preserved. After about four days' action of the battery a perfect raised counterpart of the original engraved plate is obtained. This new plate, taken as a positive, furnishes, by the action of the copper bath, any number of engraved plates like the original.

By electro-metallurgy type-metal is also coated with copper; furnishing a cheap engraved plate, which now takes the place of wood.

SECT. 9. THE PLACE OF ENGRAVING AMONG THE FINE ARTS.

Engraving, practised as a *useful art*, may become a mere trade; or it may be presided over by artists of true genius. In the German Academies, the aspirant for future practice as an engraver, is required to pass through all the schools except that of Composition. This requirement is just; for the engraver must so enter into the spirit of the master whom he represents as to be a true interpreter of his work.

Burnet, urging the dignity of line engraving, says: "We must always bear in mind that an engraving is not a *copy* of a picture; it is a *translation;* and as a picture is possessed of three properties, outline, light and shade, and color, no print can be a proper transfer, unless something is given as an equivalent for this last."

CHAPTER IV.

PHOTOGRAPHY; OR DRAWING BY LIGHT.

THE art of Photography is assuming a constantly increasing importance in connection with Drawing. Though every effort thus far made to copy *color* by the power of light has failed, yet the pencil of the sun's ray is so unerring a delineator of form that photography has taken the place very extensively of engraving in the multiplying of copies both of drawings, statuary and paintings.

SECT. 1. THE COLORING INFLUENCE OF LIGHT, WHICH LED TO THE ART OF PHOTOGRAPHY.

The effect of light in blackening the chloride of silver, or horn-silver, was known to the ancient alchemists. As early as A. D. 1722, a French chemist, named Petit, referred this effect to the crystallization of the metalic salts produced by the influence of light. Between 1775 and 1800, several German chemists investigated the different effects of the different colored rays of the solar spectrum in producing the black tint on paper saturated with a solution of chloride of silver; and ascertained that the violet ray produced the effect after fifteen minutes' exposure, while the red rays required twenty minutes.

About 1800, Wedgewood and Sir Humphrey Davy conceived the idea of copying pictures by the action of light on paper saturated with a solution of nitrate of silver; and succeeded in getting a copy in two or three minutes. Of this effort Davy wrote in 1803: "All that is now required to render these experiments as useful as they are interesting, is to find a way of preventing the subsequent coloring of the white parts upon exposure to daylight." In 1812, the existence and properties of iodine were discovered, an agent found to be most efficient in giving to the metallic salt an increased sensitiveness to the action of light; and in 1819, seven years yet later, the discovery of the hyposulphite of soda, by Sir John Herschel, furnished an agent which arrested the chemical action of light on the salt when the picture was taken.

Meanwhile, in 1814, Niepce, a French chemist, the real author of Photography as an art, began his experiments. In 1827, he obtained photographic pictures; and in 1829 he communicated the result to Daguerre, a French artist. Niepce died in 1833; and Daguerre continued his experiments till 1839, when he astonished the French Academy by the report of his perfected invention. At that time, however, twenty minutes were required to take a picture; and no living object could be copied, owing to the difficulty of securing a quiet position so long.

Sect. 2. The daguerreotype; and the early applications of photography.

The original process of daguerreotyping was as follows. The copper-plate, silvered by galvanism, was held over a box of iodine heated so that its vapor would rise to the plate. The iodine fumes, forming iodide of silver on the plate, changed its color first to a straw, then to a gold, then to a rose, then to an indigo, and finally to a blue tint. The blue tint was found to render the plate the most sensitive to light, allowing an impression to be obtained in about two minutes. At a later day the plate was dipped in water having bromine, or both bromine and chlorine, in solution; when its sensitiveness was so increased as to receive an impression in a few seconds.

The *camera* consists of a box having a double lens as an object glass in a tube and a dark square chamber in the rear. The light, admitted into the front of the object-tube, passes through it into the camera. When the object to be copied is placed in the best position for taking a good picture, the metallic plate, before prepared, is brought from a darkened room covered by a slide over its face to protect it from the light. The plate and slide are introduced through the top of the camera into the field of the object-glass; when the slide is removed, and the rays of light from the object fall directly on the plate. From the countenance, white portions of the dress, and all light-colored substances there is a strong light reflected through the tube on the plate; while from the pupils of the eyes, the hair, and all dark-colored objects the light reflected is feeble. When this action has continued sufficiently long for the proper impression to be made on the plate by the light, the plate is removed to a room into which only the yellow ray of light coming from a lamp or through a curtain, is admitted; the yellow ray not acting on the plate. Thus far the art has not changed with its advance in many particulars. In the early art the plate was next held over mercury evaporated by a spirit lamp; when the vapor of mercury so acted on the parts which had been most exposed to the light, as in the language of the art, to "bring out" the picture. To remove then the iodine still in combination with the silver of the less exposed portions of the plate, and thus in the language of the art, "to fix the picture," the plate was immersed in a solution of the hyposulphite of soda dissolved in distilled water.

SECT. 3. THE AMBROTYPE; AND PRINTING OF MULTIPLIED ENGRAVINGS BY PHOTOGRAPHY.

The photographs of Daguerre were taken on metallic plates. Davy, however, in 1800, had taken pictures on paper saturated with a solution of nitrate of silver. Fox Talbot perfected this branch of the art; and in England photographs on paper were called Talbotypes. The paper was prepared by immersion first in salt water, chloride of sodium, drying and immersing again in a solution of nitrate of silver. Talbot first used gallic acid, made of gall or oak apples, in the nitrate solution, to heighten the sensitiveness of the paper. The paper thus prepared received the picture in the camera as the plate receives it, and was, like the daguerreotype, a negative or reverse.

To obtain the positive, now specially designated as a photograph, the negative was laid upon a second paper prepared as the first; a board was placed behind the second and a glass before the first; and the whole, being then carefully pressed into contact, was exposed for some hours to the sunlight with the glass uppermost. The impression was received through the glass and the first paper upon the second; the rapidity of the process depending upon the thinness of the paper through which the light must pass, and its evenness on the purity of the paper.

The difficulty of obtaining paper free from impurities, and the slow action of the light through paper, led Sir John Herschel to use glass as the plate; hence called Vitrotype or ambrotype. Improving methods of preparing the glass plate have led to the following. Dissolve ordinary cotton fibre in an equal mixture of sulphuric and nitric acids, forming *collodion.* Dissolve iodide of ammonia and bromide of potassa in water; take equal parts of alcohol and of ether; and with these two mixtures combine the collodion. In a room to which only yellow light is admitted, pour the compound over the glass. When by the rapid evaporation of the ether the plate is dry, immerse it in a bath of nitrate of silver; which will soon form with the collodion a white film over the surface. After being placed in the camera, and removed to the darkened room, fix the picture by immersion in a mixture of acetic or pyrogallic acid, having protosulphate of iron in solution. After rinsing in water immerse the plate in a bath of hyposulphite of soda, to destroy any remaining nitrate of silver; and, if haste is required, add to the soda-bath the cyanide of potassium. Finally wash thoroughly to destroy the hyposulphite of soda.

The picture thus brought out and fixed is now used as a negative for obtaining positive pictures; the printing process being the same as that already described. In its early first use, however, the ambrotype was framed as a daguerreotype; having the double advantage of allowing the picture to be seen at any angle, and also of being reversed so to become a positive, the picture being seen through the glass, and viewed on its back side.

SECT. 4. THE CHEMICAL ACTION WHICH TAKES PLACE IN PHOTOGRAPHING.

The law of the chemical action which takes place in photographing seems to be this. The sun's rays, in which light and heat are associated with a chemical agency, weaken certain chemical affinities. When for instance chlorine is mixed with water, its affinity for hydrogen, while kept in the dark, is not sufficient to decompose the water; but on exposure to the light, the affinity of the oxygen for the hydrogen of water is so weakened that the chlorine decomposes the water, unites with its hydrogen, and sets free the oxygen. So when the Daguerrean plate is exposed to the light, the affinity of the iodine for the silver is so weakened on the parts specially exposed to the light that the silver is disposed to enter into another union. When, therefore, the plate is taken from the camera, and held over the vapor of mercury, the affinity of the mercury for the silver overpowers that of the iodine; and an amalgam of mercury and silver more perfect on the light, and less perfect on the dark parts, is formed. The iodine is thus expelled in vapor where the amalgam is complete; and the remainder is taken up when immersed in the hyposulphite of soda.

Where now, the amalgam of the mercury and silver is complete, the surface of the plate is covered with an unbroken metallic coating; thus presenting a smooth polished surface from which the light falling on the picture is reflected, and by which its light parts are formed. On the parts of the plate where shadows fall, leaving the iodide of silver undecomposed, the removal of the iodine by the hyposulphite of soda leaves the silver coating broken into minute particles; whose surface, reflecting no ray of light, forms the dark background of the picture. The intermediate shades are produced on the parts of the picture where the light is of medium intensity in taking the impression; and where consequently the amalgam on the plate is but partial.

The chemical action in the case of the ambrotype, and in photographs on paper, appears to be this. When the light has acted on the plate or paper, the affinity of the silver for the nitric acid is so weakened that it can unite with the vegetable fibre of the cotton, or the animal albumen of the egg; for both of which the acid has a strong affinity. The silver set free forms a thin film on the glass;

which, becoming a reflecting, and therefore light surface, gives the light parts of the picture where the surface of the object was lightest and therefore more reflecting. When employed in printing, this film of silver cuts off the action of the sunlight from the parts of the ambrotype that were made light by this same film; leaving the other parts to be darkened and thus shaded by the action of the light. The action of the protosulphate of iron, prior to the immersion of the plate in the hyposulphite of soda, seems to be, to take the oxygen from the nitrate of silver, prepared beforehand as it is by the sunlight to be easily decomposed.

SECT. 5. THE CLAIM OF PHOTOGRAPHY AS A FINE ART.

Photography, now extensively employed in three fields, in copying portraits, landscapes and works of sculpture and painting, may be practised merely as a trade; and yet it may rise to the highest dignity as an art. In taking portraits, positions and attitudes which will best bring out grace and characteristic features are to be sought. Hence, instead of the universal resort of a book in the hand, emblems consistent with the occupation, and accompaniments in harmony with the culture of the sitter, should be studied. Regard also must be had to the direction and degree of light best suited to the complexion of the skin, to the color of the eyes and hair, and to the style of dress to be copied. The highest genius and amplest culture in art may find a field for exhaustive employ in the photographer's gallery.

In photographing natural scenery, there is not, as in the taking of portraits, the direct arranging of attitudes and of light. Yet the artist has the power of unlimited choice as to the point from which, and the season or hour at which, he will take his view; and these two studies will be decisive as to his success.

Recent discoveries in sensitive chemicals have caused photography to become a cheap and most perfect substitute for engraving. Like the Genii with talismanic wand, it claims to be gifted with power to reproduce the finest originals in the galleries of painting, and to multiply them in such numbers that every student and lover of art can have all the best masters on the walls of his studio. More than all, cartoons by the most eminent artists, rough charcoal sketches drawn of colossal or life-size proportions, admitting, of course, of great accuracy in the detail of the drawing, have been reduced by the photographing camera; and when thus copied in miniature, the bold and rough outline assumes a delicacy and nicety of finish which no skill of the engraver can approach. The culturing influence thus exerted on both artist and people will depend for its extent and its value on the position which the photographer trains himself to take among masters in high art.

CHAPTER V.

DESIGN IN DRAWING.

A MECHANIC working after a model has nothing to do with designing; he only copies a design. So the pupil drawing after patterns set by his master, or in advanced studies from casts and even from nature, is but executing a design already prepared; he is not at all the originator of a model, much less of an ideal. As in the useful, so in the fine arts, when any new work adapted to a special end is required, the artist, like the artisan, has to design before he can execute the desired object.

The act of designing as a study naturally includes three parts; first, the conceiving of the general work by which the end is to be attained; second, the inventing of the parts of the work which is to accomplish that end; and third, the combining of those parts so that as a whole they shall secure that end. Drawing is the first of the arts of design; being the first which the child or savage learns; and also the foundation of all the other arts, sculpture, architecture and painting. The art galleries of Europe attest this. The Uffizi Gallery at Florence contains over 20,000 drawings of the ablest Italian sculptors, painters and architects, such as Raphael and Michel Angelo; and German galleries are filled with similar collections from the pencils of Albert Durer, Rembrandt and others.

Design includes conception, invention, composition and expression; which Lionardo and other eminent masters have treated of under the heads of both Drawing and Painting.

Sect. 1. Conception, or the originating of the idea to be embodied in drawing.

Conception is the originating stage in the development of form and life in all objects. The Greeks called the artist's first conception, the orator's proposition, and the statesman's purpose by the name *hypothesis.* Pliny says that Nicias, the painter, excelled in this; and he declares that a good design, *hypothesis*, is as important to the painter as is a well-conceived theme, *mythos*, to the poet. The *completed* conception Plato designated by the word, *eideia*, or idea.

The *design* of the artist takes its form from the particular object sought in the work of sculpture, painting or architecture for which the drawing is the first study. The consideration of his design leads the artist to a *conception* which he puts into a drawing. This conception, whether it embrace one or more figures, is not the direct copying of any form or forms already existing in nature or embodied by another artist. It is the originating of new forms that constitutes design.

The study of design is the great work of a true master in art. Fuseli, after devoting an entire lecture to this subject, quotes, in his next on Color, the statement of Sir Joshua Reynolds to the same effect. Though one of the ablest of colorists, Reynolds declared that this department of art in which he excelled was but secondary and subordinate to that of design in drawing, the forms afterward to be colored; and he expresses regret that his own education in this fundamental art had been pursued under such great disadvantages.

Sect. 2. Invention, or the elaborating of conceptions.

Passive imagination differs from active; some men having the power of forming conceptions, both poetical and artistic, which they lack skill to put into form. The second work in design is invention, or the power of working up the details of a fine conception.

Lionardo thus describes the labor of inventing for a single figure. "The artist should form his style upon the best-proportioned model in nature. After having taken its measure, he should take that of his own person; so as to avoid the influence of self-love in copying his own defects. He should aim at universal excellence; for one excellence in a painting only makes more manifest attendant defects." He dwells then at length on attitudes, the grace of different positions, the shape the muscles and the folds of garments assume in each position, and especially the contour of each limb when strained under any nervous excitement.

Fuseli in treating of invention suggests that its true spirit allows the borrowing of ideas, not of details, from great artists of former ages. As a Milton may borrow conceptions, not their embodiment, from Virgil or Homer, and as an inventor in the useful arts may borrow principles from a man of science, so may a truly original artist gather ideas from former great masters, and incorporate them into his own independent works. Each great master in art has his own peculiar style, as distinct from that of other leading minds, as one poet's style is distinct from another; Michel Angelo being epic in his invention, Raphael dramatic, while such an artist as Poussin is historical. In each of these styles a different order of invention is of course required. Hans Holbein is cited as remarkable for the fertility of his inventive skill.

Ruskin, urging the attaining of *truth* in drawing, says that the early Italian artists had their "judgment so tempered by veneration for old models" that they were "dull in their perception of truth;" and hence "there was little genuine invention in their works." A "particular truth" is more important than a general truth; and variety is attained "in giving a genus by individuals." "The painter and preacher are both commentators on infinity; and the duty of each is to take for each discourse one essential truth." "Primary truths, or those which belong to essence or substance, are of greater importance than secondary truths, as those of color;" an idea of Sir Joshua Reynolds as quoted by Sir William Hamilton.

Ruskin thinks the Italians excelled in their principal figures, the Dutch in backgrounds; he groups his criticisms under the headings "Truth in Space, Clouds, Earth and Water." In distant backgrounds the old masters gave no graded obscurity; "you could either count all the bricks as well in a distant as in a near house, or both alike would be a blank flat." Their clouds were separated from the blue beyond, instead of being part of the common vault. In their backgrounds the foot of a mountain comes from underneath the plains; and the summit is always pyramidal, instead of having the sharp outline always indicative of distance. After truth in cloud the rarest modern attainment is in water; especially the irregular effect of its reflecting surface when agitated. In all these nicer efforts to copy Nature it is the *principle* of truth, not any real appearance, that can be imitated; for appearances, especially in cloud and water, are so perpetually shifting, that no copy can possibly be made.

As exceptions to his general estimate of Italian art in this department, Ruskin cites Raphael and Salvator Rosa. In Raphael's drawings the dark and heavy lines are toward the light, as seen in his "Angel pursuing Heliodorus" at the Louvre; in which the dark and strong lines terminating the nose and forehead toward the light are opposed to the tender and faint lines behind the ear in the shade. Salvator "had great perception of the sweep of foliage and of the rolling of cloud;" but he "never drew a single leaflet or wreath of mist" aright.

Sect. 3. Composition, or the grouping of details when invented.

In the fine as in the useful arts the grouping of the parts invented is an added study. In composition, called by the Latins *dispositio*, Pliny cites Apelles and before him Nicias as excelling. Nicias said "that it was not a small matter in his art to take a whole forest and picture it; to delineate contests of horses and ships; to group horses in many positions, some running, some standing in battle array, and some kneeling for their riders; to represent the riders of some horses as hurling javelins, and of others as falling from their backs."

Lionardo gives the following lessons from his own life-labor. "In proceeding to composition the pupil should study every variety of form and of motion; making sketches of single figures from various different points of view. Then he may combine figures in different attitudes; as two men walking, wrestling, etc. If a historical picture, which he is studying, is to be elevated for subsequent view, the artist must place himself in the same relative position while composing. In countenances and figures he should never repeat, but always present an entirely new and original specimen. For this purpose the young artist should watch men as he sees them under the influence of varied passions; and in his note-book he should copy their expressions of countenance, their positions and gesticulations, so that when composing he may have an inexhaustible store of nature from which to draw. Each part of the body, in its anatomy and in its perspective, must be a separate study and labor. The folds of dress should be copied from nature, so as to represent real clothing, flowing and easy, not swelled as with wind, nor stiff and tight drawn. When the figure is foreshortened, there ought to appear a greater number of folds, all drawn around in circles." "In grouping a historical subject, the chief figure should stand forward and be painted in clear strong colors. In drawing trees, contrive to have them half in shadow and half in the light; selecting a day when the sun is partially hid by clouds." Hogarth says, "The art of composing well is no more than the art of varying well."

Ruskin states the following laws of Composition. *First*, Principality; there should always be a principal figure in a work of art. *Second*, Repetition; symmetry requiring that the principal figure be supported on each side by similar subordinates; as two small domes with a central one. *Third*, Continuity; the pinnacles of a Gothic cathedral having a regular ratio of increase or diminution. *Fourth*, Curvature; the tops of spires, trees, bridges and buildings, as well as clouds being drawn in curvilinear perspective. *Fifth*, Radiation; as fibres in leaves and ribs in a boat. *Sixth*, Contrast; dresses being not all of the same cut or color; and battlements of a tower not having one fixed measure. *Seventh*, Interchange: succession in change, as in colors of dresses, and in light and shade. *Eighth*, Consistency; the colors of massive and of distant objects being appropriate; the slender and graceful depending on the sturdy and rugged. *Ninth*, Gradation; the making all tints in a landscape alike shaded by a cloudy, or lit up by a bright sky.

SECT. 4. EXPRESSION; OR THE GIVING OF REALITY AND LIFE TO COMPOSITION.

In the useful and fine arts alike, the end of design is the realizing of movement, indicative of life in a labored work. To conception, invention and composition the artist must add expression; the attribute of apparent life and motion.

Socrates, as Xenophon relates, went one day into the studio of a sculptor who had admirably succeeded in representing every variety of human posture in marble, those of the racer, boxer and wrestler; and he asked, "Is it not necessary in order to give pleasure to the beholder, to imitate the *emotions* of the men performing any particular act?" Lionardo makes *character* in inanimate objects correspond to *expression* in animate beings, and says, "The artist should *express* motion in the forms he draws; old men and youth must appear to be real; those laughing and weeping should so speak as to call forth the sympathetic emotion in the beholder." "Shadows must be made to seem actual; more time even being spent upon them than upon the figures themselves. Clouds should be so detached from the background as to seem suspended in the air." Among numerous particulars he mentions, "In laughing, the brows are open and the corners of the mouth turned up; in weeping, the brows are contracted and the corners of the mouth turned down;" "Men weep from anger or fear, joy or sorrow, suspicion or compassion, enmity or tenderness;" "each mental impression has its outward expression in the form of the features;" yet more, "there is a position of each part of the body, as well as a form of the features, characterizing different emotions and each shade of emotion." Fuseli makes this striking observation: "Expression gives vividness to an image, and *interprets* composition."

BOOK III.

SCULPTURE; THE EXECUTING OF FORMS IN ALL THEIR DIMENSIONS.

DRAWING presents figures in two dimensions on a plane; only *representing* the third dimension by shading. Sculpture actually *executes* forms in three dimensions; rounding out the figure in its solid proportions. Drawing must precede sculpture; since the sculptor cannot model any form, till he has first conceived the outline from every point of view, and has elaborated each view with the pencil. A notice of the modes of executing sculpture, a sketch of the history of ancient sculpture, particularly in Egypt and Greece, and a brief glance at the sculpture of modern Europe will illustrate the nature, the principles and the progress of the art.

CHAPTER I.

GENERAL PRINCIPLES RELATING TO THE EXECUTION AND CLASSIFICATION OF WORKS OF SCULPTURE.

IN drawing, *lines* are the elements of the art; in sculpture, *surfaces.* As, however, surfaces are made up of lines, the principles of drawing enter into the study of sculpture; while new and distinct applications of those principles, new ends to be attained, and distinct methods of accomplishing those ends, are also to be regarded.

SECT. 1. TECHNICAL TERMS EXPRESSIVE OF DIFFERENT METHODS OF EXECUTING AND OF CLASSIFYING WORKS OF SCULPTURE.

Sculpture is the chief of the *plastic arts;* a designation derived from the Greek word *plasso* or *platto*, whence our word *plat* or *plait*, and also *plaster*. The terms which designate the different processes, methods or styles of plastic art have been suggeste l, either by the character of the material employed, or by the principle of design in the artist's mind.

To the first class belong the following: *Moulding* is the pressing out of forms in soft pliable material, as clay; and it designates either the finished work of the house plasterer, or the first process, usually called modeling, of the sculptor. Akin to this is *wrought* or "beaten" work; the shaping by the hammer of hard but malleable material, as the metals, into forms more or less finished, which constitutes the work of the ordinary smith, and one method of executing the most finished sculpture. *Casting* is the forming of images from material in a liquid state; as from plaster mixed with water, or from melted metal, poured into a mould previously prepared and then left to harden by drying or cooling; and it is either the second process of the sculptor in making his plaster cast from his clay model after which his marble statue is subsequently to be cut, or it is the final process of the common brass and iron founder, as well as of the ablest artists executing sculpture in copper or bronze. *Graving* is not the constructing of whole forms, but the cutting and rounding out of half forms projecting from the rough surface of material, like wood and stone, hard and friable as opposed to malleable. *Carving*, is the slighter cutting, of indented figures as opposed to projecting forms, in material with a polished instead of a rough surface, and either of malleable or friable texture, as copper or marble. The word sculpture, from the Greek *glypho* to carve *finely*, preserved in the terms triglyphs and hieroglyphs, was anciently applied to the finer works in marble. It is now the designation of a branch of the fine arts.

Forms determined rather by the idea of the artist than by the character of material, are classified by Italian terms expressive of the completeness of their execution. *Intaglio*, or form cut in, is a graving on the surface of stone without any rounding out of the figure; as in Egyptian hieroglyphics. *Basso-relievo*, bas-relief in the French, or low-relief, is the slight rounding up of figures; as seen in coins and medals of metal; and in cameos cut in shell. *Alto-relievo*, or high relief, is a carving projecting about one half the diameter of the natural object; illustrated in coarse embossed work on stoves and pitchers, and in medallion heads. Perfect or *complete relief*, presents the entire half of an object, as pilasters or half columns projecting from a wall. Finally, statuary gives an entire figure complete on all sides, as a column or human form.

The choice of material and the mode of working it have depended partly upon its character and partly upon the taste and culture of a people. Thus wood and stone must be carved, though metal may be either cast, carved, or beaten; but the rude Indian carves in wood and bone, the African in ebony and ivory; while even the Chinese carve in stone, cast in metal and mould in plaster.

The choice of style in forms has depended in part upon location and design, in part too on the cost of the work, but partly also on the taste of the age. Thus the carving on the walls of Egyptian and Hebrew temples must be low relief, and the images standing in front complete statues. The rich may have statues for funereal monuments, the less wealthy a relief upon a marble shaft, but the poor only a simple engraving on slate. Egyptian taste allowed an entire temple to be covered with carving in low relief, the Greeks admired high relief in the frieze, but modern taste excludes sculptured walls.

SECT. 2. THE MATERIAL OF SCULPTURE.

For carving wood, as the substance most abundant and readily cut, has been universally first chosen; the boy's penknife and the savage's flint easily and skillfully shaping it; while the lids of Egyptian sarcophagi, the early statues of Greek artists, and especially the elaborate oak carvings of modern times, have proved it even a noble material. Shell, ivory, and kindred substances, harder than wood, follow; the rudest tribes of Africa and the islanders of the Pacific showing true genius in this species of carving, while the master-work of Phidias gave ivory a dignity never reached either before or since. The very hardest substance, flint, has been shaped by the American Indian into his hatchet, and by the Chinese into miniature groups, having the figures in a light vein and the background in a dark stratum. The ancient Egyptians, probably because their own river banks furnished this material and their own bold ideas demanded this coarse stone, carved their statues and cut their obelisks in granite; while the Greeks found in the fine-grained marble native to their hills a material fit to set forth their refined ideals.

For moulding clay has been the almost exclusive material, whether the work were designed to be fused by heat as a work of art, or to be a pattern for a chiseler in stone, or a model for the caster in metal. The rich pottery found in the tombs of Egypt, Chaldea, Greece, Italy and ancient America, and even the famed Etruscan vases, the admiration of ancient and of modern times, are of that nicely baked clay called by the Italian name *terracotta*. The finest statuettes are formed of mere clay, coated with a silicious earth, which by intense heat is turned to glass; rivaling in beauty of material the finest Chinese porcelain. The ancient Egyptians had a composition hardened with lime, which, when laid on rough walls and sandstone columns, bore like marble the nicest touches of the chisel.

For casting brass or bronze has been used from the earliest times. Pliny's history of Grecian and Roman sculpture is an episode in his treatise on this metal. After stating that rude primitive sculpture was executed in "wood and clay," he says that the metal brass reached its glory first in "Delian," then in "Corinthian" castings. The purest of all material, however, created as it were for perfected sculpture, is *marble*, Pliny mentioning that Phidias made his Minerva of "ivory and gold," but that Praxiteles was "happier in marble."

In each class of material employed for works of sculpture there is, as Jarves has intimated, a distinctive characteristic, expressive of a correspondent idea, which in the higher development of the art has led to its special selection for specific effects. Thus, perspective and details of background, plumage and foliage, are not subjects for sculpture, since no material is fitted for them; while within the field of this art, strength and mass are for stone; lightness for wood; transparency for glass; ease and freedom for stucco and clay; and tenacity combined with ductility for metals, since they change their shape but by effort.

SECT. 3. THE OBJECTS OF DESIGN; AS SPECIALLY ADAPTED TO THE ART OF SCULPTURE.

No work of art proper can be even conceived, much less be executed, without a design. In drawing the object represented is conceived in the mind before its outline is traced. The "Arts of Design," technically speaking, are "Sculpture, Architecture and

Painting;" sculpture preceding the other two of the three, because architecture takes on as appendages the single forms which sculpture has elaborated, while painting groups and colors them.

Art proper excludes the idea of utility; and design in art is restricted to objects of beauty. The work of the architect must be founded primarily on the idea of utility. Sculpture appeals to the love of beauty alone, or through this love to sentiments of friendship or of patriotism, to emotions of human affection or of religious veneration; and its creations are either ornaments to decorate, mementos of affection to be cherished, monuments of national gratitude to inspire, funereal emblems to chasten, or symbols of religion to awaken devotion.

In sculpture the love of design has shown itself to be a universal impulse of human nature. The rudest savage, though he shows no conception of art in architecture or painting, carves his pipe and tomahawk into the image of some object of admiration or devotion, and covers it with devices of his own grotesque taste or superstitious adoration. The school-boy, who thinks of no other art, is universally a sculptor; cutting his bow or bat into a shape to please his eye, and never happier than in giving form to some bit of wood with his pocket-knife. Men of universal genius in art, like Phidias, excelling with the painter's brush and the architect's rule, have aspired to shape their purest and loftiest ideals with the chisel.

Sculpture has two fields. Single objects of personal adornment or public interest are its first creation. Beginning with the rude Indian's or African's carvings, its highest creations are funereal emblems; civic statues and monuments; and sacred images and symbols. The other form which works of sculpture have assumed is that of decorations carved upon larger and permanent structures. Such are the sculptures covering the entire walls and columns of temples and tombs in Egypt, and the reliefs on the cornices of Grecian temples.

Among the objects selected by sculptors in all ages upon which to display the beauty and grandeur possible in artistic design, the vase and the human form may be taken as climactic ideals.

The Etruscan vase, a product of mingled Grecian and Roman taste, is the masterpiece of simple and chaste beauty, upon which admirers of art have exhausted the vocabulary of words expressive of grace. The vase seems to have been designed for three purposes; for private and domestic use, as holders of flowers; for public and civic uses, as the urn that received lots and ballots; and finally and chiefly, as receptacles for the ashes of the burnt dead. The forms of manly grace and female beauty traced in miniature upon their surface, and then painted in simple black, or in dark red, have been copied and published in every country of Western Europe.

The general outlines of the vase itself most admired are those which make the human form so matchless as a work of art. There is in the lower part the same gently declining inward curve to the foot; and in the upper portion the same sharper but equally graceful slope from the shoulders to the neck, and the same rounding out again of the head at the summit. The art of design in the sculptured vase reached at once its climax because it took the Creator's most perfect work in material forms for its model. Winckelmann says, "The forms of a beautiful body are determined by lines the centre of which is continually changing. This diversity was sought after by the Greeks in works of all kinds; and their discernment of its beauty led them to introduce the same system into the form of their utensils and vases, whose easy and elegant outline is drawn after the same rule, that is by a line which must be found by means of several circles."

The human figure itself is the most perfect work of the sculptor; our impression of beauty uniting in it these two elements; that lightness which belongs to grace of form, and that perfect balance which takes away all fear as to its strength and firmness of support. In this special work of design, the distinction between Asiatic and European art is palpably manifest. The Egyptian Osiride column was the colossal frame of a Herculean warrior, holding up the crushing burden of massive blocks, all of whose weight is apparent; while the Greek column called Caryatides was the sylph-like form of a maiden flower-vender, sporting, as if it were a wreathed turban of which she was proud, the foliated and concealed burden of stone really resting upon her head. The Hebrew artist carved the cherub as an embodiment of physical perfection, but did not attempt the seraph, the type of intellectual excellence; while the Greek artist, though he began with the majestic person of Jove and the muscular frame of Hercules, soon aspired to the higher forms of spiritual superiority conceived in the Apollo and Minerva. In every department of sculpture, more truly than in architecture and painting, the power of design has sought to show itself in an effort to master that chief study among God's perfect works, the matchless symmetry of the human form.

SECT. 4. PROPORTION AS SECURING SYMMETRY IN WORKS OF SCULPTURE.

A work of sculpture is not like a drawing, a picture of an object; but it is the object itself; and its parts must not simply *seem*, but actually *be*, copies of the object. This requires not only that the general dimensions of the object be in proportion, but that the junctures and articulations of the parts be in symmetry.

In fixing laws of symmetry, the Greeks regarded *age* as well as general proportions. In man, as in the lower animals, the proportionate *length*, even more than the breadth and plumpness of the limbs, is varied by age. In the young of horses, cows and sheep, which suckle standing, the legs are disproportionately long; while in the cat, dog and other animals suckled by the mother when lying down, the same limbs are as disproportionately short. The human infant has, comparatively, the body long and the limbs short, the head large and the feet small. The Greeks chose for a Cupid the dimensions of a child; for a Hercules or Jupiter, the proportions of a man mature in body and in mind; but youth was the age chosen for the expression of beauty and grace.

As the "summetron," the "modulus," or standard of proportionate measurement, both the head and the foot were selected; the latter being preferred in sculpture, and alone used in architecture. These natural measures, the nail, digit, palm, foot, cubit, pace, ell, fathom, having their type in portions of the human body, so universally fixed in their proportions that they have become recognized standards in every nation, rule in art even when forced by legislation from the field where utility holds sway.

Vitruvius, presenting the proportions observed in Grecian statuary, says: "Nature in the composition of the human frame has so ordained, that naturally and ordinarily there should be such a proportion that the face, from the chin to the top of the forehead or roots of the hair, should be *one-tenth* part of the whole stature; while the same proportion is preserved in the hand measured from the bend of the wrist to the tip of the middle finger. The measure of the head from the chin to the top of the scalp is an *eighth* of the whole body; and the same, behind, is the measure from the bottom of the neck to the bottom of the scalp. From the top of the breast to the roots of the hair is a *sixth* of the body's height, and from the same point to the top of the scalp is a *fourth* of the stature. If the distance from the chin to the roots of the hair be divided into three parts, one of these terminates at the nostrils, the other at the eyebrows." "The foot is a *sixth* of the stature; the cubit, or distance from the elbow to the tip of the middle finger, and also the breadth of the chest, is a *fourth*. The height of the human frame is the same with the measure from one hand to the other." "The other members have certain affinities which were always observed by the most celebrated of the ancient painters and sculptors; and we must look for them in those productions which have excited universal admiration."

From other ancient authors the details thus referred to may be gathered; the following of which are important to the general student: The head is egg-shaped in the front view, and circular in the side view; the nose and forehead are nearly in a straight line in the Grecian profile; the neck is nearly a cylinder; the arms and legs tapering cylinders; and the thumb extends to the first joint of the first finger. In the female figure the height is about one-tenth less than in the male; the shoulders and loins are proportionally narrower, and the thighs much broader; while the body, limbs, hands, fingers, and nails are less flattened and more perfectly round than in the male.

Sect. 5. Position as related to balance in sculpture.

In drawing the position of objects must give the appearance of balance; in sculpture balance must be actually secured.

In order to this the centre of gravity must be sought, and all the parts be so adjusted that the weight be duly distributed around the point of support. It is necessary, therefore, to study the object from every point of view, above, below and around; observing every conceivable position of its parts, scanning the centre of support in each attitude, and remarking portions of the object lying to the right or the left of the line perpendicular to that centre.

In all simple and regularly formed bodies, as upright columns, this is an easy study; but it becomes difficult in an animal moving, in a man poised in action, and yet more in a horse rearing with his rider and balanced upon his hind hoofs. The artist's difficulty increases, according to the laws of stable equilibrium, in proportion to, first, the narrowness of the base; second, the height of the centre of gravity above the base; and third, the projection of the parts from the line perpendicular to the centre. A beer-mug stands firmer than a coffee-cup, because its base is broader; a rope-walker with his balancing-pole moves securely, because, first, the centre of his entire weight is made lower, and second, the movements of the pole readily throw a larger weight, when required, to either side. It is difficult to execute the statue of a rearing horse, both because of the smallness of the base, and of the involved curve in his unusual and momentary position.

The representations of the work of the sculptor on the monuments of Egypt show that their carvers were guided in cutting their granite statues by fixed measures as to balance and proportions. The Greek artists, as Xenophon states, studied the human frame in all its varied attitudes. They conceived the human form with the arms and limbs extended to be enclosed in a circle or sphere, whose centre was the navel. Every posture of action, as in walking, running, wrestling, boxing, was mathematically studied; the line of the centre of gravity was carefully marked; and the position of each limb and portion of the frame was located and measured with the greatest accuracy. At the revival of art, near the close of the fifteenth century, Lionardo wrote minute directions for the sculptor; accompanying them with drawings representing the male and female figure in every posture of repose and of action, and showing in each where the line of gravity would fall.

Sect. 6. Perspective as affected by distance and angular elevation in works of sculpture.

In drawing a distant or elevated object, the artist sees its aspect as actually presented; and he simply copies the appearance to his eye. The sculptor has to conceive beforehand the effect which distance and elevation will produce; and keeping this before his mind as he works, he has to form an image, which, while he is near and moulding it into form looks distorted and disproportioned, but which when elevated to its place will present a perfect outline and just proportions.

The two aspects of perspective which the sculptor is to regard are the dimness of outline produced by distance, and the shortening of dimensions from elevation or oblique vision. The former is illustrated in one of the great works of Phidias. The Athenians had desired both him and his pupil Alcamenes, more admired than his master by many of the people for the extreme grace and polish of his workmanship, to prepare a statue of Minerva of colossal dimensions and for an elevated pedestal. When completed, that of Alcamenes seemed perfect in proportion and finish while that of Phidias appeared to distort the principal features and to make the whole countenance rude and even hideous. But the master had studied the science of his art; and when the two statues were elevated to their pedestals the grand and impressive beauty of the work of Phidias stood out, and every feature was softened into grace; while the polish of Alcamenes was lost in dimness, and no feature indicating life or beauty could be traced.

In foreshortening the sculptor has a yet more difficult task. In perspective we judge of dimensions by the angle of vision filled; while, nevertheless, in real objects of known dimensions we partially correct this impression. The form of a friend on an elevation fills a less angle of vision than when seen on a level with the eye, yet we readily correct this impression. When looking, however, from a tall spire on the heads of passing men, they seem like turtles without stature; this extreme of entire foreshortening indicating its law when partial. In the statue the mind follows only partially the law of correction made in living persons. While the sculptor would greatly err who should suppose that all the difference of height which the mathematical law indicates is to be introduced into his work, he must give that slight exaggeration of the height of his figure required in a portrait or bust to sèt off any marked feature. To this principle is probably to be referred the remark of Pliny as to Lycippus, "He added much to statuary by making the heads smaller and the bodies more graceful and less bloated; through which the height of statues seemed greater." In many of the colossal statues made for elevated positions in later times this principle has been lost sight of.

SECT. 7. ANATOMY AS IT RELATES TO ACTION AND EXPRESSION IN SCULPTURE.

The proportionate length and breadth of the several parts of the human figure may be learned from exterior aspect. It is only, however, by anatomy or the cutting up of the human frame that the sculptor comprehends the contractions and swellings of the muscles, and the pressing out of the bone joints when men are putting forth their strength in action, or that he can scan the minuter workings of the muscles of the face, which give to the countenance its varied expression.

The Egyptians utterly ignored the expression of muscular action in their statues; a religious superstitition compelling the physician and the artist to abstain from anatomical dissections of the human frame. The Greeks, on the other hand, made great attainments in the practical knowledge of anatomy; accomplishing this, however, more by observation of the living than by dissection of the dead. For this purpose their artists employed living models; whose nude forms, thrown into every variety of posture, and subjected to every kind of muscular tension, were made to serve as copies from which to model. When under the Roman supremacy the dissection, and even the burning to ashes of dead bodies, was approved as religious, Galen wrote at length on anatomy; minutely describing not only the bones and muscles, but also blood-vessels and nerves; stating his purpose to write a treatise especially for artists.

The ideas of the ancients as to anatomical expression have been laboriously collected by Winckelmann and Dalloway. The parts in which beauty of design may be shown are the head, hands and feet. A straight *profile* indicates majesty in man and loveliness in woman. Their axiom founded on the supposed perfection of the *tripartite* division of the head, as also of the whole form, in which the forehead, the nose and the lips, together with the chin are equal thirds, led Grecian maidens to use a fillet or band in order to raise or bring down the hair to the proportion of beauty; an idea alluded to by Horace in his Lycoris.

The *eye* in colossal statues was deep set and darkly shaded by the brow in order to be the better seen from afar. In Jupiter, Apollo and Juno the upper eyelid is high arched, indicative of the boldness assumed by superiors; in Minerva it droops, indicating modesty; while in Venus the lower lid is raised, giving that languishing expression captivating to lovers. In the old masters the pupil was never marked; since this is an expression of color not of form. Pindar remarks the narrow eyebrow in Grecian statues, as the Niobe; now seen also in the women of the Greek Isles. Theocritus alludes to the hair of the two eyebrows meeting in a double arch as a beauty, which, however, the Roman sculptors regarded a blemish.

The *hair*, as in Hercules, was represented short, thick and low on the forehead; while Jove's was bushy like a lion's mane. In woman it was wrought into curled tresses, or in deep wavy lines giving shade and softness; and the locks behind were gathered into that simple knot admired in every subsequent age as a model of grace. Any artificial head dress, tolerated by the fashion of a day becomes hideous after a few years; a sad drawback on the value of old family portraits.

Ancient and modern taste has been divided as to the beard in statuary. The Egyptian lords were close shaven; as Herodotus affirms and the countless bas-reliefs and statues, without exception, show; a custom of court etiquette to which Joseph the Hebrew conformed. Homer, whom Phidias followed, pictures Jupiter as bearded. Virgil, however, makes no mention of this feature; and in all the finer Grecian statues, as those of Apollo and of intellectual men, the beard is omitted. Ovid, Horace and Juvenal allude to the beard as a rude relic of their uncultured ancestry, or a mark of pedantry.

The swelling of the nostrils, as in the Apollo Belvidere, indicates energy. The beauty of the chin is simple roundness; sometimes, as in the Venus de Medici, with an added slight depression. A dimple either in the cheek or chin is not a beauty in a statue. The small exquisitely curved lips of the Venus de Medici are one of its chief charms. The ear is such a test of masterly workmanship that Winckelmann made it his rule for judging of a genuine antique. The foot and the hand, next to the features of the head, show the true Grecian master in sculpture.

Lionardo has given the completest collection extant of studies in attitude and expression. Bell has done for art what Cuvier did for science; having laid the foundation of a system of comparative anatomy for artists. He thinks that no emotion but that of rage is fully expressed by the features of animals. Carnivorous quadrupeds exhibit anger by the corrugations of the lips; the horse by his ears turned back. Courage to a certain extent is exhibited in the horse by his eye and nostrils, and by his ears pricked forward. The attitudes of animals Bell regards more expressive than their features.

Hay's principles of æsthetic proportions have their most admirable applications in sculpture. In architecture the Greeks employed angles whose sines and tangents corresponded with the lengths of cords producing the tonic, mediant and dominant in music. In statuary they introduced two additional principles, employing eleven angles in all, whose sines and tangents correspond in length to concordant musical cords. The female figure is founded on the right angle; regarded by Pythagoras and Plato as the perfect angle. The male form shows a scale of angles obtained by a transposition of that on which the female figure is constructed.

Sect. 8. Practical execution of sculpture.

The study of his design, and the working up of its details in drawings, is the first labor of the sculptor. If the artist be a scientific master, every portion of the rounded form is conceived as bounded by tangent planes; whose slopes are carefully observed, and the angles of their junctions noted.

The second work is the moulding in clay of the image elaborated in the drawings. On a framework of wood and iron, with arms for the projecting limbs a dark clay of easy-moulding properties is kneaded with the hand into the general outline of the statue; when with small scrapers of wood and ivory the form is completely rounded by months of labor. When thoroughly hardened by drying, a mould in sand is made from the clay figure; in which working models in plaster are cast.

The Egyptian sculptor built a staging around the granite block to be cut into a statue, and from the sides of this staging the artist laid off the depth into the stone which each workman was to cut. The Greek artist having conceived the position of his statue in the marble block, had kindred methods of directing the workmen.

Lionardo gives this statement of the methods of sculptors at his day. "To execute a figure in marble, you must first make a model of it in clay, or plaster, and when it is finished, place it in a square case, equally capable of receiving the block of marble intended to be shaped like it. Have some peg-like sticks to pass through holes made in the sides, and all round the case; push them in till every one touches the model; marking what remains of the sticks outward with ink, and making a countermark to every stick and its hole, so that you may at pleasure replace them again. Then having taken out the model, and placed the block of marble in its stead, take so much out of it, till all the pegs go in at the same holes to the marks you had made."

The common method of modern times is to insert in an upright post on a wooden stand sliding arms graduated into minute divisions of inches. In a square marked on the floor sufficiently large to allow lines dropped from the extremities of the plaster figure to fall within its limits, the model is placed; when the sliding arms of the gauge are pushed toward the model till they touch its extreme points. The gauge is then placed before the block of marble and the stone is cut away until its arms meet the chipped block as they fitted the model. Thus every portion of the entire figure is brought to its required proportions.

The genius of the artist conceives his design, elaborates it with the pencil, and moulds it in clay. The mere cutting down of the rough stone may be performed by a common mechanic. This work, however, must be hourly presided over by the genius that conceived the ideal. No man can be a great artist who is not a man of practical science; since the workmen, literally his "hands," must be guided by his one mind.

CHAPTER II.

PRIMITIVE SCULPTURE; ILLUSTRATED IN THE EGYPTIAN.

THE earliest records of the human race, mention Tubal Cain the seventh from Adam as "an *instructor* of every artificer in brass and iron." The oldest monuments of Egypt present every form of sculpture; and the most ancient histories of Moses and Herodotus allude to perfected methods of sculpture as practised from time immemorial; Egypt being the first and chief centre of the art.

SECT. 1. CLASSES OF EGYPTIAN SCULPTURE AND METHODS OF EGYPTIAN SCULPTORS.

The Egyptians have left every form of sculpture. The *hieroglyphics* are cut into obelisks of granite in deep *intaglio;* whose sharp and clear side lines make the figure of the smallest size perfectly distinct and even beautiful in its darkness of shade. Sculptures in *low-relief* of animated battle-scenes are cut on the walls of temples in sandstone; the entire walls of "hundred-gated Thebes" being covered with these sculptures. The sculpture in the tombs, sometimes in *high-relief*, is upon a hard stucco, whose composition has not yet revealed its secret to modern analyzers. The capitals of columns called Osiride present a *perfect relief* in front; sometimes as at Aboo Simbel having a shaft wrought into a half-statue. Their *statues* of red or black granite and of a grayish porphyritic limestone, have a massiveness beyond conception wonderful. The single relic at Memphis is sixty feet high in a standing posture; the vocal Memnon and its brother at Thebes are sixty feet high in a sitting posture; while one of red granite, now prostrate and shattered, is calculated by Sir Gardner Wilkinson to have weighed over eleven hundred tons.

The work of executing these colossal statues is illustrated on the walls of the tombs. The stone, first quarried in the granite ledges of Syene, was set up on its lower end, already squared as a base. Stages were erected for the stone-cutters about seven feet above each other quite to the summit of the block. Under a chief artist as guide, hewers, with large picks and heavy mallets, succeeded by smoothers with light chisels and by polishers with rubbers, began at the head and worked downward.

When completed the finished statue was placed on a strong wooden sledge, which was made to slide on a wooden railway. Drag-ropes were fastened to the sledge at which thousands of men pulled, directed by a superintendent perched in the lap of the statue; and men with oil, or water, in pots, lubricated the rails before the sledge. These minute processes of the sculptor were, in the later ages, forgotten in the grand array of force employed in Egyptian art.

SECT. 2. THE ANATOMICAL SKILL DISPLAYED IN EGYPTIAN SCULPTURE.

In Egypt, though there were, as Herodotus states, physicians for the eye, ear, teeth, and for special diseases, the study of human anatomy related to external dimensions, not to muscular development. The stature was well-proportioned, being made seven and one-third measures of the height of the head; while the hips were at the centre of the height. The features are regularly rounded, and the expression is placid; but the same aspect is given to the Sphynx at Memphis and the Memnon at Thebes, to the king on his throne and the warrior in battle, to the mourner at a funeral and the laborer in the field.

As there was no contraction of the muscles of the face giving expression to emotion in the Egyptian statue, so there was no variation of posture in the head giving occasion for different expression. In reliefs there is always the same uniform profile view; and in statues there is no turning of the head, or bending of the neck. The proportionate breadth of the chest and hips of male and female figures is not observed; the contraction of the loins and the taper of the chest in both being exaggerated. The shoulders, too, are set off from the body as if they were appendages to the frame.

The chief defect in Egyptian sculpture is the utter extinction of life in the figures. The erect colossal statues all have the hands and feet straightened down like a corpse laid out for burial. The seated statues have both arms stretched out by the side of the leg; as motionless as those of an old man asleep in his arm-chair. In bas-reliefs the arms and legs of men in every employ, whether wielding javelins or swords, whips or hammers, whether walking, marching, running or leaping, *all* have the same stiff, motionless, petrified outline and contour. There is no bending of the neck or contraction of the muscles, no rounding of the joints or projecting of the joint bones from the strain of the muscles. The fine proportion of limb and accurate representation of features so often quoted in Asiatic and Egyptian sculpture are but the mechanical working up of a copy; there could have been no study of living models among the Egyptian sculptors. As there is no life, no elasticity of bodily frame, so of course there is no thinking soul animating the body in Egyptian sculpture.

Winckelmann has well suggested that the *aim* of the Egyptian sculptor was to impress by *magnitude*, not by expression in his figures. The characteristics enumerated are observed not only in the early and primitive Egyptian sculpture, but also in the ages of genuine development and progress. They mar even the spirited battle-scenes upon the walls of the newer portion of the Temple of Karnac at Thebes; in which the men and horses have a life and vigor if not a grace worthy of even the Grecian chisel.

SECT. 3. THE MORAL TONE CHARACTERIZING EGYPTIAN SCULPTURE.

The lack of anatomical accuracy, or rather vivacity, characterizing Egyptian sculpture, is mainly attributable to the moral spirit of the "wise men" who controlled the artist, repressing his genius. Synesius, a native Egyptian, a pupil of the famed Hypatia, after he became a Christian, stated: "Among the Egyptians the prophets did not allow metal-founders or statuaries to represent the gods, for fear that they would deviate from the rule." As a consequence statues of kings, supposed as deified to assume forms and features like to each other, must be assimilated to the common celestial model; and hence, too, even in bas-reliefs of ordinary men and animals, the people refused to allow their old favorites to be displaced by novices. The superstitious horror of marring the body of the dead by dissection, lest the soul should thereby suffer, which, even in Greece at the time of Demosthenes, compelled the student of anatomy to hide his dissecting-room in caves of the mountains, had a still greater influence in the land of embalming.

The mingling of animal and human features in statuary was an error in moral as well as æsthetic judgment. Agassiz has well suggested, that to add the wings of a bird to an ethereal image of man detracts from, instead of adding to, our conception of angelic exaltation. The *metaphors*, "he had a lion's courage, an ox's strength, and an eagle's ken," embodied in the cherubim pictured by Ezekiel, as Raphael conceived, could not be represented to the eye. The sculptors of Egypt did not discriminate between metaphor and figure, between associated symbols and actual combination of inconsistent elements. The Egyptian Sphynx, with a human head thirty feet in altitude, and a lion's body couchant one hundred and sixty-three feet long, the Assyrian winged bull with human head, the crocodile and hawked-headed deities, and kindred monstrosities, rise to the mind of Horace in the very opening of his Ars Poetica as a violation of moral propriety.

SECT. 4. THE HISTORY OF EGYPTIAN SCULPTURE; ITS RUDE NATIVE ORIGINALS; ITS ENNOBLEMENT BY SUPERIOR ARTISTS FROM ASIA; ITS REFINEMENT FROM GRECIAN INFLUENCE; AND ITS DECLINE UNDER THE ROMAN SWAY.

The observing tourist on the Nile, or student of the best writers on Egyptian art, can readily trace the prominent marks of successive stages of development in Egyptian sculpture. The age of primitive art in Egypt is very early in man's history; Sir Gardner Wilkinson fixing the founding of Memphis at B. C. 2320, the building of the Pyramid of Cheops at B. C. 2123, and the visit of Abraham to Egypt at B. C. 1921. The memorials of these four centuries of rude native art are the pyramids and tombs back of Memphis. No hieroglyphics were cut on granite; but the monarch's name was painted in red ochre. The sculptures on tomb walls were rude and simple, the figures in low relief, cut in outline rather than in rounded contour.

It is a transition to a new world to meet the life-like scenes sculptured on the temples and tombs at Thebes, whose era begins with Osirtasen I., in Joseph's day, about B. C. 1740. During this period, foreign kings and priests of a caste like the Brahmins in India, ruled in Egypt; and Rameses the conqueror brought in foreign artists. Though restrained in choice of subjects and methods by native taste, these superior masters threw a dignity and variety into their designs and execution as marked as the transition in Greece from Dædalus to Phidias.

The Greeks under the Ptolemies, at Ombos and the Isle of Philæ in Upper Egypt, reared temples truly Egyptian in architecture, yet Grecian in sculptural finish. Yet later, the temples at Esneh and Dendera, most magnificent remains of Egyptian architecture, were reared by the Cæsars; the excessive profusion of their sculptured decorations bespeaking their Roman spirit. The art of Egypt died out under succeeding Mohammedan rulers.

SECT. 5. THE SCULPTURE OF EASTERN ASIA; THE DESCENDING SCALE OF PRIMITIVE SCULPTURE; INCLUDING THAT OF INDIA, CHINA, POLYNESIA AND CENTRAL AND SOUTHERN AMERICA.

The ancient massive sculpture of Egypt and India and the modern art in China belong to the same family; as truly as do the jugglers of Cairo, Calcutta and Canton. The chief existing remains in India are two rock-hewn temples at Elephanta and Ellora in the vicinity of Bombay. At Elephanta are colossal statues and bas-reliefs on walls and columns; chief among which is the celebrated three-headed deity Brahma. At Ellora are rock-hewn tombs extending a mile and a half along a rocky hill-side; obelisks sixty feet high; colossal elephants and gigantic statues; walls covered with bas-reliefs representing every variety of scene, domestic, religious and military; all belonging to the Egyptian type.

The Chinese like the Egyptians chose the hardest stone for sculpture. Their porcelain is of the same style of workmanship as the Egyptian vitrified baked clay. Their work in miniature resembles that found in the Egyptian tombs.

Passing eastward, Humboldt traced a tide of emigration from the shores of Asia past the Pacific isles to the coast of America, finding buildings and sculpture like to those of Egypt among the Aztecs and Mexicans. The carvings on the walls of the palace of Mitla, he says, "offer striking analogies with those of the vases of lower Italy." The pen of Stevens and the pencil of Catherwood have made yet more striking this likeness to both Egyptian and Chinese types. The whole chain of specimens, half round the globe westward, is the degenerate phase of Egyptian sculpture.

SECT. 6. THE SCULPTURE OF WESTERN ASIA, THE ASCENDING SCALE OF PRIMITIVE SCULPTURE; INCLUDING THE ARABIAN, HEBREW, ASSYRIAN AND PERSIAN.

The desert of Sinai is stored with sculptured relics which form the first steps in the ascending scale of Egyptian art. In retired valleys are façades of tombs, with columns and entablatures cut in high-relief, Egyptian in origin. Surabeet el-Khadîm, southeast of Suez, is a perfect store-house of historical tablets erected by Egyptian monarchs.

Passing the desert of Sinai, at Petra, an advanced style of art is found in the rich rock-hewn temple fronts. These sculptures, whose beauties enrapture every tourist, are the first link in a chain that goes winding on through Palestine and Syria, till, circling about, it meets the artistic advancement of the Greek colonies on the west coast of Asia Minor.

Hebrew sculpture originated during the second and most advanced era of native Egyptian art; and the Hebrew artists, like the Hebrew lawgiver, were "learned in the wisdom of Egypt." The cherubs and candelabra of beaten gold, the form of which latter is preserved on the arch of Titus at Rome and described by Josephus the historian, were types of superior forms attempted in advanced ages of sculpture. Six hundred years after Moses, under Solomon, we read that the chief artist employed in decorating the Hebrew temple was a Tyrian; whose teachers were brought from Egypt. To the sculptured vessels prepared under Moses, Solomon added two colossal cherubs. The ceiling of the inner sanctuary was carved with palm-trees, cherubs and open flowers. Two pillars in front had capitals wrought with wreaths of lilies and pomegranates. The brazen lavers had reliefs of bulls, lions and eagles; and the great font stood on twelve brazen oxen.

In Assyria and Chaldea engraving on rocks was practised in the patriarchal age of Job. Daniel's mention at a later period of the golden statue of the king is illustrated in the gilded colossi now exhumed. The winged bulls uncovered by Layard are kindred to Egyptian designs. Mosaic pavements with figures in intaglio, represent state pageants and battle-scenes, in which there is the Egyptian stiffness of attitude and want of perspective. There is, however, a plumpness of the muscles, a life in the countenances and an action in the postures entirely unlike that seen in Egyptian sculptures. Layard remarks, "The principal distinction between Assyrian and Egyptian art appears to be, that in the one, conventional forms were much more strictly adhered to than in the other. . . . . The Assyrians, less fettered, sought to imitate nature more closely; as is proved by the constant endeavors to show the muscles, veins and anatomical proportions of the human figure."

In Persia ancient and modern sculpture are distinct. The modern Persians, of the ancient Caucasian stock, are the Protestants of Mohammedism; and as such retain the higher idea, belonging to their lineage, both of religious truth and of the relation of art to religion. The sculptures of ancient Persepolis have the muscular development of the Assyrian, with greater delicacy, ease and grace of finish. The men are stout and bearded; and their close-fitting military coats with capes, indicating a cold climate, show greater skill in the artist. Comparing the Persian with Assyrian sculpture, Layard says, "They exhibit precisely the same mode of treatment, the same forms, the same peculiarities in the arrangement of the bas-reliefs against the walls, the same entrances formed by gigantic winged animals with human heads, and finally, the same religious emblems. There was no attempt even in later Persian sculpture, found in Asia Minor, to impart sentiment to the features or even to give more than the side view to the face; though there was a manifest improvement in the disposition of draperies and in the delineation of the human features."

Of these general relations Layard says; "The Xanthian marbles acquired for this country by Sir Charles Fellows, and now in the British Museum, are remarkable illustrations of the threefold connection between Assyria and Persia, Persia and Asia Minor, and Asia Minor and Greece. Were those marbles properly arranged, and placed in chronological order, they would enable even the most superficial observer to trace the gradual progress of art from its primitive rudeness to the most classic conceptions of the Greek sculptor. Not that he would find either style, the pure Assyrian or the Greek, in its greatest perfection; but he would be able to see how a closer imitation of nature, a gradual refinement of taste and additional study had converted the hard and rigid lines of the Assyrians into the flowing draperies and classic forms of the highest order of art."

CHAPTER III.

CLASSIC SCULPTURE EMBODIED IN THE GRECIAN.

THE language of art given by the Greeks to the world, specially rich in terms for sculpture, indicates their special pre-eminence in this department. Homer's descriptions of the shield of Achilles, of the bowl of Helen, and of the belt of Hercules, intimate its early origin.

Winckelmann, the special student of Grecian sculpture, has divided its history into four ages; the rude style prevailing till Phidias; the grand style inaugurated by Phidias; the graceful style of the polished successors of Phidias; and, finally, the imitative style of the Grecian decline. The attentive student of ancient Greek and Latin authorities, especially of Pliny, and of modern critics like Winckelmann, aided by a careful comparison of relics of Grecian sculpture preserved chiefly in the galleries of Italy, will naturally extend this classification.

SECT. 1. GENERAL CHARACTERISTICS OF GRECIAN SCULPTURE.

The characteristics of a people's art are influenced by climate, face of country and native cast of mind. The Egyptians dwelling on a level river bottom, where massiveness and elevation were necessary to make their works conspicuous, built and carved every work in colossal proportions; and living in a climate where there was no rain, they covered the exterior of their edifices with minute and delicate sculptures which the storms of a Grecian winter would have soon obliterated. The Greeks, in a land of hills and plains, could make a temple of low proportions prominent; and could gain a rarer beauty by chastening and sheltering their nicer works. The Egyptians, like all Orientals, counted repose and impassive stolidity the highest attribute of Deity; and nature gave them along their river banks the inexpressive granite and sandstone in which to stereotype their stiff deities. The Greeks were all life and animation; and nature furnished them the almost breathing marble, whose fine texture and pure white surface seemed made to be polished into forms of beauty. It was the meeting of these external and internal causes that made the art of these two peoples such counterparts to each other.

Pliny relates that the Greeks had, first, sculptured vases, candelabras, decorated columns and furniture. After these came *imagines*, or images; by the Greeks entitled *eicones*, or likenesses, and by the Romans *statuæ*, or "standing" forms.

Religious devotion led Greek sculptors first to form deities; but as these were only heroes of earth, the transition was easy to superior men. At first only *emblems* distinguished one deity from another; Jupiter being known by his forked thunderbolt; Neptune by his trident or fish spear: and Apollo by his archer's bow.

In the advance of the art, posture, dress, sex and æsthetic ideas were studied. The natural posture of a single form was standing; but in groups filling gables, reclining became artistic. Equestrian statues began with Centaurs; and in bas-reliefs and full form, chariots with riders were cut in stone, or cast in brass.

To bring out the strength and beauty of the human form nude models were so sought as to occasion Pliny's remark, "The Grecian method is to veil nothing." Phidias, however, draped his Minerva; and Cicero remarked, "The fondness of the Romans for martial glory is observed in the fact that we generally see their statues decked in military array."

From the nude female form, first, Venus, then the Graces were studied; the Greeks selecting youth for special beauty of form, both in Venus and Apollo. Proceeding farther, the Greeks conceived the Amazon, or masculine woman, uniting to the robustness of the male the grace of the female form in Minerva and Diana; adding as a counterpart the Hermaphrodite, or Mercury-Venus, carving the manly form in lines of feminine delicacy. The centres of sculptural art were in Greece proper, Sicyon and Athens; in the Eastern Isles, Egina and Rhodes; and in the Western colonies, Sicily and Etruria. The number of works executed and preserved, as stated by Pliny, is astounding. Lycippus alone made 1500 works. At Rhodes there were no less than 3000 statues, and as many at Athens, Olympus and Delphi.

SECT. 2. THE BOLD STYLE OF GRECIAN SCULPTURE; BEGINNING WITH DÆDALUS.

Three hundred years after Cecrops founded Athens, Dædalus, contemporary with Theseus, about B. C. 1230, began the age of primitive Grecian sculpture, properly called the Bold Style; which extended to about B. C. 580, a period of 650 years.

Universally recognized as leader in Grecian sculpture and architecture in Homer's day, the name *daidalia* was a synonym for fine carvings. In the age of Augustus no less than nine famed monuments of his genius in sculpture were still admired, even by the side of the works of Phidias. Of these the naked Hercules, lost at Rome but preserved in numerous bronze copies, is still a masterpiece. The figure is nude, and in an attitude of bold advance; the right arm wields a club, and the left is wrapped in a lion's skin, while the wrinkled countenance, the swollen chest and contracted loins, the strained sinews and bulging muscles, all indicate a rare study of nature in an age of bold conception and of rude execution.

Dædalus had two classes of followers. One became mere copiers of the themes and manner of their master; while another catching his idea went beyond their leader, attempting the female as well as the male figure. To the former belonged Epeus, the fabricator of the famed colossal wooden horse, regarded as a deity by the Trojans, and therefore manifestly one of a class known to the Greeks and Trojans.

To the latter must be referred the higher yet rude characteristics illustrated by Winckelmann; the brow of Jupiter and the curl of his shaggy locks being precisely that of the lion, and the neck of Hercules just that of the bull. To this class also belonged Smilis, who carved a Juno of wood, admired in after times by the sweet poet Callimachus; and Endæus who made a Minerva, which Pausanias saw at Athens. The female as well as male deities had a bold, advancing attitude, and full muscular development; the female figures, however, being draped in robes hanging in a few straight yet graceful folds. The line of Dædalus closes with Dipœnus and Scyllis, who flourished about B. C. 580; whom Pliny mentions as "the first sculptors in marble."

SECT. 3. THE ATHLETIC STYLE, MATURED BY AGELADAS; STATUES OF VICTORS IN FEATS OF STRENGTH; ILLUSTRATED BY THE BOXER AND QUOIT-THROWER.

As Homer, advancing on Hesiod, pictured heroes in war like Hector and Achilles, so the first sculptors who dared to leave the gods and picture men, chose as ideals men like Hercules, of physical prowess.

The Olympic games, originated after the heroic age, B. C. 776, led to the athletic style in sculpture. Occurring once in four years and designed to promote skill in feats of strength, beginning with only racing, to which every variety of gymnastics was afterward added, at the seventh Olympiad, B. C. 748, crowns were awarded the victors, and at a later era statues. At the sixty-fifth celebration the athletic style in sculpture had reached its climax of perfection under Ageladas, the instructor of Phidias. At the sixty-sixth, Phidias himself made the statue of a victor in a chariot race; and Alcamenes, his pupil and rival, and other sculptors of rarest talent were proud to excel in statues of athletes.

The aim of the athletic style was to bring out the perfect anatomy of the human form, when each joint and muscle was strained to the utmost tension in every variety of gymnastic exercise. The figures were *ideal*, not likenesses of the victors; they were perfectly nude, showing every portion of the frame; the beard was either entirely removed, or cropped short; and every variety of position and expression was studied and copied. The Gladiator, called the Borghese Hero, the work of Agasias of Ephesus, who lived a century later than Ageladas, also the Boxer, the Quoit-thrower, and many kindred works, are masterpieces of this style.

SECT. 4. THE GRAND STYLE ENNOBLED BY PHIDIAS; MAJESTIC IDEALS OF HERO-WORSHIP IN THE AGE OF GREEK CULTURE; ILLUSTRATED IN THE MINERVA AND JOVE OF PHIDIAS.

Phidias, the great master of this and of all the Grecian ages in sculpture, was born B. C. 500. About B. C. 550 Sicyon, had introduced into her common schools practice in modeling; and Athens soon added the study of plastic art. The instructor of Phidias was Ageladas; Pericles was rebuilding Athens and Socrates teaching philosophy during his mature manhood. Thus a century of art training conspired to develop the master of the grand style in sculpture.

Though truly original, Phidias owed much to his teacher and his contemporaries, as well as to the people, whose criticisms he invited. Cicero says: "Phidias, when he would make a form of Jupiter, or Minerva, did not contemplate anything from which he should draw the likeness; but in his own mind there was a certain species of select beauty; gazing on which, and fixed upon it, he directed his art and hand to execute its likeness."

In Phidias, as in all truly great artists, magnanimity became a moulding power. He loved his art so much that he did all in his power to make others artists; thus increasing his own skill. All his pupils breathed into their works the lofty intellectual air caught from their master.

The greatest of his single works was his Olympian Jove of

ivory and gold, made for the temple of Elis. The image was forty-six feet high, seated upon a throne, bearded, crowned with olive, nude to the cincture, but robed below. In his right hand was a statue of Victory, and in his left a sceptre. The aweing majesty of this figure overpowered men of the noblest and sternest mind.

The comprehensive work of Phidias was the adorning of the Parthenon. The colossal Minerva peering through the roof was thirty-five feet high; the face, neck and breast being of ivory, the robe of gold, and the eyes of precious stones. Another of bronze stood in front of the Parthenon; whose spear point and helmet crest were visible to mariners as they doubled the promontory of Sunium.

In the tympanum of the principal front stood Jove receiving Minerva and the intellectual deities, who came to accept Athens, which Neptune and the rude gods of the sea were surrendering. The high reliefs in the metopes, and the low reliefs under the portico, many of them now in the London Museum, are among the richest treasures of ancient sculpture.

In the sculpture of the Parthenon, deities are full statues and colossal; while human figures are of life, or half size, and in relief. The life and grace of the human figure and also of the horses, lions, oxen and even the serpents, are as perfect as man's work can well be.

SECT. 5. THE GRACEFUL STYLE; PERFECTED BY PRAXITELES; IDEALS OF PHYSICAL BEAUTY ILLUSTRATED IN THE VENUS DE MEDICI, OF INTELLECTUAL GRACE IN THE APOLLO BELVIDERE, AND OF COMPOSITE SYMMETRY IN THE AMAZON AND HERMAPHRODITE.

Manly grandeur was perfected by Phidias; and the pupils of Phidias, who shared his genius, sought original excellence in a more delicate grace of outline and a more elaborate finish of detail, belonging to female loveliness.

Myron, a predecessor of Phidias, had cultivated the graceful style. Quinctilian characterizes his works as "more delicately wrought than those of Calamis;" and Cicero says, "Although the works of Myron had not yet sufficiently attained to truth, yet they were such as you could not hesitate to call beautiful."

Praxiteles, chief master in this style, Pliny states, "was specially happy in marble;" this material allowing delicacy of finish. His works were deities of ethereal physical mould, "Phryne," the Athenian beauty, and the goddess of sensual love, Venus. The only work of his that now exists, probably, is to be found in the bas-reliefs upon the frieze of the Parthenon.

The famed Venuses of Praxiteles exist only in the copy by Scopas, the famed Venus de Medici. Praxiteles made two Venuses, one draped, the other nude. The Cnidians bought the latter, reared a little open temple for it, and it became, as Pliny says, "esteemed before all works in the world;" many making voyages to Cnidus expressly to see it. Scopas, who lived somewhat later, and whose "fame vied with that of Praxiteles," made a kindred work, which is still preserved probably in the Venus de Medici.

In this work Venus is represented as coming from the bath; and as if startled by the approach of some one, she is turning her head slightly to one side, her eye is cast upward, as if to avoid meeting the gaze of the intruder, while her right hand is thrown forward to veil her breast, and her left to screen her middle. The artist's ideal is a girl just matured, of sanguine temperament, perfectly alive with the quick sensibility belonging to feminine delicacy; while every gesture is radiant with the grace of position and movement that attends chaste impulses.

Ovid extols the grace into which shrinking modesty has thrown her posture; and also the fascinating roll and the pinkish lustre of the eye of love in Venus, so in contrast with the yellow tinge of unimpassioned intellect in Minerva. Terence commends her full and gracefully tapered chest; condemning the mothers who, in his day, sought to enhance their daughters' beauty by "drooped shoulders and a laced waist;" as if they could thus improve on "Nature's good work." Winckelmann observes that the form of Venus is uncommonly slender, her head unusually small, and her foot long; her height being seven and a-half heads, and less than six measures of her foot.

In this age youth was selected as the model for beauty; not only Venus but Apollo being conceived as extremely youthful. The Apollo called Belvidere is an embodiment of intellectual dignity as is Venus of physical grace. It is seven feet in stature; nude, except the pallium, or small cloak, over the left shoulder and the quiver over the right. A bow is in his right hand; and his feet and arms extended, his head thrown slightly back, and his eye distended, all indicate that he has just shot his arrow. The brow, whose facial angle approaches a right angle, is expressive of the highest order of intellect. In the proportions of the Apollo as of the Venus, Winckelmann finds confirmation of the fact that the Grecian laws of symmetry were a principle rather than an arbitrary law.

The Amazon, perfected by Polyclitus, was an added step in the advance of this style. Of this, Pliny remarks, "The most lauded of Grecian sculptors came into comparison, although born in different ages, when they made Amazons." He adds that one of those made by Polyclitus won the prize over a work of Phidias; and that it was a statue which artists call a *canon* or fixed standard of the *lineaments* of art; in which he alone of men is judged to have embodied art itself in a work of art.

The final effort of the graceful style was the Hermaphrodite. The master-work of this kind, now preserved in the Villa Borghese at Rome, and often copied, is that of Polycles. The figure is reclining with the face downward, thus best presenting its rare delicacy of form. The hands Winckelmann characterizes as the most "beautiful of female hands."

Praxiteles and his school after him introduced the coloring or tinting of their statues; revived by the English sculptor, Gibson. Its legitimacy is questionable; since sculpture proper presents form alone, not color.

SECT. 6. THE HISTORICAL STYLE, DIGNIFIED BY LYSIPPUS; SCULPTURED LIKENESSES OF LIVING MEN WITH IDEAL ACCESSORIES; ILLUSTRATED IN BUSTS AND THE STATUES OF ALEXANDER.

The Hercules of Dædalus, the athlete, the creations of Phidias and Praxiteles were all *ideal*. It was a distinct and higher effort to cut exact likenesses of living men in marble, making this likeness, often ill-fitted for the attempt, to beam with an expression most characteristic and even transcending the original.

Pliny ascribes its origin to the daughter of Dibutiades, a sculptor of Phidias' day, who traced her lover's profile from his shadow on a wall, and got her father to round it out in clay.

The historic age proper commenced with Alexander the Great; from whose day correct likenesses of eminent Greeks and Romans were presented. Alexander employed Lysippus the sculptor,

Apelles the painter, and Pyrgoteles the engraver, to copy his features, Lysippus executing in marble a series of likenesses of Alexander from boyhood to manhood.

Since in man and woman the head is the *work* of the artist, busts in sculpture, and portraits in painting, came to be chosen works. Myron and Chares in marble, and Apelles in color, became eminent for executing heads only.

In Greek a head was called *protome*, and a bust *thorax;* in Latin a head *caput*, a bust *bustum*, and a portrait *vultus*. The heads of the Roman emperors were cut in white marble; the breast of colored marble being sometimes united to it as a support.

SECT. 7. THE IMPASSIONED STYLE; INTRODUCED BY SCOPAS, AND CULMINATING IN AGESANDER; STATUES EMBODYING IDEAS OF PHYSICAL AGONY AND OF MENTAL ANGUISH: ILLUSTRATED IN THE LAOCOÖN AND THE NIOBE.

As the different styles of Grecian sculpture overlap and interlace one another in point of time, so they often meet in the same artist. In fact, each class of excellences must be combined to a certain extent in every great master; while, nevertheless, every leading spirit in any sphere will excel in some one line.

The bold style of Dædalus sought to express energy and daring; the athletic style added the physical power of gymnastic training; the grand style of Phidias presented a quiet intellectual dignity; the graceful style of Praxiteles threw a charm of quiet, unimpassioned loveliness over the whole figure, especially of woman; and the historic style gave expression to the characteristic, or ordinarily moving impulse of individual men. It was a yet added department of art when passion, too overwhelming to be anything more than temporary in the sufferer, too unnerving to be endured long even by the beholder, and yet as the tragedy of art having a strange power of fascination over the minds of men, came to be cut in all its truth and life into enduring marble; giving first to physical torture its scowl of agony, and then to mental anguish its speechless voice of woe. The art maxim of Lysippus, "That Nature herself was to be imitated, not the artist," was the idea leading to the study of the expression of the intensest passions betrayed in the human countenance. Quinctilian characterized Lysippus' statues as having "natural expression," and Propertius as "animosas" or *impassioned.*

Of this style the most expressive specimen is the Laocoön and his sons, now preserved in Rome. It represents the priest of Apollo, and his two sons, struggling with the two immense serpents from the sea, pictured by Virgil after this group in marble. Pliny ascribes it to Agesander of Rhodes, with his son Athenodorus and his pupil Polydorus, who lived after Alexander. He characterizes it as a "work to be preferred to all others, both in painting and sculpture;" and a "wonder of the agreement in conception of different minds." Though in detail a work of rarest beauty, the strained muscles and the contorted features of the sufferers make it, in its main design, an embodiment of the conception of physical agony.

Next to the Laocoön as a masterpiece in the impassioned style, is the "Niobe," and her dying children; the mournfully pleasing theme of poets as the embodiment of mental anguish. It is the fruitful Lydian mother, whose children were struck with death for her irreverent pride at their number and promise, suddenly turned to stone, as if petrified in her tearless grief. Pliny says there is doubt "whether Praxiteles or Scopas made it." No sensitive observer can view this statue without carrying throughout life the idea of grief too deep for tears.

The Toro Farnese and the Dying Gladiator are admired simply for their anatomy by ancient and modern critics. They have been monuments for many an age of the powers of tragedy in sculpture.

Sect. 8. The colossal style; culminating under Chares; the effort to make gigantic massiveness truly artistic; illustrated in the Colossus of Rhodes.

Colossal proportions in a statue designed for an elevated position. when skillfully executed, have from the days of Phidias been specia. triumphs of sculpture. All Phidias' grand works were colossal. Lysippus, too, made colossal statues so large that the Romans declined to remove them. Of one of these Pliny relates, "Though it could be moved by the hand, such was the plan of its balance, it could be thrown down by no tempests." There stand now over he portico of St. Mark's in Venice four horses of most exquisite form, admired alike by artists and amateurs. They were executed by Lysippus for a chariot of the sun, in his native Isle of Rhodes. Afterward they became the glory of the Isle of Chios, thence they were borne by Constantine to his new capital; thence again by the Venetians to their Island City; thence yet again by Napoleon to Paris. Returned finally to Venice, they are now called "the traveled horses."

The famed Colossus of Rhodes, described by Pliny and criticised by Cicero, was designed by Chares, the pupil of Lysippus, to adorn the principal port of his native island. The statue was about one hundred and five feet high, and stood astride the entrance to the beautiful harbor. The statue was thrown down by an earthquake only fifty-six years after its erection. Pliny, who saw it in ruins, says, "The fingers alone were larger than ordinary statues."

Even the Roman Pliny calls the colossi, favorites after this era, works of "audacity." The climax in this degeneracy was reached by Dinocrates; who proposed to cut Mt. Athos, on the coast of Macedonia, into a head and bust of Alexander.

SECT. 9. ROMAN SCULPTURE; LINKED WITH THE GRECIAN, IN THE EARLY PERFECTED ETRUSCAN, IN THE COLLECTIONS CAPTURED IN GREECE, AND IN THE GRECIAN TASTE CHARACTERIZING ROMAN SCULPTORS.

Grecian genius, which had revealed itself first in the Asiatic provinces in the days of Homer and Thales, appeared, almost equally early, west of Greece also. The Pelasgi, driven by the Hellenes around the head of the Adriatic, seem to have brought art into Northern Italy. The famed Etruscan vases, among the most exquisite and best preserved gems of ancient art, were the fruit of their skill in sculpture.

Among the Romans themselves the ascetic principles of Numa, early fixed, checked the rising tendency toward Grecian ideas. Less, however, than two centuries after their execution, about B. C. 148, the victorious Romans bore off from Greece her most prized works in sculpture. How little they were prepared to appreciate Grecian art is illustrated in Mummius, who threatened the laborers packing the paintings and sculpture taken from Corinth, that if any were injured or lost they would have to *make others.* Even Pliny himself exclaims, "What use can be perceived as derived from them?"

The taste for art cultured by these collections at Rome is thus alluded to by Horace:

> "Græcia capta ferum victorem cepit, et artes
> Intulit agresti Latio."

Captured Greece indeed found its victor uncultured; yet she brought the arts into rustic Italy. Suetonius records the boast of Augustus, "Urbem marmoream se relinquere, quam lateritiam accepisset." The age that had developed a Cicero, a Virgil and a Horace, naturally produced an emperor proud to claim that he left a marble city where he had found a brick one.

The sculptors of the climactic Roman era were, however, Greeks in name, and probably in race. Of them Pliny only mentions three, and they degenerate.

CHAPTER IV.

MODERN SCULPTURE; PLASTIC ART AS AFFECTED BY CHRISTIAN CIVILIZATION.

THE plastic arts, declining from the days of Phidias, and for centuries lost, at length arose perfected again in Italy. A chain of causes led first to the deepening gloom and then again to the dawn; for the laws of æsthetic development operate as steadily as growth in the forest. To trace this progress in the history of Christian Europe is difficult; yet many links in the chain shine out in the mist of the ages.

SECT. 1. THE TRANSITION PERIOD FROM ANCIENT TO MODERN SCULPTURE; ILLUSTRATED SPECIALLY IN THE CHANGE OF SUBJECTS FOR ART INTRODUCED BY CHRISTIANITY.

It was a great transition in the Grecian and Roman mind when the peerless statues of gods and goddesses from being objects of religious veneration came to be relics of an idolatrous worship which was held as blasphemous.

In the rise and decline of Grecian sculpture the strength and culture of the religious sentiment was the chief fostering and refining cause. In the transition leading to modern sculpture, no less powerful influences could have wrought the change.

The spirit in man that leads to science, the tracing of effects to causes, carries the mind at once to theology or the consideration of the first cause; and material advancement reveals the greater need of moral renovation. The intellectual search for truth as to the Divine Being, first in all the questionings of Socrates and the reasonings of Plato and Aristotle, is no less the leading theme of philosophic inquiry in every cultured nation and among all studious men. The student of art who overlooks this fundamental element in human nature, no less than the artist who should ignore it, must fail of his end; as truly as would the master-builder who should deny the law of gravity, and take no account of the crush and thrust of his material.

The decline of hero-worship wrought a revolution as to the subjects of plastic art, especially of sculpture; for, as Winckelmann has intimated, sculpture is the art in which the peculiar spirit distinguishing the ancients from the moderns is most manifest. The tracing of this change bridges over the chasm that separates the two worlds and ages, that before, and that after Christ.

SECT. 2. THE CHASTE, THOUGH RUDE STYLE OF SCULPTURE, PREVALENT IN THE EARLY AGES OF CHRISTIANITY.

The decline in art following the revolution occasioned by the introduction of the Christian religion, was naturally long in operating. The development of man is as that of the plant, first the blade, then the stalk, then the ear and then the full corn in the ear. In the earliest stage of Christian development the very simplicity of its system won the rarest of Grecian genius; though it had no pomp to court the wise and noble "after the flesh."

In tracing the history of sculpture in Christian ages two things must be kept distinct, the patronage of art *in itself considered* by early Christians, and their opposition to the ancient *use of works of art* as objects of religious adoration.

Irenæus, about A. D. 175, states that the Carpocratians had both statues and pictures of Jesus. Eusebius, about A. D. 325, mentions that not only were images and pictures of Christ of great beauty and majesty numerous among Christians, but that lovers of art among the unchristianized Greeks and Romans had obtained statues of Jesus and his apostles, and that they kept them in their houses as art treasures.

In the same age Christian devices and emblems were common; such as a ship, or Noah's ark, for salvation; a dove for the Divine Spirit; a harp for worship; the cross, anchor and heart for faith, hope and love. These were carved as ornaments for the person or as funereal monuments; and Tertullian mentions embossed figures, as of the lost sheep, stitched by pious mothers on the caps of their boys. Chief among these was the cross; which to this day retains its superior place as an emblem of the Christian faith.

In the early Christian ages the images of Jesus in the churches were unobjectionable. When, after Constantine's accession, to be a Christian was to be of the national religion, and the ignorant mistaking their nature paid religious homage to these works of art, the council held at Illiberis, on the borders of France and Spain, decreed "that pictures ought not to be introduced into the churches, lest that be worshiped and adored which is painted on the walls." A generation later, when this temporary abuse had been corrected, Augustine commended the sculptor's ideals of Christ.

SECT. 3. THE ARTIFICIAL STYLE AND ILLEGITIMATE USE OF SCULPTURE CHARACTERIZING THE MEDIÆVAL AGES OF THE CHRISTIAN CHURCH.

A darker era for art, as well as science and general culture, drew on, when, two or three centuries after Constantine, the Roman Empire and with it the Christian Church, became divided; and when Gothic rudeness in the West, and Oriental gorgeousness in the East prevailed.

It had come to be popular to be a Christian; and designing men pressed into the Church to gain positions of influence and emolument, and out-voted or out-managed the lovers of the truth, beauty and glory of the Christian system. Then men without principle or genius got control of church decorations. The effect was to degrade art; the relics of which still linger in Italy, Spain and even France.

A second and most unfavorable result was the corruption of

religion itself. Our love of beauty and grandeur was given as its highest end to lead us to the Author of all. When art is accompanied by spiritual instruction it is an aid to true devotion; but when it is made the only teacher it degenerates into idolatry. When this distinction became neglected, statuary and paintings were perverted; and intelligent and spiritually-minded churchmen preferred that art should be sacrificed, since religion could not be, by true men. Yet good men sought to save both art and spiritual Christianity.

The Eastern Church rejected *carved images*, yet retained paintings of sacred personages. This distinction led in the Eastern Church to a double influence unfavorable for art, excluding sculpture from the land where classic art had reached its perfection, and degrading painting into the lifeless, meaningless objects that now hang upon the walls of Oriental churches.

SECT. 4. THE MAJESTIC GRANDEUR TO WHICH SCULPTURE AROSE AT THE REVIVAL OF SCIENCE, OF LETTERS, OF ART, AND OF RELIGION IN THE FIFTEENTH CENTURY.

It was not strange that the age of Wickliffe and Thomas à Kempis, of Luther and Loyola, of Dante and Chaucer, of Copernicus and Columbus, should fall so near that of Lionardo da Vinci and of Michel Angelo. Religion, science, letters and art, all flourish together, in the same country and at the same age, not only because they are fed from the same soil, but because like forest trees they stimulate each other's growth.

As, however, in Greece it required two centuries and a half to perfect art, so modern sculpture, revived in the beginning of the thirteenth century, did not reach its climax till the close of the sixteenth century.

In the Baptistery of the Cathedral of Pisa stands a large octagonal font, executed in marble, with fine bas-reliefs representing Scripture incidents, wrought by Nicolo Pisano, about A. D. 1250, after natural models; sacred personages assuming the beauty and life belonging to real men. The churches of the whole surrounding region now contain relics of the improved sculpture thus introduced.

When a youth M. Angelo used to stand and gaze upon the bronze doors of the Baptistery of the Cathedral at Florence, and exclaim that they were "degne d'essere le porte di Paradiso," worthy to be the gates of Paradise. Two of these were by Ghiberti, who lived one hundred and fifty years after Pisano.

About a century and a half later M. Angelo carved his Moses; whose goat-shaped and horned head has been both compared and contrasted with the lion-browed Jove of Phidias. As Phidias in his Jove, his Minerva, and his Parthenon, embodied three elements of Grecian majesty, so did M. Angelo in his masterpieces in the three departments of sculpture, painting and architecture. Spiritual Religion is speaking in his Moses through Hebrew allegory, in his Last Judgment through heathen legend, and in his St. Peter's through climactic Grecian and Roman art.

SECT. 5. THE EMBODIMENT OF CHRISTIAN SENTIMENT IN FORMS OF CLASSIC GRACE, CHARACTERIZING MODERN SCULPTURE IN SOUTHERN EUROPE.

Like Phidias, Michel Angelo was the grand representative, not only of perfected sculpture, but of revived art. Long before his time Tuscan genius had caught the spirit of the ancient Greeks, and had made it conspire to express the sentiment and advance the culture inherent in the Christian faith.

A century before M. Angelo, the first school of design, modeled after those of ancient Greece, was transforming Tuscany; two main causes giving it a Grecian cast.

In 1453 Constantinople was taken by the Turks. The few possessing the art spirit of ancient days sought the old colonial heritage of Etruria. The mingling of these fugitive Greeks among native artists gave a decided tendency to the classic taste already awakened.

Not long after, the relics of the statues of Grecian gods and heroes, buried beneath the ruins of ancient Rome, were dug up from their graves. Under Pope Eugenius IV., A. D. 1430, only five had been obtained entire. From A. D. 1480 to 1506, a large number, including the group of Laocoön, were rescued, and, deposited in the Vatican and Farnese Palaces of Rome and the halls of the Medici at Florence. The study of these ancient models, and the ambition to restore the parts of them that were lost, gave a permanent Grecian cast to Italian taste in sculpture.

Another influence arose from the Platonic club organized by the

Medici, tending to the republication of the Greek classics, the revival of the spirit of Grecian literature and art, and the harmonizing of its doctrines with the principles of the Christian faith.

The artists of that day were not great masters; as their restoration of mutilated antiques shows. The improved schools of the North did not reach Southern Italy; its style was a profuse ornament. In Naples Bernini conceived the unartistic idea of carrying the ornamented style of Corregio's painting into sculpture. The Florentine school, too, became degenerate. The opening of Pompeii, in 1740, and the treatise on ancient sculpture by Winckelmann, fanned to a flame the enthusiasm for classic sculpture. Hence obscure churches of Italy now rejoice in perfect gems, Grecian in grace and Christian in theme, the offspring of this revived taste; of which the three veiled statues, Modesty, Vice, the Dead and Christ, in the retired Church of Santa Maria della Pieta, are incomparable masterpieces.

Prominent in this new era was Canova. Born A. D. 1757, the son of a stone-cutter, in the ninth year of his age he entered the studio of a sculptor at Venice. Having visited Rome, Naples, and the new collections from Pompeii, he established his studio first at Venice. Visiting again Germany and afterward Paris, he returned to his native town, where he remained till his death in 1822.

Canova's works, representatives of modern Italian sculpture, group themselves under three classes; first, classic themes, the promptings of æsthetic cravings; second, religious studies, the suggestion of higher aspirings after moral excellence; and third, historical or private subjects, as busts and statues of living men, undertaken from the necessities of livelihood. The capitals of Austria and France have numerous memorials of the latter class from Canova's chisel; the churches of Italy abound in the second; and the collections of amateurs in almost every country in Europe have relics of the first class of his works.

Carving in marble is with the Italian a hereditary pursuit; and, as among the thousands of workmen in an English or American factory some develop great inventive skill, so among the thousands of common chippers, carvers and polishers of Italian birth, employed on great public works in almost every country, here and there a true artist is called out.

SECT. 6. THE UNION OF SIMPLICITY IN DESIGN, NATURAL BEAUTY OF FORM, AND LIVELINESS OF EXPRESSION DISTINGUISHING SCULPTURE IN NORTHERN EUROPE.

Though taste for sculpture had its rise in Northern Europe from the visits of Italian artists, yet rude native genius has been refined by the classic influences of Southern Europe.

Even Spain had a native art-taste which Italian refinement only modified. Trained amid Moorish glitter, chastened afterward at Rome, Paul de Cespides raised sculpture in that land of grand ideas to something like dignity.

The "Fountain of the Innocents," at Paris, executed by Gougon, and the works of Jacques d'Angoulême, both of the sixteenth century, the Caryatides of the Louvre, by Sarrasin at a later day, though French, show nevertheless the influence of classic Italy. In the brilliant era of Louis XIV., Girardon and Puget succeeded by Falconet, gave that yet more marked native type to French sculpture, which won for it the title "La Belle."

The master in French sculpture was Houdon. Born in 1741, inspired by Winckelmann, in youth he visited the unburied cities of Herculaneum and Pompeii, as also Rome; during which time he executed his famous statue of St. Bruno, of which Pope Clement XIV. said, "He would *speak* did not the rule of his order enjoin silence." Returning to Paris he executed busts and statues of public men. At the invitation of Franklin, then at Paris, he visited America in 1785, and took casts for the statue of Washington, now at Richmond, Va., which, when executed, Lafayette declared to be the best likeness obtained of the American patriot. He died in 1828 at the age of eighty-seven years; having passed through the most perilous national vicissitudes in quiet devotion to art.

In Germany, genius in sculpture, restricted at first by the spirit of the Reformation from religious themes, has been characterized as "excelling in funereal monuments." In the sixteenth century, Peter Vischer's group of the Twelve Apostles led the way to the works of Schlüter, Schadow, Dannecker, Rauch and others; by whom themes of classic and Christian, of national and individual interest, have been ennobled in sculpture.

In Denmark, Thorwaldsen, born 1772, the son of an Iceland

stone-cutter, sent in youth by the Royal Academy of Copenhagen to Rome, has brought more than regal honor to his native land by his works of classic and Christian sculpture. His Day and Night are gems everywhere popular. The style of Thorwaldsen is bolder and more full of passion and of majesty than that of Canova; his life-long Roman culture moulding, but not giving original shape to the peculiar type of the sculpture of Northern Europe, as eclectic in culture though independent in themes.

In Belgium the two brothers, William and Joseph Geef, have during the present generation given fine examples of the permanent union of the Christian and classic ideals, which seems a natural suggestion to artists of Northern Europe.

Sect. 7. The scope of subject and vigor of conception seen in the early growth of English and American sculpture.

Wide extent of domain, inviting genius to positions of wealth and power, has made England, like Rome, her prototype, a collector, or plunderer, rather than an originator and executor of works of art in painting and sculpture. In the time of Charles the First, about A. D. 1620, the Earl of Arundel brought from Greece those exquisite bas-reliefs, pried out from under the cornices of Grecian temples, and those matchless fragments of ancient statues, which yet adorn the British Museum. Nearly two centuries later, from 1799 to 1812, Lord Elgin, then representing England at Constantinople, made the kindred collection called the Elgin Marbles.

The early sculptures now found in the English churches were by Italian artists. From the reign of Henry VIII. the spirit of the Reformation for a time yielded to the fallacy of iconoclasm, and art was neglected; but in the eighteenth century native sculptors appeared in the persons of Banks, Wilton and Bacon. The present century has been as fruitful as the past was barren in the growth of genius for art in England. Flaxman, born in 1755, having caught in Italy the spirit immortalized on the Etruscan vases, executed his "Illustrations of Homer," which have been admired for their spirit in every country of Europe. Westmacott, born in 1774, developed an early taste for ideal creations, which impoverish the purse, though they enrich the genius of the artist. His later labor was devoted almost entirely to statues of eminent men.

Chantrey, born in 1782, having deserted his law studies at twenty years of age, made himself famous by a bust of Horne Tooke. His statue of Washington in the State House at Boston is prized by Americans.

In Wales, Gibson, born A. D. 1791, patronized by William Roscoe and Lord Brougham, trained at Rome by Canova and Thorwaldsen, devoted his early genius to ideals of ancient mythology, and statues of the living. Independent in spirit, Gibson has ventured on the hazardous attempt of Praxiteles to add tint to marble; his "Victoria" and "Aurora" being slightly tinged, and his "Venus" completely colored.

The rise of native American sculptors, though recent, is yet comparatively early; appearing as they have in the infancy of the nation, and rapidly advancing to special eminence and excellence. Hopkinson, the racy and trenchant satirist of his times, records: "there came to this country in 1783, immediately at the return of Peace, a certain Robert Edge Pine, parading the title 'Painter to His Majesty.'" Said Pine brought with him a plaster cast of the Venus de Medici; "but," says Hopkinson, "he kept it very privately, as the manners of the times would not permit the exhibition of such a figure."

The birth of the new nation, however, was immediately and in all sections of the country succeeded by an ambition for sculpture in its higher forms. The statues of Washington by the foreign artists, Houdon, Canova and Chantrey, show a universally awakened popular demand for statuary; while that of Rush, carved in 1812, at Philadelphia, is a monument of the aspiration for native art aroused by the new national life.

With A. D. 1830 begins that noble line of native American sculptors which includes the names of Greenough, Clevenger, Crawford, among the dead, and Powers, Brown, Mills, Palmer, Stone, Rogers, Story, Hosmer and others among the living.

Horace Greenough, born at Boston in 1805, left Cambridge College for Rome at the age of twenty years; where he made the acquaintance of Thorwaldsen. He established his studio at Florence. His Chanting Cherubs, Medora, Venus Victrix and Abdiel as classic, his Rescue as historic, and his Washington as ideal portrait, are master works. Greenough's cast of mind was bold and impulsive; chastened and humanized by a genial urbanity and generous sympathy. The slight draping of his Washington has called attention to the fact that Greek sculptors chose the toga for civil and the breast-plate for military heroes, because they were national; and that Phidias robed his Jove, and Lysippus his Alexander. The head of Greenough's Washington is incomparably sublime, and in itself will make the artist ever live in the hearts of his countrymen, and in the appreciation of generous critics. His "Venus," too, is of the sweetest loveliness; and the genius that could excel in such opposite styles, uniting the boldness of Phidias and the grace of Praxiteles, will shine as a rare one in the history of American sculpture.

Thomas Crawford, born at New York in 1814, trained to wood and stone carving, at twenty-one went to Rome and became a pupil of Thorwaldsen. After years of toil his Orpheus, commended by Thorwaldsen and Gibson, was ordered for the Boston Athenæum. His equestrian statue of Washington at Richmond, with the group on the pedestal, begun in 1849, forms the most elaborate composition in bronze in America. His grandest studies were his models for the group in the tympanum of the northeast portico of the United States Capitol, and for the colossal Liberty at the apex of the dome; works which have been executed by other hands since his death, in 1857.

Hiram Powers, born in Vermont, in 1805, removed early in life to Ohio. Having acquired skill in modeling, after spending seven years as curator of a museum, he came to Washington City in 1835, and gained reputation for his busts. Visiting Italy in 1837, his Eve, modeled in 1838, drew encomiums from Thorwaldsen. In 1839 he conceived his masterpiece, the Greek Slave; which has become the head of a list of kindred works wrought by his chisel. Powers' genius is of the quiet and pensive order, the natural offspring of his mild, unobtrusive nature; a trait which manifests itself in the retiring modesty and gentle grace of his female, and in the repose of his masculine forms.

Henry K. Brown, born in Massachusetts in 1814, began the study of portrait painting; but a successful attempt to model a young lady's head in clay, turned his thoughts to sculpture. After some years in Italy, he fixed his residence at New York; which city, as well as Columbia, S. C., is marked with the treasures of his skill

Clark Mills, born in the State of New York in 1815, went in

youth as a plasterer, to Charleston, S. C. His superior skill in stucco and the carving of busts led him to modeling in clay. In 1848 he received a commission for an equestrian statue of Jackson. His model, prepared from a horse trained to rear and stand poised on his hind feet, was the first specimen of its kind in the history of equestrian statuary. His genius, taking models from nature and learning methods from practical pursuits, has triumphed without an instructor in new paths of art.

Erastus D. Palmer, born in the State of New York in 1817, at the age of twenty-nine years, as a pastime, cut in shell the portrait of his wife. His success led him to cameo carving. Having modeled his own child as an infant Ceres, he devoted himself to sculpture. His carving has that exquisite delicacy acquired in cameo cutting, while his conception is most ethereal in its expression.

Horatio Stone, reared amid the scenery of the Hudson, devoted for years to landscape-gardening, has given to his countrymen in his Hamilton and Hancock most impressive monitors. A high conception of the spirituality and sacredness of the sculptor's calling characterizes his works.

Rogers, whose bronze doors for the U. S. Capitol have been admired even in Munich, where his castings were made, promises eminence in finished work. Story, Barbee, and others are destined to a high future fame.

Harriet Hosmer, born in 1831, has commenced a line, most promising, of female sculptors; Gibson, the English sculptor, being her chief teacher. Vinnie Ream is displaying rare genius, yet in its dawn.

BOOK IV.

ARCHITECTURE; OR THE COMBINING OF FORMS, WITH THE UNITED ENDS OF UTILITY AND BEAUTY.

ARCHITECTURE, derived from *architektōn*, a master-builder, is primarily a useful, and only secondarily a fine art. It was naturally the first of arts; since men require habitations before they demand any added ornaments. Hence some urge that architecture be made the first among the fine arts. In its origin, however, it was not a fine, but a technical art; simple and rude as was man himself; an art in which animals, guided by instinct alone, have excelled. Architecture becomes a fine art only when drawing and sculpture add their grace and power to the builder's skill.

CHAPTER I.

ORIGIN OF ARCHITECTURE AS AN ART; AND THE PRINCIPLES CONTROLLING ITS FORMS.

As a useful art, Architecture began with the origin of man. In Eden man needed no other shelter than the bowers formed by branching trees and creeping vines. The art of building has kept pace with human advancement in civilization.

SECT. 1. CIRCUMSTANCES DETERMINING THE STRUCTURE OF PRIVATE DWELLINGS.

The material of dwellings has always been dependent on the nature of the country and the wants of mankind. The keeper of flocks, like Jabal and Jacob, lives in a tent made of cloth easily removed. In the mountain regions in and about Palestine, the descendants of Lot, Esau and Israel, in rude times, made abodes in caves; and Homer says of the Cyclops, "Their abode is on the summits of mountains, and caverns serve them for retreats." The rude aborigines of America made huts of ice and snow in the frigid zone, of mud and bark in the temperate latitudes, and of palm branches and grass in the torrid regions. In the plains of ancient Assyria, they built of brick laid in bitumen, because they had neither stone nor lime; and in Egypt of limestone, sandstone and granite, because all these were abundant on their river's brink.

Two necessities have controlled style of building; protection from men, and from the elements of nature. Cain, with the fear begotten by crime, "built a city;" and from Job's day dwellers in Asia have built closely walled towns on precipitous hill-tops like ancient Jerusalem. The early Greeks also perched their first citadels on a jutting rock called the Acropolis; as is seen in ancient Athens and Corinth. Plato argues, "A city takes its rise from this fact; that no man can be self-sufficient; since we all have many wants beyond our own powers. Can you imagine any other principle originating the building of cities?" Aristotle, more comprehensive, urges that the inherent love of society for the sake of *aiding* others, the yearning of men to have power and repute as public benefactors, is the secret of organized society. Aristotle, therefore, and Vitruvius after him, make civil architecture cover all that belongs to the art proper.

Yet again, climate and shape of country give laws for building. Houses in India are surrounded by open verandahs for shade; and in volcanic countries they are but one story in height. Swiss cottages have sharp-peaked roofs and projecting eaves to cut and fling aside the falling snow; and on sunny plains dwellings have flat roofs as promenades in the cool evening breeze.

Since necessity originates laws of taste, to put a Swiss cottage on an open field, a grotto on a plain, a house with an open verandah in a cold clime, or to build a summer house of brick, or a castellated structure of wood, perverts the idea in which architecture as an art originates.

SECT. 2. THE DEMANDS OF MAN'S SOCIAL NATURE GIVING ORIGIN TO ARCHITECTURE AS AN ART.

When men combined in society and co-operated to rear a structure for united assembling, one superior mind naturally acquired ascendancy and assumed sway, forming the plan and regulating the many hands employed in the labor of executing the design; thus originating the office of *architect*, or chief builder. Regarding military defence its chief end, Plato calls architecture, *epistēmē*, a science; saying, "After the science of building had thus arisen," in necessity for common defence, "it separated itself from the other sciences and took the distinctive name architectural." Aristotle, confining it to civil structures, makes architecture an art, *technē*.

Human structures have three ends. Military architecture embraces the construction of forts, roads and canals; Herodotus restricting the term to this department. Naval architecture relates to structures made to float as habitations, to fly as messengers of commerce, or to sweep the ocean and command continents as moving castles and fortresses. Civil architecture comprises private dwellings to shelter families, and public halls for purposes of social enjoyment or improvement.

The leading uses of public buildings grow out of man's material, intellectual and religious wants. The principles that should control their structure, according to Greek architects, are these five; *first*, *taxis*, or order, the proper arrangement of parts before putting them together; *second*, *symmetria*, proportion in size; *third*, *euarithmia*, harmony in number, and in the adjustment of the parts both in their separate dimensions and in their interlocking junctures; *fourth*, *diathesis*, or composition, the disposing of the portions of an extended edifice so that they shall be beautiful as a whole; and *fifth*, *oikonomia*, or economy, the securing of the useful ends for which the building was erected. Ruskin, in his "Seven Lamps of Architecture,' presents five purposes and seven guides to their accomplishment. The *purposes* of edifices are: first, "devotional," for religious worship; second, "memorial," as private and public monuments for the dead; third, "civil," as public edifices for business and recreation; fourth, "military," for defence against armed foes; and fifth, "domestic," for family abodes. The seven lamps or seven *guiding principles* that control the architect are these; *first*, "Sacrifice," under which the Jewish temple is considered; *second*, "Truth," which leads to the discussion of the propriety of Gothic drops, frescoed domes representing the open sky of a hypæthral temple, and the use of iron as material for building; *third*, "Power," which embraces massiveness as an element of architectural effect; *fourth*, "Beauty," relating chiefly to architectural decorations; *fifth*, "Life," the making of an edifice the exponent of living things and of the men who rear it; *sixth*, "Memory," as monuments of history, conservators of old ideas and relics of the past; *seventh*, "Obedience," respect for great men and their plans, as opposed to empiricism and striving for novelty.

Among buildings to promote material ends are markets, the *agora* of the Greeks and *forum* of the Latins. The Forum was an elliptical enclosure, surrounded by covered sheds or porticoes two stories in height, with projecting galleries where men of leisure could saunter. The pillars in the Grecian agora were close set; but in the Roman Forum more open. The lower porticoes were occupied by bankers and tradesmen;. and the upper balconies contained seats for spectators of the diversions of the Forum. The Basilica, or Royal Hall, was a rectangular building, with a lofty portico, having inner halls and outer galleries.

The buildings designed to meet intellectual wants are of two classes; educational and æsthetic. Those for *instruction* proper embrace schools, colleges, lecture and lyceum halls, libraries and halls of collections in science and art. In ancient Greece practical instructors, like Socrates, used the *stoa*, or covered porticoes around the *agora;* while for select pupils the *Academia* of Plato, the *Lykeion* of Aristotle, and the *Mouseion* of Alexandria were erected. Structures designed to minister to the *sensibilities* were the theatre and the amphitheatre. The amphitheatres furnished exhibitions addressed only to the eye; while the theatre, both among the Greeks and the Romans addressed the mind through the ear as well as the eye. The study of acoustic effects, based on mathematical calculations, secured in these immense areas the requisites for audience-halls.

The moral ends sought in public structures are two; civil and religious. The *Pnyx* for popular oratory, the Areopagus for judicature, and the Acropolis covered with temples to the gods, were alike moral powers. The Capitol of Rome was at once the seat of law and of religion.

The structures erected for religious ends are *temples* and *tombs*. In rude ages, religious worship is held in the open air, under shady trees; alike by ancient Druids and modern Christian worshipers. Afterward Pagan and Jewish temples, Christian churches and Mohammedan mosques were erected in a large enclosure. The Grecian *temenos* or Roman *delubrum*, with its grove and open field was requisite for the slaughter of bullocks and the smoke of burning flesh; while the *naos* or *templum*, within this enclosure, was the shrine of devotion. From the times of the rearing of Egyptian temples down to the building of Christian churches, sacred architecture will be found to be the central interest in the history of the art; and often entirely to absorb it.

SECT. 3. PRINCIPLES ORIGINATING AND GIVING FORM TO COLUMNAR ARCHITECTURE.

Columnar appendages to edifices, originating in necessity, came to be the chief field in which genius and skill sought their highest triumphs. As the face in the human portrait, so the façade in the public building is, as their common derivation indicates, the chief work of the artist. Public and private edifices need projecting porticoes as a shelter from sun and rain; and these must have columnar supports.

Vitruvius hints the origin as to material and shape of columns first used. Sections of the trunks of trees, first employed as corner-posts, gave proportions for rude columns suited to, as it was suggested by the kind of tree selected. The bulging stump and projecting branches formed a natural base and capital. The style of columnar decorations has been suggested by favorite plants; in Egypt, destitute of trees, the water-lily winning the post of honor; in India the banyan; in China the palm; in Greece the shade trees of academic groves; and in France the monarchs of Northern forests.

As all structures are built by men for mankind, so the human stature has ever been the naturally chosen modulus for entrance doors and interior elevations. Columns have conformed to this law; not only true human figures, as the Egyptian Osiride and

Grecian Caryatides directly showing this, but also the general proportions of the orders in architecture making it manifest.

SECT. 4. LOCAL CIRCUMSTANCES, AND NATIONAL PECULIARITIES OF ÆSTHETIC CULTURE AND MORAL CONVICTIONS, GIVING ORIGIN TO LEADING STYLES IN ARCHITECTURE.

The parts of every building are the walls, roof, platform and porticoes; the modification of which, through the influence of local, national, æsthetic or moral causes, have led to diversity of styles and schools in architecture.

Local circumstances, to a great extent, determine the material of buildings. In a new and wooded country the walls and roof are from necessity of perishable material. In Assyria, destitute of wood and stone, burnt brick was used; in Egypt, abounding in stone and having no rain, stone for temples and unburnt brick for huts were employed; while in Europe and America iron is becoming common.

The slight showers of Northern Africa and Western Asia allow roofs to be flat for promenades; while from Greece northward through Italy to France the roof pitch constantly increases the steepness. The breadth and height of porticoes decrease with latitude. The temple of Egypt on a plain needed no raised platform; but a Grecian temple on a rounded eminence must have a flight of steps around the depressed border.

Forms of religious belief and æsthetic culture have had an influence yet more decided. The reptile-worshiping Egyptian made his shrines dismal cells; but the hero-worshiping Greek reared in their place cheerful open halls. Hebrew and Christian sanctuaries have sought broad, elevated, airy and well-lighted audience-halls, since their services are chiefly addressed to the mind through written records. Very generally, therefore, the student's cloister is an attachment to their precincts.

CHAPTER II.

EGYPTIAN, THE TYPE OF ASIATIC ARCHITECTURE, IN WHICH MASSIVENESS IS THE AIM.

THE ancient relics of Asiatic architecture seem by their massiveness to have been prompted by the spirit of the men who, just escaped from the deluge, said, "Let us build us a city and a tower whose top may reach unto heaven." The massive was certainly the aim in this early structure; and in less than two centuries it is found transferred to Egypt as its native home.

SECT. 1. THE USES OF EGYPTIAN STRUCTURES CALLED TEMPLES; GIVING CHARACTER TO THEIR FORMS OF ARCHITECTURE.

There are two classes of structures in Egypt, whose vastness in their ruins still fills the world with admiration. The first reared above ground, called temples, answered the three-fold purpose of palaces for royalty, of fortresses in war, and of shrines for religious worship. The second constructed under ground, called tombs, were burial-places for the dead.

Both the style and design of the Egyptian temples are illustrated in the modern cities of India. In Lucknow, above whose square miles covered with mud hovels massive fortresses, called *Bagh*, are scattered at distances of from one-half to three-quarters of a mile from each other, a perfect counterpart is seen to the "hundred-gated Thebes," mentioned by Homer.

On the eastern bank of the Nile stands first the temple of Luxor, covering a quarter of a mile square; and distant from this a mile and a half to the northeast is the temple of Karnak, covering half a mile square. On the western bank, half a mile from the river, is a third temple; a third of a mile farther, a fourth; and so on till even a seventh and an eighth are passed. Of these the fifth is the celebrated Memnonium, before whose portal stand the vocal Memnon and his brother; and the sixth, "Medinet Aboo," famed for the beauty and perfection of the bas-reliefs on its walls.

SECT. 2. GENERAL ARRANGEMENT, THREE ORDERS OF COLUMNS AND CORNICE OF THE EGYPTIAN TEMPLE.

In the temple of Karnak the largest of the number, the original shrine was reared by a Pharaoh of Joseph's day. The foundations are of limestone, not disintegrated by moisture. The walls are of sandstone, easily cut by the chisel with the sculptures which cover them. The roof is of immense blocks of sandstone laid across from wall to wall. The interior facing is of granite, which received a polish like that of marble. In front of this first shrine two massive walls, from thirty to forty feet high, form the sides of a hollow square, whose back is the shrine and its front a castellated gateway one hundred feet high, called a pylon, from the Greek *pulē*, a gate; enclosing an area of three or four acres. Along the sides of this open court is a covered colonnade; and in front of the temple a portico with a double row of columns. Before the pylon towered a pair of lofty obelisks, or of gigantic statues, or of both; the obelisks being of red granite from sixty to one hundred feet in height, and from twelve to fifteen feet square at the base, tapering gradually till near the top, where they terminate in a pyramidal point; and the statues being of red granite or grayish porphyry, and rising sixty feet in a standing or seated posture.

In the temple of Karnak, covering half a mile square, portion after portion, halls, porticoes, obelisks, enclosing walls and pylons, were added during a period of 1800 years, by Egyptian, Grecian and Roman occupants. In the grand hall of this structure is a forest of columns covering an acre of ground; two rows of which are twelve feet in diameter, and sixty-six feet in height. Over the entrance passage at the east the roof is formed of blocks of sandstone five feet in thickness, and thirty feet long, raised thirty feet high, and laid across from wall to wall. A pair of obelisks in front of the grand hall of Karnak measure ninety-two feet in height.

In Egyptian structures, temple walls and pylons, as well as obelisks and pyramids, slope inward from the base to the summit; according to the law of strength giving beauty, and of stability ensuring grace. In this the Egyptians, unlike the Grecians, exaggerated nature so much as to falsify her law. In Egyptian, as in Grecian columnar orders, three ideas prevailed. These columns were styled by the savans of 1798 according to the model of their capitals, the lotus bud, the lotus flower, and the Osiride or head of Osiris; but they have been better classified by Dr. Walter, the American architect, as the *robust*, *medium* and the *delicate*, corresponding severally to the three Grecian orders. In the robust the height is about five diameters, in the medium six, and in the slender seven diameters; though no two specimens agree in every respect. The robust has its shaft sometimes smooth and sculptured, but generally reeded and banded like a bundle of lotus stalks; its capital a lotus bud either smooth or slightly foliated; and its base rounded and foliated like a tuber root; copies of which are seen in Philadelphia and New York prisons. The medium has its shaft plain or sculptured; its capital has four human faces with cows' ears; while its base is a plain projecting foot-slab. The delicate has its base rounded and foliated as a tuber root, and the capital an inverted bell or open lotus flower, sometimes smooth, sometimes slightly foliated, and sometimes with leaves deeply cut.

A mixed or composite order grew up after the Grecian conquest, the capitals being both Osiride and foliated; specimens of which are found in the Isle of Philæ, at Dendera, at Karnak, and at Apollinopolis. The knowledge of geometrical proportions known to the Egyptian is seen by cutting a horizontal section of one of these columns. The depressions or grooves in the reeded shaft, and the periphery of the capital, are found to be included within a series of overlying squares inscribed in a circle; showing the nicety with which every part of the surface of the shaft and capital was calculated from the centre of the column.

The cornice of the Egyptian temples projected one-half its height. Its lower half is flat; the upper curves outward, the curve being a quarter cylinder, having one-half the height of the cornice as its radius; a feature often overlooked in copies after the Egyptian style. A plain fillet or band runs along the top of this curve or cavetto, and an ornamental bead along its base; the bead extending also down the corners of the pylon in the more finished Egyptian structures. The contrast between Egyptian and Grecian art is seen in this; that while the Greeks employed the more elaborate curves of the conic sections, as the ellipse and parabola, in moulding architectural ornaments, the Egyptians used only the simpler curve of the circle.

SECT. 3. THE STRUCTURE OF EGYPTIAN TOMBS, THE FAÇADE OF ROCK-HEWN TEMPLES AND THE LABYRINTH.

The tombs of Egypt are back of the large cities, excavated into the limestone walls of the ravine in which lie the river Nile and its alluvial banks. Large halls were cut with lateral passages and rooms along each passage; and the walls coated with cement, were then covered with sculptures and paintings representing all the scenes of active business life. The coffins of the dead were placed in a standing posture around the walls, and the chambers successively walled up. The reigning king's name was written in hieroglyphics at the portal. Finally the exterior entrance in the mountain wall was closed by an immense stone, and the desert sand heaped over it.

In Nubia, above Egypt, where the sandstone allowed it, immense temple fronts with columns and architectural ornaments were cut in the solid rock. In the façade of the temple of Aboo Simbel are statuesque columns, the most beautiful in all Egypt, about sixty feet high.

The famed Labyrinth, the most remarkable specimen of Egyptian underground architecture, situated about fifty miles above ancient Memphis, consisted of twelve palace-temples above ground, with twelve corresponding tombs below ground; including in all one thousand five hundred rooms. Virgil's picture of the one with a "thousand passages," built in Crete by Dædalus, through whose windings even the artist had to guide himself by a thread, has given a fabulous air to this wonder of Egyptian art.

SECT. 4. THE OBELISK AND PYRAMID AS TYPES OF THE MASSIVE IN THE ARCHITECTURE OF EGYPT.

The obelisk in temples and the pyramid among tombs are characteristic features of Asiatic architecture. The obelisks placed in pairs before temple entrances are needles of red granite with a base about one-twelfth of their height, polished to a mirror-like smoothness, and covered with hieroglyphics. Of these forty-two were conveyed to Rome between the times of Augustus and of Constantine; and Constantinople, Paris and other cities have so followed up the plunder that only eight are now left in Egypt; namely, two at Alexandria, one at Heliopolis, and five at Thebes. The largest remaining are ninety-two feet high, and eight feet in diameter

Of the largest removed, one at Rome is seventy-eight feet, and one at Paris seventy-six feet high. Those at Thebes are still perfectly mirror-like in polish after the lapse of ages; but Cleopatra's Needle, at Alexandria, is much defaced on the seaward face by the salt spray. The faces of some have a convexity of 3°, which prevents a complete shadow on the entire face, and the consequent hiding of the sculptures when the face is shaded.

The form of the pyramid, like that of the obelisk, represents, as its name intimates, a tongue of flame, the emblem of the spirit ascending. They were a very ancient conception, and laid aside in the advance of the race; all being completed in the early patriarchal age. The oldest and largest is seven hundred and sixty-four feet square at the base, covering over thirteen acres, and four hundred and eighty feet nine inches in height. The slope of its side, therefore, is an angle of 51° 51′; a steepness of inclination which makes it difficult and even dangerous of ascent. The pyramid stands with its faces due north and south and east and west. The entrance passage declines at an angle of 27°; and as the latitude of the pyramid is about 30°, this, with other like indications, have been regarded as an index to the Egyptians' knowledge of astronomy as well as of geometry. Early historians agree in the statement that the pyramids were designed to be the tombs for kings; while ancient tradition hints a theory, revived by modern savans, that the granite-cased inner vaults were meant to contain standard weights and measures.

SECT. 5. THE HISTORY OF EGYPTIAN ARCHITECTURE; THE PERMANENT TYPE, MASSIVE IN MATERIAL AND PERMANENT IN ITS RUDE AND SOMBRE CAST; ITS SIMPLE MASSIVE ORIGINALS; ITS ASIATIC GORGEOUSNESS; ITS GRECIAN REFINEMENT; AND ITS ROMAN GRANDEUR.

Egyptian architecture, having a long history and well-preserved monuments, furnishes a most striking exhibition of the power of national conceptions in controlling foreign ideas introduced, and of preserving substantial types, while it may be modified in external aspect by an improved civilization. The Egyptian palace-temples and tombs, so well preserved that the works of different ages are readily recognized under rulers of varied nationalities, never departed in plan or principle from the early model. Though entirely unlike their own religious shrines, Asiatic wise men and Grecian and Roman conquerors, reared temples having the same flat roof and circular cornice, with porticoes having columns of one of the three Egyptian orders, fronted by immense open courts surrounded by colonnades, and having obelisks and colossal statues standing or seated before their portals, as well as avenues of guarding sphynxes leading to their outer entrances. All the foreign possessors of the land, too, went back to the line of desert mountain rock into which to cut their tombs; they excavated the branching passages; they stuccoed and carved the walls; and they drew pictured and painted scenes of life in a style perfectly Egyptian: denationalizing themselves to become ministers to ruder conceptions.

The four eras already marked in the history of Egyptian sculpture are to be noted in its architecture. The first is the age of rude native taste. The pyramids built of limestone and having chambers lined with granite, and the inner shrine of the grand temple at Thebes, with plain octagonal columns of sandstone, are the only monuments of this age.

The second era was that of Asiatic gorgeousness; the age of commerce and foreign influence, extending from Osirtasen I., in the days of Joseph, to its culmination under Osirei and his famed successors, Remeses I. to IV. Its matchless monuments are the grand hall of the temple of Karnak, the Remesium and the Memnonium, and the richer tombs of Thebes. Any one of the forest of columns in the grand hall of Karnak, twelve feet in diameter and sixty-six feet high, embodies the idea of the age; Egyptian massiveness with Asiatic gorgeousness.

The third or Grecian era, had as its centres Alexandria in the north and Philæ at the south. Its grand works at Alexandria were the Pharos, or light-house, the library and museum reared by the Ptolemies. The beautiful temples on the Isle of Philæ are its preserved memorials; showing how even Egyptian heaviness was made light and graceful by the touch of Grecian genius.

The last and Roman era has its two grand monuments in the temples of Dendera and of Esneh. Both are simple shrines, without enclosing courts, pylons or obelisks; but loftier and grander than any earlier covered structure in Egypt. That at Esneh has columns with the lotus capital; those at Dendera are Osiride; both have a screen exquisitely wrought in a sort of lattice running be tween the outside row of columns and rising to half their height. The zodiacs on the ceilings of both seem a suggestion of the Julian period in astronomy. The absence of surrounding pylons, obelisks and statues is a feature of the independence of the Roman sway; while the perfectly Egyptian idea and style of the shrine itself is an interesting comment on Roman policy, which not only recognized but adopted the religion, as well as the local customs and state institutions, of every conquered nation.

In the single temple of Karnak there is an epitome not only of all the four eras, but of several stages in some of these eras. The improvement of art is specially conspicuous in the second era, the age from Joseph to the successors of Moses.

SECT. 6. THE ARCHITECTURE OF INDIA, EASTERN ASIA AND WESTERN AMERICA; THE DECLINING PHASE OF THE MASSIVE STYLE.

As in sculpture so in architecture a resemblance with growing degeneracy can be traced eastward from Egypt through India, China and Polynesia to America. Its ancient relics in Hither India, Polynesia and America, and its modern representatives in Farther India and China, are degenerate specimens of the same style.

In India the most interesting relics are found at Elephanta and Ellora, already referred to. On the isle of Elephanta the entrance to a rock-hewn temple is sixty feet wide, and eighteen feet high; the grand hall, one hundred and twenty-three feet wide and one hundred and thirty feet long is cut into the solid rock; and the walls are covered with sculptures in relief. At Ellora a line of similarly excavated temples run along a mile and a half on a hill-side, most of which are one hundred feet in depth; while one has a pagoda-like roof cut into the rock ninety-five feet high, differing from the pyramidal roof in being circular.

In Farther India the pagoda is characteristic; a steep pyramid in shape, having numerous stories each of less area than the one next lower. The Burmese pagoda, generally square, resembles in general outline the Pyramid of Sakkhara; its proportionate height being much greater than that of the pyramid. One at Pegu is three hundred and sixty-one feet high, and its base only three hundred and ninety-five feet broad. One at Ava has in the colonnade of its first stage eight hundred and two columns of sandstone, each five feet high.

In China the bell-shaped flare of the curved roofs, in the style of a tent with pavilioned covering, adds grace to their pyramidal pagodas. To this class belonged the famous porcelain tower of Nanking, finished A. D. 1431. This pagoda, recently destroyed, octagonal in form, and two hundred and thirty-six feet high, was of brick covered with plates of porcelain. From its spire and projecting balconies forty-four bells of sweet tone, suspended by chains, kept up a musical chime as they swung with the wind.

In the islands of the Pacific are ancient architectural relics in the style of Burmah and Egypt. Among these is a pyramid fifty feet high with a base two hundred and seventy by ninety feet. In Western America, as Mexico and Peru, truncated and terraced pyramids abound; which Humboldt declares must have been built by a people whose culture was derived from Egypt. That at Cholula has a base 1426 feet broad, four times that of Cheops in Egypt, and an altitude of 162 feet. In later times Stephens has described many others.

SECT. 7. THE ARCHITECTURE OF ARABIA, PALESTINE, SYRIA, ASSYRIA AND PERSEPOLIS; THE ADVANCING PHASE OF THE MASSIVE STYLE.

In tracing the progress of the art of architecture, as well as of sculpture, along the eastern borders of the Mediterranean, the successive influence of several cultured nations is to be carefully discriminated.

In the peninsula of Mt. Sinai the tombs cut into the mountain sides are Egyptian. At Petra the massive rock-hewn temples with flat or pyramidal roof-peaks show Egyptian mingled with Grecian taste. Entering Syria, sacred as well as secular history, points to a long history of sacred edifices. Jacob's "pillar," called *Bethel*, the exemplar in name as well as character of the Celtic "Bothel" at Stonehenge, was succeeded by the temples of Baal in the north and Dagon in the south, of which Lucian says, "The Phœnicians built in the Egyptian style, though the people were of Dorian origin."

The Hebrew temple of Solomon, reared in an enclosure a quarter of a mile square, was planned by a Phœnician architect. Being ninety feet long, thirty feet broad, and forty-five feet high, having a tower one hundred and eighty feet high and two columns in front, it was manifestly Egyptian in type. The courts surrounding the house, with their porticoes, and the chambers for the college students, are in keeping with the Egyptian, Indian and Arabian sacred enclosures. The capitals of the two columns, seven and a half feet high, decorated with lily-work and pomegranates, and the carvings on the inner walls of palm trees and cherubs, are in keeping with the same central model. The reconstructed edifice built by Ezra, B. C. 530, was of the kindred Assyrian order; while the later structure of Herod, begun B. C. 15, was of the mingled Grecian and Oriental type favorite among the Romans..

Baalbek, built by Solomon in the valley between the Lebanon ranges, exhibits the architecture of three ages. The massive foundations of the great temple are of Hebrew origin; the ruins of three or four porticoes and colonnades are Greek Corinthian; and a small octagonal temple is of Roman construction, In the foundation are stones larger than in any known structure; three of these built into the wall twenty feet above ground being about sixty-four feet long, twelve feet wide, and twelve feet thick. The winged globe with encircling asps sculptured on the walls shows an Egyptian influence coming through Tyre.

A line of cities on the Euphrates and its tributaries, from Babylon to Persepolis, reveals a growing transition from Egyptian to Grecian ideas. Fergusson traces the introduction of the Ionic capital and other architectural ornaments from Persia to Asia Minor and thence to Greece.

CHAPTER III.

GRECIAN ARCHITECTURE; CHARACTERIZED BY MATHEMATICAL EXACTNESS IN FORMS AND DELICATE GRACE IN ADORNMENT.

THE germ of mathematical science, learned by the Greeks as their historians agree in Egypt, was applied with surpassing nicety by Grecian architects in the construction of their masterpieces. As in sculpture the Greeks secured life and expression, so in their architectural works they sought a lightness and grace inconsistent with Egyptian massiveness.

SECT. 1. THE INFLUENCE OF FACE OF COUNTRY AND MATERIAL IN GIVING CHARACTER TO GRECIAN ARCHITECTURE.

The Greeks lived in a mountain region; their citadels rose on rocky promontories such as the Acropolis of Athens and Corinth; and their temples, standing unenclosed, required a kindred finish on all sides. Their structures were but one story in elevation, with a low, gently sloping roof, and without tower or pylon in front.

The chief charm of the Grecian temple was its gable. The columns of the portico rose to the eaves; the slope of the roof above was the least possible to allow the shedding of rain; and the tympanum or open triangular space at the end of the roof furnished a sheltered niche for finely carved statuary.

The material for building furnished to Greek architects, white marble of the finest texture, aided the realization of their ideal.

SECT. 2. THE PERMANENCE AND COMPLETENESS OF GRECIAN COLUMNAR ARCHITECTURE.

Pliny, speaking of the labyrinth of Crete, says that Dædalus its architect "closely imitated in this structure the celebrated labyrinth of Egypt." Yet the earliest temples executed by Grecian architects were as distinct in their type as those of the day of Phidias. The beautiful and romantically situated temple of Jupiter Panhellenicos, on the elevated eastern shore of the island of Egina, which commands a panoramic view of Greece, built according to Pausanias before the Trojan war, is of the oldest and most massive columnar order.

The architectural works of Greece, alike in all their main features, have three distinct orders of columns. These orders, though their names, Doric, Ionic and Corinthian, are all found in the same age at Athens, are borrowed from three types of progress in culture; the purest specimen, the Parthenon, being of the oldest or most massive order. Their ideas and general features are graphically presented by Thomson:

> "*First* unadorned
> And nobly plain, the *manly Doric* rose;
> Th' *Ionic* then, with decent *matron* grace
> Her airy pillars heaved; luxuriant, last
> The rich *Corinthian* spread her *wanton* wreath."

The Doric derived its name from the Grecian colonists of Doris in Asia Minor; whose people surpassed even those of the mother country in art and science. Vitruvius says, "They sought that medium which should make these columns sufficiently strong to sustain the front of the edifice, and at the same time should render them agreeable to the view. In order to do this they took the measure of the foot of man, which is the sixth part of his height; upon which measure they formed the height of their column." The Ionic column originated among the Ionian islanders west of Greece. "They sought to introduce a new order of columns by giving to them the proportions of the female figure; and, that they might be emblematical of female delicacy, the height of the columns was eight times the lowest diameter. Bases also were given them in imitation of sandals, and volutes were sculptured in the capitals, in allusion to the ringlets which fell down on either side of the face." "And thus," he adds, "were two species of orders invented: one representing the strength and simplicity of man, the other the fine proportions and the elegance of woman."

The Corinthian column, whose proportions vary from eight to ten diameters of the lower part of the shaft, was suggested, as Vitruvius records, to Callimachus, the compeer of Phidias, under these circumstances: The nurse of a lovely maiden, who had died suddenly, placed her trinkets in a basket on her grave, covering it with a tile. In the spring an acanthus root beneath the basket shot up its tendrils, wound its leaves around it, and its branches were bent into spirals under the projecting tile. Callimachus passing by the spot, and observing the basket and the beauty of the young foliage entwined about it, adopted it in the columns of edifices at Corinth; which were thence called Corinthian.

The three orders of Grecian columns, because of their exhaustive analysis, have become comprehensive types for all succeeding architectural works. The proportions of the male and female form, like the letters of the alphabet and tones in the musical scale in all lands, have, in all ages, been observed and fixed. So in the principles of columnar architecture the Grecian artists reached an exhaustive analysis which allows no additional type to be conceived. As, however, in language and music there may be new study of details and new arrangement of parts, so in architecture there may be new groupings of previously recognized harmonies, and an introduction of new emblems selected from the productions of different climes.

The Greeks themselves have left no two specimens even of the same order alike in all their parts. Thus the Doric or robust order has at Pæstum in Italy four diameters as its modulus, and the portico of the Agora at Athens six; while in the monument of Lysicrates, and the tower of Andromicus, the foliated ornaments of the Corinthian capitals belong to flowers most unlike. As the Egyptian which preceded, so the Roman and Gothic which succeeded, recognized the *canon* of symmetry established by the Greeks in their orders; while the revived Grecian of M. Angelo, now a ruling type in modern architecture indicates the decision of great artists as to the completeness of Grecian analysis.

This, their own *canon*, guided the ablest Grecian builders. Thus in the Parthenon, elevated on the Acropolis, to be seen at such a distance that the finer ornaments would be lost, the Doric was used by Phidias; while in the sheltered vale below, the temple of Jupiter has the slighter and more elaborate Corinthian. The same principle of adaptation has led the architects of the Madeline at Paris and of the Girard College at Philadelphia, both modeled after the Doric Parthenon, to select the elaborate Corinthian capital; while, too, the architect of the U. S. Capitol has inwrought into the ornaments of Corinthian capitals, the corn of the northern sections, the tobacco of the middle latitudes, and the cotton of the Gulf States.

SECT. 3. THE ARRANGEMENT OF COLUMNS, WITH THEIR INTERCOLUMNIATIONS, ON WHICH THE DESIGNATION OF STYLES IN GRECIAN ARCHITECTURE IS FOUNDED.

The Greek temple, according to Vitruvius, should have a breadth equal to half its length. Columnar appendages may consist of one or more rows of columns placed in front, in front and rear, or on all sides of the temple; and they may be differently arranged and bestowed both as to number and to width of intervening spaces. The word style, from the Greek *stylos*, a pillar or column, as applied to an edifice, indicates the order of its columnar arrangements. The simplest style is that of the temple *in antis*, from *anti*, in which two columns stand in a recess in the gable front. The second, called *pro-style*, has a portico in front alone; the third, named *amphi-style*, has a portico at both ends; and the fourth, termed *peri-style*, has a colonnade on all sides; these names being successively derived from the Greek prepositions *pro*, *amphi* and *peri*, with the noun *stylos*. According, again, to the intervening distances of the columns, called *intercolumniation*, there are five different styles. Those having their columns one and one-half diameters apart are named *pycnostyle*, or close-set, from *pycnos*, the clenched fist; those two diameters apart *systyle*, or near-set, from *syn* together; those two and one-half diameters *eustyle*, or well-set, from *eu*, well or beautifully; those three diameters *diastyle*, or open-set, from *dia*, through or between; and those four diameters *areostyle* or wide-set, from *araios*, broad. According, once again, to the *number* of columns in the front row of the portico, temples were designated *tetrastyle*, *hexastyle*, *octostyle*, etc., *i. e.* four-columned, six-columned, eight-columned, etc.

The term *pteros*, a wing, properly applied only to circular buildings, originating among the Romans, was by them also applied to rectangular buildings, having no wings proper. A temple having a single row of columns on all sides was called *monopteral*, or single-winged; one having two rows on all sides was named *dipteral* or double-winged; and one having one row of columns and a corresponding row of pilasters, or half-columns fastened upon and projecting from the walls, was designated as *pseudo-dipteral*, or false double-winged. A temple having an open or unroofed centre was called *hypæthral*, from *hupo*, under, and *aithēr*, the air.

SECT. 4. THE SEVERAL PARTS OF THE GREEK TEMPLE, CONSPIRING TO GIVE GRACE TO GRECIAN ARCHITECTURE.

The three parts of an edifice giving character and expression to its architecture are the *columns;* the *entablature* or table capping, the columns, and the *pediment*, or roof-angle resting upon the entablature; to which may be added the *platform*, or surrounding ground-steps.

The parts of the column are the *base* or foot, the *shaft* or body, and the *capital* or head. The base of the columns is either square or round, plain or carved. The Doric column has properly no base; the Ionic and Corinthian base is a rounded and slightly projecting foot.

The shaft slants upward in a parabolic curve so slight that, like that of the tree, it denies its reality to the ordinary eye, but yet reveals itself to the searching analysis of the architect's measuring gauge. The *modulus* of the column, as of all portions of the Grecian temple, Vitruvius teaches, was the radius or half-diameter of the lower part of the shaft; and this was subdivided into sixty minutes, or equal minute parts. By application of this nice measure to the shaft of the column at different successive heights, passing from the base upward, it will be found to taper not in a straight slope, but in a parabolic curve.

The *fluting* of the shaft, the concave of the reed or flute, may be omitted in Doric and Ionic columns; or they may be fluted only at the top, leaving the exposed space at the bottom guarded against chipping. The flutes of the Doric are made to meet each other, leaving only a sharp intervening edge; but in the Ionic, they have a sharper curvature, leaving a narrow central band between them. The Corinthian, always fluted, has its grooves separated, as in the Ionic, by fillets or bands.

The extent to which philosophic study was carried by Grecian architects is illustrated by statements of Vitruvius. "The columns at the angles of buildings should have their diameters enlarged by a fiftieth part, because, being from their situation more immediately contrasted with the light, they hence appear less than the others." "The diminution of the shaft in its taper from the top to the bottom is to be thus regulated. To the eye the diameter of the column diminishes as its height increases; hence to preserve the same apparent proportion of the diameters it becomes necessary to increase that of the upper portion of the shaft. If, therefore, the height of the shaft be fifteen feet, the upper diameter should be five-sixths of the lower; if the shaft be from fifteen to twenty feet high, the upper should be eleven-thirteenths of the lower; if thirty feet high, the proportions should be thirteen-fifteenths; if from thirty to forty feet high, the diminution should be one-seventh; if from forty to fifty feet high, the decrease should be one-eighth." "If the width of the temple be more than one-half its length, the proportion should be apparently restored thus. Columns should be placed within and opposed to those between the antæ. These should be of correspondent height; but their diameters should be less in the following proportions: if the columns in front be eight times their diameter in height, the inner ones should be nine diameters; if the exterior be nine or ten diameters in height, the interior should preserve a proportionate augmentation. The difference in the bulk of the columns will not be apparent, because they will not be seen contrasted with the light. If notwithstanding they should appear too slender, the number of flutings should be increased. Thus if the columns in front have twenty-four flutes, the inner ones may have twenty-eight, or even thirty-two; so that what is in fact taken from the bulk may be restored by the additional number of flutings. This optical deception arises from the idea of greater magnitude which is impressed by the transit of the visual rays over a greater surface. For if the peripheries of two circles of equal diameter, one of which is fluted and the other not, be measured by a line which is made to be in contact with every point of the peripheries, the length of the line will not be the same in both cases; because in one it has been made to touch every point in the concave surfaces of the flutings in the intervals between the fillets. Since this deception therefore may be accomplished, it is allowable to make columns which are in confined situations and little exposed to the light less massive than the others, because their want of bulk may be rendered imperceptible by augmenting the number of flutings as circumstances may require."

The capital, as the column, has properly three divisions of its parts; an upper and a lower tablet and the moulding between. In the Doric capital the lower tablet is wanting; as the base is wanting in the Doric column. The moulding of the Doric is a plain ovolo; a curve named from its egg shape, and limited in size to a quadrant, whether the curve be a quarter of a circle, of an ellipse, of a hyperbola, or of a parabola. The ovolo of the Doric moulding has always the curve of a parabola, or hyperbola, never of a circle; the design being to reflect light to the eye looking from below in the most perfect manner.

The Ionic moulding consisted of two volutes, or scrolls, representing the curls of hair on each side of the female head; between which was a band, like the fillet worn on the brow of Grecian women, having as pendants from it two egg-shaped ovals, separated by triangular tongues, these pendants seeming to be the ornaments of jewelry strung upon the fillet. In the original Ionic, as employed in the Asiatic provinces of Greece, the capital had but two faces, a front and a rear face, while at the side the volutes rounded downward and inward like the smooth-combed puffs behind the curls of female hair; and the capital thus constructed had a finished character because it was always placed between *antæ* or other columns, and never at a corner. In Greece proper, however, where the Ionic column was used in porticoes, it was customary for the sake of harmony to give its moulding when standing at a corner, a side as well as a front face; a modification, as we shall see, still farther extended by the Roman architect.

The moulding of the Corinthian was a bell-shaped basket as a foundation, overlaid with intertwining stalks and leaves of the favorite acanthus, or of some other plant; as of the fern or the olive. The upper points of the leaves and stalks were represented as bent downward into curls from the resistance of the tablet or tile laid above them.

Above the columns the *entablature* is the second study in the Grecian temple. The entablature is to the range of columns what the capital is to the single column; it is the coping or capping of the entire work. The greater or less elaborateness of its finish was made to correspond with that of the columns in the same edifice. The entablature consists of three parts; the architrave, frieze and cornice.

The *architrave*, from *archē* and *trabs*, or main-beam, is the timber or row of stones laid immediately upon the caps of columns, and uniting them together. It projects slightly in front of the columns, whose capitals are its rests. In the Doric, the architrave is plain; but in the Ionic and Corinthian it is more or less elaborate.

The *frieze*, so called from the verb freeze or frizzle, to be contracted, is the middle and retired member of the entablature; corresponding to the shaft of the column, whose surface is depressed behind its base and capital. The surface of the frieze is divided into compartments, or panels, separated by small squares cut into three perpendicular bars with grooves between, and called triglyphs. One of these is placed over each column, and one or more between the columns; which squares project in front of the depressed face of the frieze, and represent, according to Vitruvius, the projected ends of rafters in the log cabin after which the Doric order is modeled. The intervening spaces between the triglyphs are called the metopes, or openings-between. These spaces, originally left open, were afterwards filled with slabs, as in the Parthenon, having sculpture in high-relief.

The *cornice*, or corona, is the projecting crown serving as the coping or cap of the entablature. The cornice is divided into its three parts; and these again in elaborate specimens, each into their three subdivisions; this tripartite division of the Greeks being carried into the minutest parts of their work. Underneath the projecting cornice are always to be noted the mutules or square blocks corresponding to the trygliphs over the columns, and having on their face small circular pendants called drops, because representing the rain drops, hanging over the triglyphs whose grooves serve as gutters for their descent. In later periods of the history of architecture modillions and brackets take the place of the mutules and triglyphs.

Yet above the entablature, as the third characteristic study of Grecian architecture, is the *pediment*. The base of the pediment is the upper part of the entablature; the sloping sides of the gable or roof-angle rest upon the cornice, projecting forward even with it and being finished in harmony, if not in perfect uniformity, with the cornice. The central triangular space called the tympanum, or drum, offering a deep and sheltered niche for sculpture, was regarded as the feature of the Grecian temple, giving it a celestial aspect. Thus Cicero remarks of the Capitol of Rome, "This same roof-peak of the Capitol and of other edifices, not grace, but necessity itself constructed. For when the reason of the case had suggested, how from each side of the house the water should be made to glide, thus securing utility to the temple, the idea of dignity attached to the roof-peak; so that if in heaven a capitol should be erected, where rain could not occur, it would seem that it would be regarded as not possessing dignity without a roof-peak."

An indication of the philosophic spirit that guided the Greek architect is hinted thus by Vitruvius: "All the members placed above the capitals of the columns, as the architrave, frieze, cornice, tympanum, etc., ought to be inclined forward each the twelfth part of its height; since, if a person looking at the face of an edifice conceives that two lines separate from the eye, one of which touches the bottom the other the top of the object of vision, it is certain

19 *

that which touches the top is the longer; and the farther up one line extends, the more it makes the upper part appear to tip backward; so that if the members which form the face of the upper portion are made to lean a little forward, the whole appears to be perfectly upright and plumb."

The platform, or steps which form the ascent to the Grecian temple, adds greatly to its beauty. Unlike the Egyptian, the floor of the Grecian temple was raised some feet above the ground; and the broad and easy flight of steps, with their slant as graceful as that of the roof-peak, formed a pedestal on which the fair structure stood. In a prostyle temple these steps went up only at the front; but in a peristyle structure on all sides.

Sect. 5. The Parthenon as the Embodiment of Grecian Genius in Architecture.

The Parthenon or temple of Minerva, the virgin patron of Athens, is perhaps the completest, as it was the most finished specimen of Grecian architecture. Standing as it does on the lofty rock of the Acropolis, in a position where it is exposed to the rudest blasts which sweep over the plains of Attica, its low massy Doric columns when seen in the distance, seem to be happily chosen as the order of its architecture; while its graceful roof, sloping upward at an angle of only 14°, allows the hurrying gales only to kiss its gently inclined face. As the observer approaches and climbs to the Acropolis enclosure through the Propylæa suddenly the whole peerless structure in one enchanting view breaks on his gaze. The temple stands about two hundred feet back from the Propylæa, about one hundred feet to the right, and raised some twenty feet above the beholder, presenting its southwest corner; thus permitting the eye to take in at a glance its entire length, breadth and height. It is now sadly shattered and dilapidated, its centre having been torn open by a Venetian bomb, A. D. 1687; but the large portion yet standing, together with the particular descriptions of such men as Vitruvius who saw it in the days of the first Roman emperor, and of Sir Geo. Wheeler who visited it as late as A. D. 1676, bring all its glory fresh before the gaze of the modern traveler.

This peerless model is two hundred and seventeen feet long and ninety-eight and a half feet broad. It is pure Doric; its columns being six diameters in height, each having twenty flutes, no base, and as a capital-moulding a simple ovolo. It is peristyle having columns on all sides; monopteral, its colonnade being a single row of columns; octo-style, having eight columns in front; pycno-style, the intercolumniations being one and a half diameters; and hypæthral, its inner shrine opening to the heavens, from whose floor the colossal Minerva lifted her majestic form thirty-eight feet. The architrave was plain and chaste; the metopes filled with the richest sculpture in relief; the cornice rich but not gaudy; and the tympanum of the pediment ornamented with majestic statuary. Finally the graceful slope of the low graded steps, ascending on all sides, gave a finished elevation to the entire structure.

Minute measurements of the Parthenon indicate two funda mental principles. The science which gave proportions requisite to strength and beauty in Grecian structures did not dictate mechanics' patterns, but hinted principles to save genius from error.

Again, every line in the stretch of the platform, in the taper of the column, in the sweep of the entablature, is a parabolic curve The centre of the platform on the sides of the temple is elevated twenty inches above the level of the ends of the same range, while the centre of the end range, or of the platform in front and rear of the temple, is correspondently raised; the effect of which is, in conformity with the laws of curvilinear perspective already considered, to give to the eye as it courses over the curved surface the impression of greater extent. To adjust the upward taper of the columns, each is made up of twelve separate blocks, whose outer side is about one inch thicker than the inner side; thus offsetting the slope of the platform, and giving the column a graceful slant inward.

As no tree or man has a fixed measure of dimension, either absolute or relative, so no two Grecian edifices are modeled one after another; nor is any one rigidly conformed to any fixed measure. This is strikingly seen in comparing any of the details above given as to the measurements of the Parthenon.

To describe every particular of the wonderful science entering into the art of the Grecian architect, would be as endless as was the ever-widening study and ever-growing perfection of the artist himself.

SECT. 6. HISTORY OF GRECIAN ARCHITECTURE TILL ITS DECLINE.

The history of Grecian architecture, as of sculpture, begins with Dædalus, before the Trojan war. An Athenian by birth, his first great works were a labyrinth and temple in Crete, then under the reign of the famous Minos; a river reservoir, and a mountain-fortress in Sicily; several palaces in Sardinia; and temples of Apollo at Capua and Cannæ in Southern Italy. Their names indicate that Egyptian ideas, to a considerable extent, prevailed.

The next stage is the introduction of the columnar orders. To this age belongs the Panhellenicon, on the island of Egina, and the early Ionic temple of Diana at Ephesus; the first two orders appearing together. The era of these finished architects is about the first Olympiad or B. C. 776.

The era of discussion as to the orders is the next advance. Vitruvius mentions Pytheus, who contended that the Doric column was not adapted to sacred edifices, "because deceptions and inconsistent proportions are executed in this order." Greek architects generally agreed that the Ionic should be employed only *in antis*, where its face alone was seen; though it was also used in full porticoes.

The culminating era of the Doric at the rebuilding of Athens about B. C. 450, was the climactic era of Grecian architecture. Phidias was general superintendent, Ictinus and Callicrates chief architects, when, about B. C. 438, the Parthenon, the peerless master-work, was finished.

The introduction of the Corinthian order, in the age succeeding Phidias, by Callimachus, a comprehensive genius in art, marks the final stage of the history of Grecian architecture. Though favorite in the provinces, Greece proper, especially Athens, was slow to admit the Corinthian. It was not until about B. C. 175, that the temple of Jupiter Olympus on the plain under the Acropolis was erected after the Corinthian order; while the Choragic Monument, so exquisite a gem of the same style, was of a still later date.

The celebrated Temple of Diana, at Ephesus, embodied the history of Grecian architecture. The first rude edifice was Asiatic in style. The second, begun about 776 B. C., was four hundred and twenty-five feet long, and two hundred and twenty feet broad; its peripteral portico embraced one hundred and twenty-seven columns sixty feet high, each composed of one block of Parian marble with Ionic capitals; and the whole exterior was enriched with the most costly decorations. When burned by the wretch Herostratus, Alexander, on his Eastern expedition, directed Dinocrates to rebuild it with more than its former magnificence. Restored and made the treasure-house of the gems of art left by such sculptors as Praxiteles and Scopas, and of such painters as Parrhasius and Apelles, it continued even for ages after the Christian era, one of the glories of the world.

CHAPTER IV.

ROMAN ARCHITECTURE; CHARACTERIZED BY STATELINESS IN DIMENSIONS AND PROFUSE ELEGANCE IN ORNAMENTATION.

THE Greeks were ideal, the Romans eminently practical. In sculpture, therefore, the Romans never approached the Greeks. In architecture, whose end is utility, the Romans originated new principles, invented new styles and employed new methods.

The Roman architects aimed at elaborated strength; not the mere massiveness of the Egyptians. Hence among their earliest as well as latest triumphs in architecture, were military constructions such as bridges and aqueducts.

When the age for added refinement came, their effort at finish showed itself in what Cicero calls "a manly and robust ornament." It added to the light grace of the Grecian columnar capitals greater strength to sustain a heavier superincumbent weight; leading naturally to an excess of ornament. This departure from the chasteness of "learned Greece," who gave rules "when to repress and when indulge our flights," led to the style called in the Latin, "elegant."

These two characteristics, strength and elegance, and their application by the Romans to different classes of structures reared in their own city and in other climes, through succeeding ages of culture and of decline, hint a natural division of the subject of Roman architecture.

SECT. 1. THE INTRODUCTION OF CURVED LINES IN GROUNDPLOT AND ELEVATION, GIVING BREADTH AND STATELINESS TO ROMAN ARCHITECTURE.

In sculpture the Greeks perfected the beauty of the curved line; while in their rectangular temple fronts they gave such mathematical nicety to straight-line combinations, that Cicero said these could not be improved in heaven itself. The Romans first employed curved lines, not simply as had the Egyptians and Greeks in the ornaments of capitals and cornices, but also in the groundplot and elevation of edifices. The two ends sought were spaciousness and elegance.

Nearly all the architectural works of the Greeks were temples; and these had a rectangle for a base. The Pantheon, and the tomb of Marcellus, now the Castle of St. Angelo, still standing at Rome, are specimens of a complete circle as a groundplot; the Coliseum, the most majestic pile in the world, has an entire and perfect ellipse as its base; while many of the smaller Roman temples are circular, and most of their theatres have a half circle or half ellipse as their ground-outline.

The Egyptians even under a flat roof and straight lintel, secured breadth of hall and door-way by the immense length of the overlapping stones which they raised and laid across their side-walls. The Greeks used a sloping roof as a water shed, giving its pitch for beauty's sake the slightest slant possible; occasioning thus, however, an almost direct outward thrust, to overcome which without outside props they built up inner supporting walls, whose intervention allowed a limited breadth of interior. The Romans wished broad gate and door-ways, and lofty spreading roof-elevation, without the clumsy Egyptian method of securing the former, and vastly beyond any invented power to attain the latter; and they dared to use, if they did not invent, the circular arch, by which the former end was accomplished, and the dome by which, for all the world and for all time, the latter aim was realized.

The Brahmins of India knew the principle of the circular arch; and understanding the law of its constantly pressing and dislocating lateral thrust, they embodied their objection to its use in larger edifices in the maxim, "the arch never sleeps." All the so-called arches used by the ancient and modern Asiatics, as in pagodas, are built after the plan of a boy's cob-house; by pinning beam after beam in layers above each other. In the circular arch, curved into a half-cylinder, each course of stone rising from the foundation has the outer rim higher than the inner, the upper and lower faces of its blocks lying in planes cutting the axis of the cylinder; and when the keystone is fitted into the apex the several tiers are sustained by their own pressure against each other.

In the dome, again, curved into a hemisphere, while the upper and lower faces of each course of stones conform to the law of the arch, the side faces lie in planes cutting the axis of the hemisphere at its zenith, perpendicular to its base, each course of stones being supported by the pressure of its faces on each other. As there is in the arch and dome both a downward and outward pressure, there must be in its foundation, both a mass and disposition of material, which shall secure a perpendicular support and a lateral bracing adequate to serve as a counterpoise to the crush and the thrust. The very earliest great architectural works of the Romans show their thorough and practical understanding both of the nice theory, and of the nicer execution essential to this end.

SECT. 2. MODIFICATIONS OF THE GREEK COLUMNAR ORDERS; GIVING INCREASED PROFUSION OF ELEGANT ORNAMENTATION TO ROMAN EDIFICES.

The plain walls of a rectangular building have a chaste beauty requiring no ornamentation. The walls of a towering circular edifice, however, require the relief of projecting pilasters or columns; as is seen in the elaborately ornamented Coliseum. The Roman architects resorted to two modifications of the Grecian styles; the use of pilasters or half columns merely projecting from the exterior wall, instead of complete columns standing out as supports of a portico at some distance from that wall; and the employ in their elevations of successive stories having columns of different orders.

The first of these modifications affecting the styles of Greek architecture arose from the fact that a dome-roof must rest directly on the side walls of the edifice and cannot project beyond them so as to cover a portico; while pilasters or half columns, built into the wall, require only a slightly projecting cornice. To give prominence to the entrance, a purely Grecian portico with columns, entablature and pediment, was projected in front of a circular edifice, as in the Pantheon. In smaller edifices, like the shrine of Vesta at Rome, the light roof of wood, projecting over the wall, formed a rotunda, sustained by a circlet of delicate Corinthian columns. Behind these columns, both in the Grecian portico and the Roman rotunda, instead of a second row of columns, corresponding pilasters were fastened upon the circular wall. Carrying this idea still farther, the walls of rectangular buildings were ornamented with false pilasters; mere flat slabs carved with the flutes, the cap and the base of a column fastened to the plain straight wall in place of the rounded half column projected from the circular wall; as is seen constantly illustrated in every modern European and American city.

The second modification affected the *orders* of Grecian columnar architecture. The Grecian temple had only one story, its columns rising to the eaves. The greater elevation of the Roman edifice demanded different stories, each with its own columnar decorations. Grecian taste, revived under M. Angelo, might have taught that the same order of columns should be employed in each story. The Romans, with a less chastened love of simplicity, used different orders of columns at different elevations; and since the three Grecian orders did not furnish the variety their method demanded, they invented two additional ones.

The Tuscan order was nothing else than an improved gate-post of the carpenter, boxed and capped. Vitruvius fixed as its height seven diameters; the taper of the shaft one-fourth of its diameter; the base in two parts, the lower one-half the diameter of the shaft in height; the capital of the same height as the base. The plainness of the Tuscan has made it in modern Roman basement stories, and in Romanesque buildings, the chosen order. The Doric, used by the Romans in arcades allowing only a half column, for uniformity with the other orders had a base. The Ionic, made stouter than the Grecian, having at its corners, front and side, curls clustered and projected diagonally, was used sometimes in porticoes, but generally in elevations between the Doric and Corinthian. In the Corinthian, in order that the capital might seem adequate to the heavier weight imposed upon it, the Romans entwined with the Greek leaf decoration strong spike-shaped horns. They also retained a fifth order, the composite; whose capital unites to the volutes of the Ionic the foliate decorations of the Corinthian. In the Coliseum the lower stage is Doric, the second Ionic, the third Corinthian, the fourth Composite. In the façade of one of the older college edifices at Oxford, England, the five orders, with the Tuscan below, are presented together.

SECT. 3. VARIED CLASSES OF BUILDINGS AND MODES OF STRUCTURE REQUIRED BY THE CIRCUMSTANCES, CHARACTER AND HABITS OF THE ROMAN PEOPLE.

The climate of Rome, more inclement than that of Grecian cities, required walls and roofs more enclosed. The Roman Forum had arcades with closely-clustered columns, requiring a modification of its model in the Greek agora. The Roman baths, with their broad arched chambers, required by their climate, were a field for architectural adaptations unknown in Greece.

The peculiar relations socially of the Roman patricians to the plebeians called for the basilica; at first a hall in the mansion of the patrician, then a separate edifice. It usually consisted of a central hall two stories high, with wings one story in height, giving double area for the audience room. A row of short strong columns, not obstructing the view and hearing of the auditory, sustained arches in the central wall. In front was a Grecian portico. The basilica thus constructed has become the chosen model for Christian audience-rooms.

The Roman theatre and amphitheatre, of immense area, and necessarily uncovered, except by small awnings, are, in their vast proportions, monuments of the grandeur of the Roman conception of architectural proportions.

Many of the Roman temples were of Grecian type, though more adorned; as is seen in their remains along the Roman Forum. Others were of circular form; as the temple of Vesta on the Tiber, twelve feet only in diameter, with straight wooden rafters; and the Pantheon spanned by that wonder of the world, a dome one hundred and thirty-two feet across at its base.

SECT. 4. HISTORY OF ROMAN ARCHITECTURE; THE CURVILINEAR ETRUSCAN UNDER THE KINGS; THE RECTANGULAR AND COLUMNAR GRECIAN UNDER THE REPUBLIC AND EARLIER EMPERORS; AND THE ADAPTATION OF BOTH THESE UNDER THE CHRISTIAN EMPERORS, TO NEW RELIGIOUS USES.

Three periods in the history of architecture at Rome correspond to the three great eras in her political history. The first is the Etruscan age covering the age of the Roman kings; having the Greco-Asiatic type of the primitive Romans. The second is the Grecian age beginning under the Republic, and culminating under the first emperor, the era of Greek columnar ornamentation. The third began with Christian civilization, giving a Roman cast to church architecture.

The Etruscans, coming from Western Asia to Northern Italy about B. C. 1200, brought in mingled Asiatic and Grecian ideas in sculpture and architecture. Their tombs were circular and arched above; one at Vulci being two hundred and forty feet in diameter and one hundred and twenty feet in height. Their temples were, as Vitruvius states, of two kinds, circular and rectangular. The rock-hewn amphitheatre of Sutri, in form an ellipse of slight eccentricity, has as its diameters two hundred and ninety-five and two hundred and sixty-five feet.

At the founding of Rome, B. C. 753, the Etruscan builders were employed as architects. The Cloaca Maxima, or great sewer, executed as early as B. C. 616, extending as a drain from the Forum, or market, to the river Tiber, is fourteen feet in diameter and seven feet in height. The arch is double; the rows of stones about five feet long and three and a half feet in thickness, though laid without cement, having retained their place for two thousand five hundred years. The Capitol, dedicated about B. C. 507, and the Pantheon, with an exterior diameter of one hundred and forty-four feet, and a dome one hundred and thirty-two feet in breadth and elevation, resting on walls six feet thick, were built about the close of the age of the Roman kings.

The republic, Grecian in its idea, and having the laws of Solon as its code, invited Grecian taste in architecture. As early as B. C. 500, Greek artists were employed at Rome; and Grecian culture, growing in the best days of the republic, culminated under the first emperor, Augustus, about B. C. 31. A few years later the theatre of Marcellus was built, the portico of the Pantheon was added, and several of the rectangular temples, whose noble columns now stand along the old Forum, were reared; works whose relics justify the boast of the first emperor, "That he had found the city built of brick, and he left it built of marble." The Coliseum, built under Vespasian, the Arch of Titus, the Basilica and Column of Trajan, Hadrian's temple of Jupiter Olympus, the Arch of Septimius Severus, the Baths of Caracalla, and finally the Basilica of Maxentius, following each other, down to A. D. 306, indicate the sway of Grecian taste under the emperors. The noblest of these was the Coliseum, an elliptical amphitheatre, with its diameters six hundred and twenty, and five hundred and thirteen feet, having an exterior wall elevated to the height of one hundred and fifty-seven feet, adorned with four stages of pilasters, with seats supported by arcades, sloping downward from the wall's giddy height to the arena in the centre, and accommodating one hundred and seven thousand spectators.

At the introduction of Christianity private houses for a time served as places for religious assembly. The Roman basilica was naturally the first model when structures specially designed for Christian worship were reared. When afterward the religion of Christ became the State religion, temples of the deities, the circular Pantheon and the rectangular temple of Jupiter, were devoted to Christian purposes; while also special forms adapted to the new faith arose.

SECT. 5. INFLUENCE OF THE ROMAN CIVIL DOMINATION ON THE STYLES OF ARCHITECTURE IN THE ROMAN PROVINCES.

Rome had no native ideal in sculpture; but it originated masterly types in architecture to extend and transmit. Its influence on religious structures was only modifying, not originating. The Roman idea that every country has its own native deities, led them to build Grecian temples in Greece, and Egyptian in Egypt. On neither of these fixed types in their native home could it do more than add its own idea of ornament.

In Arabia Petræa, Palestine and Syria, however, true Roman ideas are met. The Roman method permitted Doric and Corinthian pilasters, surmounted by either the Egyptian abacus and pyramid, or the Roman arch. At Jerusalem the golden gateway with its circular arch and Corinthian pilasters, the tombs with Ionic pilasters and pagoda-shaped domes, were executed by Roman artists between the times of the Jewish Herod and of the Emperor Hadrian. At Baalbeck the long range of Corinthian columns standing on old Asiatic foundations, reveal even in the rudest engraving, the influence of the Roman colony, planted by Julius Cæsar and fostered by the Antonines.

While in Africa Roman influence in architecture was modifying, and in Asia controlling, in Northern Europe it was originating. In Spain, France, Germany and England, the Roman arch and pilaster still rule in every class of structures.

CHAPTER V.

SACRED ARCHITECTURE, AS CONTROLLED BY THE SPIRITUAL WORSHIP AND THE PRACTICAL CHARITY OF THE CHRISTIAN FAITH.

THE progress of Christianity, first among Asiatics, then among Greeks and Romans, strikingly illustrated as it is by the relics of Christian literature, is equally marked by remains of varied styles in sacred architecture.

Living under the Roman civil sway, proud as some were to claim, "I am a Roman citizen," it was natural that the early Christians should in things not inconsistent with their religious principles follow Roman ideas. The two main characteristics in sacred edifices required by the Christian faith were already associated in Roman structures; the securing of a broad ground floor for large audiences; and the attaining of lofty elevation expressive of the exalting influence of the Christian faith. Art conceptions already prevailing in the three distinct regions where Christianity had its early seat, led to three preferred styles of Church Architecture; the Romanesque dominant in Southern Europe; the Byzantine in the East; and the Gothic in Northern and Western

Europe. In respect to time four eras are marked; *first*, the classical from A. D. 100 to 323, during which old forms without special adaptation to new ideas, prevailed; *second*, the Romanesque and Byzantine, from A. D. 323 to 692, during which the rivalries of the Eastern and Western Empires stimulated a rivalry for architectural supremacy in the two branches of the Christian church; *third*, the Gothic, from A. D. 692 to 1400, beginning with the settlement of the Ostrogoths in Northern Italy; and *fourth*, the revived Grecian, commencing with M. Angelo and the incomparable St. Peter's at Rome. Intervening between the Byzantine and Gothic, the Saracenic or Mohammedan sacred architecture claims notice. Finally the multiform styles introduced by the Reformation in Northern and Western Europe close the history.

SECT. 1. THE ROMANESQUE STYLE OF CHURCH ARCHITECTURE; FOUNDED ON THAT OF THE ROMAN BASILICA.

As the modern Greek language was half a century ago called Romaïque, from the modifying influence which Roman conquest and succeeding Italian supremacy had for ages exerted upon the spoken tongue of old Greece, so the Roman cast given to the first Christian sanctuaries, was called in early Christian art Romanesque, to distinguish it from later fixed and finished styles.

Modeled after the basilica, already described, the churches of the Romanesque style, common in Northern Italy, have this general form. In the earliest, built at Rome, the main roof, which in true Roman had a pitch of 45°, took a slope of about 25°; the walls supporting the central roof had a very slight elevation above the shed roof of the wings; and the exterior was perfectly unadorned. Northward the roof-slant became steeper, as in the Lombard, till under the Alps it approximated the wedge-shaped roof of the Gothic. As taste suggested, and wealth allowed, the elevation of the central portion over the side wings was increased; and the unseemly obtuse angle, formed between the wall of the upper story and the roof of the wings, was filled in with a shield presenting the form of an immense double scroll.

At an early day Christian sentiment gave to the groundplot of the basilica the form of the cross. In the cross, or tree, to which the victim was nailed, the longer portion of the post against which the body was hung, below the cross-beam to which the arms were fastened. In sculptural and architectural representations, art naturally fixed a rule of definite proportions for the length of these parts; this proportion in the groundplot of a Roman church, established by a canon in the "Apostolic Constitutions," being an equal measure for the projecting head and arms of the cross, and twice that common measure for its foot. As this cross section interfered with the side wings, these were gradually diminished in width; till, lost for a time in the early Gothic, they reappeared in the flying buttresses. The figure of Noah's ark suggested the designation *nave*, from *navis*, for the longer portion or body of the church, occupied by the people; the upper portion, occupied by the priests, was called the *choir;* and the two arms were named the *transept*, from the cross-hedge or screen separating them.

Tertullian, in the second century, mentions superb church edifices, which, as works of art, won Greeks to the Christian faith. Under Diocletian, a magnificent Christian sanctuary stood nigh the emperor's palace in Nicomedia, riv ıling it in architectural merit. Early in the fourth century, no less than forty church edifices at Rome claimed esteem for Christian art. The Basilica or Romanesque style had elements which made it worthy of perpetuation in Northern Italy.

SECT. 2. THE BYZANTINE STYLE OF CHURCH ARCHITECTURE; HAVING THE GREEK CROSS FOR ITS GROUNDPLOT, AND THE ROMAN DOME FOR ITS ELEVATION.

The Romanesque or Basilica, first used in Christian sanctuaries, gave one of the two Christian ideas, breadth but not elevation. The Roman Pantheon embodied both; and, transferred by Constantine to his new city on the Bosphorus, the dome became glorious in the church edifices of the East.

The outward thrust of the hemispherical dome, met in the Pantheon by the extreme thickness and mere massiveness of the circular walls, was sustained in the Byzantine church by eight bracing walls meeting in four right angles at the intersection of the nave and transept. Greek symmetry suggested that the concentring arms of this cross thus supporting the dome should be of the same measure; the nave being made equal in length to the choir and arms of the transept.

Constantine employed this style at his capital, and his mother

Helena in Palestine. Its noblest monuments now existing belong to the era two hundred years later. The mosque el-Aksa on the south of the temple area at Jerusalem, a structure two hundred and eighty by one hundred and ninety feet, reared and dedicated to Sophia, or Wisdom, by Justinian, about A. D. 529, preserved by the Mohammedan conqueror of the city about A. D. 685, and consecrated as a Mohammedan mosque, is to this day reverenced alike by Christian and Mohammedan.

The magnificent mosque of St. Sophia at Constantinople, whose splendor led to the boast of Justinian, the builder, *Nenikēsa sē Salomon*, "I have surpassed thee, Solomon," consecrated as a Christian church, A. D. 527, was, at the taking of Constantinople by the Turks, A. D. 1453, made a Mohammedan mosque. The length of each section of the cross is two hundred and sixty-nine feet, the breadth one hundred and forty-three feet, the diameter of the dome one hundred and fifteen feet, and its apex one hundred and eighty feet above the floor. The edifice is of brick, the inside walls are ceiled with marble, and the floor is inlaid with variegated marble tesseræ. Around the walls runs a gallery supported by forty columns, eight of white porphyry from the Temple of the Sun at Rome, eight others of serpentine, from the Temple of Diana at Ephesus, and twenty-four of Egyptian red granite. The interior of the dome was carved and painted in the richest style of the times with Christian themes; all of which were covered with stucco by the Mohammedan proprietors.

The Church of the Holy Sepulchre at Jerusalem, towering over the western foot of the northern mountain ridge called Millo by the Hebrews, and Akra by the Greeks, covering the jutting rock called Golgotha in the Hebrew, *kranion* in the Greek, *calvarium* in Latin, and *skull* in English, and also the valley where was an ancient "garden," embodies the history of the style of architecture to which it belongs. On the site thus hallowed, marked from the age of Titus to Hadrian by the northern wall of Zion, then till Constantine by Hadrian's temple to Venus, Helena, the Christian empress, about one hundred and fifty years after Hadrian, reared a small chapel over the tomb, and a large Basilica on Golgotha; which existed till destroyed, A. D. 614, by Chosroes, the Persian. Rebuilt on the plan of Helena, respected by Omar at the Mohammedan conquest of Jerusalem, A. D. 686, they stood till razed by a new invader, A. D. 1010. Byzantine art now triumphed over Roman, and instead of two Romanesque structures, one immense domed structure arose, finished by the Crusaders A. D. 1099; which is still standing, about three hundred feet long, by two hundred wide, covering the entire garden, embracing thirteen chapels, the chief of which are over Golgotha and the tomb. The Byzantine of the East was the preferred and controlling form with Western Christians at Jerusalem; who went home to rear churches of a far different style among their Gothic ancestry, and amid their native mountains.

SECT. 3. THE GOTHIC STYLE OF CHURCH ARCHITECTURE; CHARACTERIZED BY STEEPNESS OF ROOF WITH BRACING BUTTRESSES, AND BY POINTED SPIRES AND WINDOWS FOR ORNAMENT.

While the Byzantine style was rising in the East, the Roman Basilica, even in its Italian home, was for two causes declining. First, genius was attracted from Rome to the new capital; second, a new race of men, the Goths, independent in sentiment, resisting invasion of their own native customs and taste, but taking on a moulding influence from Roman culture, gradually developed a new type of architecture which reacted across the Alps.

The elementary features and essential principles of architecture, belonging to every age and every school, have been, with exhaustive analysis, applied to the Gothic by M. Viollet le Duc, the present chief architect of the French government. These elements are the walls and roof, whose strength and pitch are controlled by climate; the doors, windows and columns, whose measure is taken from man, for whose convenience and to whose dimensions they must be adapted; and the sculptured decorations of interior and exterior, whose types have been drawn from the two fields of human and Divine workmanship, the geometric and arborescent.

A pencil sketch may indicate how the roof, beginning with the level Egyptian has grown into the low Grecian, the medium Roman, the steeper Lombard, and finally the sharp-peaked Gothic. This latter, beginning with the Swiss cottages of the Alps, is traced to the inclement north through Switzerland, Germany, France and England. The support of this steep roof called for a modification of the circular Roman arch; and the high-pointed arch, probably unstudied at first, reached a perfection which bears the test of the most rigid mathematical analysis. The Gothic arch is made up of two arcs of a circle, each having its lower end resting upon a side wall, while the two upper extremities lean against each other at the apex. The downward and lateral pressure of the circular arch may be reduced to two resultants, one on each side, lying in the direction of chords of 60° passing through the extremities of the diameter; while that of the Gothic arch lies in the direction of the chord of two-thirds of the arc forming either of the two sides. To sustain the Roman arch, whose outward thrust is in a line departing at an angle of 60° outside of the wall, requires great solidity in the wall, or a strong outside bracing. The lateral thrust of the Gothic roof is less than the Roman; but its downward pressure is greater because of its great height.

The much criticised suggestion of Warburton, that the idea of Gothic architecture was derived from the intertwining of the boughs of forest trees forming natural arches, M. Viollet le Duc has no hesitation in announcing as to the interior decorations. Indeed the Gothic architects show a profound study of embryologic types as well as of floral, orchard and forest varieties in their arborescent ornaments. Even the curves of re-entering arches called *trefoil* and *cinqfoil* seem in their very name to assert this analogy.

Gothic architecture never prevailed south of Milan; whose cathedral mingles Grecian window-caps and statues with Gothic ideas. Working northward, the Gothic pervaded Switzerland, Germany, France and England.

In England there have been three eras in the history of Gothic. The pointed Gothic arch was an angle very acute; the pure Gothic was fixed at 60°; and the Tudor, going to an opposite extreme, used an obtuse-angled arch. Dalloway has compared the first with the Doric, the second with the Ionic and Corinthian, and the third with the Composite in Roman architecture.

The earliest style was the "pointed," called in its extreme the "lancet." It was the arch of a window cut under the sharp roof of a Swiss cottage. Introduced into both England and France under Stephen, the last of the Normans, about A. D. 1150, it prevailed about a century. The thick side walls made the entrance seem a deep, cave-like recess. The door was very low; at each side were very narrow windows called in the Italian *lanceola*, or lancet; and above the door one much wider. The pinnacles, already existing in Norman architecture, were repeated in the early Gothic.

The second or pure Gothic, prevailed from about A. D. 1240 to A. D. 1380, till the reign of Henry IV. The angle of the roof and of the arch was 60°; buttresses were projected, supporting flying buttresses; brackets were added under the cornice for relief; and pinnacles were raised above the buttresses, having niches often for statues. The walls consequently were made less thick, the doorway was higher and the entrance-way less deeply recessed; the windows had greater width; the mullions, or bars between the panes, were broad and delicately fluted like columns; and trilobe and rose windows were introduced. The columns of the interior, also, as well as the archings, were lighter and more airy.

The third style, called "obtuse" from the angle of its arch, and "florid" from the superfluous ornament heaped upon it, began to prevail about A. D. 1380, ran into the Tudor about A. D. 1420, and held sway till A. D. 1550. It depressed the Gothic arch and introduced projecting portals over the doors; it divided the windows by horizontal transoms, made the mullions elaborate with carvings, and pierced their paneled hoods with tracery-work; while it divided the area of the windows into trefoils and quatrefoils, and inserted in them armorial bearings. Finally, in the Tudor proper, it introduced projecting bay-windows, corresponding to the projecting portals.

Along the Rhine the Cathedral of Freiburg is one of the purest specimens of a single Gothic spire; that of Strasburg has two towers, the loftiest of which is four hundred and sixty-six feet in height; and that of Cologne, finished after six centuries, is the grandest in design. The old Cathedrals of Aix la-Chapelle, of Paris and Rheims, are most expressive of the gloomy sentiment to which this style of church architecture may be adapted. The ceiling of the Chapel of Henry the Eighth in Westminster Abbey, London is a perfect wonder of science and art; the laws of pressure in the arches by which its pendants are supported being now an inextricable puzzle.

SECT. 4. THE SARACENIC, OR STYLE OF MOHAMMEDAN SACRED ARCHITECTURE; HAVING THE HEBREW GROUNDPLOT AND THE BYZANTINE ELEVATION.

The Saracenic style of architecture prevailing in Western Asia, Northern Africa, Spain and European Turkey is a striking illustration of the mingling of Hebrew and Christian ideas introduced by Mohammed into the Koran, to commend his religion as the restored primitive worship of the patriarch Abraham. The first sacred structure worthy of mention erected by the followers of Mohammed was reared on the very spot where the Hebrew temple had stood, and conformed strictly to its groundplot. Its architect had on the south of that same area the Byzantine church of Justinian as a model; and only varied from it by filling up the four entering angles of the Greek cross, so as to form an octagonal edifice.

The mosque has always around it the open court-yard of the Egyptian and Hebrew temple. It grafted the conical pagoda spires of India upon the Roman dome; and added tall towers, like the Chinese in form, called minarets. Into the arches of the gateways and surrounding colonnades the features of the Roman arcade were introduced; whose arches afterward assumed the pointed form like the Gothic. In the Saracenic, too, the mitre and acorn-shaped arches, afterward used in Gothic architecture, received their highest perfection of form. The suggestion is not without foundation that the perfected Gothic borrowed many of its features from the Saracenic between the age of Charlemagne and the close of the Crusades.

In the later and more elaborately ornamented style, called "Moorish," ranges of arches of horse-shoe form are introduced into the parapets and balcony railings; sometimes merely cut in wood, sometimes also built in brick and stone. At the era of the advanced culture of the Moors in Spain, a style called "Arabesque" because of its Arab origin, grew up, which loaded the Saracenic arch with an excess of ornamentation, illustrated in the Alhambra, and akin to the embossed work now bearing that name.

SECT. 5. THE REVIVED GRECIAN STYLE IN SACRED CHRISTIAN ARCHITECTURE; HAVING THE LATIN CROSS AS ITS GROUNDPLOT, THE BYZANTINE DOME AS ITS ELEVATION AND THE PURE GRECIAN ORDERS IN ITS COLUMNAR DECORATIONS.

The pure Grecian columnar orders, first modified by the Romans, then successively displaced in Byzantine, Gothic and Saracenic structures, were as truly forgotten as was Grecian art in sculpture. A series of progressive steps led on to its revival with entirely new applications in the St. Peter's of M. Angelo.

The merchants of Venice and Pisa, borrowing from the East, mingled Saracenic and Byzantine elements and embodied them in sacred structures. St. Mark's in Venice, begun A. D. 976, has a Byzantine groundplot and dome; and the Cathedral of Pisa grafts these features on a Roman Basilica.

The merchants of Florence, determined to outrival both their sister cities, secured in 1294 a plan of a basilica five hundred feet long, three hundred and six feet across the transept, and one hundred and fifty-three feet in elevation. Through the death of the architect the work failed for four generations; until a young artist, Bruneschelli, had the daring not only to attempt the work before planned, but to erect over it a dome like the Pantheon in grandeur. For months the city authorities spurned the young artist as a visionary; but, yielding, Bruneschelli completed a dome one hundred and thirty-eight feet and six inches in diameter, one hundred and thirty-three feet and three inches in height, and three hundred and eighty-seven feet in elevation. When yet a child M. Angelo studied this work; and at seventy-two years of age he surpassed it in St. Peter's. This dome rests on a drum or circular wall, built on immense piers, with concentric arches spanning the openings below leading into the nave, choir and transept, and is braced outside by abutting arches springing from the drum to the walls.

The Cathedral of Florence was scarcely finished when, in 1450, the ecclesiastical authorities at Rome began, as Gibbon says, "the most glorious structure that has ever been applied to the use of religion." In honor of St. Peter, who, from the baptism of Cornelius, A. D. 43, to his death, A. D. 68, a period of twenty-five years, was, as Jerome says, eminent at Rome, the spot northwest and outside of the ancient city where he was crucified was covered by his friends with a small oratorio. This, Constantine, A. D. 306, caused to be replaced by a basilica; which stood, occasionally renovated, for twelve hundred years. The foundations of the new church were laid A. D. 1506; eight years after which the original architect, Bramante, died.

About A. D. 1540, Michel Angelo, then in his seventy-second year, was called to undertake the work from which other artists shrank. He enlarged Bramante's plan, adding to the transept so as to make the form a Greek cross, and giving strength to the piers supporting the dome, uttering the memorable declaration, "I will hang the Pantheon in the air." M. Angelo died A. D. 1563, when the drum was ready for the dome. Succeeding architects extended the nave, restoring the form of the Roman cross. In 1626, the structure was dedicated; the circular colonnade being added forty years later.

The length of this immense edifice is six hundred and thirteen and a half feet; its breadth through the transept is four hundred and forty-six and a half feet, and the height of the ceiling is one hundred and fifty-two and a half feet. The exterior breadth of the dome is one hundred and ninety-five and a half feet; its interior one hundred and thirty-nine and a quarter feet; the height of its apex is four hundred and five feet, and the elevation of the top of the cross four hundred and forty-eight feet. It covers two hundred and forty thousand square feet, or about five and a half acres of ground; a village of mechanics live on its roof; and the ball accommodates eight persons. Its original cost was nearly $47,-000,000; the annual expenditure for its care is about $30,000.

As Byron intimates, at first "its grandeur overwhelms not;" because every part is equally colossal, and, like Niagara, each detail must be viewed alone before the whole can be appreciated. Its true beauty is the feature called "Revived Grecian," the employ at every stage in the exterior of the same order of columns.

St. Paul's in London, built by Sir Christopher Wren, from A. D. 1666 to 1696, has a length of five hundred feet, a width of two hundred and eighty-six feet, and a height to the top of the cross of four hundred and four feet. The impression of vastness is greater than in St. Peter's, since the interior is less obstructed by columns, galleries and chapels. In the Pantheon at Paris, in form a Roman cross with Corinthian porticoes, the nave is three hundred and two feet, the transept two hundred and fifty-five feet long, and the dome two hundred and sixty-eight feet high. In England and America this style has been much more copied in secular than in sacred edifices.

Sect. 6. The modifications of form and style in church edifices suggested in the progress of Christianity.

The spread of Christianity, gaining sway purely by the moral conviction it awakens, has been like the growth of a tree, by stages. The early Christians, energetic in their spiritual work, had little time or means to devote to sacred art. In the progress of Christian culture under Constantine and Chrysostom, Justinian and Augustine, Charlemagne and Alcuinus, Leo and M. Angelo, the four styles of sacred architecture mentioned arose; the spirit of centralization culminating in St. Peter's. The spirit of the Reformation, associated with that intense sentiment of personal independence belonging to the Germans and Anglo-Saxons, forbade the concentration of interests and material resources in a few grand edifices. At the same time this independence has led to great variety in selection of styles for church edifices.

In Switzerland the prevailing type is Gothic, often rude; the Cathedral of Geneva illustrating the early, and that of Constance the later type. The Cathedrals of Zurich and Schaffhausen are Romanesque; while at Basle, near Germany, the Cathedral, though Gothic in general, is without the range of classified art. In Germany basilicas are met in old cities; the Cathedrals of Vienna and Freiburg are Gothic; while in Protestant Germany no settled taste has yet been developed.

In France, the oldest churches are Romanesque; the finest Cathedrals, as of Paris and Rheims, are Gothic; while French love of change may be traced in the Romanesque of St. Germain de Prés, the early pointed Gothic of Notre Dame, the medium Gothic of St. Sèverin and St. Germain l'Auxerrois, the latter florid Gothic of St. Gervais and St. Merri, the revived Grecian of St. Eustache and St. Etienne du Mont; Palladio's Italian, or the Elizabethan of St. Paul et St. Louis, and the Louis Quatorze of the Val de Grace, and Hôpital des Invalides. The religious spirit of the French Revolution expressed itself in the "Pantheon," or temple of *all gods;* and its speedy return under Napoleon to the Roman faith and Grecian culture culminated in the Madeleine, uniting the idea of the chaste Minerva and the reformed Magdalen.

In England and America, the united stimulus of religious freedom and of princely wealth, guided by general culture and religious enlightenment, has called forth special devotion to church architecture. The cathedrals of England present a complete history of the Gothic. London alone has the noblest Gothic in Westminster Abbey, the grandest Byzantine in St. Paul's, and the most perfect union of the Grecian columnar edifice with the Gothic spire in St. Martin's and St. Pancras'. America, pre-eminently rich in its variety, furnishes in almost every city specimens of the Basilica, Romanesque, Byzantine, Gothic, Norman, Saxon, and even of the amphitheatre styles. The favorite type is a sort of Roman Gothic; an edifice with a gable front, a Grecian entrance portico, side pilasters, and a central spire; while the interior, with side galleries, resembles the basilica.

CHAPTER VI.

SECULAR ARCHITECTURE AS INFLUENCED BY THE SOCIAL AND INTELLECTUAL, THE CIVIL AND DOMESTIC WANTS INDUCED BY CHRISTIAN CIVILIZATION.

WHILE Christianity influencing man's religious nature has led to new forms in sacred structures, its precepts, arousing to social and intellectual life, have prompted to improved secular edifices. Even under Christianity a special charm has clustered about castles and fortresses reared for defence from evil men. On the other hand, the Christian faith, seeking to forestall evil or alleviate its consequences, has prompted special provision for the education of the young, for the relief of the suffering, and for the restraint of the vicious. Yet again, Christian truth, making civil government a more cherished interest of the people, has led to new adaptations in structures requisite for its assemblies. Finally, Christian grace, furnishing security to individual wealth, has given to private dwellings a new character for sumptuousness and artistic merit.

The classes of buildings thus suggested may be grouped thus: *first*, Castellated, *second*, Capitoline, *third*, Conventual, and *fourth*, Villa and Cottage styles.

SECT. 1. CASTELLATED STYLES; AS A MODEL FOR PALATIAL RESIDENCES.

The spirit of civil independence, carried to an excess, studded Germany, France and England with feudal castles. As in the infancy of Asiatic civilization, Canaanite and Hebrew tribes under petty dukes and chiefs crowned the hill-tops east of the Mediterranean with rude fortresses whose character is still a study, so the early history of Northern Europe has left its monuments on the "castled crags" of the Rhine, and along the cliffs of English and Scotch Highlands.

These castles belong to civil architecture, since, when inadequate as military defences, they became palatial residences. Reared by German and Saxon nobles, their walls were built of coarse stone, with a Roman circular arch over the gateways and loop-hole windows. Dalloway ascribes the improvement of architecture in England to "the *security* of edifices for *religious* purposes, and the *insecurity* of structures for social uses," and divides its progress into three distinct eras; the first from Egbert to Alfred, A. D. 598 to 872; the second from Alfred to Canute and Harold, A. D. 1036; and the third to the Norman conquest, A. D. 1066. The Saxon improvements were chiefly Roman pilasters at the sides and Roman arches over the heads of gates and windows.

The Normans made the arches over gateways and windows of broad, semi-elliptical form, and crowned the wall with a battlement. In these, as in the Saxon improvements, there were three stages; first, from William the Conqueror to Stephen, A. D. 1050 to 1154; second, from Edward I. and II., A. D. 1272 to 1327; and third, from Edward III., A. D. 1327 to 1377. The Norman castles in the first age were either square and elevated, or circular and low; and as improved beyond the Saxon by Edward I. during the Crusades, they had complete columns for Roman pilasters, more ornamented capitals and arches, sculptured panels in the walls, towers and battlements projecting over the walls, and ceilings vaulted instead of flat. The Norman differed from the Gothic in having no exterior pediments or pinnacles, and no interior ribs or fretwork on the ceiling. The four castles in Wales erected by Edward I., including Caernarvon, Conway and Harlech, remain as monuments of this style.

The Norman improvements of English castles prepared them for residences. The widened doorways and windows, the projecting corner towers and the interior arcade balconies, furnished facilities for a family residence; the tower of London becoming the court residence of the Norman kings, from A. D. 1066 to 1135. Under the Plantagenets, from Henry II., A. D. 1154, to Richard III., A. D. 1483, the Norman improvements consisted of an enlargement and adornment of the Saxon structure. Under Edward I. exterior changes better adapting castles for defence, and under Edward III., about A. D. 1350, most important interior arrangements fitting them for sumptuous abodes, were made. The extension of the outer fortress-walls enlarged the inner court; large Gothic windows, made double or treble, to give increased light and air, opened from high-vaulted halls into the court; and projecting galleries and corridors with arcade arches afforded an open promenade and an airy lounge. The castles of Windsor, Kenilworth and Alnwick belong to this age.

The accession of the Tudors under Henry VII., A. D. 1485, originated the style, having three eras, called the "Tudor proper" of Henry VII., the "perfected Tudor" of Henry VIII., and the "Elizabethan;" to which, after Elizabeth, was added the "Louis Quatorze." Introduced about 1450 in Northern France by the Duke of Burgundy, later into England, the Tudor prevailed for two centuries. It aimed to furnish halls spacious and with high ceilings, while it added an exterior breadth and elevation that should be in harmony. It added to the exterior small octagonal towers with mitre-shaped cupolas, skirted underneath with fringes of rich crotchets borrowed from Saracenic minarets; also intervening turrets tipped with spires and gilded vanes, copied from the pointed Gothic; and finally bay or angle windows, serving as inviting side look-outs and reliefs to the blank castle wall. Richmond, in Surrey, built under Henry VII., illustrates this style.

Henry VIII., breaking off, A. D. 1509, from the Roman Church and excluding foreign artists, invited the genius of the Eastern

Church to add its ornamentation to the Norman Gothic. The gateways became lofty and crowned with the broad, semi-elliptical, obtuse-pointed arch; whose directly lateral thrust forbids its use except in an extended and massive wall. Embossed panels, with reliefs in wood or *terra cotta*, were inserted in the broad doors and blank side-walls. The windows, increased in breadth and height, were relieved by a dividing transom, and a miniature battlement called "crenellated." The chimneys were clustered, raised to the height of towers, and ornamented with an embattled cornice; and a notched parapet ran above the wall.

After Henry VIII., Holbein, the painter, and Inigo Jones, the architect, restored Italian culture and classic forms, especially in architecture. Born in 1572, Jones studied his art in Italy, brought home in 1613 Palladio's new treatise on architecture, and, till his death in 1652, fostered the taste for that mingled Grecian and Gothic, Roman and Tudor style, called "Elizabethan;" which, begun when the English nobles under Henry VIII. returned, rich in treasure and in new ideas, from their conquests in Northern France, was stimulated by the genius of such men as Shakespeare and Raleigh, and prevailed, including the reign of Elizabeth from 1558 to 1603, more than a century.

The castles of the "perfected Tudor" style had grand halls, with high pitched rafters of unpainted oak and chestnut, supported by brackets; at the end opening into the court large bay-windows adorned with armorial bearings; and on its sides wide galleries, having broad cornices lined with oak, and adorned with carved tablets, scrolls, escutcheons and grotesque figures in high relief. The Elizabethan introduced inside classic or grotesque figures, rectangular for curved and scroll panels, and outside, Roman porticoes with classic columns; leaving, however, many Gothic features.

In the "Louis Quatorze," prevailing in his reign, A. D. 1643 to 1715, the classic superseded the Gothic, introducing a basement truly Roman, with circular arches and square pilasters; a main story with Roman porticoes, pediments, corridors and columns; adding the scroll-work of the Tudor, sometimes the pinnacles of the Gothic, and as a crowning feature the double-slope roof, now gracefully curved, of the French architect, Mansard. It was an easy transition from this style to the classic Roman-Grecian prevailing in France, England and America. In London this history may be traced in the Gothic of Guildhall, the plain Gothic with Tudor battlements of Westminster Hall, the Tudor of St. James' Palace, the Roman Ionic and Corinthian of the Treasury and Whitehall, and the almost pure Grecian of Cumberland Terrace and Buckingham Palace.

While palatial edifices in Western Europe were thus modified, those of Italy at Genoa, Pisa, Florence and Venice retained the Roman arcade style; sometimes modified by Saracenic tracery-work. The Palace of the Grand Duke at Florence, built by Arnolfo in 1298, and the Farnese Palace at Rome, by M. Angelo, are true Roman. As a specimen of the influence of Saracenic taste, grafted upon a Roman foundation, the Palazzo del Commune, built at Piacenza, about A. D. 1281, has Saracenic corridors with arches of oval horse-shoe form.

SECT. 2. CAPITOLINE STYLES FOR STATE-HOUSES AND HALLS OF LEGISLATION.

In monarchical and aristocratic governments, castles or palaces are the natural residences of hereditary rulers. In representative governments edifices accommodating large deliberative assemblies must be provided. Halls designed for speakers occupying every portion of an audience-room must differ in construction from churches and theatres in which the speakers occupy one position.

At Athens the people met in the basin west of Mars-hill; at Rome the *comitia* assembled in the Forum or Campus Martius; always in the open air. In France, Germany and England, covered halls for even popular gatherings have been sought. The old Palais de Justice at Paris was Elizabethan in style; the present Palais du Corps Législatif, under Republican influence, has a Grecian façade. In England the popular element reared Westminster Hall, two hundred and seventy feet long, seventy-four wide, and ninety high, now Tudor in its façade; in which Richard II. feasted ten thousand guests, and where the early Parliaments of England met. In comparatively recent times the gorgeous new Parliament Houses have been elaborated in the most florid Gothic style.

In the North American Republic, made up of many States, a style of public buildings has arisen properly designated *Capitoline.*

As at Rome the names "Capitol" or head and "State-House," are significant. A few States, as Virginia, have selected the Grecian temple, the model apparently of the Roman Capitol, as alluded to by Cicero; but generally the Roman basilica, crowned with a dome and adorned with a Grecian entrance, has been preferred.

The National Capitol at Washington, D. C., first built by B. H. Latrobe of Baltimore, but reconstructed by T. U. Walter of Philadelphia, was originally three hundred and fifty-two feet and four inches long, one hundred and twenty-one feet and six inches broad, with a dome ninety-six feet in diameter and one hundred and forty-five feet high. It is now seven hundred and fifty-one feet and four inches in length, three hundred and twenty-four feet in extreme breadth, covering one hundred and fifty-three thousand one hundred and twelve square feet; the summit of the dome above the pavement being two hundred and eighty seven feet and five inches. Its basement is Roman, its porticoes the purest Grecian Corinthian, its dome Byzantine, and its exterior columnar ornamentation the revived Grecian of M. Angelo. In the old interior the columns are Doric in the basement, and Ionic in the second stage; but in the new portions the columns within, as without, are pure Corinthian. The artist, in true adherence to the Greek's idea, has allowed each sister State to twine her own favorites, leaf and flower, about the clustered capitals.

SECT. 3. CONVENTUAL, INCLUDING COLLEGE, HOTEL, HOSPITAL AND PRISON STYLES; DESIGNED AS CONGREGATED HOMES FOR THE EDUCATION OF YOUTH, THE ACCOMMODATION OF TRAVELERS, THE CARE OF THE INFIRM AND THE RESTRAINT OF THE VICIOUS.

While men devoted to the defence and regulation of society congregate in castles and palaces, the young, the traveler, the sick, the vicious, are gathered in colleges, hotels, hospitals and prisons. Under the early influence of Christianity the name "Conventual" was given to the style of architecture appropriate to buildings designed to supply these ends; convents being the chief schools, inns and hospitals.

The Hebrew, Mohammedan and probably Egyptian colleges were gathered in rooms clustered under colonnades surrounding the inner courtyard of temples and mosques; after which the cloisters of ancient Christian churches were modeled. Among the ancient Greeks, Socrates had no school building; Plato was favored to use the groves and porticoes of the country-seat of Academus; Aristotle was a peripatetic in the fields, or sought shelter when necessary in the temple of Lycæan Apollo; while the Stoic Zeno loitered under the *stoa* or porticoes of the Agora. The later Grecian schools at Athens, Pergamos, Tarsus and Alexandria, seem to have gathered in rooms connected with temples; while the Romans had Grecian teachers and temples.

In Christian lands convents became early the seats of learning. In the East these are castle-like structures, with high, blank unadorned exterior walls, and a large open court and garden within. In later days they became plain brick edifices, providing in the simplest form the needed rooms. In the revival of art, college structures in Europe became more elaborate, taking the characteristics of the early Saxon, Roman, pointed Gothic, Norman, Tudor, or revived Grecian; the castellated style seeming most appropriate.

Hotels designed for travelers or associated families, naturally taking the form of a hollow square, were, in early ages, like convents mere castles with plain walls. As leading ornaments of modern towns, hotels have usually a Roman basement, with a façade varying from plain Grecian Doric to exuberant Louis Quatorze.

Hospitals proper, for the diseased, the maimed and wounded, yet more permanent asylums for the insane, the indigent, the disabled, deaf-mutes and blind, are specially the offspring of Christian civilization. The Greeks and Romans had houses of entertainment called *Xenodocheia* or *Hospitalia;* but neither corresponded to the modern hospital. The first hospital proper met in history is a Christian provision for the poor pilgrims of Jerusalem, erected in Constantine's day. During the Crusades the famed Hospital at Jerusalem was a new feature in military history. About the same time hospitals at different points grew up on the route of Christian pilgrims, fostered by Christian women, commended by Jerome; as that of Fabiola at Rome, another at Constantinople, and others in Asia Minor planted by Paula. Yet later they are found in Northern Europe; the famed "Hospices" in the passes of the Alps. being specially noteworthy. All these took the character of convents; their design requiring openness of structure and airiness of location. The plain Norman, the more adorned Tudor, or, as in the hospital for invalids at Paris, the Byzantine is adapted to their object.

Even prisons as architectural works are the product of Christian civilization. The ancient prison was a cell dreadful to the occupant. The prison vaults of ancient Jerusalem, the Mamertine cave-prison at Rome, and the Black-hole at Calcutta, as compared with prison edifices in modern Christian countries, indicate how pure religion is the moving stimulus even of the spirit of art. Not until the present century has the idea of *reforming* the vicious, suggesting *palaces* of the most adorned castellated style as penitentiaries, begun actually to adorn cities with such structures as the Egyptian, the Norman, the Gothic prisons, now found in Philadelphia and New York.

SECT. 4. VILLA AND COTTAGE STYLES DESIGNED AS PRIVATE RESIDENCES, SUBURBAN RETREATS AND COUNTRY RESIDENCES.

The mass of mankind in cities and country live in cabins and garrets; and even princely wealth cannot in cities secure sufficient breadth for the highest architectural art in private residences. In suburban villas, wealth and taste united find ample scope for artistic skill.

Among Asiatics there are no country residences; all living in closely-walled towns on hill-tops; while for miles around no abode for man is seen except the shepherd's tent. The huts of the poor are without windows, and even the mansions of the wealthy are in narrow alleys. A blank wall two or three stories high faces the street; a low portal leads into a cave-like passage-way; and a side door opens into a broad unroofed courtyard. The lower story is occupied by stables and servants' rooms, and for storage. On the second floor, the family abode, large windows screened by lattices project into the court; over which an awning is drawn. The roof, coated with gravel-cement, has a slight slope, furnishing a promenade in pleasant weather and a water-shed for rain. At its centre is often a "summer parlor," open at the sides.

Grecian and Roman city-mansions were deeper but not wider than Asiatic. The entrance door was set back, leaving an outside vestibule. The court within called *aulē* in Greek, *atrium* in Latin, was covered, except a central opening, by rooms above; whose floors were supported by rows of short columns. Around this court were offices and other rooms for men; and back of it was another court similarly disposed for women. The roof gathered the rains into a cistern in the centre of the court; whose floor was paved in mosaic and its centre adorned with a small fountain and miniature statuary, illustrated in the descriptions of Cicero and Pliny and in unburied Pompeii. The slant of the Grecian and Roman roofs forbade promenades on the house-top; but the security of private property allowed suburban retreats. The German habit, however, of building private houses in the country wherever a cool spring, a shady grove, or a pleasant vale invited, was unknown in Italy, and a surprise to the historian Tacitus.

The Romans, unlike the Greeks in fondness for variety, excelled in suburban retreats; the hills about Rome for ten or twelve miles, and towns thirty or forty miles distant, being dotted with villas described by Cicero, Vitruvius and Pliny. These were of two classes. The *villa urbana* was near the city, and modeled like a town residence except that it had side, as well as front, balconies and porticoes. The *villa rustica*, distant from the city, was a farm mansion; having *cellæ* for servants, an *ergastulum* or night lock-up for convicts hired out as laborers, cellars for wine and oil, and extensive stalls for horses and other domestic animals; the details of whose grouping belong to Landscape Gardening.

The modern "Italian villa" is, in groundplot, the old Roman; its style of architecture being that mingling of Roman and Gothic perfected by Palladio, called in England "Elizabethan." It has a straight roof without parapet above, but with brackets underneath, clustered chimneys and an entrance tower at one side, also arcade-balconies and bay-windows. The "French Chateau" is substantially the "Louis Quatorze," with roof of double pitch, without towers or battlements; and it is adapted to a city, as the "Italian villa" is to a suburban residence. The "Swiss cottage" has a steep projecting roof, with no exterior colonnade; and it is adapted to a hill-side. The "verandah" of India is a square house, with low roof, and a wide circling piazza; and is appropriate to a lawn having a sunny exposure. The "kiosk," or Turkish summer-house, is octagonal with mitre-shaped roof and latticed sides; and is appropriate only as an arbor.

BOOK V.

PAINTING; THE ADDING OF COLOR TO FORM.

THUS far form alone, aside from color, has been considered. In drawing, light and shade require the employ of only white and black; in sculpture every work is of the hue of its material; and in architecture, color is always secondary, generally accidental, and only occasionally artistic.

Painting follows drawing, sculpture and architecture; *first*, because it requires an acquaintance with all other arts; and *second*, because to accurate execution in them all painting must add just color to form. Lionardo, said "A painter ought to be well instructed in perspective, to be a master of anatomy, and also to be a good architect;" perspective being the final attainment in drawing, and anatomy in sculpture. In order to success in landscape painting a knowledge of gardening is equally essential.

In fact painting is the "art of arts;" for drawing is a part of the painter's work; and while sculpture and architecture actually *make* forms, painting, *without making* them, must present them to the eye. The blind man's judgment was just, when having felt first a statue, and then a painting of the same figure, he remarked, "If this flat surface *looks like* that round one, then this is the greater art."

CHAPTER I.

THE ANALYSIS AND COMPOSITION OF COLORS.

NOT only the general student, but also the practical artist, is called to regard, first, the analysis and synthesis of colors in themselves; and second, the combination of colors existing in nature.

His main subsequent toil is to gain the power of copying existing colors, and of conceiving and executing new hues, shades and tints.

Sect. 1. The simple or elementary colors.

The pure rays of the sun's light are white; retaining this hue even when reflected from polished black iron. Substances reflecting none of the sun's rays, really unseen, seem black; the color of darkness, where we see nothing. Substances between black and white in color, reflect a part only of the light. White is the combination, black the absence of all colors; their mixture is *gray;* and these three are in art called *neutral*, or negative colors.

From the earliest times the decomposition of sunlight into varied colors by passing through ice or amber, and in the rainbow, was observed. The Chaldean and Indian philosophers counted seven distinct colors. The Greeks, Pythagoras and Aristotle, regarded color "superficial," dependent on the reflection of light; and the rainbow as "solar rays reflected by vapor." Sir Isaac Newton's practical division of the colors of the prismatic spectrum into seven—red, orange, yellow, green, blue, indigo, violet—were, by Sir David Brewster, reduced to three, yellow, red and blue; experiments showing that all other colors are compounded of these three; which are hence called *essential*, or, as opposed to negative, *positive* colors. The important fact thus established, so far as painting is concerned, is, that all hues, shades and tints, in coloring are to be attained by admixture of the three elementary colors; while at the same time these three are so intermixed in nature, as in the solar spectrum, that in none of his pigments can the artist expect to find, as he could not with truth to nature, employ any pure elementary color.

Sect. 2. The artificial or compound colors.

The simplest admixture of colors, that of black and white, produces the variety of which Sir Isaac Newton remarks, "These gray and dun colors may be also produced by mixing whites and blacks." The history of language from the time Hesiod applied the term "*graiai*" to the "fair-cheeked Greek women," as well as the demands of analysis in art, require that a distinction be made between *gray*, a combination of simple black and white, and *grey*, an admixture into which blue and its compounds enter.

The positives, blue, red and yellow, are found to have fixed proportions essential to beauty in the compounds formed by them; that law requiring for yellow three, for red five, and for blue eight. With reference to their proportionate admixtures, yellow, red and blue, are called *primary* colors; and these proportions their "equivalents."

The union of primaries in their proportions forms secondaries; the three being orange from red and yellow, green from yellow and blue, purple from red and blue. The equivalent of each secondary is the sum of the equivalents of its elements; of orange eight, of green eleven, and of purple thirteen. The admixture of the secondaries in their proportions forms three tertiaries; citrine from green and orange, russet from orange and purple, and olive from purple and green. These proportionate admixtures are called *pure* colors. Their combinations in *indefinite* proportions give the *dirty* or *impure* colors; which, as to their effect in nature, are called *semi-neutrals*.

In the practice of the art of painting, it is important to note this order of the colors. Yellow, next to white, mixed with it gives the faint hue straw-color; it is the ruling element in the tertiary citrine, and enters largely into buff, bay, tawny, tan, dan, dun, drab, chestnut, roan, sorrel, hazel, auburn, Isabella, fawn and feuille morte. Red, the central color, is a leading element in orange and scarlet, in purple and crimson; it controls in russet; it enters largely into marrone, puce, murrey, morello, mordore, pompadour; and is found also in browns. Blue, the primary nearest black, regarded by Lionardo from observation as a mixture of white and black, abounds in the green of the earth's covering; it is the ruling element in olive; and it enters largely into the semi-neutral greys, as slate and lead colors.

Among the secondaries, orange, when inclined to red, gives scarlet, poppy, coquilicot; and when tending to yellow is gold. Green, the central secondary, tending to yellow is pea-green, and to blue is bottle-green; while in every land foliage is called green from the lightest poplar to the darkest fir, from the greenish yellow of Italy and Mexico to the blue-black of Ireland and Greenland. Purple, the extreme secondary on the dark side, when tending toward red is rose, when toward blue is lilac or violet, and when toward black is indigo.

Among the tertiaries citrine having most yellow, and least blue, succeeds first to the green of summer as autumn comes on. Russet, the central tertiary, follows citrine in autumn tints. Olive, the darkest of the tertiaries, prevails in foliage designated as greenish, in sky characterized as greyish, and in earth styled ashen.

The semi-neutrals, into which black enters, are of three classes; brown, maroon, and grey. Brown, an indefinite class of colors in which yellow predominates, including yellow-browns, red-browns, orange-browns, purple-browns, but no blue-browns, embraces, also, dun, hazel and auburn. Marrone, or maroon, including a class of impure colors in which the red predominates, derives its name from the color of the wine of ancient Maronea, resembling claret, and is applied to the copper-colored mixed breeds of Central America. Grey embraces a class of impure colors in which blue predominates; including blue, olive, green, purple, but no yellow or red greys; a distinction of special importance in studying the grey tints of cloud, earth and water.

Black, in admixture with colors, does not alter the hue; it only deepens the shade.

No painter in ancient or modern times has passed beyond the rudiments of his art without knowledge of, and careful attention to this analysis of pigments and of the law of their harmonious admixtures. The knowledge of the Greeks, who so excelled in this art at his day, is thus alluded to by Aristotle: "The many other colors besides white and black are multiplied in number by proportionate admixtures; for they can be formed by uniting them together in the ratio of two to three, of three to four, and of other numbers. Other colors, however, are formed by admixture without ratio; having a disproportionate amount of some and an absence of other elements." No one can successfully trace the history of painting, from the glaring yellow, crimson and blue of the ancient Egyptians, till the consummation of the art of coloring in the mellow tints of Raphael and Guido, without a careful preliminary study of the analysis of colors.

SECT. 3. COMPLEMENTARY AND CONTRASTED COLORS.

Colors in proportionate admixture, by their very name, "pure,' indicate that man's nature is formed to prefer them. Aristotle observes, "the colors most accurately proportionate in their admixture, as purple and light-red, are the most delightful colors." That we are equally made to prefer complementary and contrasted colors is seen in the variety sought in dress among all mankind; and in the hues of sky, cloud, earth, foliage, flowers, insects, birds and animals ordained by the Creator.

The *complement* of a color is that which it lacks of being pure white; the complement of yellow being a due proportion of red and blue; the complement of orange a due proportion of green and purple. The study of complementary colors in its lower applications has a relation to scenic and decorative painting; but its profoundest analysis has been sought in the Gobelin tapestry works at Paris as well as by the ablest artists in different ages.

That we are made for this law of complementary colors, nature without and within us both attest. The blue sky is so compensated by the complementary yellow and red on the earth, that few blue flowers, and those chiefly poisonous, are found; while the glowing crimson of the evening sunset in the West is set off by a greenish grey in the East. If, again, the eye has been fixed on a red wafer, when suddenly turned to a white page it sees a circular spot of a bluish-green color, the complement of the red; the health of the organs of vision, as well as the demands of our intellectual nature, requiring compensation in colors.

Colors in *contrast*, when their differences are not precisely complementary, are pleasing; the principle of compensation, however, both in nature and art, being the foundation of the pleasure thence derived. The purple flower has generally a centre of yellow, the purple inclining to blue or red as the yellow tends to orange or green; while in the few flowers that are blue, the centre is orange. Green, as central, is in accord with almost all the colors of nature; while citrine the first, and russet the second tint of autumn, following green, keep up the contrasts making the harmonies of nature.

SECT. 4. THE DISTINCTION BETWEEN HUES AND TINTS; AND THE NATURE AND LAWS OF TONE AND OF HARMONY IN COLORING.

In nature there is no marked line separating between colors, complementary or contrasted. In the rainbow one color shades off imperceptibly into another, and sunset reflections from sky, cloud, earth and water, are so thrown upon each other in the glow of evening twilight that language lacks words by which to depict their varied and ever-changing aspects. The terms shades, hues and tints, indicate variations in the coloring of single objects; and tone, expression, harmony characterize special effects of coloring as a whole.

The word hue designates the proportion of any one color entering into an admixture; shade the degree of darkness or light given to that color; and tint the overlaying of a foreign hue thrown upon the principal color. The color blue has as its shades, dark, medium and light; as its hues, indigo, violet and azure; while we speak of the rosy tint of morning, the purple tint of evening, and the brown tint of autumn cast on the distant blue hills. Shade is varied by adding black or white to the principal color; hue by increasing the proportion of any one of the elementary colors; while tints are laid upon hues already executed, by rapid and light touches of the artist's brush tinged with a contrasted color.

The terms *tone* and *harmony* as applied to painting, are borrowed from the kindred art of music. Tone expresses, literally used, the adaptation of sound to sentiment; as when we say of a piece of music, "Its tone is grave, and it should be performed in a subdued tone of voice." Physicians, using the term figuratively, speak of "the tone of the vital organs." Raphael Mengs, to illustrate its use in painting, alludes to the common statement that the Italian artists, using the warm colors yellow and red, the Germans cold blue and black, Caravaggio sober grey and brown, and Rubens gorgeous orange rose and purple, have respectively a lively, severe, gay and sombre "tone." Ruskin embraces harmony in tone; making it consist in "the just relation of the *shading* of all the parts to the chief figure," and "the just *coloring* of the lights and shadows in their relation to each other."

While tone relates to the æsthetic impression made by a picture taken as a whole, "harmony" relates properly to the artistic relation of the parts to each other, separately regarded. Mengs, treating at length upon harmony as he does upon tone, says: "The artist will observe that by harmony we designate what the Italians call *accord*. As accord or harmony in music produces an agreeable effect on the auditory nerves, so does harmony in painting on the optic nerves." As to the method of securing harmony, he says, "The lighter colors have more effect, because

22 *

they produce quicker vibrations upon the organs of vision." "The purest and most glaring colors, as possessing more strength than the pale ones, must be used in principal figures. The use of either white or black has a tendency to subdue and diminish the power of the pure or primary colors; while the latter also darkens all these colors." Rembrandt secured the finest gradation and thus harmony, by simple black; and Boccacio by pure white; the effect being kindred to that produced in music by a single instrument as the violin, or one voice in a solo.

Even in interior views, hues are varied without end by in-door and out-door lights, by bright sunshine and dense clouds; as well as by the reflected tints of morning and evening, of daylight and twilight. When any one of these myriad phases of light is chosen by the artist, he must retain the recollection of each separate hue and tint belonging to that selected moment, and preserve each variety throughout his entire work; for thus alone can harmony be attained.

It is in landscape, however, that the principles of harmony have their special application. Ruskin thinks that the chief superiority of modern over ancient painters is their attaining the two requisites of tone described by him. His numerous suggestions as to the method of executing the varied shadings of refracting and reflecting media, his nice discriminations between the hues, tints and shades of light as they stream through clouds, glance from water, and rest on the soil, his pencil-tracings of outlines in foliage, cloud, and even of granite boulders, group themselves under the topics here considered.

CHAPTER II.

GENERAL PRINCIPLES AS TO THE EMPLOY OF COLORS IN PAINTING.

As in drawing, so in painting, the pupil proceeds from the simpler to the more abstruse principles of his art. Among the higher aims in coloring are the securing of special æsthetic effects by colors; the attaining of "aerial perspective;" and finally in landscape, the blending of shades, hues and tints in distant prospects.

SECT. 1. THE COLORS OF OBJECTS IN NATURE TO BE COPIED IN PAINTING.

The analysis of colors in themselves prepares the eye to trace their distribution in nature. Ancient philosophers and poets aided painters in minute observation of minor distinctions; Aristotle asking, "Why have white men and white horses for the most part azure eyes?" and Ovid in his Metamorphoses, alluding to the "blue" hue of nymphs floating "in the sea."

The snow is white, the sky blue, and the grass green; but upon these are reflected a thousand differing shades, hues and tints; of which the ordinary observer is not really aware, though he looks directly upon them. The painter must learn not simply the characteristic features, but the peculiar shades of colors. The farmer calls foliage green, and soil brown; yet he has no distinct words to represent the distinct hues which he would blame the painter for overlooking. The mariner never separates the white foam on the wave-crest, the light pea-green of its head, the deep blue of its body, and the dense black of its foot; but the artist must analyze and copy them all, or he can never satisfy his sea-bred critic. The hunter, the drover, the hostler, never have thought of the nice varieties of color in fur; but the artist must understand every varied hue, and never paint two animals alike. The mountaineer who never saw a painting is quickest to note if the artist has caught the rosy tint of morning on the mountain peak, the slaty grey of its rocky pinnacles, the lively blue of its sunlit slopes, the sombre of its shaded gorges, and the deep green skirting of its base. The artist must have *seen* all that other men in varied pursuits ever look upon; and must besides have mastered the secret methods by which all he has seen is to be reproduced.

The painting of a basket of fruit or flowers gives the range of livelier colors; and a bunch of autumn leaves furnishes a series of soberer shades. The study for an hour of any single landscape, or a rapt gazing at the shifting tints of a waning twilight, indicates that the range for this observation is inexhaustible.

Two centuries before Newton analyzed colors, Lionardo, the art-teacher, thus wrote: "One painter ought never to imitate the manner of any other; because in that case he cannot be called the child of Nature, but the grandchild. To have recourse to Nature, which is replete with such abundance of objects, is always better than to go to the productions of old masters, who learned everything from her." His three hundred and sixty-five chapters are mainly hints for the successful study of Nature. He teaches the distinction between transparent and opaque colors; the former showing, the latter hiding opposite colors beneath them; and he illustrates their effect by colored glasses held between the eye and landscape, as also by the influence of smoke, which before a black chimney is bluish, but in the air is a reddish brown. Red on blue lake becomes violet; yellow upon blue is green; while to be pure, each transparent color should be laid upon a white ground. Red rays reflected on a red object give lustre to its hue; while the cutting off of the sun's light darkens any color.

The thorough student may find in the pages of Lionardo, Ruskin, Leslie and kindred authors, an exhaustless mine of suggestions as to methods of studying the tints of Nature. The works themselves, however, from which they borrowed all their hints, are the learners' true field.

Sect. 2. The relation of color to form; and the demands of anatomy and general symmetry in painting.

Shading with black crayon gives a less distinct impression of solidity than colored shades furnish. The sun's disc is more complete when seen through haze than in a clear atmosphere; and a snow-capped mountain top, or chalky cliff, is less distinct in the clear noonday sunlight than when set off by evening tints.

A painted portrait ought to present truth even in form more fully than a crayon drawing, an engraving, or a photograph; for though these may give the perfect outlines of form, while no skill of art can attain like truth in coloring, yet if the coloring be that of a master, it will enhance the vividness with which form strikes the eye. Two causes contribute to the definiteness which color gives to our impression of form. First, the idea of *substance* is more vividly presented when color is added to a form; for while spectres are always conceived as white or colorless, the very idea of color in cheek or mantle would be conceived as an attribute of a real being.

Second, as shade alone indicates the projection of the dimension perpendicular to the line of vision, and as color alone even without shade gives the impression of substance, when these two, as in a painting, unite, the impression of form is enhanced by the combined address to the eye of shade and color.

The pupil in drawing and sculpture, having only form to represent, may study the human figure in plaster casts alone; but the painter must have as his model the human form itself, or some former master's work founded upon such a study. Colored shades alone assure the beholder of the correct anatomy of figures.

The great painters of ancient and modern times have studied flesh-color and its shades with special care. Parrhasius and Apelles painted from living nude models; the former indifferent to the piercing shrieks of the captive old man on the rack as he sought to catch the hues, now flushed, now livid, of dying agony; the latter insensible to the blush of shrinking modesty in his lovely maiden captive, while he only thought of transferring the tints of that blush to his canvas. Lionardo mentions: "Black drapery will make the flesh of the human figure appear whiter than it really is; white will make it appear darker; while yellow will render flesh more highly colored, and red paler than it is." Vandyke following this hint chose black velvet as the dress of a lady whose complexion he wished to make of a tint specially delicate.

SECT. 3. THE RELATION OF COLOR TO LIGHT AND SHADE, AND THE EXECUTION OF CHIAROSCURO IN PAINTING.

Color brings out form, and heightens its effect in landscape as well as in portrait. The half shade which gives a delightful softness to objects in the distance at noonday becomes enchanting when, at sunset, this delicateness takes on the richest coloring. The landscape painter, therefore, must study chiaroscuro in respect to coloring as well as to shading. Though observed and commented upon by the ancient Greeks, yet color in chiaroscuro was first analyzed by Lionardo; it attained impressive majesty in Michel Angelo, and magical life in Correggio; three artists of the same age.

Lionardo conceived the idea of concentrating the chief radiance upon the central figure, gradually diminishing the light upon remoter objects. The effect of colored shades may be seen by placing a light blue cylinder between a black and a white wall. To execute the gradation of shade thus produced on the cylinder, three parts of black and one of blue must be taken to begin the dark side of the cylinder, blue being constantly added to this mixture, until it alone is used to complete the semi-circle. Numberless hints are given by Lionardo: "The shadow of every white body must have a tinge of blue, which it receives from the air. When one white body terminates on another of the same color, as may be seen by holding one sheet of white paper a little before another, there is an edge of shade cast by the foremost upon the hinder sheet, which makes it stand out from it. In general, a light-colored object before a light background looks darker than it is; while the same object before a dark background looks lighter than its natural shade."

Germany, England and America have added to the teachings of the Italian school. The poet Goethe was remarkable for his personal observations and instructions as to the means of making varied colors meet and blend with each other. Fuseli regards Lionardo's study of colored reflexes as the climactic work of the revival of art. He pronounces the head of Jesus in the Last Supper of Lionardo, from which as a centre the light is made to radiate, the first, as it is one of the most finished masterpieces of chiaroscuro; he characterizes the boat of Charon, the centre of M. Angelo's Last Judgment, as the perfection to which Lionardo's teaching led the bold genius of his pupil; and he counts the entrancing fascination of Correggio's sky the most perfect illusion of modern art. Ruskin dwells on the distinction between in-door and out-door sunlight, and between the action of clear white sunlight in bringing out local tints, and that of the light of a clouded sky in modifying local hues. Leslie, though an ardent admirer of Raphael, places him low in the rank of colorists, because he did not study and practice the art of chiaroscuro as developed by his contemporary, Lionardo.

Sect. 4. The relation of color to perspective; and aerial effects in painting.

Opaque-colored objects reflecting colored lights and shades make the study of chiaroscuro difficult. Besides this, however, transparent air throws on every distant object the tinge of its own blue, making aerial perspective an added study. Like chiaroscuro the attainment of aerial effects in painting seems to be a triumph of modern art. Yet the Greeks had knowledge of the theory of aerial perspective, as is manifest from the following language of Socrates: "A magnitude seen at a distance is not the same as when seen near to us. Objects strike our eyes in different ways according to the medium through which we see them. Our senses are deceived by color, and this deception is transferred to the mind. The art of painting, taking advantage of our liability to this deception, does not hesitate to practise enchantment and to dazzle our eyes."

Lionardo, after treating of "Linear Perspective," considers "The Perspective of Colors." The lighter a color is in nature, the darker it will appear when removed to a distance; but with dark colors it is the reverse, since the blue of the atmosphere lightens colors darker than azure, and darkens colors lighter than itself. Hence the foot of a column or distant mountain appears less distinct, and farther off, than its top. Colors seen on a level with the eye change more than when seen from an elevated height; the air being denser in its lower strata.

Lionardo illustrates the distinction between linear and aerial perspective by their effects. "A thick air renders the outline of an object undetermined and confused, and makes it appear larger than it is, because the linear perspective does not diminish the angle which conveys the object to the eye. The aerial perspective carries it farther off; so that the one removes it from the eye while the other preserves its magnitude.

Ruskin argues: "It is not tint, but depth and softness that represent distance. A mountain near is green or gray; afar off it is purple. A yellow box is soft yellow at a distance. Distance alone only softens colors."

Sect. 5. The relation of color to human sensibilities; and the address of varied emotions by painting.

Colors, both in nature and art, affect the sensibilities; poets appeal to this law; but it is the artist's office so to analyze both these effects and their causes as to be able to copy the special hues which produce special impressions.

The dark colors in general are expressive of gloom, and the light of cheerfulness. Black is the garb of mourning; and in nature the storm cloud, the darkening eve, instinctively beget gloom. White, the emblem of joy in bridal robes, the symbol of peace and purity in priests' vestments, speaks at a child's burial of innocence prevailing over corruption. Man's out-door toil makes the graver colors fittest for his garb; while for woman's in-door adornment the gayer hues seem essential.

The dicta of fashion sometimes overcome the teachings of true culture. Fuseli remarks, "Glare is always the first feature of a savage or infant taste." Yet European, and even English taste clings to gold and scarlet as the dress appropriate to royalty and the court; and it doubts the legitimacy of the American use of black as the garb appropriate to civic ceremony and social festivity. It certainly is a mark of semi-civilization when the Oriental chieftain flaunts woman's gaudy colors in his robe and turban; and there must be a lack in true culture when the gorgeous coloring of Rubens is preferred to the quiet tints of Lionardo. There is a speechless power in the sunny glow on the "glistering white" of the robes of Jesus, of Moses, and of Elijah, in "Raphael's Transfiguration;" in the dreary "blackness of darkness" shrouding the condemned in Angelo's "Last Judgment;" and in the soft and mellow evening radiance falling on the faces of Jesus and the "beloved disciple," in Lionardo's "Last Supper;" and they subdue every beholder to the sentiment of each scene.

SECT. 6. THE RELATION OF COLOR TO DESIGN, AND ITS SPECIAL APPLICATIONS IN PAINTING.

Painting, like sculpture, is an in-door adornment; being excluded from the field of out-door art, such as funeral or civic monuments and landscape ornamentation. It has, however, its own field of design, from which sculpture is excluded. An altar-piece, or a mural tablet may be sculptured; but the broad field of historical illustration, the boundless expanse of landscape representation, and the pervasive panorama of wall and ceiling decoration which may bring the life of an age and nation into a single chamber, belongs to painting alone.

A higher order, also, as well as a wider field of design can be sought in painting. An engraving fails in its effect unless the engraver has the genius to give to his work those speaking touches which go beyond the mere enunciation of form, and furnish an expression kindred to that of color. Guizot, probably extreme in his view, thinks that sculpture can only express strength and beauty in objects at rest; leaving the whole field of action in art as the peculiar province of painting.

The work of *conception* with the sculptor ends when his model is complete; and a common marble carver might cut an Apollo Belvidere from the cast before him. No artist ungifted and uncultured in design, however, could copy in Guido's Crucifixion the hues of cloud and tints of flesh; in which the light struggling with the darkness throws its uncertain gleam now on the radiant form of the sufferer and now on the shifting mist around. In *invention* the sculptor directly executes dimensions viewed obliquely, while the painter, by a skillful gradation of colored shades on the retiring limb, foreshortens it. In *composition*, again, so few figures can enter into even a bas-relief, that the Greeks seem never to have used the word except for the groupings of painting. Yet, again, *expression* is pre-eminently the province of the painter; for, from the day Apelles made the arm of Alexander seem even to a Cicero to stretch forth from the canvas, painting has been the art that has seemed able to impart actual life to its creations.

In fact, in ancient as well as in modern treatises on design, the full import of the term forbids its employ except when painting is the subject considered; as appears in Lionardo's summary of design. "The first thing to be regarded is the relief; that the central figure from which the light is cut off by those on the sides have the deepest shades around it. The second is that the order and disposition of the figures be accommodated to the subject. The third is that the figures be alive to the occasion, with expressions suited to their attitudes."

CHAPTER III.

MATERIALS AND SPECIAL METHODS OF USING THEM IN COLORING; AND CONSEQUENT CLASSIFICATION OF AGES, STYLES AND SCHOOLS IN PAINTING.

THE history of painting indicates that the hinging principles on which classification of ages and of schools turns, relate to pigments or coloring materials, vehicles or mixing agents, tablets or substances on which colors are laid, subjects or themes to be represented, objects or the purposes for which paintings are designed, and styles or the special manner of execution practised by different schools and by rival artists.

SECT. 1. PIGMENTS; OR MATERIALS USED AS COLORS.

As outlines, cut with a hard, sharp pencil into the material on which the picture was to be drawn, such as wax, stone or copper plate, were the germs of sculpture, so drawing executed with a soft pencil of adhesive texture, such as crayon, charcoal or chalk. which left a line of its own substance on the material, was the first stage of painting. These primitive pictures were called *skiagrams* by the Greeks, because they were drawn in shade; which were followed by *monochromatic* pictures, or those executed in one color with simple ochres or vegetable tints. In the climactic age of painting in Greece, a large number of different pigments were tested and either adopted or rejected as experience developed their merit.

Pigments have been classified according to color, as blacks and whites, reds, yellows and blues, alike by Pliny and by modern writers. The nicer analysis of a cultured age classifies coloring materials according to their chemical elements, as vegetable and mineral; the latter being subdivided into earthy and metallic.

Modern chemistry has enlarged the number of articles used as paints; it has led to a knowledge of the elements of which compounds are made; it has enabled the philosophic artist to effect new combinations, to form new theoretical conclusions as to the durability of different pigments, and to enlarge the list of varying shades, hues and tints; yet the same natural and artificial colors which by practice the ancients found to be the best are still retained, and are generally acknowledged to be superior. The following, as examples, now employed in China and India, may be historically traced through the Middle Ages to Greece and Rome, and thence to Assyria and Egypt. Among vegetable pigments the English *madder*, a bright red extracted from the root of a plant, is the *rubia tinctoria* of the Romans, and the *eruthra* of the Greeks; among earthy the ochre is the Greek *ōchros*, (pale opposed by Aristotle in complexions to *eruthros* ruddy), a term applied to earths of various dull colors, all produced by that common coloring ingredient of fertile soils, the oxide of iron; and among mixed pigments, lake is the Indian word *lacca*, a designation of the combination by boiling of vegetable tinctures with clays. Besides these, Linton has shown that of forty-two metallic pigments mentioned by Pliny and other ancient writers, thirty-one are now employed by painters.

Chemists, who have analyzed Egyptian pigments under the direction of Sir Gardner Wilkinson and Assyrian under Dr. Layard, have arrived at the following conclusions. The blues all appear to be oxides of copper. The reds were three; one brownish, an iron oxide; another brick-red, an earth tinctured with iron; a third scarlet, a madder, the vegetable *coccus*. The yellows were ochres on grounds, and vegetable on cloths. The greens were blue glass mixed with ochres; or a vegetable yellow mixed with copper blue. For blacks, calcined bones, lees of wine, asphaltum or burnt pitch, charcoal and soot were used; and for whites, a very pure chalk, lime and gypsum. The unbroken history of pigments is illustrated in the "vermillion" mentioned by Hebrew writers; ancient translations compared with Strabo, Dioscorides and Pliny, showing that the Chaldee *shashur* of India is the *miltos* of the Greek, and the *sinopis* of the Latin.

The study of the nature of pigments was in ancient as in modern times an experimental science; as is seen in the allusions of Greek and Latin writers from Herodotus to Pliny. Thus Hippocrates, about B. C. 420, remarks that "the writings of physicians, or physicists, had less regard to medicine than to arts of design."

The works of Pliny and of Galen show how, from every land and nation, Grecian and Roman artists sought new materials for coloring. The celebrated Byzantine manuscript, discovered among the monks of Mt. Athos, indicates how genius as well as learning lingered in the cloister, enamored of the charms of art. Even after all the advances made by the great masters, Vasari mentions Raphael's delight that the Pope had appointed "an aged friar" to assist him in the decorations of St. Peter, because he expected to "learn some secrets of the art from so experienced an associate."

The ambition of modern painters to secure improved pigments, rivaling the ardor of men in the Middle Ages in search of the philosopher's stone, has proved, as Eastlake's investigations show, that the thorough study of the writers on Greek painting points out the paths which have been most thoroughly searched through, and those which invite farther scrutiny.

SECT. 2. VEHICLES AND VARNISHES; OR MATERIALS USED FOR SPREADING COLORS AND GIVING THEM CLEARNESS, BRILLIANCE AND DURABILITY.

Pigments, chiefly in a solid form, must be converted into a semi-fluid condition in order that they may be spread; and, as the art has advanced, the search for fit *vehicles*, or carriers of colors, has been as earnest as for worthy pigments. The first and essential quality in a vehicle is ease of flow and smoothness of spread, as opposed to daubing and pasting, in laying on colors; a second and important characteristic is adhesiveness to the ground on which they are laid, and consistency with themselves, so that they shall not scale or crumble; while a third and desirable property is lucidness and transparency, the vehicle not covering so as to hide the color, but giving its own sparkling lustre to the dull metallic or earthy pigment which it allows to be seen through itself.

Water, the natural and universal solvent, was universally first selected in rude ages for mixing paints. It is the simple liquid which the child and savage use; it was the only solvent employed by ancient Egyptian and Grecian painters even when considerably advanced in art; it has always proved the only vehicle proper for fresco painting; and to this day painting in water colors is an important branch of the finished art.

Water dries rapidly, so that by its employ the perishing flower may be completely copied ere the special hue and fresh brilliance of its prime are gone. Pure water being only a vehicle, and evaporating completely, has no tendency to change the hue of pigments. All water, however, is liable to be affected by acids or alkalies, taken on from the air or earth; and hence in the advance of art filtered rain water or distilled spring water has been sought. Water colors, too, are easily removed; a quality most undesirable in permanent works; though very convenient in designs to be changed; as was illustrated when Apelles placed his paintings in the window of his study, seeking from the criticism of passers-by hints for their improvement; as also was amusingly exemplified in Buffulmacco, so called from his fondness for buffoonery, who loved to provoke the horror of pious ecclesiastics by painting in water colors on altar-pieces, a bear's cub in the arms of the Virgin, or St. Luke blowing the ink out of his pen.

The first improvement on water as a vehicle was the adding of a glutinous vegetable substance, or gelatinous animal gum to the water to temper, or give it consistency; called *temperata* in classic, *tempera* in mediæval, and *distemperata* in modern Latin. In modern distemper any glutinous substance which will make the colors laid on adhere to the ground and cohere in their own layers, either gums or glues, either vegetable juices as wine, vinegar and fig juice, or animal liquors as the white of eggs, the serum of blood and cow's milk, have been employed.

Pliny mentions a great variety of preparations of gums, resins, oils and mixtures with milk, honey, fig-juice, etc., employed by Greek artists; referring to Egyptian varieties of many of them as especially valuable. At the revival of art in Italy, Cimabue restored the *tempera* of the Greeks; and in Italy honey, and in Germany "the parings of parchments boiled in water," tragacanth, arabic, or ammoniac gums and isinglass, also albumen, serum and milk, have been used for admixtures. To give adhesion in painting on ivory or glass, animal gall, borax, or a mild alkali is employed.

Though gums and glues thus used in the mixing of paints gave to pigments coherence in themselves and adherence to grounds, they did not furnish transparence to the colors floating in the vehicle, nor a varnished gloss and protection to the surface of the picture. The Divine painter of the broad face of Nature hinted a supply for this lack in the wax which coats the upper surface of leaves, giving them a smooth polish to resist dampness, and a gloss to furnish them lustre.

The use of wax, *keros* in Greek, *cera* in Latin, as a vehicle for mixing pigments, originated, at a very early day, with the painters of the prows of vessels; who observed how the sun's heat caused the wax used in caulking ships to flow over the painted surface, and to give a firm and glossy surface. Three methods grew up in the progress of the art; in the first, the pigment was plastered upon the ground with a scraper called *rabdion;* in the second, the method afterward called *niello*, it was laid in engraved lines cut into the ground, and impressed with an iron graver called *kestron;* and in the third it was spread, as with other vehicles, by the brush called *penicillum.* When laid on by either of these methods, a heated iron was held over the surface to burn in the pigment; this finishing process giving the name *encaustic*, from the Greek *enkaio*, to this style of painting. Its discovery was to the Greeks what oil-painting was to moderns; Lycippus, the predecessor of Apelles, writing upon his wax-paintings instead of the *epoiëse*, or *fecit*, of ordinary artists, the word *enekause*, burnt it. The advantages of encaustic painting were, the distinctness of hue caused by the floating and consequent glistening of the particles of pigment in the dissolved wax; and the protection of the color from the action of moisture and from friction in cleaning the surface. Horace and other Roman critics extol the masters in this art; Chrysostom, the great preacher, practised it as an accomplishment; the Byzantine painters continue it to this day; and the Venetians surrendered it only for a superior invention.

The chief disadvantages of wax as a vehicle and varnish were its extreme gloss and consequent excess of reflection, which prevented the painting being seen to advantage except in one light; its stiffness and consequent exposure to crack from bending of the ground; and especially the want of an easy flow, which might allow the particles of different pigments so to intermix as to give gradation of hues. Another vehicle, eagerly and perseveringly sought by able artists, was at length found in oil; the history of whose use in painting Eastlake has traced back into Grecian and even Egyptian history. Vasari records the discovery of John Van Eyck, A. D. 1410; who, after numerous experiments, found that linseed and walnut oil were more drying than any others, that they gave a firm consistence to colors mixed with them, allowed their blending better than tempera, lit them up with a radiant gloss-like varnish, and protected the ground from damp. Van Eyck's secret afterward spread to Italy and thence to all Europe. Scientific masters like Lionardo, perfected the use of oil; introducing gums, turpentine, alcohol and other ingredients to hasten its drying.

The last requisite in painting was a varnish whose smooth polish should at once protect and beautify the colors employed. The Egyptians gave to sculpture, even in coarse granite, a polish such that its lustre still mirrors the sunlight. Grecian statuaries not only gave to ivory and marble the most exquisite polish, but Praxiteles even added a varnish to increase their finish. Painted Egyptian sarcophagi still show the varnish laid upon them. Praxiteles and Apelles spent years in search of a varnish at once firm and transparent, which, as Pliny's word *circumlitio* implies, gave a projection of the figure from the canvas. Gum dissolved in oil by the ancients, and in turpentine by the moderns, has always been the main constituent of varnishes; Indian lac in every age being in use.

SECT. 3. GROUNDS; OR SURFACES ON WHICH PAINTINGS ARE EXECUTED.

The American Indian daubs bright colors on his buffalo robe, on his buckskin moccasins, and even upon his face, arms and breast; the Ethiopian adorns baskets and trinkets with colors; the grounds on which painting is first executed being articles of personal adornment.

As art became perfected, paintings were classified, virtually according to their grounds, into miniature, wall and easel. Ivory became the chosen material for the former; a stucco of lime for the second; and wood and afterward linen for the third.

Miniatures are so called from *minium*, red lead, first used as a flesh color in small portraits. The outline was scratched upon ivory with a sharp pencil, then traced in *carmine*, or crimson. In the Middle Ages parchment served as a ground for miniatures painted in tempera; especially in limning or the adorning of manuscripts. The name *vignette* was given to small heads wrought into the delicate vine borders of manuscript pages.

Wall-painting in Egyptian tombs and Assyrian palaces was exe cuted on a cement which received the nicest touches of the chisel, and was a firm ground for rich coloring. The principal ingredient of this cement, as the ancient Chaldee and Greek words show, was lime. Pliny mentions that in preparing stuccoed walls for painting, the lime, chalk or gypsum was beaten in a mortar and mixed with gum-water or milk. In marshy ground a first coat of brick-dust was laid on to arrest dampness. Pliny mentions what pigments were not affected by the lime of the ground. The walls of houses at Pompeii show the extent to which among the Romans this art was carried.

Ancient wall-painting seems to have been in *secco*, or on dry plaster. In *fresco*-painting, of modern origin, pigments are laid on when the mortar is fresh; the colors sinking in so as to resist the wear of time and of frequent cleaning. As in fresco the painter's work must be executed in sections, no more space being prepared than the artist can finish at a sitting, to prevent the junctures of the work of succeeding days from showing it is a study with artists to have the lines of each day's work fall in the shades, where the darker colors hide them. Some have supposed that the walls of ancient Pompeii show these junctures; indicating that *secco-fresco*, or the wetting of a dry wall already prepared, was practised by Greek painters.

Cimabue, reviving the art, painted dry walls in tempera; Giotto employed *intonacco*, or painting first on a lower then on an upper coat of cement; while Orvieto, a successor of Giotto, A. D. 1390, seems to have been the first to use *fresco* proper. Lionardo's chief works were in fresco; and M. Angelo admired it as "large-hearted."

For easel-pieces *wood* and *canvas* have been used as grounds alike in Egyptian, Grecian, Byzantine and Italian art. The qualities requisite in a tablet are "durability, infrangibility and inflexibility." Metallic tablets expand too much by heat; parchment bends easily; and both thus cause paintings to crack. Wood and canvas best meet the three requisites.

The ordinary Egyptian coffins were of wood, covered with a thick paint. A cheaper coffin was made of layers of linen cloth, united by intervening coats of lime-cement about one-fourth of an inch in thickness, the surface being covered with paintings. So common was wood for grounds that the Latin word *tabula* became a synonym for easel pictures; *machina* being the name for easel. Canvas or linen cloth was used by the Greek painters; Pliny speaking of a *linteum pictum* of Parrhasius; and mentioning that "Nero had ordered a colossal painting of himself one hundred and twenty feet high to be executed *in linteo*," or on canvas.

SECT. 4. SUBJECTS OF PAINTING; THE OBJECTS IN NATURE AND THEMES IN THOUGHT OR HISTORY SUSCEPTIBLE OF BEING REPRESENTED BY THE PAINTER.

The mind of man derives pleasure from things perceived by the senses, from ideas conceived in the understanding and images framed by the imagination, and from remembrances recalled and reproduced by memory. In the youth of an individual or of a nation things are the objects of thought and effort; in the maturity of a man or a people ideas are the study and the employ of human reason; while old age, be it that of an individual or of society, lives in the memories of the past. From these three fields of human thought, emotion and action, the artist must select his subjects; and in these three departments the spirit of art in every age and nation has shown progress.

The child draws simple objects such as houses; while the genius of a Giotto or West may sketch a sheep or a babe. The savage and half-civilized paint single objects; the American Indian, coloring the objects themselves; the Egyptian laying colors on pencil drawings of objects; and the artists of the Middle Ages illuminating manuscripts with vignettes.

In the age when thought begins, the idea of a Deity and of duty seems to arise; and the first effort of art is to carve and paint images of gods; the progress of this first stage of development culminating in ancient Egypt in pictured deities covering walls and tablets. Advancing intelligence, analyzing distinct attributes, has at length made not only the marble of Phidias, but the pigments of Apelles create a Jove that seems to speak from his pedestal, and to hurl his thunderbolt from the canvas. In this stage different tendencies in human thought lead to new varieties of subjects for the brush. From gods, painters have passed to men, ennobled by various classes of qualities and illustrious in different spheres. In this field Egyptian grossness and Chinese stolidity, Greek philosophy and Christian faith, have shown in human subjects chosen for the brush, the type of their own intellectual advancement. The last stage in this line of progress has been landscape painting; in which the highest science as to mathematical realities and optical illusions, causing mountains to tower, clouds to float, and water to ripple and foam, has made the artist's power seem magical.

Memories of the past have furnished painters their richest themes, and have filled picture galleries with their choicest gems. First came family portraits; which, presenting the features of an individual in his quiet life, but perpetuate a simple memory. Then, when the painter seeks to embody some elevated sentiment by fixing some characteristic expression, the superior range of subjects called "historic" is reached; the highest to which the Grecian painters aspired. Under Christian civilization the inimitable moral beauty pictured in the lives of Old Testament "friends of God," and the unapproachable spiritual grandeur everywhere manifested in the life of Christ, has furnished a fertility and fascination in subjects touched by the genius of modern art beyond the conceptions of the ancients; the variety of themes called "scriptural illustrations," developed by artists during the last eighteen centuries, being the most remarkable, as it is the all-pervading characteristic of modern painting. The height of human conception in exalted forms was perhaps reached when Lionardo, almost despairing of ever realizing his ideal of the countenance of Jesus, for weeks now roamed the crowded streets of Milan, and then sat for hours absorbed in efforts of imagination. When to this perfection of form attained in sacred themes by the Italian masters shall be added, what has never yet been fully attempted, truth to landscape views in the Holy Land, a new if not the climactic subject for the painter will have been reached.

SECT. 5. THE USES OF PAINTING; THE ENDS SOUGHT BY PAINTERS, AND THE CLASSES OF WORKS DESIGNED FOR DIFFERENT EFFECTS.

Human wants, individual, social and religious, existing in the early history of individuals and of nations, and calling for works of art when men are yet rude in their conceptions and coarse in execution, increase their demands as mankind refine in culture. In this progress three stages in the uses of painting are to be observed.

The demand for personal ornaments makes the field for works of art of limited extent and perfection. Even the religion of men, in this lowest type of humanity, seems to be an individual interest, showing itself unsatisfied with the idea of a spiritual being everywhere present, or even of a common and public deity far off in some distant temple; and seeking an embodiment of a supernatural power in some shrine in the family dwelling, or some image worn about the person.

The second stage, when the mind takes in the broader relation of a state or nation, is in nothing more marked than in the demand for new works in the department of painting. When the Egyptians, after two centuries of tribal life, reared the Pyramids, when the Hebrews sought a capital and temple, when Greeks, Romans, Arabs, Franks and Saxons attained civil union, then a new type of painting and new uses for this climactic art arose.

The architectural age of a nation calls for paintings of two classes; columnar decorations, and fresco, including panel and ceiling paintings. In Egypt, when architecture became truly an art, the columns of temples and the walls of tombs began to be covered with the rarest variety of painted objects and scenes. The Athenians, at the era of Pericles, sent as far as the Isle of Rhodes for painters competent to execute the wall paintings worthy of the Parthenon; while the Romans, yet rude, brought painters from Greece to fresco the walls of their Capitol at the early date of its erection. The history of church architecture is yet more significant; commencing with rudely-colored altar-pieces in the Western, and stiff though gorgeous pictures in the Eastern Church; maturing in frescoes, till under Raphael, Lionardo and Correggio, the walls of churches seemed to re-enact the scenes of Christian history, and their ceilings to open Heaven with its ethereal inhabitants; and finally, when oil-painting came to rival fresco, making the panels of churches, picture galleries of historic and sacred themes.

The highest advance in the art of painting is the age of "easel" or "cabinet" pieces, denominated by the ancients "tablet" paintings. When walls are all covered with frescoes, and temple niches and panels are filled with wall paintings proper, the spirit of art-creation is not exhausted, but is nerved for yet higher designs and efforts. Science, philosophy and literature, still advancing, present new subjects for embodiment, and improved taste demands more perfect execution in painting. Works of every variety, fruit pieces, animal sketches, portraits, historical pieces, Scripture incidents, landscape, fill wide halls and long galleries. For this end Zeuxis and Parrhasius, Apelles and Protogones stretched their canvas and smoothed their wooden tablets, giving the last glory to Grecian art. So now this climactic era of the painter's skill rules in the collections of the Vatican at Rome, of the Pitti Palace at Florence, of the Louvre at Paris, and of the National Gallery at London.

SECT. 6. STYLES OF PAINTING; THE METHODS OF COLORING CHARACTERIZING DIFFERENT AGES AND NATIONS, AND ORIGINATING DIFFERENT SCHOOLS AMONG PAINTERS.

The Asiatic, as represented by the ancient Egyptians and by the modern Chinese, never has attained to the higher principles of the art of painting, such as perspective in drawing and gradation in coloring. The European, as seen in the ancient Greek and modern Italian, has, from his first essays, recognized the laws of excellence, and after long practice has reached perfection in execution. Thus *ages* in design and execution are marked. Even in Egyptian painting eras of improvement are visible; in Greece no comparison could be made between the early essays of the hero painters and the finished ideals of Apelles; and in the history of Christian art no transformation could be greater than that in painting from the age of Cimabue to Raphael. Yet, again, in the last stages of the art, *schools* of painting have arisen; determined by the mental cast and consequent taste of the people of different sections and of the artists of different sects in the same country and at the same age.

The causes of these differences are various. Progress in painting has depended in part on the materials employed. Pliny marks the era between the monochromatic painters and those who, like Apelles, used four or more colors. Yet more as to the vehicles employed, water-color sketching, the clear and open lines of fresco, or the deep round moulding of oil-painting, artists have separated into classes and schools; Raphael, M. Angelo and Lionardo, with all their great skill in oil-painting yet loving the free scope, the quick execution and the striking effects of fresco.

In Asiatic painting there has been no division of schools. The earliest division in Greece, the Hellenic or Greek proper, and the Asiatic or provincial, was made after painting had been recognized as a sister art with sculpture and architecture; the freedom in conception, and adherence to nature in execution, peculiar to the Greek coming in this art into most marked contrast with the stereotyped and trammeled spirit of the Asiatic. The second division, that of the Athenian and Sicyonic schools, arose from the commercial and literary spirit of Athens, in contrast with the rural aristocratic conservatism prevailing at Sicyon. A double tendency widened the breach between the two schools: the taste of the people leading them to patronize their preferred style; while artists from distant provinces, according to their cast of mind, were drawn to one or the other of the two centres.

In the Augustan age three distinct schools again arose, nearly akin to the three Grecian schools just mentioned; namely, the Byzantine, the Grecian and the Etruscan. The Byzantine retained the stiffness in form and gorgeousness in color belonging to the old Asiatic school. The Greek proper aspired after the grace amid the departed glory of their native land; seeking to be masters in ideal and spiritual themes. The Etruscan, Grecian in spirit and Roman in patronage, uniting the ideal and practical, inaugurated a natural school; adhering to truth in form and color, and adding life and expression.

In modern times Italy alone has developed numerous divisions and sub-divisions of schools; as the Florentine, the first to return to nature as a model; the Venetian devoted to color, the Roman to form, the Lombard to expression, each with its sub-divisions; then the Neapolitan borrowing from all; the Bolognese Eclectic; and the Spanish, of the same cast with the Neapolitan, but more sombre in tone. All these leading schools devoted themselves almost exclusively to Christian themes; the Florentine taking living men and women as models for apostles and saints; the Paduan substituting classic forms in place of traditional or living personages; and the Sienese guarding the ecclesiastic traditions both as to form and color.

In Northern Europe the Flemish, living under a sky murky yet healthful, among a people cheerful almost to levity, pictured cheerful home and sportive pot-house scenes in dingy smoky rooms; while the German blended Dutch cheerfulness with classic grace and Italian brightness. In the French school among a people fickle and mercurial, genius is seen ever on the wing; taking a start with Giotto, and again from Lionardo, yet never guided by a steady fixedness of aim for generations. In England the influence of a cosmopolitan life, with the old Roman yearning after a broad domain, has bred artists persevering and steady, but over-conservative; like the Romans, too, more ready to accumulate by power and fortune than to create by patient native toil. Finally in America among a people made up of all nationalities, and gathering artists from every country in Europe, no decided national style, except in distant mountain scenery, has yet been established.

CHAPTER IV.

ASIATIC PAINTING; RUDIMENTARY COLORING DEVOID OF TRUE ART IN FORM AND SHADING.

As in sculpture and architecture, so in painting, the Asiatics have been true to the traditions of their fathers. As instructors of Africans, quick in rudimentary conceptions, docile as learners, and untiring in application, Asiatic masters taught in Egypt. In India, Persia and the Greek provinces, they gave a spring to minds more active than their own; the pupil advancing most after being separated from his teacher. The study of this field requires, *first*, a survey of rudimentary painting; *second*, a notice of Egyptian painting as the type of its class; *third*, a glance at the declining phase of this order of art as we turn eastward; and *fourth*, a reference to the westward advance, opening into the grand vista of the Grecian art.

SECT. 1. THE RUDIMENTARY STAGES IN THE EARLY HISTORY OF PAINTING.

The childhood of an individual is illustrative of the childhood of the human race. In Asiatic painting the germs of the art are readily traced.

A child's first effort at painting is a mere laying of color upon some object. The simple, uncompounded colors, red, yellow and blue, are his first delight. The Asiatic painter has retained permanently this first characteristic of rudimentary painting.

The second stage is entered when desire for contrast introduces more colors than one into the same picture. In this essay no idea of propriety has been conceived; for a tree is painted red, a cow blue, a hat yellow, without regard to *the* color which each object really has in nature and should have in art. This stage, again, becomes permanent in rudimentary art.

A third stage is reached when the idea of distinctive colors arises; though only approximate in its conceptions and partial in its applications. For the human countenance, peculiar in its hue, an approximation is sought in the color red; the whole face, lips, cheeks, forehead, having no gradation from the ruby-red of flesh-tint proper to the white of the eye. This germ of the idea of propriety in color, influencing the artist's choice of colors only in parts of his work, such as blue for a coat, and red or yellow for a vest or trowsers, becomes a permanent one in Asiatic painting.

The last stage of advance in rudimentary painting has been a simple increase in the number of pigments. The Egyptians used six different colors; the Japanese employ a greater variety. These varied colors were not graded admixtures; but they were substances found colored in nature, and used as found; having no definiteness of hue, and incapable of representing nature. Gradation of hues, secured by the continual addition to the fundamental color of a lighter or darker pigment, is never seen in Asiatic coloring.

SECT. 2. EGYPTIAN PAINTING; THE TYPE OF SIMPLE COLORING, WITHOUT PERSPECTIVE, SHADING OR PROPRIETY OF HUES.

The abundant relics of Egyptian paintings, executed centuries before those of the Greeks, surviving them for ages, preserved by the peculiar dryness of the climate, have given a rare opportunity for the study of the methods of those ancient artists.

Asiatic influence on painting in Egypt is alluded to by Pliny, who states that "Gyges the Lydian introduced painting into Egypt;" and he adds, "the Egyptians affirm that it was invented among themselves six thousand years before it passed over into Greece;" which he regards "a vain boast."

Pliny alludes to Egyptian varieties of ochres and metallic pigments used by the Greek painters; while also he describes their mode of painting on silver, and of fixing colors in dyeing. Wilkinson states "That the Egyptians possessed considerable knowledge of the metallic oxides is evident from the nature of the colors applied to their glass and porcelain. They were even acquainted with the influence of acids upon colors; being able in the process of dyeing or staining cloth, to bring about changes in the hues by the same process adopted in our own cotton works." Egyptian artists painted statues and columns; they laid metallic pigments on pottery and mouldings in clay to be burned in; and their frescoes covered walls and coffins coated with a lime cement.

The general characteristics of Egyptian painting are expressed in Pliny's picture of the rudimentary art just cited; he himself saying of the art in Egypt, "such it continues even now." Upon an outline drawing, destitute of shading, Egyptian painters laid their six colors with ungraded hue. They gave, however, a definite, if not accurate hue; distinguishing most perfectly the dark African, the brown Asiatic, and the straw-colored superior race of the North. Wheat is recognized by its reddish and barley by its gray tint; while gold and other metals are distinct in hue.

The fixed type they maintained in their art is thus commended by Plato in his "Laws:" "The art we have proposed for the education of youth was known long ago to the Egyptians. This people, having fixed by statute what forms and what music should be licensed, they had them represented in their temples. Nor was it lawful for painters or other inventive artists to make the least deviation from the authorized standard. Upon careful examination, indeed, it will be found that the pictures and the statues made by this people ten thousand years ago are neither an advance upon, nor inferior to those which they now execute."

Sect. 3. The Painting of Eastern Asia; the Declining Phase of Rudimentary Coloring.

Eastward from Egypt, painting, like sculpture and architecture, preserves its primitive type. In China most of the painting abundant in every mart, is of two of the classes already mentioned as found in Egypt. Wall painting has less place in this northern climate. Most of the Chinese painting is executed upon paper, cloth, glass or porcelain. The colors used are chiefly vegetable, sometimes ochre, with water as a vehicle. The ground often lacks the consistency essential to prevent the spreading of the pigments. Costume differs in hue; but there is no variation in expression, nor gradation of tint in flesh or any other color.

The Japanese painters have learned the rudiments of admixture and gradation in colors, of perspective and of chiaroscuro. In addition to black, white, red, yellow and blue, they employ the intermediate hues, crimson, scarlet, pink, rose, purple, saffron, purple-maroon, light and dark blues, and also various shades of brown. In their landscape views, rivers with groups of men in front, boats on the stream, and trees and mountains on the opposite side, are sketched with manifest though not accurate diminution from distance. They have mastered also the first principles of aerial effects, painting clouds in the evening twilight, below of a pink, and above of a purple tinge; water near the shore, of a saffron, and farther off of a maroon or brown tint. In neither clouds, water or flesh tints, however, is there any gradation proper.

The smaller isles of the Pacific and the coast of America, with a population evidently Asiatic, present only the rudest attempts at coloring.

SECT. 4. THE PAINTING OF WESTERN ASIA; THE ADVANCING PHASE OF RUDIMENTARY COLORING.

A line of improving art in painting may be traced northward through Arabia and Syria, which yet lives in the unburied monuments of Assyria; having relics also in Persia and Asia Minor. All these show a progress advancing in perfection toward Greece. The style of coloring now met in this region is no index to its past character; since Greece itself has for ages followed the Asiatic type.

In Hebrew painting there are three eras; that of Moses or the Egyptian, that of Solomon or the Phœnician, and that of Herod or the Roman. In the first age not only the simple colors, red and blue, but also scarlet and purple, were employed; but the pigments used were, as Josephus states, chiefly vegetable. In the second era, Hebrew, like Grecian and Italian art, had introduced mosaic inlaid with "glistening stones of varied colors." In this age, too, wall painting existed; ceilings being "painted with vermilion." In the third or Roman era no painting proper is found in the sacred temple; but the curtains were adorned with "purple flowers."

In Assyria the palace of the ancient Medo-Persian king was adorned with curtains "white, green and blue, fastened by cords of purple;" and had "a pavement of red and blue and white and black marble." Layard says, "The only colors first used by the Assyrians were probably blue, red, yellow, black and white." "These colors alone were used in the painted ornaments of the upper chambers of Nimroud." "The tints formed by their combinations may have been introduced at a later period." "The Assyrian red exceeds in brilliancy that of Egypt." "It nearly approaches to vermilion on the sculptures of Khorsabad; and has a bright crimson or lake tint on those of Nimroud." At this day, he adds, "Dyes of the finest qualities, particularly reds and greens, which even European ingenuity has not been able to equal, are obtained by the inhabitants of Koordistan from flowers and herbs growing abundantly in their mountains."

Statues, also, were colored by Assyrian artists. Layard remarks, "No trace of paint except in the eyes and on the hair has yet been found on the human body in Assyrian sculpture;" and he adds, "On the colossal lions and bulls, forming the entrances to temples, color only remains in the eyes; the pupils having been painted black and the rest filled with a thick white pigment."

Wall painting also was introduced into Jerusalem from Assyria; the Hebrew prophet, Ezekiel, mentioning "idols and men portrayed on the wall, after the manner of the Babylonians of Chaldea."

Layard also states of Assyrian palaces, "The ceilings were divided into square compartments painted with flowers or the figures of animals." A method apparently peculiar is alluded to by Diodorus, who states that "the figures of men and of animals seen on the walls of the palace of Semiramis at Babylon, were painted on the bricks before they were put in the furnace."

The advance of the Persians in this art, indicated by their superior work now met at Constantinople, may be traced to Homer's day among this Northern race. Pliny, the chief historian of ancient art, to confirm the very early and Arian origin of painting, appeals to Homer's mention of several varieties of the art existing among the Greeks and Trojans at the time of the siege of Troy.

CHAPTER V.

GRECIAN PAINTING; NATURAL COLOR UNITED TO IDEAL FORM.

THE Greeks, having attained ideal form in sculpture, united this in painting with true naturalness in color.

To analyze the history of painting among the ancient Greeks is difficult for three reasons. First, the relics of Ancient Grecian painting, unlike their sculpture and architecture, have nearly all perished; and it is only from scattered allusions by Plato and Aristotle, Cicero and Horace, Pliny and Pausanias, that material for such an analysis can be gained. Second, the technical terms employed by these authors, illustrated in sculpture and architecture by the works themselves, are unexplained in painting. Third, while able critics like Winckelmann have thoroughly classified works of Grecian sculpture and architecture, no kindred analysis in the department of Grecian painting has been furnished to modern students.

Pliny thus indicates the progress of the art in Greece: "The art of painting was discovered, some say at Sicyon, others among the Corinthians; all affirm that it began with the mere shadow of a man around which lines were drawn. The second stage was in single colors called *monochromaton*. At length art invented light and shade; the employ of different colors, alternating with each other, producing this effect. Afterward again there was added lustre; this being another thing than light; which, since it is between light and shade, they called *tonos;* while they named the commingling of colors *armogē*." These steps of progress, are, first, shading in colors; second, the conjunction and inter-blending of hues; and third, gradation of lights or chiaroscuro, producing tone and harmony.

SECT. 1. THE FORMATIVE PERIOD OF GRECIAN PAINTING, DURING THE AGES OF THE GREEK LYRIC AND EPIC.

This period covers about seven hundred years; from the fall of Troy, about B. C. 1184, to the restoration of the Athenian Democracy, B. C. 510. It began with Euchir, the beautiful-handed; whom Aristotle mentions as a near relative of Dædalus. A century later, about B. C. 1068, four eminent painters grew up as rivals; to three of whom, Philocletes, and Cleanthes and Crato, has been attributed the origin of drawing in outline; while two of them were painters of merit. The first was an Egyptian, the latter two were native Greeks, one born at Corinth, the other at the rival city Sicyon. The paintings of Cleanthes in the temple of Diana in Elis, Strabo says, were admired in the Augustan age; and they were quoted yet later by Greek sophists and Christian apologists as indices of the religious spirit of the early Greeks. A century later, in the ballad age, Ardices of Corinth and Telephanes of Sicyon were rivals for the invention of rudimentary *shading;* which invention Pliny regarded an era in the history of painting.

Next followed improvement in *coloring;* the *mixing* of colors for gradation of hues being introduced by four artists. Cleophantus, a Corinthian, about B. C. 655, used "ground earthenware" as a flesh color. Yet later, Eumarus, the earliest painter mentioned at Athens, "was the first to make a distinction of sex in painting."

The last step in rudimentary Grecian painting was the executing of likenesses; Leon painting a portrait of Sappho, who flourished about B. C. 600.

While noting this progress of the art in Greece proper, Pliny remarks of an eminent painter who flourished about B. C. 720, in the Greek provinces of Asia Minor: "Surprise need not be felt at the dignity to which this art so early attained in Greece, when the picture of the battle of the people of Magnesia, in Lydia, against the Cimmerian barbarians, executed by Bularchus the painter, was purchased for its weight in gold by Candaules the king of Lydia."

SECT. 2. THE ADVANCING DEVELOPMENT OF GRECIAN PAINTING UNDER AGLAOPHO AND DAMOPHILUS IN THE AGE OF THE GREEK DRAMA.

In the united progress of poetry and plastic art in Greece, the drama had more influence than the lyric and epic. In the sixty-first Olympiad, or about B. C. 535, Thespis first introduced science representations into Athens; Æschylus, Sophocles and Euripide succeeded; and for more than a century Athenian genius was devoted to the histrionic art.

A double influence was exerted by this new bent of the Athenian mind; the people demanded finely executed scenic representations, and a taste for large and extended paintings, to be seen at a distance, was awakened; which led on to fresco or wall painting. A cluster of artists arose who developed both these departments; the artists in higher walks being the leaders, the scenic painters but imitators.

The great early master in easel studies, or in historical subjects associated with higher portrait, was Aglaopho, contemporary with Æschylus; who, with his son Aristopho, painted the heroes of Troy. Cimon, of the same age, attempted portraits at oblique or quarter views, to bring out characteristic beauties of form. Alluding to the excellences of Aglaopho and his son Polygnotus, Quinctilian says that their "uncompounded color so captivates the minds that study it, that those almost rude first steps, as it were, in the future art are preferred to the greater masters who lived after them on account of a certain natural yearning we have to learn originating elements."

Wall painting was introduced about B. C. 493, from Greece into Rome, by Damophilus and Gorgasus, eminent in both stucco-moulding and coloring; who adorned the temple of Ceres in the Circus Maximus at Rome with both these arts.

At this era, during the age of Grecian supremacy in Southern Italy, at the home of the Greek philosopher Pythagoras, there appeared an eminent wall painter named Sillax; whose frescoes became famous.

Meanwhile artists devoted to *scēnographia*, or scenic decoration proper, flourished; then, as now, employing gaudy "uncompounded colors," without finished gradation or blending of hues; of one of whom, Serapio, Pliny says, "having proved unsuccessful at portrait-painting, he turned his hand to scenic painting, in which he attained eminence." Among others of this class the daughter of Cratinus was eminent; to whose lewd "comic scenes" the able Christian Father, Clement of Alexandria, alludes with disapprobation.

SECT. 3. THE RECOGNITION OF PAINTING AS A SISTER ART UNDER MICON AND POLYGNOTUS IN THE AGE OF PERFECTED SCULPTURE AND ARCHITECTURE.

The age of perfected sculpture and architecture covering the lives of Pericles and Phidias, from about B. C. 500 to B. C. 430, exerted a direct influence on painting. From stage decoration the decoration of works of architecture became the absorbing end of this art. Historic paintings, as rich in color and expression as th. genius devoted to that art could make them, began to cover th(inner walls of the Propylæa, of the Poicile and of other porticoe' about the Acropolis and Agora of Athens. Mathematical science, perfected by Pythagoras, was now directed to the fixing of proportions in forms; chemical knowledge was devoted to the improvement of pigments; and the germ of the study of proportion ir colored hues and shades is indicated by the azure backgrounds introduced into marble niches for statues, to set off their virgin whiteness. Pliny remarks that the picture of the battle of Marathon, painted on the Poicile, illustrated how far "the use of color had improved," and to what an extent "the art was perfected."

The first artist of this age, Micon, painted on the Poicile and in the temple of Theseus, legendary themes. With Panænus, the cousin of Phidias, he attempted a theme of recent history, the battle of Marathon, on the Poicile; in which having the independence to paint the Persians of larger stature than the Greeks, he was fined by the fickle democracy of Athens.

Polygnotus, born in the island of Thasos, was brought to Athens by Cimon, the Athenian General, to adorn the new temple of Theseus. Afterward he was employed by Pericles. Of his style, Pliny records, "He first painted women with transparent dress, and ornamented their heads with parti-colored turbans; and he added very much to the art of painting since he introduced the partial opening of the mouth so as to show the teeth." Aristotle ranks Polygnotus among *ethical* painters; thus alluding to the intellectual cast of his ideals: "Polygnotus painted objects superior to nature."

Panænus, the cousin of Phidias, who himself began his career as a painter, introduced an improved method in fresco; washing "the plastered wall with milk and saffron." Of his works, Strabo relates, "Panænus, the painter, worked much with Phidias, being his brother and fellow-laborer in the finishing of his carved work, by decorationg it with colors, and especially by painting drapery."

Aglaopho the second, nephew of Polygnotus, won that encomium of Cicero "that no lover of art would wish to have him other than he was." Athenænus, the sophist, with a spice of irony, mentions a picture of his in flattery of the young Athenian demagogue; in which was "seen Nemea seated, and upon her knees Alcibiades himself, more delicate in features than any woman."

SECT. 4. THE FIRST RECEIVED SCHOOLS OF GRECIAN PAINTING, UNDER APOLLODORUS AND EUPOMPUS, IN THE AGE OF GREEK PHILOSOPHY.

Plastic art having reached its climax, and filled Athens with the choicest works in sculpture and architecture, Socrates, born B. C. 470, trained as a sculptor, turned the Athenian mind to philosophy, already ennobled by Thales and Pythagoras. Under Plato, born B. C. 430, ideal philosophy, fitted to the genius of the Greek people, began to exert a controlling influence over the creations of art.

Discussions in philosophy originating rival schools, artists following the thinking men of their time, sought, according to their bent, to excel in the ideal, or in the natural; while many aspired to be teachers of art.

Among leading teachers appearing at this era was Evenor, "the father and preceptor of the painter Parrhasius," author of an "exposition hastening to the lights of art." Next came the resplendent Apollodorus, of whom Pliny records: "He first introduced the method of expressing splendor in sky," and was "the first of men to discover the mixture of pigments and gradation of shade." He excelled in "skiagraphy" or "shadow-painting," in which there is "contrasted aspect in color;" as opposed to "scenography," or scenic painting, which has no sky, and no alternation of light and shade. Fuseli says of Apollodorus: "He originated local color and tone; not light and shade in themselves considered; but as regulated by the medium which tinges both. . . . This was the element in the ancient *armogē*, that imperceptible transition, which without opacity, confusion or hardness, unites local color, demi-tint, shade and reflexes."

The great analytic teacher of this and of all ages in Grecian art was Eupompus, who taught Pamphilus, the preceptor of Apelles;

these three artists being leaders in the three climactic ages of Grecian painting. Pliny says of him: "So great was the authority of this artist that he divided painting into three schools; whereas before him there were two only, called the Grecian and the Asiatic. On his account, he being a native of Sicyon, the Grecian was by popular assent divided, so that three were established; the Ionic, the Sicyonic and the Attic." The Ionic was the old Asiatic; the philosophic spirit of the age of Eupompus having led to analytic instead of national names, by which to designate different styles in art. Eupompus taught Lysippus the sculptor, "that nature herself was to be imitated, not any artist." So perfectly absorbed was he in his work as teacher, that only one work of his is referred to by any ancient author.

SECT. 5. THE PERFECTING OF GRECIAN PAINTING UNDER ZEUXIS AND PARRHASIUS IN THE AGE OF GRECIAN ORATORY.

The era of the decline of the Grecian republics called forth Æschines and Demosthenes; and two classes of influences on art were thus called into exercise. The demand for practical oratory revived the popular taste for histrionic art, the orators resorting to rhetoricians and actors for training in elocution; and a style of painting hence originated corresponding to the "dramatic" of modern Florence.

In Greece as in other lands the age of the written drama was not the era of superior acting. Æschylus, like Shakspeare, waited long for a Garrick worthily to enact his conceptions. Two centuries after their dramas had immortalized Greece, the orator Lycurgus secured a decree of the Athenian people that authentic copies of the tragedies of Æschylus, Sophocles and Euripides should be deposited in the public archives.

As the influence of the dramatic age had been felt on the painters of that era, so the double stimulus of the age of oratory and of the histrionic art in two respects led to improved painting; first, giving added culture to artists, and second, suggesting new themes for the pencil. The inspiring appeals of Demosthenes to the works of art wrought in the times of Pericles, recording the deeds of the heroes of Marathon, roused artists as well as warriors; and the portrait of the orator Lycurgus in the glow of action by Ismenius was a new attempt in art.

Under Philip of Macedon, when at Athens the theoretical philosophy of Plato was yielding to the practical logic of Aristotle, Pamphilus, a Macedonian was teaching art; whom Pliny characterizes as "first in the art of painting to be learned in all that liberal art, especially in the science of numbers and of geometric measurements; without which he declared that art could not be perfected." His terms of tuition, a ten years' course, and "a talent" or about $1000 as a fee, indicate his eminence. "By his influence," following up the idea of Eumolpus of Sicyon, who nearly two centuries earlier had introduced the study of drawing and moulding into common school education, "the plan was effected, first at Sicyon, then in all Greece, that boys of free birth should be taught before all things complete drawing, including painting on box-wood." Pliny adds: "Pamphilus caused that the art should be received into the first rank of liberal arts."

The second great master, Zeuxis, came from Magna Græcia, the western province. His works were in *still life;* such as fruit and domestic scenes. In a contest with him, Parrhasius presented a curtain, and Zeuxis a cluster of grapes. When the birds pecked at his canvas, assured that he was victor, Zeuxis called on Parrhasius to remove his curtain and show his painting. Aware of his deception "He yielded the palm with ingenuous modesty, since he had deceived the birds, but Parrhasius the artist himself."

Pliny states that in his female figures Zeuxis "gave undue size to heads and joints." Quinctilian says: "Zeuxis gave more fulness to the members of the body; preferring it broader and more close-set; and, as it is thought, he followed Homer in this, to whom the most robust form, even in females, was favorite." Italian artists would censure with Pliny, and German commend with Quinctilian this plumpness of figure. Of his methods Pliny records: "He painted also *monochromata* in white."

Parrhasius, grand master in the impassioned style, is thus characterized by Pliny: "He first gave symmetry in painting, liveliness of expression, elegance to the hair, grace to the mouth; by the confession of artists having won the palm in terminating lines. This is the highest perfection in painting. For to paint bodies and the central parts of objects is indeed a great work; but one in which many have attained eminence. To execute the extremities of figures, and to round in the terminal line, is rarely discovered in the success of art. For the extremity itself ought to enfold itself; and so terminate that it shall project other parts behind itself, and also show what is concealed." Pliny adds, indicating how excellences are carried to excess: "Nevertheless he seemed to fall below himself in bringing out the central parts of his figures."

Parrhasius became an authority in painting; leaving "specimens of his drawings on boards and parchments which made him," Quinctilian says, "the founder of laws; because other artists, as if by necessity, follow his models." "He painted," Pliny relates, "an assembly of the Athenians," showing "varied expressions; the angry man, the unjust, the inconstant, as well as the yielding, the humane, the sympathizing, the high-minded, the conceited, the cringing, the overbearing, the shrinking; and all these expressions equally vivid."

Excessive vanity led him to vaunt himself to be "prince of art," and that "art was consummated by himself." Like too many men of genius Parrhasius gave way to degrading appetites and unmanly passions, painting "libidinous scenes on small tablets." Four centuries afterward under the Roman Emperor, Tiberius, these licentious works were exerting their corrupting influence. Seneca, father of the moralist, censures his inhumanity in his great work; stating that "when Philip sold the captured Olynthians, Parrhasius bought one old man among them, brought him to Athens, tortured him on the rack, and from him as a model painted Prometheus. The old Olynthian died under the torture; the artist deposited the picture in the temple of Minerva; and he is accused of having thus defamed religion."

Euphranor in this age was eminent for richness of color, and especially the softness and naturalness of his flesh-colors. He wrote a book on "Symmetry," which became a standard among sculptors; adding one on "Colors" equally authoritative with painters. Pliny and Plutarch regarded his Theseus superior to that of Parrhasius; he himself boasting, "that of Parrhasius was rose-color, but his own was real flesh." Of his Twelve Deities Valerius Maximus says: "He set forth Neptune in the most transcendent colors of majesty possible; having still to represent Jove yet more august. But every power of thought being exhausted upon the superior work, his after efforts were not able to rise to the point which he sought to attain."

A single picture of Timanthes is eulogized in like terms by Cicero, Valerius Maximus, Quinctilian and Pliny. The scene is the sacrifice of Iphigenia, daughter of Agamemnon, to appease offended Diana. Quinctilian's comment is: "In elaborating an oration there are things which either ought not to be presented plainly, or cannot on account of their dignity be expressed. Thus Timanthus, when in his Immolation of Iphigenia he had painted Chalcas sad, Ulysses more sad, and had added to Menelaus the highest expression which art could effect, the range of human affections being exhausted, not finding in what worthy manner he could express the countenance of the father, he veiled his head and left each beholder to form his own conceptions of it."

Among others eminent in this age was that Nicias; "concerning whom" Pliny says, "Praxiteles spoke when being asked which of his own works in marble he most approved, he replied, 'Those to which Nicias has given his touch;' so much did he attribute to his shade-tint."

SECT. 6. THE CULMINATING ERA OF GRECIAN PAINTING UNDER ITS GREATEST MASTERS, APELLES AND PROTOGENES, IN THE AGE OF THE POLITICAL UNITY OF GREECE UNDER ALEXANDER THE GREAT.

Under Alexander, the fresh and vigorous genius of Macedon, meeting the cultured refinement of Athens, Sicyon and Corinth, called forth the great practical teachers in science and art, Aristotle and Pamphilus. The ambition of the young Alexander, not only to be first of all the Grecian race as a military leader, but also as a fosterer of science and art, awakened the aspiration to show himself worthy to have such a city as Athens in all its glory brought under his sway.

The galaxy of masters in four departments of art. Dinocrates in architecture, Lysippus in sculpture, Pyrgoteles in engraving, was completed by Apelles, so unrivaled for ages that painting was called "The Apellean Art." Pliny mentions of this group: "Dinocrates laid out Alexandria when Alexander was founding it in Egypt; and this same emperor issued an edict that no other than Apelles should paint himself; none but Pyrgoteles engrave his likeness, and none but Lysippus cast his form in bronze; which arts these men have made illustrious."

In this age experimental science had perfected form in sculpture and had improved pigments and vehicles in coloring; while exact science had given the last power in perspective and grouping. Yet more at this era the true method of studying nature was realized under the teachings of Aristotle; and its employ by artists secured wonderful success in aerial effects. To this that great philosopher, teaching and writing in this age, refers, when, having alluded to skill in proportionate admixture of colors as "one method by which special hues are produced," he adds, "but another method is to make colors appear through each other; which painters employ when they place a second color over one more vivid; as when for example, they would make an object apparent in water or in a dense atmosphere; as too in nature the sun in itself appears to be white; but through a dense atmosphere, or through smoke seems to be red."

Two causes conspired to the superiority of Apelles; his untiring industry and the new methods which his studied efforts to aid other artists, and also the criticisms he invited from the common people suggested. As a specimen of his diligence, Pliny states: "He singly transmitted to his successors more improvements in painting than all other artists combined; he also brought together in published volumes what might serve for instruction in its theory." "He never spent a day so occupied that he could not practise his art by drawing a line; which habit of his passed into a proverb." In his disinterestedness, "he yielded the palm to Melanthius in grouping, and to Asclepiodorus in proportion; admiring the latter in symmetry." Pliny relates at length how he taught the people of Rhodes to appreciate Protogenes. Having on his first visit inquired of the modest artist for how much he would sell his pictures, he circulated the report that he had bought them for the enormous sum of fifty talents, or about $45,000, and intended to sell them at a profit; when the Rhodians bought them at his price, thus giving at once fortune and fame to their obscure townsman.

Apelles used to expose his finished pictures in the window of his studio, and avail himself of the suggestions of passers-by. Pliny relates that "being censured by a cobbler because in some sandals he had made one stitch more inside than outside, when the same man on the next day, boastful on account of the correction the artist had made on his former suggestion, caviled about the ankle, Apelles indignant stuck up this notice, 'Ne sutor supra crepidam judicaret, Let not the cobbler criticize above the sandal;' which also passed into a proverb." Pliny adds: "His society was very attractive to Alexander the Great, who often came into his shop. But, when Alexander gave opinions as to many things of which he was ignorant, Apelles courteously advised him to silence; saying that the boys who ground his paints were laughing at him. So great of right was his authority toward a king." "When he had ordered that one of his concubines, a special favorite of his own, Campaspe by name, should be painted naked by Apelles on account of his admiration of her form, when it became apparent that Apelles had fallen in love with her, he gave her to him as a present."

Among special methods invented by Apelles, "of great profit to others devoted to art," was the bringing out and softening of his colors with a minutely thin coating of black pigment, which no one succeeded in imitating. Apelles was remarkable for accuracy in likenesses and for skill in securing the best views. In painting King Antigonus, who had lost an eye, "he made the view oblique, so that what was wanting in his face seemed rather the necessary lack in the picture." He painted Hercules with his back toward the beholders; in which "this most difficult result was obtained; he showed his face more truly than if it were a front view." His skill in aerial effects is thus recorded: "He painted what cannot be painted, sheet-lightning, chain-lightning and heat-lightning." To two of his Venuses, preserved at Rome, one injured and the other unfinished, which no artist of any succeeding age was able to touch, Pliny and Cicero allude; the latter making one of them the turn of a sweetly sad sentiment.

Next to Apelles in this age of great artists was Protogenes, whose excellences were the exquisite delicateness of his lines and the body he gave to his color; both of which made his labor slow and the number of his finished works few.

Born in Rhodes, in his youth a ship-painter, he was brought out by Apelles. Having heard of his merit, Apelles visited Rhodes to seek him out, called at his studio, and learning that he was out, drew a fine colored line on a picture he was painting. Protogenes returning exclaimed, "Apelles has come!" then drawing a yet finer line in another color at its side he concealed himself, when, as he had promised, Apelles again called. Irritated at being refused a second time an interview, and piqued at being excelled, Apelles drew a third line yet finer, between the two, and hastily left. Protogenes hurried after him; and a friendship began that made Protogenes in fortune and fame second only to his benefactor.

Drawn to Athens, Protogenes painted frescoes on the porticoes of the Acropolis, yet waiting for a master-hand. Aristotle admired Protogenes' finished art; he painted "the mother of the philosopher;" and he was urged by him to attempt a work half-real, half-ideal, "the deeds of Alexander the Great." Pliny adds, "The impulses of his spirit and his peculiar bent in art impelled him the more to these works." Protogenes began this work, executing "reliefs in bronze;" probably designing a column similar to those of Trajan and of Napoleon, executed the one four, the latter twenty centuries later.

Returning to Rhodes in later years, his "Ialysus," described by Pliny, affords an epitome of the Grecian artist's life-labor. "When painting it he lived on boiled pulse, since this diet would sustain at once hunger and thirst, lest he should dim his perceptions by too great delicacy in food. He laid on four thicknesses of color as a protection against injury and age; so that the lower coat might succeed when the upper gave way." In it he sought to represent the foam issuing from the mouth of a panting dog. When, "despite his torturing anxiety of mind, though often he had wiped off the paint and had changed his brush," it still "seemed to be painted, not to be born from the mouth. At last enraged at art, he struck his sponge on the place, from it replaced the colors taken off just as he had desired, and fortune created nature in the picture." Only ten finished works of Protogenes are mentioned by ancient admirers of art; this fact explaining the allusions of Quinctilian, Petronius and Pliny to the excessive labor bestowed on his works.

To this age belonged Aristides, who in expression excelled Apelles. Pliny records: "He first painted passion, expressing those emotions of men which the Greek call *ēthe;* or violent affections." One of his master-pieces admired by Alexander, was a picture of a battle in which "a child is creeping to the breast of its mother dying of a wound, while the mother is understood to perceive it and to fear that it may lap blood, her milk being dried up."

In this age Pausias of Sicyon perfected the art of enamel painting. His power of contrasting and grouping was acquired from a flower girl whom he loved; "by imitating whose work he advanced that art to the employ of a most numerous variety of flowers." His power in foreshortening, shading and transparence is described by Pliny and Pausanias. "When he wished as the chief thing to show the length of the ox, he painted him with his head, not his side, toward the beholder, fully representing his size in both dimensions." "While all painters made of a glistening white the parts which they wish to appear prominent, and finished with black, he made the whole ox of a dark color, and gave body to the shade from itself; thus with great art representing all portions projecting forward in due proportion and in a bent form as if solid;" evidently introducing the light from behind the object. In a celebrated picture of his, "wine is flowing from a goblet, the goblet is of transparent material, and the face of a woman is seen through it." Of this era, too, was Nicias; whose teaching as to composition has already been quoted.

This culminating era was the age of writers on art. Apelles in his gathered volumes was the leader in this department. Melanthius also, among others, wrote a treatise on painting; of which Pliny made extended use in his history.

SECT. 7. THE DECLINING PERIOD OF GRECIAN PAINTING IN THE DECLINE OF GREEK POLITICAL SUPREMACY AND OF GREEK CULTURE.

Political domination awakens in a conquered nation a prejudice against the culture which gives the ruler superiority. Among the selfish and tyrannical successors of Alexander, only the Ptolemies of Egypt preserved the love of culture belonging to the true Greek. The history of Grecian painting, after Alexander, shows a steady though fluctuating decline, like the fading of a sunset sky, radiant at moments with scattered lines of rarest beauty; while, however, the gray is fast consuming the gold.

During this era, succeeding the ideal Plato and comprehensive Aristotle, the sensual philosophy of Epicurus was antagonistic to the spirit of true art. Yet the Eclectic schools of Athens, Pergamos

Tarsus and Alexandria gave to Greek genius in every department after Alexander's, and even after Christ's day, a congenial home. The appreciation, too, of Grecian art shown by the early Roman conquerors under the Republic, as well as by the first emperors, who not only transported to Rome works of ancient art, but invited Grecian artists as their teachers, acted against the tendency to degeneracy.

The first stage of decline manifested itself in the abuse of the imagination; the *phantasia* of Plato. The second cause of corruption arose from Roman fondness for decoration. An arrest of these degenerative tendencies acted for a time when Ptolemy Philadelphus was enriching the Museum of Alexandria with collections of literature and art, and the poet Aratus, a man of broad and refined general culture, was acting as his agent in gathering up in Greece the works of the best masters. Nealces, a special friend of Aratus, restored injured pictures of the old masters bought for Ptolemy's Museum. His skill in invention was shown in a picture of a naval battle on the Nile; whose breadth "like to a sea," was indicated "by the device of a little donkey drinking on the shore and a crocodile lying in wait for it."

A century of decline succeeded to the age of Aratus and of Ptolemy Philadelphus; revived at the Roman conquest of Greece, B. C. 168, by Paulus Æmilius; who, appropriating to himself nothing but the library of the usurper Perseus, was ambitious that the spirit of Grecian art should become the public treasure and renovator of the Roman people. The two lights of this age were Heraclides and Metrodorus; the latter "a painter and a philosopher," whom, when Lucius Paulus desired from the Athenians to send to him a most approved philosopher to educate boys, and also a painter to furnish decorations for his triumph, the Athenians chose as most eminent in each of the desired qualifications. The decline of fresco under Augustus alluded to by Vitruvius as stupid and libidinous, finds abundant illustration in the frescoed walls of Pompeii, now unburied.

The last in the line of the Greek painters proper was a Byzantine employed by Julius Cæsar at Rome, noted for his Ajax and Medea. Pliny, however, crowds into the close of his brief history the names of several artists, whom he groups in the last or declining age; his remark about them being, "Up to this point the chief leaders in each kind of the art having been presented, those next to the first will not be passed over in silence." He closes his history with the mention, "Women also painted," adding five names. Of these we observe that nearly all are daughters of painters, who from their fathers caught their devotion to art; their themes are generally ideal and religious; and they attained a grade of eminence which led Pliny to place them among painters of the lower rank.

CHAPTER VI.

ROMAN AND MEDIÆVAL PAINTING; CHARACTERIZED BY ARTIFICIAL COLOR AS AN ADJUNCT AND ORNAMENT OF ARCHITECTURAL FORMS.

AMONG the Romans painting was a mere adjunct of Architecture. Not only were walls and ceilings adorned with fresco on plaster, and with encaustic enameling on wood; but, Pliny says, "we begin even to paint stone." On the door-posts of private houses portraits of deceased ancestors in stucco took the place of statuary in marble and bronze preferred by Grecian taste.

It constituted a new era when, at the conquest of Greece, the cabinet paintings of the great Grecian masters were brought to the Roman capital. Pliny's memoir is studded with the frequent mention that such a painting executed by Zeuxis or Parrhasius, by Apelles or Protogenes, and even by earlier artists, were in this or that temple at Rome, either still seen or burned in the destruction of the edifices.

These collections from Greece awoke in a few Roman minds an ambition to rival these works of the Greek masters. Some of these Cicero found occasion to commend; but in general their genius produced only works of an inferior cast.

While Pliny was writing, a new spirit was coming over thousands of the Roman people; a quiet leaven. beginning in the insignificant Christian gatherings which Trajan directed this literary favorite of his to watch as novelties, was spreading its influence, destined to mould art in the two centres, Rome and Constantinople.

The eras in the history of Roman painting take their character from the series of events thus noted.

Sect. 1. Collection of Greek Paintings and Employ of Greek Painters at Rome.

A line of Grecian painters, beginning with the two who adorned the first capitol, is found at Rome during the ages of the Kingdom and of the Republic. One of the best was Eumælus; and the last Hilarius who flourished about A. D. 364.

The Romans, however, were eminently collectors of cabinet or easel paintings. About B. C. 167 Æmilius conquered Macedon, enriched by Alexander's influence with the best works of the Greek painters; and these movable paintings transmitted to Rome, whetted the appetite for a more extensive plunder. About twenty years later, Mummius, having subdued Achaia, bore off countless stores of statues and paintings. At a later period these were gathered in public repositories such as libraries and picture-galleries. Of these Pliny beautifully remarks: "In libraries are reverentially preserved not only true likenesses of the men whose immortal spirits are still speaking in the same places, but also human desire produces portraits not historically preserved, as happens in the case of Homer." Pollio, a consul under Augustus, began these collections, while Agrippa, who built the magnificent portico of the Pantheon, recommended to his countrymen "that the works of art they had gathered should be devoted to public use; and that to this end they should be placed in public repositories for the improvement of those who devoted themselves to the pursuit of art, as also for the pleasure and admiration of all."

Sect. 2. Native Roman Painters and their Productions.

As to the antiquity of Roman painting Pliny records: "There are in existence in the sacred structures of Ardea, paintings that are more ancient than the city of Rome. Among the Romans honor at an early period attached to this art." Of the source of this devotion, having mentioned that art in other nations declined "because as there were no images of souls, those of bodies were neglected," Pliny adds: "On the other hand, among our ancestors in the doorways might be seen not the works of foreign artists, either in bronze or marble, but busts in wax with curved borders drawn around these images and painted portraits."

Akin to these ovals at doorways were the painted shields called *clypeus* from the Greek *glypheos*, with the portrait of the owner in the centre, after the manner of the Carthaginian captured from Hasdrubal; these decorated shields naturally suggesting the oval form for a class of cabinet paintings.

As early as B. C. 300, the chief of the noble family of the Fabii, illustrious for generations under the title "Pictores" or Painters. decorated the temple of Safety at Rome. After the Fabian family, Roman painters of less merit succeeded. An interesting instance is mentioned of a mute, son of a man of consular rank, whom "Messala the orator thought should be taught painting; which the Emperor Augustus approved. The boy, having greatly advanced in this art, died."

Under Nero flourished three painters of native birth; under Vespasian, Pinus, and Mallius noted for his scurrility as well as ability; and under Trajan, Turpilius, a Roman knight, a native of Venice, of whom Pliny records, "his beautiful works are to this day extant at Verona. He painted with his left hand; which is related of no one before him."

SECT. 3. ROMAN TASTE IN PAINTING CHARACTERIZING EARLY CHRISTIAN ART.

In the early Christian church the ecclesiastical power of Rome gave to taste in art the same direction which the Roman civil power had inspired. The characteristics of early Christian painting may be gathered, first from the relics of this age preserved at Rome; and, second, from the writings of Christian fathers who allude to the paintings and artists of their times.

A succession of Greek painters, flourishing from about A. D. 100 to 350, is alluded to and criticised by Greek scholars and Christian fathers in terms so kindred that it is manifest appreciation of true art formed one of the peculiar characteristics of early Christianity. Thus Tertullian in the third century, in a controversy on the Stoic philosophy with Hermogenes, a Greek poet and artist, is not only most courteous in argument, but highly complimentary to the artist.

Very early, artists themselves Christians, and painting Christian themes, are met. The eras of this Christian art are differently marked by critical writers. Kugler, borrowing from architecture, styles the painting of this age "Romanesque." Mrs. Jameson, followed by Lady Eastlake, distinguishes between paintings of *supernatural* scenes, adapted to inspire religious awe, and *natural* scenes in the life of Christ and his apostles. Jarves styles the age of symbols and ideals of the supernatural *theological;* and the age when models for Scripture themes could be chosen from among living men *historical.*

The development of Christian painting makes prominent these four elements and ages. First, the *symbolic;* simple signs of ideas and instruments depicting an office; practised by Christian artists for three or four centuries. Second, the *mystical;* the representation of supernatural beings; a style culminating in the Byzantine church, and fixed to this day; ruling also in the Western church with occasional intervals during eight or nine centuries, till the revival in Italian painting. Third, the *ascetic;* natural personages in an unnatural state of dejection or exhilaration, a style originating in Italy, holding sway till the age of Raphael and finding its congenial and permanent home among the Spanish painters. Fourth, the *historical;* in which incidents in the lives of the patriarchs and of Jesus find natural representation; an era commencing with the great masters of Italy and becoming the very life of Christian art in modern Europe. All these styles had a germ nurtured in the field of Roman painting.

Kugler makes the earliest period of Christian painting end with the invasion of Rome by the Lombards in the sixth century. He classifies its subjects and objects in five groups; *first*, emblems proper, such as the cross, the anchor, etc.; *second*, funeral inscriptions and symbols; *third*, paintings of Christ's features or form; *fourth*, miniatures of eminent Christian men; *fifth*, mosaics, beginning in the fourth century with the decoration of walls instead of pavements. These divisions are made on diverse grounds; the first relating to objects colored; the second to the location and use of the painting designed; the third to subjects represented; the fourth to the size of the works executed; and the fifth to material employed. The consideration of the first and last of these groups belongs to the subject of decorative art; the second third and fourth are the painting proper of this age.

The Catacombs of Rome, like the tombs of Egypt, are the permanent gallery of early works in Christian painting. About sixty of these ancient burial-places remain; the most interesting of which are on the old Appian Way. The themes relate to the Christian's trials and rewards; among the former Adam and the serpent, Moses smiting the rock, Daniel among the lions, the three children in the furnace and Jonah in his arbor; among the latter Adam and Eve in Eden, Noah and his dove, Moses at Sinai, Elijah ascending, the Good Shepherd and the raising of Lazarus.

A head of Christ illustrates the artistic execution of these paintings. The face is oval, the nose straight, the eyebrows arched, the forehead high and smooth, the hair parted on the forehead and hanging in long curls on the shoulders, the beard thin, short and divided, the expression mild and serious, the age between thirty and forty years. These artists never represented the Divine Being but in a symbol, such as a finger pointing from a cloud; and they placed no *nimbus*, or circle of light, about any head but that of Jesus. They represented historic scenes of the Old and New Testaments with the naturalness of true life; borrowing from classic art such models for ideals as Mercury and Orpheus.

At an early period a tradition prevailed that Luke, like other Greek physicians of his day, was a painter. Irenæus, who lived as near to Christ's apostles as we do to Washington, attests that pictures of Christ were found in the hands of lovers of art, as well as of Christian believers. As Origen, Clement of Alexandria and Tertullian in the next generation intimate, at first these representations, corresponding with the sad history of the Christian Church, embodied the image of the "Man of Sorrows." When, however, under Constantine, Christians were the happy instead of the unfortunate of earth, then, as Jerome and Eusebius state, artists made Jesus the reflex of their own changed aspect, painting him as "the one altogether lovely." A generation yet later, so intelligent and devout a man as Augustine, alluding to the pictures of Christ then multiplied as "varied in expression and composed after innumerable conceptions," argues that all these are legitimate and true, since they give the ideal best suited to aid the mind of each student of his character. In the early days of the Church no thought is hinted that pictures of Christ, in ideal representations, were anything else than contributions of art to general culture, and an aid to the study of Christian truth.

When, however, thousands who had been trained to worship images of Grecian deities nominally avowed themselves Christians, the paintings, then frequent in churches, naturally became objects of religious reverence, leading to restrictive canons. The fact that the churches at this era were filled with paintings liable thus to abuse is the strongest possible testimony as to the purity, as well as to the extent, of the culture of this art among the early Christians.

SECT. 4. THE BYZANTINE STYLE OF PAINTING; RIGID IN OUTLINE AND EXCESSIVE IN COLORING; PERMANENTLY ESTABLISHED IN THE EASTERN CHURCH.

As Christianity came from the East and the first Christian Emperor established a new capital on the borders of Asia, it was natural that Asiatic ideas in art should influence even the Greek. The style of painting, Asiatic in caste, though Christian in sentiment, called Byzantine, which began at the Eastern capital in the fourth century after Christ, had characteristics both of form and color which live on the walls of Greek churches to this day.

In form the Byzantine designed only single figures, and hence had no perspective; it did not attempt portrait; and it had no background or shadow giving projection to the figure. In the posture of the head there is a rigid stiffness without any expression; the cheeks are lank and corpse-like; the body is thin and lifeless; and the dress is stiff as with starch, having no flowing grace. Restricted to sacred persons, the Byzantine represented Christ on the cross as sinking, his head hanging, his knees relaxed and his body swayed to one side; while the Italians always in the crucifixion pictured Jesus vigorous with life, erect and victor over suffering.

In color the Byzantine painters are yet more Asiatic. They use the pure colors without gradation of shade or hue; flesh color is cherry-red, with no variation for forehead, cheek, neck or hand; and dress is glaring yellow or blue, pink or purple. Though the colors are laid on with thickness, they have no transparence; and though the polish is perfect, it is the burnish of metal, not the irradiation of color reflexes. The striking peculiarity of the Byzantine is the golden background forming the halo-relief to sacred heads. Only occasionally, in the age of Constantine, and later, as in the tenth century, did genius assert its sway in this style.

The differing positions taken by the Eastern and Western

churches as to images and pictures in sanctuaries gave the leadership to Byzantine art. In the age of Constantine, at a council of the Western Church held at Illiberis in the south of France, a town then decayed but rebuilt by Constantine in honor of his mother, a decree was adopted to the effect, "that pictures ought not to be in the church, lest what is painted on the walls should be superstitiously reverenced and worshiped." A reaction naturally followed; and about A. D. 590, Gregory the Great, wrote, "Paintings ought to be retained in the churches, in order that those ignorant of letters may as it were, read by looking on the walls what they are not able to read in the manuscripts."

Meanwhile in the Eastern Church painting became even more cherished from the order of Justinian, A. D. 692, forbidding images. The rich coloring of the Byzantine spread westward, and became a fundamental characteristic of the subsequent Venetian school. During ten centuries Greek ecclesiastics of culture, as Chrysostom, the Demosthenes of the Grecian pulpit, were "devoted to encaustic painting." Down to this day the chief seat of this art has been the promontory of Mt. Athos; on which no less than twenty-two convents, occupied by over four thousand monks, are consecrated to the art so much in demand in the Greek Church.

SECT. 5. THE ROMANESQUE, OR RUDE NATIVE STYLE OF PAINTING LONG PREDOMINANT IN NORTHERN ITALY.

The demand in the Western Church for sculpture made form rather than color to be the aim of Roman painters. As distinguished from the Byzantine, the style called Romanesque was statuesque in form; while in color it introduced a subdued and lack-lustre tone, the cloudy gray of a time-worn marble statue, rather than the gaudy sky-blue, crimson and purple of an Oriental grandee.

The seats of this style were Rome and Parma, the Umbrian valleys and Lombardy. In Umbria it was rigid in outline and lifeless in color; while in Lombardy it became more truly a copying of nature. Under Charlemagne it reached its highest stage of development; specimens of which improved style are preserved at Rome, Paris and Munich.

Its gems in Italy were the fine old mosaics now met in the most ancient churches, executed between the fifth and ninth centuries.

Usually located in the arches of the choir back of the altar, they represent Christ with an expression placid and gentle, and his garments hanging in plain folds. The excellence both in outline and coloring of these mosaics, which could not perish with time, is a testimony to the merit of painting proper, which must have decayed.

Prevailing until the eleventh century, the Romanesque was first modified by the introduction of the Byzantine style of coloring into Venice; then, finally superseded by a return to the method of drawing from nature in Florence, Padua, Milan and other cities where there was special freedom of thought in science, philosophy and religion.

CHAPTER VII.

THE RISE OF MODERN PAINTING IN SOUTHERN EUROPE, INCLUDING ITALY AND SPAIN; PRE-EMINENTLY RELIGIOUS IN ITS THEMES, CLASSIC IN FORMS, AND SPECIALLY CHARACTERIZED BY PERFECTION OF LIGHTS IN COLORING.

In modern painting, more than in literature, the progress of Christian thought is to be traced. For centuries only symbols, then portraiture, at first placid, next ascetic, again sensuous, and finally natural, were leading on to higher art.

The new spring given to science and philosophy in the eighth and ninth centuries under Alfred of England and Charlemagne of France, showed fruit from the fourteenth to the sixteenth centuries. In England, Roger Bacon in science, Chaucer in letters and Wickliffe in religious inquiry, opened the door for Lord Bacon and Newton, Shakespeare and Milton, and the lights of the Anglican Church; in France and Germany, Copernicus and Tycho Brahe, Rabelais, and Thomas Aquinas led on to Descartes and Leibnitz, to Luther and Pascal. In Italy, the land pre-eminent in art, Columbus and Galileo, Lorenzo and Machiavelli, Dante and Petrarch, Savonarola and Leo X. were products of the age of Giotto and

Brunelleschi; opening the way for Lionardo, Raphael and M. Angelo.

In the progress of painting in Italy from the twelfth to the eighteenth centuries, native temperament distinguished the Tuscan of Grecian descent from the Umbrian of Italian lineage; commerce with the East made the Venetian most unlike to the agricultural Sienese; and the republican Florentine and the hierarchical Roman, the scholastic Paduan and the romantic Neapolitan necessarily belonged to different schools in art. The cosmopolitan and comprehensive leaders, Giotto, the originator, and Lionardo, Raphael and M. Angelo, the finished masters, influenced all the Italian schools. Five leading divisions are recognized: the Tuscan, Roman, Bolognese, Venetian and Lombard; and as subdivisions in the Tuscan, the schools of Florence, Siena and Pisa; in the Roman, the Roman proper and the Neapolitan; in the Lombard, the schools of Milan, of Parma, of Mantua, of Cremona and of Verona; to which some would add those of Genoa and Piedmont. A classification founded upon periods of historical development and predominance of methods, may be more serviceable to the ordinary student.

Italian painters have had three leading characteristics. Their themes have been pre-eminently Christian; in form the classic has been preferred; while in coloring, including the rich, deep twilight hues of the Venetian, the pale, hazy morning shades of the Umbrian, and the clear, bright noonday radiance of the Florentine, all in keeping with the transparence of their sky, they have excelled in light and brilliant colors.

To trace these features of Italian painting as they began with Cimabue, gained ascendancy under Giotto, and developed to perfection of expression in the Tuscan, of form in the Paduan, and of color in the Venetian schools, as they were combined in the three great masters modifying through their influence all the schools, and controlling even the mystic Neapolitan and superstitious Spanish schools, as they were revived aspiring to a union of excellences in the Eclectic and ambitious of a new youth in the Natural schools, and finally as they declined till their light went out for generations, will be the instructive history of this chapter.

SECT. 1. THE EARLY REACTION OF THE LOVE OF NATURE AND OF GENIUS IN ART AGAINST FORMALISM AND DOGMATISM IN NORTHERN ITALY.

In the age called Romanesque, from the fifth to the twelfth centuries, painting was assimilated to the style of church architecture. Occasional artists, as Giovanni, about A. D. 960, and Petrolino, A. D. 1110, executed frescoes still admired at Rome by the side of later works. Yet later the celebrated Monk Bernhard, alluding about A. D. 1125, to the paintings on convent walls representing "pagan and sensual subjects," indicates that a corrupted classic taste was prevailing.

In the early part of the thirteenth century the arched panel pictures of the Romanesque churches at Pisa, Lucca, Siena and Florence, began to display an improving taste. These new artists drew portaits of saints, not emaciated and cadaverous like corpses, according to the Latin method; nor as painted puppets decked for a show, after the Byzantine style; but as beings of flesh and blood, "men of like passions with us all."

The leader in this formative era, Cimabue, was the originator of the natural school. Vasari, the historian of Italian art, says of Cimabue's portrait of St. Francis, "He drew that which was a new thing in those times from nature as though he knew her the best model." In the fields and crowded streets, he sought models which he studiously copied; and he established a school of drawing which became the germ of modern academies of art.

The faults of Cimabue's style were emaciation and stiffness in his figures; which faults, transmitted to his pupils, are illustrated in the celebrated Beatrice of Dante.

SECT. 2. THE NATURAL STYLE ESTABLISHED UNDER GIOTTO, AND THE RISE OF DISTINCT SCHOOLS UNDER ITS INFLUENCE.

As Cimabue was riding one day into the country, he saw a shepherd boy reclining on the ground, engaged in drawing with a bit of slate on a smooth stone, while his flock browsed around. Alighting and looking at the boy's picture, Cimabue found that he had executed a most natural and admirable likeness of a sheep standing nigh him. The marks of superior genius in the boy, now only twelve years of age, were so manifest that the artist prevailed on his father, but an humble peasant, to allow him to take him with him to Florence and train him in his school of drawing and coloring. His proficiency appeared when one day he painted a fly on a half-finished picture of his master, so life-like that on his return he brushed his hand over the shrewd boy's work to drive the supposed intruder away.

The age was prepared for an independent leader; the Dominicans, the conservators of art, as the Benedictines were of literature, being eager for improvement; while the political disputes of the Guelphs and Ghibellines led Rome to court the good-will of Northern Italy. Giotto, like Apelles, was laborious and courteous; he traveled south to Naples, then north to Piedmont, and over the Alps into France; seeking out everywhere the best artists, inquiring into their methods and explaining his own. His good nature extended even to brutes; a pig who threw him down in a gala-dress receiving this laughing address: "You are quite right, brute. I, who have gained so much by your bristles, have never given you even a dish of soup." This equanimity carried Giotto through the political conflicts of his day, preserving the good-will of all parties as a man who could best serve his country by entire devotion to his profession.

The style of Giotto had its faults as well as its excellences. His excellences were, conformity to nature in attitudes, dramatic energy in expression, and effective grouping. His St. Francis in attitudes, his Dante in enthusiastic expression, his Last Supper in grouping, and his allegorical paintings in the Campo Santo of Pisa in dramatic power, are his master works. Like other leading artists, Giotto was a comprehensive genius; excelling in drawing, sculpture, architecture, painting, music and poetry. When Pope Benedict IX. sent to him to furnish a plan for a new church, Giotto, pausing a moment in his work, took a pencil, with a sweep of his hand drew a perfect circle, and handing this to the messengers, told them to bear it back to the Holy Father as his reply. The Pope construed aright this testimonial to his general power, and employed the artist in his proposed work.

Giotto executed fresco, tempera, mosaic and miniature; making great improvements in materials and methods. M. Angelo used to study with admiration his preserved works, and his frescoes recently uncovered at Pisa have opened even in modern days a new field of art study. Giotto left at Florence not less than one hundred pupils. In Naples he formed, with Simone, an undying friendship, greatly to the advancement of Neapolitan art. A generation after his death his method was introduced into Milan and Venice.

SECT. 3. THE TUSCAN SCHOOLS; THE DRAMATIC OF FLORENCE AND THE CONTEMPLATIVE OF SIENA.

The influence of Giotto was greatest in his native Tuscany; two classes being roused by his spirit; the commercial class of Florence, cosmopolitan in character, and moved by the dramatic action accompanying passion; and the quiet, thoughtful, agricultural people of the valleys about Siena, who loved the contemplative and nature in still life.

The secular spirit of the Florentines is seen in the following decree appointing Arnolfo as the architect of their magnificent cathedral: "Whereas the chief aim of a people of illustrious origin should be to act in such a way that from its seen works every one should recognize its wise and magnanimous councils;" following which preamble is the order to restore the edifice, "in the style of the greatest magnificence which it is possible for human genius to conceive."

When, on the other hand, Duccio of Siena was called to execute his celebrated altar-piece, he pledged himself in his contract, dated October 9, 1308, "I will execute it according to my best ability and as the Lord shall grant me skill." In the decree passed A. D. 1438, concerning the architect of their Cathedral, the proviso is inserted, "no one even suspected of immorality shall be eligible."

These two Tuscan schools of painting, existing before Giotto's day, though taking their cast from his influence, true to the spirit of their ancestry, resorted like the ancient Greek to the ever-varying field of nature itself. Since, however, the fields of nature seen by the Florentine and the Sienese were most unlike, the Florentine style was dramatic, the Sienese contemplative. The themes of both were religious; but the Florentine sought to make sacred scenes stirring and splendid, while the Sienese sought to render his pictures a sermon full of solemn thought; one gave a lively cheerfulness, the other a grave and even sombre hue to the real saints he depicted. In the Florentine school, Spinello Aretino, born

A. D. 1308, more bold and less tender than Giotto, gave the impassioned action of the drama to Florentine painting. Associated with him, as a sort of counterpart, was Buffulmaco; so fond of the sportive that sacred themes could not put restraint on his wit.

Orcagna, born A. D. 1329, under the influence of the perfected sculpture of Ghiberti, attained a sublimity of action which made him the precursor of M. Angelo. As the feminine counterpart of the masculine Orcagna, Angelico, born A. D. 1387, added as a new element, intense earnestness of manner and unearthly etherealness of mould. There is a bewitching fascination about his frescoes of the Madonna which never fades from the memory when once viewed.

Massacio, born A. D. 1402, having studied architectural perspective under Brunelleschi, became noted for scientific accuracy of form. He drew from nude figures, both male and female; as did also Ghirlandaio, born 1449, the teacher of M. Angelo; whose servant women even are princesses in mien and bearing. From him the Florentine school caught this, its last characteristic feature.

In Siena, a hundred years before Cimabue, a fraternity of artists chiefly sculptors existed, out of which grew the order of St. Luke, whose bond of agreement had this preamble: "Since we are teachers to ignorant men," and "since in God every perfection is eminently united," "we will in our work earnestly ask the aid of the Divine grace."

Among this fraternity in the age of Giotto was Simone Martini, born 1284; whose style under Giotto's teaching was transformed into that natural sweet expression which became a leading type in the established Sienese school. After Simone was Ambrogio, born 1265; in whose greatest work, "The Career of a Franciscan Missionary," the picturing of a terrific hurricane, with lightning and hail, anticipated the most difficult attempt of later landscape painters. In its decline the Sienese was lost for a time in the Umbrian school.

SECT. 4. THE SCHOOL OF PADUA DISTINGUISHED BY CLASSIC FORMS, THE DIRECTLY ASSOCIATED SCHOOL OF VERONA AND FERRARA, AND THE INDIRECTLY CONNECTED SCHOOLS OF MILAN, BOLOGNA, MODENA AND PARMA.

In the broad long valley between the Alps and the Apennines, embracing all Northern Italy, are four cities, Padua, Verona, Mantua and Milan, and four small States, Ferrara, Bologna, Modena and Parma, closely associated in the history of art.

The special pride of Padua was its University, exalted by the genius of Galileo about the close of the sixteenth century. The tendency of science is to precision in form, and under its shadow artists strive after geometrical and anatomical exactness.

Giotto visited Padua, and his principle that nature should be made the painter's model, led Guarcento, about A. D. 1350, to add to the special study of form the dramatic expression of the Florentine school and the brilliant coloring of the Venetian.

The great master who fixed the style of the Paduan school was Squarcione, born A. D. 1396. Regarding the ancient Grecian models as a truer type for imitation than living men, since they were ideals founded on the real, he traveled as far as Greece, collected specimens of the antique, made numerous drawings, and, returning, established an academy of design, into which not less than one hundred pupils were gathered. His teaching cultivated a classic style and a preference for mythological themes; giving an excellent training to young sculptors, but leading in painting to statue-like forms ghostly in aspect.

At Mantua, about a generation after Squarcione, Mantegna, called the successor of Squarcione in the Paduan school, improved on his style, giving grander and fuller proportions to his figures, and a greater richness to their drapery. His best works, now at Paris and at Hampton Court, England, exhibit elegance as well as breadth of design.

At Verona and at Ferrara a double influence was exerted; the Venetian school prompting brilliance of coloring, and the Paduan inspiring grace in form among its artists. Even Milan in the extreme west adopted the Paduan model; a tendency which at a later period invited Lionardo, the most thoroughly Grecian of the great masters.

The classic spirit was yet more marked at Bologna; da Gubbio, a contemporary of Dante and Giotto, being ranked by Raphael between Perugino of Umbria and Bellini of Venice. During the youth of Lionardo, Melozzo was the recognized head of the style of ceiling painting, called by Italian artists "Sotto-in-su;" or below-in-above; in which figures are represented ascending erect, with their feet toward the beholder, the most difficult of foreshortening. The schools of Modena and Parma were unimportant until the age of Correggio.

SECT. 5. THE SCHOOL OF VENICE; DEVOTED TO THE ATTAINMENT OF RICHNESS AND BRILLIANCE OF COLORING.

Through the trade which had enriched in turn the Egyptians, Greeks and Romans, the Venetians gained a taste for Oriental art. In architecture the Saracenic-Byzantine, and in painting the rich coloring of the Byzantine became favorite. Under the influence of a more refined culture, gold, crimson and azure, softened into the darker but even richer purple and maroon. The habits of the people revelling at night in the subdued glare of torch-light on the water, cultivated a fondness for that bewitching fascination of dim outline in gorgeous shade which is the prevailing cast of Venetian painting.

While that early taste came from the East, its improved culture was derived from Germany. Commercial intercourse, political affiliation and kindred love for festivities and parades, tended to this latter association. Antonio, a pupil of Giotto, attempted in vain to supplant the Byzantine; the clear outline and transparent color of the Florentine not commending itself to either people or artists. The dark shading, however, of the German, and the cheerfulness of the Dutch, introduced by Giovanni Alamanus, or John the German, early in the fourteenth century, became nationalized among the lagoons of the island city. Gentile da Fabriano, born A. D. 1370, highly dramatic in his themes and in the posture and expression of his figures, yet rich and even gay in coloring and fascinating in aerial effects, became an authority not only at Venice, but also at Rome; M. Angelo, a century and a half later, regarding him as a prophet of the future; saying that "Gentile's works as well as his name were his autobiography."

The Venetian school attained superior rank when about A. D.

1450, oil was introduced as a vehicle. At an early period the Venetian painters had followed the Greek method, of laying on their canvas first a dark background, adding next their darker shades, and then making their lighter hues and tints superficial; the use of wax as a vehicle giving a partial transparence which allowed the underlying colors to show through and modify those above them. The revived Italian and Flemish method made the foundation-color light; since, with a gummy vehicle having little transparence, an underlying white gave relief and softness to darker colors above. The use of oil permitted a return to the Greek method, allowed by its transparence, depth and blending of overlying colors, and giving the soft, dark shade and indistinctness of outline preferred at Venice. From this era dates the superior success of the Venetian school; the Florentine being averse to the sluggish flow and labored kneading peculiar to oil as well as to the darkness of shades produced by it. The themes of Venetian artists still called for a quiet dignity; even their scripture personages being merchant princes.

Bellini, born A. D. 1501, the great master of this school, excelled in architectural backgrounds; a feature natural to a city having no streets or suburbs adorned with foliage. This influence, associated with the "alluring color at Venice," begun by Gentile and perfected by Titian, Fuseli thinks, led the way to landscape painting; since it demonstrated the methods of securing its two leading characteristics, "the harmony due to balance of colors," and the "breadth of local tints."

Sect. 6. The Umbrian school of Central, and the Neapolitan of Southern Italy; formal in style and mystic in religious spirit.

In common with the North the style of painting prevalent in central and southern Italy was in drawing formal as opposed to natural, and in design mystic as contrasted with the practical. Two causes contributed to maintain these characteristics. As in Egypt so at Rome, the Orthodox models for religious themes being fixed, a radical revolution alone could produce the requisite change. The old Latin, as opposed to the Byzantine, prevailed; destitute of anatomical correctness in expression, and lacking both body and distinctness in color. The Roman people, moreover, unlike the commercial and adventurous inhabitants of Pisa, Florence and Venice, never went abroad to borrow ideas from other nations.

The spirit of mystery, fostered during the crusades, had its special seat in the retired valley of Umbria, north of Rome; whose people, Pliny states, were regarded the aboriginal tribe of Italy; the Greek colonists of Etruria calling them Ombrioi, as remnants of the antediluvian race. This ancestral tradition, making them special objects of Divine interposition, fostered by their seclusion, made Umbria the natural home of the ascetic and mystic brotherhood of the Franciscans. The art-spirit of this order invited visits from Cimabue and Giotto: and subsequently three currents of influence modified the school; one from Florence, leading to the study of nature's models; a second, through Ancona, introducing Venetian taste in coloring; and a third, through Urbino, prompting to themes of the supernatural.

The head of the Umbrian or early Roman school was Piero, of the Franciscan brotherhood, born A. D. 1400. Trained at Florence; settling first at Perugia, on the Tuscan or western side of the Tiber, he afterward crossed into Umbria. He excelled in the three features of the natural style introduced by Giotto: perspective, foreshortening and the securing of breadth between his figures. Among his pupils, the precursors and instructors of the great masters, were Luca, who in his "Last Judgment" anticipated M. Angelo; Antonio, noted for his dissections and anatomical exactness in drawing; and Verrochio, who had as his pupils Lionardo, the first of the three great masters, Perugino, the teacher of Raphael, and Lorenzo di Credi, one of the chief lights in the future of the Umbrian school.

Perugino, so called from his native town, born A. D. 1446, trained first in Umbria then at Florence, was devoted entirely to religious themes; his early works being of the ascetic Umbrian type; those of his mature years of the secular Florentine cast, while some works of his later life were wanton and vulgar.

The most finished and pure of the school was Lorenzo di Credi, born 1459. Opposed to Perugino's wantonness, he rejected the nude entirely; taking as the moral law of his art this sentiment of the reformer, Savonarola: "Creatures are beautiful in proportion as they participate in and approximate to the beauty of the Creator; and perfection of form is relative to beauty of mind. Bring hither two women equally perfect in person; let one be a saint and the other a sinner; you shall find that the saint will be more generally loved than the sinner, and that on her all eyes will be directed." The sweetest of the galaxy of Umbrian painters, was Francesco Francia, born 1450; the congenial companion, the virtual master and afterward the friendly rival of Raphael.

The Neapolitan, from the earliest times associated with the Roman school, shared with it the influence of the Florentine. Tomaso de Stefani, contemporary with Cimabue, and Simone with Giotto, caught the spirit of the revived natural style. In the fifteenth century Antonio Solario, and Antonello da Messina, the introducer of oil as a vehicle, gave character to the art of Southern Italy. The characteristic style of this school was established by Andrea Sabbatine, a pupil of Raphael, and a true Umbrian; its chief features being an unearthly calm, devoid of passion in forms, and a faint ethereal hue in coloring.

SECT. 7. THE AGE OF THE THREE GREAT MASTERS, LIONARDO DA VINCI, MICHEL ANGELO AND RAPHAEL SANZIO.

As in Greece Phidias and Apelles were produced after ages of development, so the three great masters in Italian painting appeared after two centuries of the continued impulse given by Giotto. In themselves paragons of industry, they excelled because they entered the field at an era when Italian intellect had in every department of human pursuit reached its acme.

Lionardo, called da Vinci, from a small town near Florence, where he was born A. D. 1442, placed at an early age under the tuition of Verocchio, after some months showed his power in painting by an angel in this artist's Baptism of Christ; which led Verocchio to throw down his brush in chagrin, "that a child should so excel him."

Lionardo was noted for personal beauty and strength; he mastered the abstruse laws of the mathematics, anatomy, optics, chemistry and mechanics as they applied to art; and became a voluminous writer in varied science, as well as a skillful musician and poet. In drawing, his industry knew no limit; his pocket sketch-book receiving daily new contributions from his rambles and reveries. In sculpture his nude Leda is admired for its chaste expression and exquisite symmetry, especially in the head. At the age of thirty-one he was at the same time head of the civil engineers building at Milan the aqueduct so famed; and also planning the fresco of "The Lord's Supper," perhaps the highest work of Christian art.

The character and method of the great artist were illustrated when the prior of the convent on whose wall it was executed complained to the Duke of his dilatoriness. Lionardo wrote to the Duke that he was "still in want of two heads." One of these, the Saviour's, he "could not hope to find on earth." For the second, that of Judas, he said he "would make diligent search; and, if he could not do better after this effort, there would still remain to him the head of the impertinent and annoying prior." Lionardo represents Jesus in the act of saying, "One of you shall betray me." On his right sits, first, grieving John; second, suspicious Judas, clutching the bag; third, impulsive Peter, reaching behind Judas to whisper to John; fourth, cautious Andrew, with both hands raised; fifth, stern James the Less, pressing Peter forward in his inquiry; and sixth, guileless Bartholomew, standing and leaning on the table. On Christ's left is, first, doubting Thomas, appealingly raising his finger; second, conscientious James the Greater, starting back; third, anxious Philip, laying his hand on his breast; fourth, astute Matthew, informing the two disciples beyond him of Christ's remark; fifth, tragic Thaddeus, passionately gesticulating; and sixth, nervous Simon, listening to Matthew.

Spending his life between Florence and Milan, dying at last near Paris, Lionardo accepted few public contracts. His characteristic excellences were his delicate taste in design, the anatomical correctness of his drawing, the faultless gradation of colors in shade and tint which made him the father of chiaroscuro, and the labored finish of every part of his work. Lionardo was pre-eminently the scholar-artist; the monuments of his perfected genius being few, but models for all time.

Michel Angelo Buonarotti, of noble parentage, born A. D. 1474, was trained by Ghirlandaio, from fourteen to seventeen years of age, in drawing and coloring. At this era the Medici were collecting exhumed statues, and sculpture was the love of Angelo's boyhood. He contended against the critics that the moderns could equal the ancients. To test his principles he executed a statue, broke off and hid one arm, and had the statue buried; his gardener pretending afterward that he had found an antique. When his opponents were sufficiently committed in its praise, Angelo brought out the arm; showing that the two were made by the same, and that a modern hand.

Devoting himself for a time to this art, Pope Julius insisted on employing him to fresco the ceiling of the Sixtine Chapel in the Vatican Palace; and in twenty months his series of matchless conceptions were finished. Never had such unearthly scenes, chaos and restored earth, Paradise and infernal gloom, been made so real. The impatient Pope insisted again and again on the temporary removal of the scaffolding that he might anticipate the effect of the completed works; while Raphael, then in his prime at thirty years of age, was in ecstasies of unselfish admiration, and exclaimed that "he thanked God he was born in the time of Michel Angelo Buonarotti!"

The end opposite the entrance was reserved for the Last Judgment. For twenty years Angelo was employed on varied works; when he began this master-piece, devoting to it only hours of choice leisure. Paul III. criticised the nudity of the figures; without effect on the high-spirited master, for forty years acknowledged monarch in the kingdom of art. The master of ceremonies annoyed him; but the next day he found his unmistakable portrait borne by one of the lost in the infernal regions, with asses' ears on his head and a serpent twined about his body. The Pope besought the despot in art to relieve his victim; but he replied to this effect, "Your Holiness may release a man from purgatory but not from the lower prison-house."

The special characteristics of M. Angelo as an artist were the grandeur and boldness of his conception, which made him seek the majestic in sculpture, the grand in architecture, and in painting the awful. He was impatient of the restraint and labored kneading of oil, and preferred fresco; in which he could lay on his colors at a dash of the brush. He was overbearing toward rivals, and terribly severe on disparaging censors; yet he was genial and generous to appreciative critics and to aspiring pupils.

The third of the galaxy of great masters, Raphael Sanzio, born A. D. 1483, was early trained by his father, an indifferent painter; from twelve to twenty he was under Perugino, and practised his art for some time in Perugia, following the stiff ascetic style of the

Umbrian school. At twenty-one he visited Florence; when a new world opened to him in the cartoons of Lionardo and M. Angelo. Self-reliant, in three years he painted about thirty altarpieces; executing most of the portraits and Madonnas which now make his fame.

At twenty-five Raphael was called to Rome. In Umbria he had surpassed his master in the dreamy supernatural; and at Florence he had rivaled Lionardo in naturalness of expression and in exquisite moulding. At Rome, studying the nude, he caught the energy and breadth of M. Angelo, adding to it a classic grace; and in this third and climactic style his manly genius and womanly heart so won on M. Angelo that the aged master commended Raphael to the Pope as his superior in his special art. The frescoes known as the "Stanze" or chambers of Raphael, in the Vatican palace, were commenced while M. Angelo was painting the ceiling of the Sixtine Chapel; and "The School of Athens," the admiration of critics and artists of succeeding generations, shows the progress of the maturing artist.

From this time private orders crowded upon Raphael; and he became the head of a school, whose master-spirits he employed to work up his designs. His sketches and unfinished drawings, after his early death at thirty-seven, more valuable without color than if finished by his pupils, are among his choicest works. Though not, like Lionardo and Angelo, a master in sculpture and architecture, in painting Raphael perfected one department after another, conceiving his ideal from real scenes. His method he thus explained to a friend: "To paint a figure truly beautiful it might be necessary that I should see many beautiful forms; but I avail myself also of certain ideas that come into my mind." He exemplified this statement when he drew on a barrel-head the exquisite form of a peasant mother and her child, the model for his Madonna della Seggiola.

As Mrs. Jameison and others have well urged, Raphael was pure in morals. The rise together of three men like Lionardo, Angelo and Raphael. all comprehensive masters and all capable of such labor and attaining such skill because none of their powers were weakened and wasted by sensual indulgence, indicates that no artist, however great in genius, can be a leading master, unless, as Cicero declared of the orator, "he be a good man."

SECT. 8. THE SCHOOLS OF NORTHERN ITALY AS INFLUENCED BY LIONARDO, AND OF CENTRAL AND SOUTHERN ITALY BY M. ANGELO AND RAPHAEL.

The superiority of the three great masters was only the culmination of an improvement that had been steadily progressing for two centuries. The Florentine had reached a standard which could only receive a finishing touch; the Umbrian, which had succeeded to the Sienese, through Lorenzo had felt Lionardo's influence; while the schools of Northern and Southern Europe, especially of Venice, more out of the centre of gradual advance, were in a condition to receive a new and decided forward impulse.

The influence exerted by the three masters was widely dissimilar. Lionardo, quiet and scholarly, gave a higher intelligence and a more finished execution to artists already able, and awakened a general spirit of culture among the artists of Italy, France, and even of Spain and Germany. At Milan a school of finished artists arose like Luini and Oggione, who followed his style; while at Paris he left a marked impress on French painting. Michel Angelo, a man of towering genius rather than of labored culture, would not condescend to take pupils; yet he had imitators beyond even professed instructors. His grandeur of design and intense action aroused to new life the waning dramatic school of Florence, and broke in upon the stereotyped pomp of the Venetian school, leading Titian, Giorgione and Tintoretto to make M. Angelo's drawing underlie their gorgeous coloring. Raphael, learning from every master by intuition, and unable to teach the principles of his own success, since he could not himself analyze them, attracted pupils of genius kindred to his own, who by intuition like his caught his style. In the Florentine school, Fra Bartolomeo, in the Venetian, Fra Sebastiano, and in the Sienese, Francesco Francia admired and copied his method. At Rome kindred spirits were employed by him in working up his designs, who after his death established the Roman school; while at Naples one of his pupils became the head of the modern Neapolitan school.

Commencing at the North, five centres illustrate this influence. Correggio, born at a little town of the same name, after studying a short time at Mantua met some works of Lionardo and Raphael; when, inspired by the industry of the one and the intuition of the other, he exclaimed while looking at one of Raphael's masterpieces, "Anch' io son pittore!" "I also am a painter." His excellences were, breadth of view between his figures, a peculiar power of gradation in light and shade, united to M. Angelo's form, Raphael's expressiveness and Titian's hue. Self-educated, he went to Parma, and left those monuments of genius which have given that little city an undying fame. His easel-pieces at Parma and Rome have a fascination beyond Raphael's; while his frescoes in the convent and cathedral of Parma seem like the very opening of heaven, so transparent is the sky, so sweet are the cherubs and so seraphic the saints floating above.

In the Tuscan school Fra Bartolomeo attained Lionardo's finished conception; Raphael drew him from his seclusion; and his nude St. Sebastian stamped him as an original and able Florentine. With less judgment most Tuscan painters chose M. Angelo as their model; and unable to apprehend his spirit verified the remark of Fuseli, that "M. Angelo lived to see his style perverted in the Tuscan as well as in the Venetian school."

In the Venetian school the influence of the three great masters is most seen. Prior to this age the Venetian painters, absorbed wholly in study of color, designed nothing beyond "fine old Venetian gentlemen." The genius of M. Angelo and of Raphael awakened other ideas of men and of women; and led to the grand action of the former, and the expressive loveliness of the latter. Giorgione, born 1477, trained under Bellini, the last of the old Venetian masters, studied Lionardo's works and attempted his boldness of outline, action and expression, adding also his grading of colors; introducing an entirely new style of Venetian painting.

Tiziano, born also A. D. 1477, becoming intimate with Giorgione, caught the impulse of his genius, and at his early death finished his pictures left incomplete. His first success was in portrait; his happy choice of attitudes, freshness of expression, and finish of features making him a favorite with royal sitters. Visiting Rome, M. Angelo brought to view Titian's failure in forms; exclaiming, "What a pity that Titian does not draw as well as he paints!" and declaring "Titian would have been the first painter in the world had he only been early grounded in correct drawing." Improving on this criticism, Titian devoted himself to landscape; attaining in ideal background what Kugler calls "the glorification of earthly existence;" adding also real scenery, prompting Fuseli's declaration, "Landscape, whether it be considered as the transcript of a spot, or the rich combination of congenial objects, or as the scene of a phenomenon, dates its origin from him."

Titian's fault, jealousy of rivalship, made Jacopo Robusti; called "Tintoretto," or the little dyer, from his father's occupation. Born A. D. 1512, entering at an early age Titian's studio, he was soon dismissed with the master's stinging remark, "That he would never make anything but a dauber." Conscious of genius, Tintoretto by self-culture attained such success that he dared to write over his door, "Il desegno di Michel Angelo; il colorito di Tiziano;" "the drawing of Michel Angelo, the coloring of Titian." He studied perspective and foreshortening by suspending plaster-cast models and drawing them in varied positions; and he attained chiaroscuro by suspending those same models at night and painting their shadows cast by lamplight on a richly-colored background. With an imagination almost rampant in design, especially in composition, retaining the gorgeous Venetian coloring and adding his new power in drawing and shading, Tintoret fascinated the lively and fantastic Venetian people. His Paradise fills the largest canvas ever covered, being eighty-four feet three inches broad and thirty-four feet high. Though painting in oil, he worked so rapidly that he was called "Il furioso Tintoretto." Of his fertile invention his admirer Ruskin, says, "There is not the commonest object to which he will not attach a range of suggestiveness almost limitless; nor a stone, leaf or a shadow, nor anything so small, but he will give it meaning and oracular voice."

The last leader in the Venetian school was Paul, called Veronese from his native city Verona. Born A. D. 1528, he studied at Venice the works of Titian and Tintoret, and united some of their improvements to the old Venetian ideas. In place of their open sky, he returned to architectural backgrounds. His immense canvas, picturing incidents in Jesus' life with Oriental gorgeousness, mark the decline of the Venetian school.

From Rome, Giulio, called Romano, the virtual head of the new or Roman school, four years after Raphael's death removed to Mantua. Withdrawn from his master's chastening influence, he adopted a style of coarse elegance, akin to that of the ancient Roman; and found a host of followers to perpetuate this perverted modern Roman school. At Bologna three followers of Raphael, Primaticcio, Tibaldi and Nicolo dell' Abate, prepared the way for the Eclectic school. The other pupils of Raphael gave character to the Neapolitan school; Penni, the first, dying just as his influence was established; Sabbatini, its virtual head, introducing the natural drawing and winning sweetness of his master; while Polidoro Caldara fell into the later and easily perverted style of Raphael's pupils, a copying of the antique in form with an ill-associated picturesqueness in grouping.

SECT. 9. THE SPANISH SCHOOLS; FORMAL AND MYSTIC IN STYLE; HISTORICALLY ASSOCIATED WITH THE SCHOOL OF SOUTHERN AND CENTRAL ITALY; CULMINATING IN VELASQUEZ AND MURILLO OF SEVILLE.

In Spain the demands of religion raised up native artists in every age; but it required the later power of Spanish nationality to give dignity to Spanish art. It was under Charles V. and Philip II., who in their long reigns, from 1516 to 1598, were devoted to art as well as to general progress, that artists like Velasquez and Murillo arose, that Madrid was made the national capital, and the first stone laid in the Escurial, destined to be the receptacle for generations of the best works of Spanish artists.

Pacheco, the father-in-law of Velasquez, himself a painter and author of a history of Spanish painting, is a living embodiment of the spirit of Spanish art. Praising the idea of drawing from nature, he yet boasts of his authority from the Holy Inquisition to visit the studios of artists, galleries of paintings and printshops, and to see that nothing not in accordance with the rules of the Catholic faith should appear in the representations made by artists of sacred subjects. Condemning the nude, he criticised with a double-pointed logic M. Angelo's license in his Last Judgment, in picturing "the angels without wings and the saints without clothes;" adding, "although the former do not possess the one and the latter will not have the other, yet since angels without wings are not known to us, and our eyes do not allow us to see the saints without clothes, as we shall hereafter, there can be no doubt that this representation is improper." Finally warning his brother artists of even that advanced day, he cites a case of a painter subjected to a severe penance for painting the blessed Virgin "with a hooped petticoat, a pointed spencer, a saffron-colored head-dress, pantalettes and a fringed doublet."

In its early history the Gothic or Romanesque prevailed in the North of Spain, and the Byzantine among the Moors of the South; Saragossa being the seat of the former, Seville of the latter, while Valencia was intermediate.

The Cathedral of Saragossa, decorated by Torrento, illustrated the style prior to Giotto; Gothic influence prevailing in Spain as in Northern Italy. At a later period German artists added naturalness in drawing, the sombre Spanish cast still prevailing; of which Bermudez, a Spanish writer on art, says, "The coloring is not so bright as that of the old German painters; but there is in it a sort of softness like in effect to a veil thrown over their pictures." Yet later an Italian spirit prevailed at Saragossa.

The school of Aragon and Castile proper began with Pedro de Aponte, under Ferdinand and Isabella, when, in 1479, the seat of the court was removed to Castile. Charles V., a little later, brought the best Italian artists to Castile, he himself having become enamored of the style of Titian. The Escurial Palace at Madrid is now rich with Titian's finest works. The pride of this school was Morales, born about A. D. 1500; called "the divine" because of the ethereal aspect of his suffering Jesus and "Madonnas dolorosas." Pacheco compares his rich and mellow coloring to that of Correggio; styling the expression of his Christ a "sublime spirit of self-sacrifice and resigned love." The truly religious painters of Spain, and the school of old Aragon and Castile, closed with Morales.

At Valencia, an ancient seaport, whose cathedral stands on the site of a Roman temple to Diana and of a Moorish mosque, Byzantine and Venetian influence prevailed until Joanes, born A. D. 1523, introduced into religious themes the natural style, akin to Raphael's. After him followed Navarette, born A. D. 1526, called "El Mudo," the deaf-mute; another illustration that a special gift for plastic art is bestowed on the deaf, as a special gift for music on the blind. Having studied under Titian, he was employed by Philip II. His fondness for drollery is shown in the order as to some of his sacred pieces obtained by the Inquisitors: "the artist shall not introduce any dog or cat, or other unbecoming figure; but all shall be saints, or such as incite to devotion." When

Titian's Last Supper, painted for the refectory of the Escurial, was found too large and Philip ordered it to be cut to fit the space. El Mudo by signs begged the king to spare it and place it elsewhere; pledging himself in six months to make a perfect copy of the requisite proportions, or to lose his head if he failed. Among the able artists of this school was a Greek called "El Greco." The most noted was Ribalta; who, stung by his master's repulse on asking the hand of his daughter, went to Italy for some years, returned, and in his master's absence, painted a hasty sketch on his easel. The old man coming home gazed at the painting with admiration, and exclaimed to his daughter, "That is the man I would have you marry; and not that dauber Ribalta!"

At Seville, Pedro Campaña, born at Brussels A. D. 1503, but educated in Italy, executed a Descent from the Cross, whose two Spanish characteristics are illustrated, by Murillo gazing at it for hours and exclaiming, "I am waiting till these men have taken down our Lord!" and by Pacheco who said, "One would be afraid to be alone with it in a gloomy chapel." Luis de Vargas, born 1602, forming in Italy a love for the natural, was the real founder of the improved school of Seville; an almost Raphael-like loveliness characterizing many of his figures. In Pablo de Cespedes, born 1538, the Spanish Correggio, this school culminated. Having acquired in Italy the method of Correggio, he engrafted its features upon Spanish art. Pacheco calls him "one of the best colorists in Spain;" and says, "The school of Andalusia owe to him the fine tone of their flesh tint." Roelos, born about A. D. 1560, was in design and color the Spanish Tintoret. In his St. Anne he pictured youthful Mary in a rose-colored tunic and a blue mantle studded with gilt stars, with a cat and dog and basket of playthings near her. Next came Pacheco, born about A. D. 1579, more of a critic than an artist, but a good teacher. With him flourished Turbaran, born A. D. 1598, who painted from nature and excelled in drapery; and whom Philip IV. complimented with the title "Pintor del Rey y Rey de los pintores," "Painter of the King and King of the painters."

Diego Velasquez, born A. D. 1599, a youth of bold and independent genius, entering the studio of Pacheco, found the gentle rules of the academy the easy bridle his free spirit needed. At the age of about twenty he had originated improved methods; training a boy to act as a model in postures and expression, and sketching from him heads in charcoal on white or blue ground and painting in colors.

In 1628 Rubens visited Madrid, met Velasquez and gave him hints. The next year he visited Italy and studied Tintoret at Venice, and M. Angelo and Raphael at Rome. Returning, Philip IV. gave him a studio in his palace, in which he would sit for hours to see him work. In 1648 he employed him to visit Italy and purchase paintings for the Escurial Palace; and during this excursion he executed his famed portrait of Pope Innocent X. In 1656 he painted his masterpiece, "The Theology of Art," noted especially for its linear and aerial perspective; with which the king was so delighted that taking up a brush, he painted upon the artist's breast in the picture the cross of St. Iago, the highest honor in his gift.

Bartolomé Esteban Murillo, the second of the two great Spanish masters, was to Velasquez, both in friendly intercourse and in style of art, what Raphael was to M. Angelo. Born at Seville, A. D. 1616, he learned to execute coarse sketches for the country-people at fairs. Hearing of Vandyke's visit to Madrid, he painted a large number of cheap pictures for traders to the American colonies; which realized the sum needed for his tour. These are now treasured in many an old church in Spanish South America. Received with great kindness by Velasquez at Madrid, Murillo was permitted to copy the best paintings of Titian, Rubens, Vandyke, Ribera and Velasquez; when, returning to Seville, he spent the remainder of his life a self-taught artist.

Like Raphael, Murillo passed through three different styles; the first entitled "frio," or cold; the second "calido," or warm; the third "vaporoso," or misty. The first, practised about three years, was vigorous in design but coarse in color and finish. At thirty-two Murillo married an Andalusian lady of rank and fortune; which marriage gave a new character to his mode of life and equally to his style. His vigorous drawing was softened by a polished finish, which continued for ten or twelve years. In 1658 he planned an art academy; in whose atmosphere the vigor of his youth returned, and freed him from the trammels of artificial society imposed by his marriage. To the bold design and vigorous drawing of his first were united the finished coloring and sweet grace of his second style; while over both was thrown by his genius a dreamy mist of fascinating attractiveness.

Murillo's works were almost numberless. Like Raphael's, his paintings were preferred to those of his more scientific rivals; for while Velasquez was beyond rivalry in all the higher walks of art, Murillo's scenes of social life and themes of sentiment were more winning. War, too, gave a wide dispersion to the works of Murillo; and though a critic like Ruskin may protest against the comparatively high rank assigned to Murillo in France, England, Germany and even Russia, and call him a "base" artist, his style will always be a favorite with popular observers.

SECT. 10. THE ECLECTIC SCHOOL OF BOLOGNA, IMITATIVE THOUGH SELECT; ESTABLISHED BY THE CARRACCI, ADORNED BY DOMENICHINO AND GUIDO, CLOSING WITH CARLO DOLCE.

Kugler argues that when the culminating and climactic period of art has been reached in any country nothing else than a decline can be expected. In Spain the reaction, after the two great masters who could not be rivaled, was immediate and almost complete. In Italy the decline took another turn.

As in Greece men of genius turned to a new field when any one was exhausted, the epic, lyric and dramatic in literature, and architecture, sculpture and painting in art, successively culminating and declining, so was it with successive styles and schools of painting in Italy. When decline began, two classes of minds struggled against the downward tendency; the Eclectic school of the Carracci, and the Naturalistic school of Caravaggio. These schools had a merit, and their history an instruction worthy of special consideration.

While in every school of Italy, except Venice, the followers of Lionardo, Angelo and Raphael were becoming mere copyists, at Bologna, Lodovico Carracci, born A. D. 1555, became possessed with the idea, that, since the great masters had perfected painting each in one line, the way to improve art was to select and combine their several excellences. Two nephews, Agostino, self-taught, and Annibale, a student of varied styles, united with him in establishing a school at Bologna; which received the derisive sobriquet of *Incamminati*, or, Walkers in leading strings. Lodovico, popular and impressive, was the presiding head; Agostino, theoretic and analytic, was the chief teacher of principles; and Annibale, ready and skillful with the pencil and brush, was the practical illustrator of the system. The models of the school were set forth by Agostino in fourteen lines of Italian verse; including "the drawing of Rome, the action and shading of Venice, the dignity in coloring of Lombardy, the terrible energy of M. Angelo, the true natural of Titian, the sovereign purity of Correggio, the exact symmetry of Raphael, the decorum and foundation color of Tibaldi, the invention of the learned Primaticcio, the grace of Parmigiano;" while Nicolo, an imitator of Raphael, was made the model of all excellences.

The finished works of Lodovico were few, and excelled only in certain details. The two principal works of Agostino show the labored effort of a theoretic teacher to be true in every respect to his principle. Annibale's numerous paintings display excellences of the great masters, but have an artificial aspect akin to a theatrical style in public speaking. The great merit of Annibale is the landscape background in his historical pieces.

English critics have appreciated the Eclectic school more highly than have the German. Sir Joshua Reynolds wrote: "Style in painting is the same as in writing; a power over materials whether words or colors by which conception or sentiment is conveyed. And in this Lodovico Carracci, I mean in his best works, appears to me to approach the nearest to perfection. His unaffected breadth of light and shadow, the simplicity of coloring, which, holding its proper rank, does not draw aside the least part of the attention from the subject, and the solemn effect of that twilight which seems diffused over his pictures, appear to me to correspond with grave and dignified subjects better than the more artificial brilliancy of sunshine which enlightens the pictures of Titian." Of Annibale's "Descent from the Cross," John Bell says: "The drawing of the figure of our Saviour is at once the most learned in point of anatomy and the truest to nature of any that I have ever seen."

In the Eclectic School pupils excelled their masters. Zampieri, called Domenichino, born A. D. 1581, developed a style of artless loveliness in drawing and coloring so akin to that of Raphael that Poussin ranked him next to that master. Albani, born A. D. 1578, attained a peculiar finish in style; his themes, such as Venus and the Graces, gaining him personal admirers and pupils. In his old age a deeper sentiment possessed him, and his themes became Christian. The star of this school was Guido Reni, born A. D. 1575. To natural vigor in drawing he added that joyousness of expression which characterizes his principal works. In his "Aurora" the impression of swift motion in the galloping steeds, the rolling wheels, the torch of Lucifer blown back, and the forward strain of Aurora in her chariot, fascinates the beholder as if the scene were real. In his last days Guido painted rapidly for money; taking on a third style, often devoid of sentiment and unfinished in execution, while yet his instinctive conception of beautiful forms gave a charm to his works.

Next after Guido, Barbieri, called Guercino or Squinter, held the palm at Bologna, despite his defective sight. Like Raphael and Guido, he developed three different styles at different periods of life; a fact which had a natural cause. Youth of genius both as writers, speakers and artists, develop an unstudied power, attractive for its naturalness and impressive from its energy; but which does not bear too frequent repetition. Such minds, finding themselves soon outstripped by mere plodders whose every effort is an advance, either sink into listless inaction, or nerve themselves to the thorough study and practice of a second or manhood style. Returning success and consciousness of increasing power invites to princely expenditure; and a rapid instead of finished execution is demanded. Guercino, like Raphael and Guido, began with a style of unchastened vigor; as he advanced he sought the finished culture of established schools; and when overburdened with pecuniary demands, he became unfinished in execution. Guercino's first style was an exaggerated natural, violent in action and crude in execution; his second adds to vigor in drawing and harmony in coloring, a masterly power of light and shade, giving such a relief to his figures, that they seem separated from all behind and suspended in the air; a power which gained him the title of the "Magician." His third style, like Guido's, lacks distinctness in aim, and has a soulless beauty which speaks only to the eye of sense.

While Eclecticism had its chief seat at Bologna, its spirit pervaded Italy. Fifty years before the Carracci lived, Giulio Campi, of Cremona, a pupil of Giulio Romano, aimed to combine the excellences of Raphael and Correggio. At Milan, Procaccini, educated at Bologna, founded a school, mingling the grace of Parmigiano and the breadth of Correggio; Crespi being its ornament. At Rome, Baroccio attempted a similar method; but his effort died with him from the violent opposition of his associate artists.

At Florence, even during the life of M. Angelo, a degeneracy had begun. Vasari, while embalming for all time the memory of the great artist, discloses how unconscious of its decline inferiority is. "We," says he, "paint six pictures in a year, while the earlier masters took six years to one picture; and yet these pictures are much more perfectly executed than those of the early school by the most distinguished masters." Certainly a reform was needed when such a statement could come from a Florentine. The Eclectic Florentine began with Cigoli, born A. D. 1559, admired for his attractive warmth in coloring; and it was adorned by Allori, noted for his Judith and Holofernes, Empoli, who reproduced Venetian princes, set off with Florentine lights, and Rosselli, who with his pupils gave to portraits a life-like freshness. The favorite master, with whom the eclectic spirit expired in Italy, was Carlo, called Dolce. Born at Florence, A. D. 1616, he early painted a St. John, and a portrait of his mother, which brought out the fascination of his developing style. Adopted by the Medici family, he painted single figures and heads; chiefly Magdalenes and Madonnas, whose winning sweetness of expression gave him his name. Dolce had but one style, as he had but one ideal; and his numerous works are each admired where it is a separate treasure. Being, however, all reproductions of the same type and easily copied, Dolce's daughter Agnese became his most efficient aid in working up his designs.

SECT. 11. THE REACTIONARY NATURAL SCHOOL PRECEDING THE DECLINE OF ITALIAN ART; ORIGINATING WITH CARAVAGGIO, AND ADORNED BY SALVATOR ROSA.

The aspiration for originality, leading artists to nature for new themes and methods, became as much bound by the rules of the Eclectic as of partial schools. The tendency to mere imitation culminating in Carlo Dolce, led to the Reactionary Natural school.

M. Angeli Amerighi, called Caravaggio, from the town where, A. D. 1569, he was born, in youth a paint-grinder for an artist at Milan, studied at Venice the works of Giorgione. Being of a passionate temper and dissolute in habits, he commenced a wandering life, and adopted a style of painting in keeping. He painted, indeed, from nature; but chiefly scenes of passion and lust met in the dens of infamy, seldom seen and scarcely dreamed of by the mass of virtuous society: such as Schiller's early literary fancies. In themes of a religious cast, his style was most inappropriate; Kugler saying of his "Entombment of Christ," "it is too like the funeral ceremony of a gypsy chief."

Caravaggio had numerous imitators, as Vouet and Valentin of France, and Corenzio, a Greek; but the special seat of his school was at Naples, where its way had already been prepared. Shortly after Raphael's death, one of his pupils, Polidoro Caldara, at first an imitator of his master, going to Naples, broke suddenly into a style quite opposite; his designs being pictures of passion in excess and his coloring in deep brown hues, grand but gloomy. Ribera, called "Lo Spagnoletto," the little Spaniard, born A. D. 1593, a pupil of Caravaggio, became the leading spirit in his school, spending forty years at Naples. Most of his works are scenes of horror, such as martyrdoms and executions.

The school closed, as it began, with a wild adventurer. Salvator Rosa, born near Naples, A. D. 1615, at eighteen made an art-tour to the mountain dens of banditti. Returning, he was drawn to the school of Ribera. Visiting Rome at twenty, he assumed the threefold character of actor, musician and painter. During a political revolution at Naples he joined the insurgents, fled to Florence, and finally settled at Rome, where he remained till his death. In his "Conspiracy of Catiline" the figures are Neapolitan insurgents. His head of a warrior, fearfully gloomy, is a specimen of his power in dark portraiture. His landscapes are true works of genius; dark, dismal mountain ravines and forests, with a lonely hermit or robber band in the gloom.

Art in its childhood effort imitates its teacher instead of nature; in youth it discards too much the bonds of authority; brought back in manhood to system again, it works too much like the man of settled and driving business, ever in the same rut; until the son fails where the father succeeded. The natural style prompting genius in its early aspirings, is only the first stage in the true artist's progress. Its early effort under Giotto was an advance; but its reflection of the long line of successful teachers was a decline. The school of the naturalists, though noble in its aspiring, was composed of men like Byron and Shelley in poetry; whose fiery spirits burnt rapidly to the socket the candle of their existence, and then left the world all the darker for their having shone in it.

CHAPTER VIII.

THE ADVANCE OF MODERN PAINTING IN CENTRAL EUROPE; INCLUDING GERMANY, THE NETHERLANDS, HOLLAND AND FRANCE; EMINENTLY SECULAR IN SUBJECTS, NATURAL IN STYLE AND CHARACTERIZED BY PERFECTION OF SHADES IN COLORING.

IN Germany as in Italy, commerce introduced art and led to its advance. In the days of Cimabue the Hanse Towns were leagued to protect the trade from the Mediterranean to the Baltic, between Venice and Oleron; and when Albrecht Dürer, the founder of the German school, visited Venice, it was to paint his St. Bartholomew for an association of German merchants.

In the revival of art in Italy ancient masterpieces checked independent study; and the controlling influence of a dominant Church made religion the chief theme of art. The Germans had no ancient glories in art to check the untrammeled aspirings of nature, nor any hereditary religious associations to guard the tendency to secular subjects. Yet more, the German sky in the centre as well as the lowlands, wore a sober gray which made utterly impossible the conception of the clear transparence of an Italian daylight and the gorgeous glare and curtained purple of Venetian night-shades. These three peculiarities distinguish the German from Italian painting.

The order of location mainly, but in part also the order of time leads to the notice, first, of the schools of Germany; then of the Netherlands or of the Flemish race; next of the Dutch in modern Holland; and finally of the schools of France; all of which were associated with the old German Empire.

SECT. 1. THE RUDIMENTARY HISTORY OF PAINTING IN GERMANY TO THE SIXTEENTH CENTURY.

The works of the first native German artists exhibit the stiff angular drawing of the Romanesque rather than the rounded contour of the Byzantine, and the cold gray tints of the West instead of the warm hues and glittering gold pigment of the East. About half a century after Giotto, appeared Wilhelm, of Cologne; four of whose paintings are at Cologne and four at Munich. The latter are groups of saints and apostles painted in Gothic niches; three of which have a golden Byzantine, and the fourth a dark background. Wilhelm established a school of art; in which Meister Stephan succeeded him, whose altar-pieces, executed A. D. 1410, in the cathedral of Cologne, and a picture of St. Veronica in the Pinacothek of Munich, are among the finest relics of ancient art. Wilhelm's school was celebrated for a century.

Early in the fifteenth century schools of art existed in Westphalia and Nuremburg; the former the precursor of the Flemish schools, the latter culminating at Munich in Bavaria. In the line of Nuremburg painters were the family called Schongauer from the beauty of their style; under one of whom, in 1492, Dürer studied. The most eminent before Dürer was Michael Wohlgemuth, born A. D. 1434; his early and efficient teacher. Four of his pictures at Munich, a Nativity, Crucifixion, Deposition and Resurrection, show that religious themes prevailed. Of them Lord Lindsay remarks, that though uncouth in general design, attitude and drapery, there is a heavenly expression about the countenance of Jesus.

SECT. 2. THE ESTABLISHMENT OF THE NATIVE GERMAN SCHOOL UNDER ALBRECHT DÜRER AND HANS HOLBEIN.

Albrecht Dürer, in English Albert Durer, born at Nuremburg, A. D. 1471, at fifteen years entered a studio; and spent four years under Michael Wohlgemuth. At twenty-one he went to Germany and the Netherlands; and studied for a time under the Schongauers. At twenty-four he settled at Nuremburg as an engraver and a painter: soon attaining the highest reputation with the Emperor Maximilian I. One day, as Dürer was tracing on a wall in the palace one of his designs, the ladder slipped. The Emperor beckoned one of his suite to hold it; and when he hesitated the Emperor himself held it till the drawing was completed. When finished he conferred a title of nobility on the artist; saying: "Know that this painter is already more than a noble by his talent. I can easily make a peasant a nobleman; but with all my power I should never be able to make a nobleman such an artist as Albrecht Dürer."

At thirty-five Dürer visited Italy. At Venice he painted St. Bartholomew; at Bologna he studied perspective; at Florence he made the acquaintance of Raphael; but he returned home the next year with no characteristic of his style essentially modified. His faults were an excess of the dramatic and of fancy in composition, a stiffness in drawing, and a lack of breadth affecting his perspective. Most of his studies were Scripture themes. He became an adherent of the Reformers, and painted the portraits of their leaders. In Christian themes he rejected the classic, and was sometimes too independent in his creations.

In 1520, at the mature age of forty-nine, Dürer made a second visit of four years to the Netherlands; spending some time with Lucas of Leyden. On his return his style was subdued to sober simplicity; Melancthon stating that Dürer confessed to him he had gained new conceptions of the simple spiritual majesty belonging to sacred themes. Dürer's female associations, especially his marriage, proved unhappy. This seems to have worn upon his sensitive spirit; and he died at the age of fifty-seven years.

Contemporary with Dürer, was Lucas Cranach, court painter to three electors of Saxony, accompanying the first to Palestine. His style had less of grandeur and more of grace and simplicity than Dürer's. He delighted in the anachronism of introducing Luther and his associates into scenes such as the Crucifixion and the Last Supper; a fault opposed to the professed spirit of the Reformation. Altdorfer, a pupil of Dürer, perverted his master's style by romantic associations clustered about secular and sacred themes.

Hans Holbein, born 1495, belongs to the early English rather than the German school.

SECT. 3. THE REVIVAL AT THE CLOSE OF THE EIGHTEENTH CENTURY OF THE IDEAL HISTORIC BY CORNELIUS; OF THE FORMAL AND MYSTIC STYLE BY OVERBECK; AND OF THE NATURAL STYLE BY THE DUSSELDORF SCHOOL.

The religious reformation of the fifteenth century had men of extreme views among its leaders; it was continued by men of calmer spirit; while many opposed it by a reactionary movement. Art in Germany, subjected to this reaction, showed three tendencies; first, the rationalistic, founded on extreme independence of thought; second, the conservative, leading to a return to old ecclesiastical associations; third, the intermediate, retaining what was valuable in the past, and adapting it to the new spirit of progress.

Though Dürer's visit to Italy and intimate acquaintance with Raphael wrought no change in the vigorous but unclassic drawing peculiar to German art, yet Melancthon's scholarship chastened his method. Toward the close of the eighteenth century the impulse to general culture given by Niebuhr, and the two Schlegels, was communicated to artists. The return to ancient authority led some to the standard of Roman ecclesiastical art, and others to the Grecian classic; while at a later period the school of Lessing became devoted to the real in contrast with the ideal, and allied to the Reformed rather than the Roman Church.

Early in this period appeared Raphael Mengs; cosmopolitan in nationality, encyclopedic in learning, and eclectic in art-methods. Born A. D. 1728, in Bohemia, early promoted to be royal professor in his native country, appointed painter to the king of Spain in 1761, and head of the Academy of Florence in 1769, he acquired extended reputation as a teacher and writer, inaugurating a new era.

Peter von Cornelius, born in 1787, at Dusseldorf, caught at first the style of Rubens; but at nineteen he revealed a fondness for the style of Raphael in fresco, assuming the bold, free, open method of drawing which fresco encourages. Going to Rome in 1810, as leader of an artistic German brotherhood he established a European reputation as the restorer of fresco painting. Becoming in 1819 the head of the Dusseldorf Gallery, in ten years Cornelius wrought an entire revolution in that school; during four subsequent years he reorganized the efficient academy of Munich; after which he spent some years at Rome and Berlin. His illustrations of the Nibelungen Lied, the Iliad of Germany, though classic in spirit, are so thoroughly national that they are the delight of the common people. As the restorer of the ideal historic in fresco, Cornelius is the great master of Modern Germany.

Friederich Overbeck, born A. D. 1789, at Lübeck, studied at Vienna and Rome, and imbibed at first the classic spirit of Cornelius, Schadow and others. At twenty-five he united with the Roman Church, and devoted himself to religious themes; his style assuming the dreamy mystic cast peculiar to his own spirit.

Under Karl Lessing, born 1808, the independent German style of Durer, Protestant in themes and characterized by bold naturalness and nationality in drawing and accessories, has been revived. After studying at Berlin, he entered the Dusseldorf Academy, then under Schadow, who had succeeded Cornelius; from whom he borrowed a style ideal and classic. At twenty-four he departed entirely from his master; selecting themes of the intensest modern interest, throwing into them energy and passion. Lessing's methods lack the grace in outline and the mellowness in hues, belonging to the Dusseldorf school in historic themes; but in landscape he is a perfect master of local hues and shadows.

SECT. 4. THE ESTABLISHMENT OF THE FLEMISH SCHOOL BY H. AND J. VAN EYCK; CHARACTERIZED BY LIFELIKE NATURALNESS AND LABORED COLORING.

In the Lowland commercial towns of old Flanders, now in the kingdom of Belgium, the spirit of art early manifested an independent development; the Flemish schools being established during the age when the schools of Northern Italy were taking form.

Hubert Van Eyck, born A. D. 1366, and John or Jan, his abler brother, about A. D. 1370, were sons of a painter of the Byzantine type. With their sister Margaret, also an artist, the brothers settled at Bruges; and at Ghent united in an altar-piece embracing three hundred figures; which work, painted in sections, is now divided between the Berlin Museum, the Gallery of the Louvre at Paris, and the Cathedral at Ghent. Hubert and Margaret died early; but John lived long, honored with official position. The Van Eycks were masters in landscape; John, especially, excelling in aerial perspective. It was to John's persevering efforts to find an improved method of giving transparency to atmospheric effects that the world became indebted for the method of employing oil as a vehicle in mixing pigments. The characteristic of Flemish landscape, a dark shading admirable in twilight scenes, the natural suggestion of their murky lowland sky, is departed from by John in his grand work; as Humboldt in his "Cosmos" intimates. The Latin epitaph on his tomb describes his power: "He painted breathing forms, and covered the earth's surface with flowery vegetation, perfecting every work to very life."

The style of J. Van Eyck was transmitted for more than a century; Roger of Bruges, becoming a noted teacher; Hans Hemling, a soldier-artist, painting chiefly altar-pieces; while Jan Mabuse, contemporary with A. Dürer, found his way to England under Henry VIII., and painted portraits at court.

The spirit of the Flemish school appeared at Antwerp in Quentin Matsys, whose genius in art was roused by admiration of a young lady above his condition in life; and at Leyden, in Lucas, whose sober naturalness influenced Dürer more than the grace of Raphael.

At a later period Michael Coxies, a Flemish pupil of Raphael, sought to incorporate his methods with the Flemish; when its glory declined, quicker than the Italian schools where Raphael's imitators had influence.

SECT. 5. THE CULMINATING ERA OF THE FLEMISH SCHOOL UNDER RUBENS; DISTINGUISHED BY BOLDNESS OF INVENTION AND RICHNESS OF COLORING.

The people of the Lowlands, fond of rustic fêtes, and accustomed to a murky sky, could not appreciate at once Italian methods. A master who could lead the popular taste into a new channel must unite boldness in invention and skill in execution.

Peter Paul Rubens, born in 1577, at Cologne, was, when a child, carried to Antwerp. By his mother's solicitation at thirteen he was allowed to study painting. At twenty-three he visited Italy. At Venice he studied Paul Veronese and Tintoret, and as Fuseli says, "compounded the splendor of the former and the glow of the latter." Sent to Spain as ambassador of the Duke of Mantua, he won at Madrid royal patronage in portraits. Returning to Italy, he studied Raphael and M. Angelo at Florence, Bologna and

Rome; where his Flemish cast, modified by Italian study, gave him numerous orders. Subsequently visiting Milan and Genoa, he returned and settled as court-painter at Antwerp, his early home. Marrying A. D. 1609, he lived in elegance; and excepting visits in 1620 to Paris to decorate the palace of the Luxemburg, in 1628 as ambassador to Spain, and in 1629 to England, he steadily pursued his profession at home till his death in 1640.

Rubens united the natural life in drawing of the Flemish school with the gorgeous coloring of the Venetians, and the harmony of lights of the three great masters of Italy. His invention was boundless; scenes, sacred, historical and domestic, landscape, animal and human subjects, being equally mastered. He had industry and system, rising early, attending church, drawing alone till breakfast, then meeting his pupils. Those skillful in special subjects, animal or human, flowers or fruit, landscape or sky, he employed on his own works; overseeing and directing the work of numerous hands. Many of his fourteen hundred paintings were thus executed. Skilled as a collector, he sold to the Duke of Buckingham, in England, his first gathering. In making up a second he patronized young artists of promise; giving Vandyke his first reputation.

Jacob Jordaens, born at Antwerp A. D. 1594, employed as a pupil and worker by Rubens on small pieces, succeeding in low sportive scenes, began an independent and sometimes antagonistic career. He lived to a great age, wrought with industry and rare inventive skill; but devoted his powers largely to gross subjects.

Anthony Van Dyck, afterwards Sir Anthony Vandyke, born at Antwerp, A. D. 1599, was at sixteen a pupil of Rubens. His genius was first brought out by an effort to relieve the anxiety of a fellow-pupil who had brushed against a freshly-painted arm; young Anthony restoring the injured painting so perfectly that their master, not discovering the change, called his pupils' attention next day to the arm as a happy effort of his own brush. At the age of twenty, he went to Italy; at Venice studied the coloring of Titian and Paul Veronese, and modified the Flemish cold hues by the rich and mellow Italian tints. Returning after seven years to Antwerp, for five years he industriously employed his brush on portraits and altar-pieces. Invited by Charles I. to England in 1632, ten years of eminently successful toil, attended by a sumptuous style of living, undermined the artist's constitution and brought him to an untimely grave.

In the Belgian school, successor to the Flemish, Gustavus Wappers, born 1803, imbibing the taste of the later French school, has devoted himself to modern scenes of Belgian and French history wrought in the gorgeous fête style. Louis Gaillait, born 1810, is also one of the ablest modern historic painters.

SECT. 6. THE DUTCH SCHOOLS; THE EXAGGERATED NATURAL STYLE ORIGINATING WITH REMBRANDT; THE LOW LIFE OR "GENRE" WITH THE BREUGHELS; AND THE PASTORAL LANDSCAPE FAVORITE WITH THE DUTCH MASTERS.

The effort to represent the ludicrous and grotesque, in itself a genuine aspiration to copy Nature in real scenes among the happy though uncouth laboring people, an aspiration dignified in the early efforts of Apelles and Lionardo, became the pervading genius of the Dutch masters, when, led by Rembrandt, they separated from the Flemish school.

Paul Gerritz Rembrandt, born on the Rhine near Leyden, A. D. 1606, the son of a miller, having studied art at Amsterdam, at twenty made his father's mill his studio. The sale of one of his pictures for one hundred florins led him to make Amsterdam his residence. Marrying into a family of low rank, his associates were the common people met at the ale-house; where he learned to copy the grotesque attitudes and uncouth habiliments of his jocose companions. A rapid composer, he executed historical and scriptural pieces, portraits, and especially mirthful scenes of low life, introducing the attributes of this style even into sacred themes. His magical skill in chiaroscuro, learned in the badly-lighted garret of his father's mill, made him as Fuseli says, "a meteor in art." Rembrandt left able pupils; among whom Gerard Dow, too labored to be popular, in portrait wearying his sitters by his slowness, delighted in domestic scenes, where his power in grouping and shading could be displayed.

Jan Breughel, born A. D. 1510, preceding Rembrandt, though fond of village, gipsy and bandit scenes, remained associated with Flemish artists. His two sons, Jan, born in 1565, and Peter, in 1569, were influenced by Rembrandt. The elder, called "Velvet Breughel" from his soft touches in coloring, after a tour in Italy, became eminent as a colorist of landscape backgrounds. The younger, called "Hell Breughel," from his fondness for witches, sorcerers, robbers and devils, gave encouragement to an extravagance in picturing the darker features of human nature; which, added to the coarseness in form encouraged by Rembrandt, tended to a degeneracy in the Dutch school.

A happier tendency began with David Teniers. Born A. D. 1610, trained under his father of the Dutch comic school, afterward attempting unsuccessfully the graver style of Rubens, at thirty Teniers entered on that fascinating style of *genre* or home scenes which he pursued till he was eighty. His methods have been minutely scanned. In essaying a graver manner he made his ground of a dark-brown; but in his new style he changed this to a silvery light-gray, and later to a tremulous yellow-brown. Upon a ground prepared with chalk or plaster, he first scumbled tints of brown or pearly gray; second, sketched the figures and chief accessories, and third, the principal shadows in bistre; fourth, threw in the half tones with delicacy and labored transparency; fifth, worked up the prominent figures, giving them a thick body of color to indicate solidity; and finally, sixth, added sparkling touches and glaring tints. Teniers was patronized by the Spanish and Swedish courts; he painted about one thousand pictures, whose value varies from one thousand to ten thousand dollars each; and many able masters became his followers. Teniers is the link between the Flemish and Dutch schools.

Besides *genre* or home scenes the Dutch school has been eminent in pastoral landscape, with the accessories of animal, bird, fruit and flower painting. Both Cuyp and Ruysdael in wild, native scenery, excelled in ideal landscape; W. Vander Velde in marine views; Wouvermanns in hunting scenes; Snyders in animals; and Van Huysum in fruit and flower-pieces.

SECT. 7. THE EARLY HISTORY OF THE NATIVE FRENCH SCHOOL; ITS MODIFICATION UNDER GIOTTO AND LIONARDO; THE CLASSIC STYLE OF POUSSIN AND THE LANDSCAPE OF CLAUDE, IN THE SEVENTEENTH CENTURY.

The French people, mediate between the North and the South, possessing the physical hardihood of the German and the passionate impulse of the Italian, borrowing much from intercourse with and employment of the artists of other countries, have had in every age native artists of great independence in their methods. The eras of their civil and commercial advancement mark very nearly the stages of progress in the history of French painting.

Under Charlemagne French painting was associated with the German; the missal illumination of the day, Byzantine in coloring, showing in the drawing of figures a native French vivacity. Flemish artists afterwards wrought in the North; a brief visit of Giotto to the South introduced naturalness in design; and an impulse began which culminated under Louis XI., A. D. 1461, the era called the "Renaissance." The consolidation of the French nationality and the extension of French commerce gave greater comprehensiveness to French artists. Jean Fouquet, court-painter to Louis XI., excelled in animal and human figures in repose, though not in action and expression, and also in perspective and chiaroscuro. Rève, of Anjou, followed Van Dyke; this age being but preliminary.

The French school proper opened, A. D. 1515 to 1547, under Francis I., whose conquests in Italy brought Lionardo and other Italian artists, as well as valuable art collections, to the French capital. Its founder, J. Cousin, born A. D. 1462, by his writings awakened the French people to love of art; and his "Last Judgment," now in the Louvre, shows that the French people appreciate the serious as well as the frivolous. Vouet, born A. D. 1582, aiming at the rude vigor of Caravaggio, softened by the sweetness of Guido, increased the tendency French genius in art was taking.

The first great master of the French school was Nicolas Poussin. Born 1594, deriving his early idea of expression and grouping from engravings of Raphael and Romano, at the age of thirty he went to Rome, where Marino introduced him to Cardinal Barbarini with the expression, "Vederete un giovan che a la furia del diavolo," "Behold a young man who has the furor of the devil." For six years he studied Titian and Raphael, and devoted himself to drawing from antique sculpture; the latter most modifying his native French style. His themes were chiefly historical, both civil and sacred; his composition shows extended learning; in attitude and expression his designs have French vivacity; while in coloring his method was intermediate between the dark Flemish and the light Italian. Fuseli says: "Poussin painted basso-relievo;" but Reynolds attributes to him, despite his faults, these three excellences: "correct drawing, forcible expression and just character."

The counterpart of Poussin was Claude Lorraine, born A. D. 1600. Sent by his brother in early youth to Italy, he studied architectural drawing at Naples and landscape coloring at Rome. Making a tour through Northern Italy and visiting his home on the Rhine, he returned and spent his long life at Rome. His themes were landscapes, pastoral and classic. He spent months studying architecture in the cities and scenery in the mountains of Italy. He often sat whole days and even nights intently watching every change in the aspect of the sky and earth; preferring the hours of morning and evening twilight. He made his ground color a light gray; laying on warm colors thinly for the distant semi-transparent half-tints; and giving a full body to the principal lights and prominent figures. The bewitching illusion of his atmospheric effects gives him universal popular favor. In drawing, however, he was defective; sensible of which, he would either employ another artist to work up the figures, or with his peculiar suavity he would humorously remark to purchasers that he charged for the landscape and threw in the figures.

Sect. 8. The operatic style of Le Brun under Louis XIV.; the fête style of Watteau under Louis XV.; the temporary reaction of the natural style of J. Vernet, Greuze and others; the gross tragic style of David during the Revolution; and the restoration of the natural style under De la Roche and H. Vernet.

Under Louis XIV., whose long reign extended from 1643 to 1715, the military power of France was extended by conquests in Spain and Flanders; its widening commerce led to the incorporation of a French East India Company; and its advancing culture suggested the establishment of the since celebrated Academies of Belles Lettres, Inscriptions and of Science. Painting in this era took character from the style of architecture called Louis Quatorze.

Charles le Brun, a companion of Poussin in Italy, called to adorn the extensive walls of the palace of Versailles, revealed a style like that of Louis himself, forced by the spirit of his age to an artificial grandeur, and to act a part on a stage of fictitious elevation; as is seen in his series called the Life of Alexander. His Scripture themes are natural and truly expressive; and of his family portraits, Schlegel remarks: "A painter, essentially a mannerist. though really a man of genius, may in single works attain the highest excellence, if he be only forcibly driven from his ordinary style;" a remark suggesting a most important principle of criticism both in art and literature.

In the age of Louis XV. commerce reached China; the manufacture of silk, porcelain and of tapestry was largely introduced; the Jesuits were meeting such men as Voltaire; and the leading spirit in art was Watteau. In him religious themes proper were superseded by scenes at festivals. Horace Walpole hinted that the artificial style of Watteau was really an excessive imitation of the natural around him; his figures being fac-similes of the conventional society in which the artist lived, and the stiff trees and walks of his backgrounds being copies of the clipped and squared landscape then in vogue about Paris. Reynolds recommended "attention to the works of Watteau for their excellence in the florid style of coloring." A degeneracy in such a style was the natural result; culminating in the wanton Boucher, of whom even Diderot writes: "I am bold to say that this artist in reality knows not what grace is; that he has *never* known what *truth* is; that all ideas of delicacy, purity, innocence or simplicity have become entirely strange to him; that he has never for one moment seen nature. The debasement of taste, of color, of composition, of character, of expression, and of drawing has followed step by step on that of morals."

During the era of Louis XVI., men of true genius in science, philosophy and art, numerous and worthy, retired to the pure retreat of quiet academic shades. Among the artists Claude Joseph Vernet, born 1714, the second in the line of four generations devoted to painting, first instructed by his father Antoine Vernet, at eighteen went to Rome. The study of Salvator Rosa led him to love marine views. After twenty years of devoted diligence he ranked as the best landscape painter of his age. Invited to Paris by Louis XV., in the midst of a terrific storm he insisted upon being lashed to the mast, that he might study the features of the sea in a tempest. Ten or twelve years were devoted to those fifteen grand masterpieces, the views of the principal ports of France. Nearly every one of his two hundred or more landscape views have been copied in engravings and published in different countries of Europe.

Greuze, born A. D. 1726, became a master in an entirely different department. The sweet grace of two of his early domestic scenes, "The Father explaining the Scriptures to his Children," and "The Paralytic Father," led the French Academy to suspend their rule requiring a historic painting for admission; and to receive Greuze for his success in "genre." His paintings numbered about one hundred and seventy-five. Waagen, the German critic, compares him to Sterne, and adds: "The natural characteristics of France are seized by Greuze with the same success as those of England by Wilkie."

David, born in 1748, is a monument of the power of adaptation characteristic of true genius. Having at the age of twenty-seven partaken of the general enthusiasm for the antique, he devoted himself to classic themes; his "Horatii" making him a favorite with Louis XVI. During the Revolution his pictures of "Tullia" commended him to the school of Robespierre. Under Napoleon his "Leonidas" and "Crossing of the Alps," familiar in the engraved copy, added to his popularity; and even in the retirement of age, still master of the situation, his "Wrath of Achilles" and "Mars discerned by Venus," proved themes for the times. Among his pupils, Gros, born A. D. 1771, merely modernized his severely classic style by employing his method on themes of contemporaneous history. His "St. Genevieve protecting the French Monarchy," brought him one hundred and fifty thousand francs and the title of baron.

At the restoration, three schools, the product of the times, divided popular favor. De la Croix, born 1799, characterized by brilliance of color, opposed to the sober hues of the classic, sketching in Morocco every variety of gay costume, employed then to decorate the Bourbon palace, was the head of the Romantic school. De la Roche, born 1797, a master in drawing, design and coloring, and excelling in almost every department, winning popular esteem by his scenes in English and French history and his portraits of Guizot, Thiers and Lamartine, enshrined in the heart of Christian sentiment by his head of Jesus, became head of a French Eclectic school. Horace Vernet, fourth in the line of family artists, born 1789, spending two years in the army to learn details essential to his art, devoted himself to picturing the rapid military successes of his country. Honored equally by Napoleon I., the Bourbons, Charles X., Louis Philippe and Napoleon III., less gorgeous than De la Croix, less dreamy than De la Roche, he is the head of the modern French Historic school.

CHAPTER IX.

THE LATE DEVELOPMENT OF MODERN PAINTING IN ENGLAND AND AMERICA; COMPREHENSIVE IN SUBJECT AND AIM, AS WELL AS IN THE NATIONALITY OF ITS ARTISTS; NATIVE IN CONCEPTION, BUT CULTURED IN STYLE.

ENGLAND has been late in developing native genius in art; her Shakespeare being in advance of her sculptors and painters, as Homer antedated Phidias and Apelles. The English, too, like the Romans, sturdy in practical pursuits, have been contented with imported rather than with native art. The Americans, besides partaking of the national traits of their mother-land, have had a new land and nation to mould. Both England and America have thus opened an inviting field to artists of foreign culture; whose influence has awakened the germs of a peculiarly vigorous native art.

SECT. 1. THE EARLY ENGLISH TASTE IN PAINTING AS DEVELOPED FIRST BY ITALIAN AND LATER BY FLEMISH ARTISTS.

As in architecture so in painting, Roman vied early with Saxon taste in England; then Italian religious and German secular artists succeeded; till native masters were called out.

The oldest English portraits and altar-pieces are on wood and in the stiff Lombard method of drawing. Improved Italian art was late in being appreciated. When Francis I. had brought Lionardo to Paris, Henry VIII. was trying, though unsuccessfully, to bring both Raphael and Titian to London. At this period, from religious reasons, artists began to be looked for from another quarter than Italy. Under Henry VIII., John of Mabuse, a Flemish artist, came as a youth to England and became portrait painter for the court. He also executed altar-pieces, which drew Albert Dürer to England to examine them. About 1527 Holbein, influenced by Erasmus, the scholarly Dutch Reformer, coming to England, became a precursor of the English school proper, established two centuries later. From Henry VIII. to Mary, Holbein was honored as an artist, leaving such pupils as Sir Anthony More. Holbein's chief success was in portrait; the expression and relief of his dark backgrounds being chief excellences. His exquisite skill in engraving, seen in his "Dance of Death," awakened in England a germ of native art afterward to be matured.

Under Elizabeth architecture, and under James I. and Charles I. painting began their native history. About 1622 the Duke of Buckingham established a gallery, purchasing the entire collection of Rubens. Charles I. took lessons in drawing and oil painting. In 1629 Flanders sent Rubens as ambassador to England; whom Charles received with enthusiasm, and for his fine painting of "Peace and War," conferred on the artist the order of knighthood. In 1632 Vandyke, invited by Charles, was appointed court-painter, soon knighted, and pensioned for life. The touching emotion of his Scripture themes, and the fascinating animation of his portraits, formed an English taste.

While the sojourn of three Flemish masters, and common sky, habits and cast of mind made the English and Flemish taste in art correspond, the collections of the Duke of Buckingham and of Charles I. kept alive a love for Italian art. The vandalism of the Revolution scattered these treasures; and a decline in art followed, whose repressing influence was felt during the reign of four successive sovereigns of the house of Stuart.

SECT. 2. THE EARLY NATIVE ENGLISH MASTERS, BEGINNING WITH HOGARTH; THE FIRST ENGLISH SCHOOLS ORIGINATING WITH SIR J. REYNOLDS IN PORTRAIT AND GAINSBOROUGH IN LANDSCAPE.

The dawn of native English art was gradual. Nicolas Hilliard, born A. D. 1547, limner to Queen Elizabeth, excelled in miniature portraits. In the next generation Isaac Oliver and his son Peter were eminent, the former as a miniature painter in oil and water, the latter as a copyist of larger paintings. Wm. Dobson, born A. D. 1610, made court-painter at Vandyke's death, whose style and self-culture won for him the title of the English Tintoret, might have proved, but for his early death, the father of English painting.

Wm. Hogarth won this honor. Born A. D. 1697, noted when a boy for the drawings covering his school-books, employed as engraver by a silversmith, at twenty-one years he began to attend lectures on art, and to draw from life at the London Academy. Devoting himself for some years to portrait painting, engraving became his master art. His style in satire, or mingled tragic and comic, led Walpole to pronounce him "no painter;" while Charles Lamb regarded him the true type of an English artist; remarking, "Other pictures we look at, Hogarth's prints we read." His "Analysis of Beauty," published A. D. 1753, has many practical suggestions of value, though faulty in its leading principle. His familiar portrait, a hale, jovial, somewhat haughty English face, with his favorite dog perched by his side, is suggestive of his place in English art; the rude but powerful genius who broke loose from the trammels of mere Flemish and Italian copyists, and by his pen and brush originated an English school.

The recognized founders of English portrait and landscape reached the maturity of their powers while Hogarth was still living. Sir Joshua Reynolds, born 1723, educated in a school kept by his father, at eighteen years placed in the studio of a portrait painter, after two years' study and six years' practice studied in Italy Venetian coloring and Correggio's transparence. At thirty-one, returning to London, he secured rank as the best of English colorists; though the neglect of his early training left an abiding defect in his drawing. Social in disposition, literary in his tastes, he shone in the galaxy of Johnson, Burke, Goldsmith and Garrick; the English club reviving the associations of ancient Greece and modern Tuscany. Devoted chiefly to portraits, he found time for historical and devotional themes; his "Holy Family" and his "Kneeling Samuel" being familiar in thousands of Christian households. Masterly as were the effects he sometimes attained in coloring, Reynolds declared that the results he achieved were but chances; that he knew no *science* of coloring; a fact confirmed by the fading of some of his newly-tried pigments.

Thomas Gainsborough, born A. D. 1727, at ten years of age was remarkable for capacity in drawing, and at twelve had learned coloring. He early obtained proficiency in portrait, but overshadowed by Reynolds, his retiring nature found rarer delight in landscape. True English scenery first smiled on canvas at his touch.

Contemporary with these leaders were other able artists; Richard Wilson in landscape, John Opie, called the "Cornish wonder," in portrait, and James Northcote, more eminent as an author. In addition to these native artists Ireland gave Barry, sent as a genius by Burke to London, whose "Victors of Olympia" Canova said he would have traveled as far as England to see; while Switzerland furnished the Italian Fuseli, who has done much for the just criticism of art.

SECT. 3. THE ENGLISH SCHOOLS, MASTERS AND CRITICS IN PAINTING IN THE NINETEENTH CENTURY.

During the last half century in England ideas of former ages and schools have been revived; the extreme natural of the Pre-Raphaelites, and the value of oil as a vehicle, have been newly tested; portrait, low-life, history and especially landscape, have received comprehensive study; while artists and amateurs have employed the pen equally with the pencil to advance national art.

In portrait Sir Thomas Lawrence, whom George III. appointed court-painter, was employed by the princes of Europe to paint the portraits of the generals prominent at the battle of Waterloo. Sir Henry Raeburn, born at Edinburgh, has left portraits of Sir Walter Scott and other Scotsmen eminent in literature, philosophy and politics, which are treasures in history as they are gems in art.

In historic fiction Etty has won the reputation of being the best of English colorists; his Cleopatra, radiant in nude loveliness, heightened by the contrast of the gorgeous equipage around her, beginning his fame. Sir David Wilkie, of Scotland, the leading artist of the age in "genre," or low-life, will live as long as the remembrance of his "Sir Walter Scott" and "Chelsea Pensioners." Stothard, the illustrator of the English poets, noted for richness and exhaustless fertility of invention, constantly rambling in the fields, not only with his pencil to sketch the form of every striking grace in the bend of stalk or tendril, but also with his box of colors to copy every new variety of rich hue in insect or flower, is prince in this humble walk of loveliness.

Joseph M. W. Turner, born 1775, at five years of age beginning to draw and paint in water-colors, showed early a skill in the management of his lights from which his future success in landscape was predicted. His style was first modeled after Wilson and Gainsborough. A visit to France, the study of Claude, and a foot journey through Switzerland, gave him an independent style of truth to nature in sky and cloud, in foliage and in water, surpassing perhaps the attainment of any other artist, ancient or modern. His later style, founded on the idea of sketching only what the eye sees in one line without turning it, giving vivid distinctness to a narrow tunnel-like vista, encircling this with a cloudy indistinct rim, and leaving the corners of his canvas a perfect blank, though eulogized by his panegyrist Ruskin, is regarded by most critics as a degeneracy from the true ideal of his prime.

After Turner followed Constable, especially successful in transient aspects of landscape, such as dew on foliage, and falling rain; Morland, who excelled in portraying domestic animals, especially the pig; Collins eminent for coast-views of fishermen and their families; and Charles L. Eastlake, the most thoroughly cultured of English artists, an able master in Scripture and classic themes, as well as a profound critic. Most admired of all is Edwin Landseer, whose father, when he was a child, led him into the pastures to copy the form and study the color of different animals in varied positions. At sixteen he executed the famous St. Bernard dogs rescuing a traveler from the snow; and his fame culminated in a succession of landscape sketches relating to the chase and the habits of wild animals, which have made him the most popular because the most life-like of delineators.

The English school in "Water Colors," established about 1750, by Sandby, adorned by Turner and Prout in architectural views and Fielding in wooded scenery, sought at first the peculiar freshness and clearness of hues afforded by water as a vehicle; which, as we have seen, led M. Angelo to prefer fresco to oil coloring. A later method inaugurated by W. H. Hunt, born A. D. 1827, and an association called the "Pre-Raphaelite Brotherhood," proposes a return to the themes as well as the style introduced by Giotto; its subjects being either religious or exhibitions of high virtue; and its methods of drawing and coloring being derived from direct study of nature.

The progress of art in England has been especially influenced by critical writers; Lord Kames and Burke, belonging to the school of Locke and Reid, and Alison to that of Berkeley. The more prac tical works of Hogarth, Fuseli, Reynolds, Hay, Eastlake, Ruskin and Jamieson show that critical judgment is in advance of practical execution.

SECT. 4. THE HISTORY OF AMERICAN PAINTING PRIOR TO THE WAR OF AMERICAN INDEPENDENCE; WITH ITS CHIEF MASTERS, WEST AND COPLEY.

The rise and progress of painting in the United States of America, while colonies of Great Britain, was specially associated with that of the mother-country. In 1728, John Smibert, accompanying Dean Berkeley to Rhode Island and seeming to partake the enthusiasm of Berkeley's famous stanzas, beginning, "Westward the star of Empire takes its flight," became eminent at Boston as a portrait painter. Other foreign artists aided in the development of a native taste in Wollaston and Blackburn, in Copley and Trumbull.

Portraits of eminent men were first in demand; Robert Edge Pyne, M. du Cimitière, Joseph Wright and other foreign artists, receiving sittings from Washington when no native artist had yet been developed.

Benjamin West, born at Springfield, Pennsylvania, A. D. 1738, was, when a child, fond of drawing and painting; his brush being of his own manufacture from the hair of a cat, and his colors some red and yellow ochre obtained of the neighboring Indians, and indigo given him by his mother. At seven years he surprised his mother, a Friend in religious profession, by a drawing of the babe in the cradle. Sent before he was sixteen to Philadelphia to study art, his early religious connections were severed; and at twenty-two some New York merchants sent him to Italy; where, in three years, he was elected a member of the Art Academies of Florence, Bologna and Parma. Settling in England in 1763, for fifty-five years, until his death in 1820, West practised his art in London; leaving about four hundred finished works, many of large size. His themes were ancient, modern and sacred history. In his "Death of Wolfe," breaking over the scruples of Reynolds, and picturing English heroes in their national costume, he formed an era in British art. West's color, a monotonous reddish brown, is faulty; but his correct drawing, chaste design, and admirable grouping have ranked him as a master. Though English in his predilections, West, in respect for his countrymen, declined the order of knighthood, when, in 1792, he succeeded Sir Joshua Reynolds as President of the Royal Academy.

John Singleton Copley, born at Boston, Massachusetts, in 1737, sent at twenty-two to the Royal Academy at London, attracted special notice by his coloring. In Italy he studied the styles of Correggio and Titian. Devoting himself at London to English history, his "Death of Chatham" won him esteem with the British public, though a memorial of his country's defender. Copley had West's correct drawing; he fell short of him in design; but excelled him in brilliance of coloring.

SECT. 5. THE AMERICAN PAINTERS OF THE HALF CENTURY SUCCEEDING THE ERA OF NATIONAL INDEPENDENCE.

Immediately after American Independence, the spirit of the South, ardent and refined, that of the North, bold and inventive, and that of the Middle regions, staid and allied to the past, seemed to call for a native art in history, domestic scenes and landscape. The plain modern costume introduced by West was demanded by the American habits and character; while the wild forest scenery of the New Continent, especially in the gorgeous dress of autumn, opened an entirely new field in nature for the artist's study. The Northern, Southern, Middle and Western States, all combined to supply this national demand.

Gilbert Charles Stuart, born at Narragansett, Rhode Island, in 1756, having received early instruction from a Scotch painter, went to London in 1778, where West became his teacher. In 1781 he developed such power in portrait that George III., Sir Joshua Reynolds and Louis XVI. sat for him. Returning to America in 1793, he executed that master work, the head of Washington, of which he afterward made several copies. Living till 1828, the great men of two generations in the American republic have been preserved in memory by his art. Stuart excelled in seizing the characteristic expression, and in the life-like freshness and glow of his flesh color. The head was always his chief study; the drapery he often left unfinished, or threw it into deep shade to give greater prominence to the strong light on the features.

John Trumbull, born at Lebanon, Connecticut, in 1756, was led by the paintings of Smibert and Copley to devote himself to art. Entering the American army at nineteen, his skill in drawing influenced Washington to appoint him one of his aids. In May 1780 he sailed for France, went to London and became a pupil of West. Shortly after the war he painted "The Battle of Bunker Hill," and "The Death of Montgomery;" which subjects not altogether suiting the English taste, he painted "The Sortie at Gibraltar," whose exhibition gave him a wide reputation as excelling in battle scenes. Returning to America in 1789, he devoted his life till his death at New York in 1843, chiefly to portraits. In 1817, he began the four historic pieces in the rotunda of the National Capitol. The Trumbull gallery of Yale College contains fifty-seven of his pictures. The figures in Trumbull's pictures have more merit than the backgrounds; their chief value being the correctness of the portraits introduced.

Edward G. Malbone, born at Newport, Rhode Island, in 1777, learning his art from watching the work of scene-painters, at seventeen began miniature painting at Providence; whence in 1796 he removed to Boston. With Washington Allston, he went in 1800 to Charleston, South Carolina; after which he visited London and several American cities. Allston, his admirer, speaks of his portraits as "elevating the character without impairing the likeness."

Samuel Finley Breese Morse, afterward famous as the inventor of the electric telegraph, born at Charlestown, Massachusetts, A. D. 1791, after graduating in 1810 at Yale College, went to London to study art under West; where he modeled a dying Hercules which won the gold medal at the Adelphi Exhibition in 1813. Returning home in 1815, he aided in the organization of the "National Academy of Design," in New York; spent some years in Europe, became a professor in the University of New York; and having done much for the general advancement of art, devoted himself to his great work as inventor of the electric telegraph. Among other New England artists, Chester Harding, Alvan Fisher and Gilbert Stuart Newton, adorned their profession in the early part of the present century.

In the Middle States, Charles Wilson Peale, born in Chester, Maryland, 1741, having received some instruction at home, went in 1770 to England. Returning, he painted portraits chiefly at Philadelphia. He contributed much to the advancement of art by the establishment of a museum and the founding of the Pennsylvania Academy of the Fine Arts. Rembrandt Peale, son of the former, born 1778, at eight years was skilled in drawing, and at eighteen years was engaged in portrait painting at Charleston, South Carolina. In 1801 he went to London and studied under West, then to Paris. Returning in 1809, he settled in Philadelphia. Portrait was his chief field; as also of his cousins, Sarah and Ann.

John Vanderlyn, born at Kingston, New York, 1776, at sixteen years began study under Stuart, and in 1796, under the patronage of Aaron Burr, went to Paris. His "Marius at Carthage" won the gold medal at Paris in 1808, and an encomium from Napoleon. In 1815 Vanderlyn settled in New York. His "Landing of Columbus," in the Capitol at Washington, is one of his best works.

Asher Brown Durand, born in Jefferson, New Jersey, in 1796, by his famed engraving of Trumbull's Declaration of Independence, was brought into public notice. In 1835, abandoning engraving, he began to paint portraits, then devoted himself to historic themes, and then to ideal and natural landscape. He excels in idyllic expression, and is distinguished for truth in color and tone.

Charles Robert Leslie, born in 1794, residing from early childhood in Philadelphia, at nineteen visited England and studied under West and Allston. Choosing the humorous writers of England and the Continent for his study, his scenes from Shakspeare and Sterne, Cervantes and Molière, gave him a wide popularity. His composition is expressive, and his execution elaborate in finish.

Henry Inman, born in Utica, New York, A. D. 1801, trained to portrait painting for seven years, after an eminent practice visited England in 1844, where he painted the portraits of Macaulay, Chalmers and Wordsworth; sketching also in landscape Wordsworth's favorite haunt, "Rydal Water." A series of historical works for the U. S. Capitol was left unfinished at his decease, in 1846.

Washington Allston, born at Waccamaw, South Carolina, in 1779, fond of art in childhood, associated at college and after his graduation with Malbone, first gave his genius its bent in sketching comic and tragic scenes, especially pictures of bandits in wild caves. Going with Malbone to London in 1801, he studied three years under West, then spent some months in the galleries of the Louvre at Paris, thence again repaired to Rome, where he became intimate with Coleridge, the poet, and Thorwaldsen, the sculptor, remaining four years. At London his early Scripture themes procured him princely patronage, revealing exalted imagination. Returning in 1818 to Boston, religious themes occupied him for twelve years; his method being subdued by the chastening of age and experience. A design conceived in 1817 as a great life-work, "Belshazzar's Feast," led him to decline filling a panel in the National Capitol with a historic picture. On Saturday night, July 9, 1843, after a week of constant toil on this work, and an evening of pleasant converse with his family and friends, he suddenly and gently fell asleep in death. The unfinished picture, now in the Boston Athenæum, is a monument symbolic of its author's life; glowing with unearthly loftiness of sentiment, the effort at whose utterance exhausted the spirit that sought to give it form.

After Allston, Sully and Fraser brought credit to the State of South Carolina. Thomas Sully, born in England, A. D. 1783, brought at nine years to Charleston, S. C., at twenty settled in Richmond, Va., as a portrait painter, and six years later removed to Philadelphia. His "Washington Crossing the Delaware" is a gem of his leisure. On a visit to England he painted a portrait of Victoria.

Thomas Cole, born in England in 1801, in 1819 was brought to Steubenville, Ohio. An acquaintance with an itinerant portrait painter led him, with colors and implements of his own manufacture, to attempt landscape sketching. At twenty-one, after a tour on foot of about two years amid the bold scenery about Pittsburg, he came to Philadelphia as a landscape painter. Proceeding to New York in 1825, Trumbull and others recognized him as one of Nature's great masters. Here he originated the American school in landscape. Rambling for weeks among the Highlands, and extending his tours even to Niagara and the White Mountains, he sketched the varied forms and hues with a simplicity and truth, with a living expressiveness in outline, and a naturalness of color that captivated every beholder. Attempting ideal themes, as the "Garden of Eden," the popular taste preferred his home scenes. In 1829, Cole visited London and painted there two years; and in 1831, roamed in Italy till its sublime mountains and magic atmosphere were photographed on his memory. Returning to New York in 1832, he executed five large pictures, styled "The Course of Empire," for Lyman Reed, of New York; adding those gems the "Dream of Arcadia" and "Voyage of Life." In 1841, revisiting Italy and Sicily, he attempted a succession of views, which hastened his death in 1848. His last works, like those of most men of ripest genius, assumed a religious turn.

SECT. 6. THE CHARACTERISTICS OF AMERICAN NATIONALITY AND CHRISTIANITY, AS DEVELOPED IN A COMPREHENSIVE TYPE AND ELEVATED STYLE OF NATIVE ART IN PAINTING.

As in the African colonies of Phœnicia, and the Asiatic colonies of Greece, the highest national energy in science, art and literature, was developed, so the first emigrants from Spain, France, Germany, Holland and Great Britain to America, were the more energetic, not only of the middle or civilizing, but also of the noble or ruling classes in European society. Their civil government and their religious associations have taken, as a natural consequence, a peculiarly independent cast; which necessarily has reacted upon the style of their art.

The artists of America, German and Italian, English and native, have shown the peculiarities of their nationalities; the German revolutionary, the Italian conservative in political and religious tendencies; the English less distinctive in caste. American scholars and artists naturally tend to comprehensive views, and to a conservative course in both politics and religion; the reflex of which spirit is taking form in their works of art.

Without invidious comparison, a few artists must be named as examples of classes. As copies from old masters, Paul Balzé's "School of Athens," and some of J. K. Fisher's later Venetian masters, have long been admired. In portrait every leading city has its favorite artists. In aboriginal history Stanley's Indian portraits are invaluable; while in American history proper Weir's "Embarkation of the Pilgrims," and Walker's "Battle of Chapultepec," are links in a series. In genre, Huntington has won praise. In higher passion, Rothermel is showing decided genius; his "Paul before Agrippa," being, unlike Raphael's ideal, true to tradition; while his "Christian Martyrs in the Coliseum," in architectural background, in the action of the picture, in the expression of the chief figures, and in the aerial effects, is a master-work. Fresco is attaining in Brumidi a worthy American character.

In landscape, especially in distant aerial effects, American artists have originated a distinct school. While Leutze has recast Venetian sky, a class of artists have caught the mantle of Cole in American scenery. The twilight landscapes of Weber are fairy-like in aerial and ground tints; the sky of Church's "Cotopaxi," "Heart of the Andes," and "Niagara," is as rare in art as the subjects of his sketches are in nature; and Bierstadt's master-works, uniting both these fields, have established a new school in the history of coloring.

The lack of the religious element in the designs of American artists is calling forth frequent comment. Allston, drawn by his early affliction to religious studies, and for it sacrificing public patronage and popular fame, is an exception in American art. The devotion, however, of West and Cole in their advanced and declining days, like that of Newton, Grotius and the mass of the ablest men of science, and statesmen in France, England and America, indicates that when American genius is directed to this field it will show a depth of conviction, an intelligence of faith, an inspiration of hope, and a zeal of love entirely new in the history of Christian art. As American scholars, aside from the prejudice of national and ecclesiastical predilections, have analyzed Christian traditions, local and historical, with an independence and candor of judgment impossible in men of any European nationality, so, with their skill in natural landscape and their personal intelligence in Christian truth, the climactic field of art, the union of a lofty ideal of the Divine "Word made flesh" with the perfect transcript of the scenes of his actual life, may be realized by American painters.

BOOK VI.

LANDSCAPE-GARDENING; THE GROUPING OF NATURAL OBJECTS TO SECURE ARTISTIC EFFECTS OF FORM, COLOR, RELATION AND MOTION.

A GARDEN is a work of man designed for utility; a *landscape* is a creation of the Divine hand moulded and grouped to produce the impression of beauty. A *landscape-garden* is a composite creation; the artist availing himself of the outline already furnished by Divine skill, removing the defects of Nature's decay, and adapting for dwelling-places what otherwise would be fitted only for the abode of animals. Lord Kames says, "Gardening is not an inventive art, but an imitation of nature, or rather nature itself adorned."

Landscape-gardening appeals primarily to the eye, presenting the united beauties of form, of color, of relation, and of motion; yet addresses the other senses; adding the odor of flowers, the flavor of fruits, the refreshing of shade, and the charm of the insects' hum and of the birds' warble. It is an art open in its treasures to all; the flower-beds of the cottager and the park of the noble feasting the eye alike of every passer-by. The garden, too, is the first and the last of human delights; the traditional abode of man in his purity and perfection, before sculpture and architecture existed; the home of the blest hereafter in the Greek Hesperides, the Roman Elysium, the Mohammedan Paradise, and the Apocalyptic Christian Heaven.

Not only passive enjoyment but delightful employ is furnished in the landscape-garden. As in Eden, the first pair were to "dress and keep" the garden, so in all cultured ages and nations it has been the art earliest practised because of its utility, yet last perfected as a work of beauty. Lord Bacon's philosophic statement is, "Man came to build stately sooner than garder finely; as if gardening were the greater perfection."

CHAPTER I.

THE EFFECTS TO BE SOUGHT IN LANDSCAPE-GARDENING.

LANDSCAPE gardening, broad in its sensual appeals, is restricted in its spiritual addresses. All the varied impressions of the mind made through the eye, the beautiful, the grand, the picturesque, the novel, the grotesque, the tragic and the comic, belong to this art; as also the appeals to all the lower senses. The range of moral impressions, however, is restricted in landscape-gardening; its delights awakening less directly than other fine arts the emotions called forth by human associations, by the higher social virtues, or by the religious affections.

SECT. 1. THE GENERAL END OF ORDER AND SYMMETRY, COINCIDING WITH UTILITY, IN LANDSCAPE-GARDENING.

The first element of beauty in a garden is, as Kames and other critics agree, order in the arrangement and symmetry in the proportion of parts. Order demands that paths have a central dividing avenue with equal subdivisions, and that plants be ranged in beds according to their size, increasing from the centre. Symmetry demands that in rectangular plots a fixed measure control the length and breadth.

In the broader work of laying out a public garden, park or cemetery, winding avenues must so intersect as not to mar each other's outline; and the clumps and lines of trees of different sizes and forms must so succeed as to aid each other's effect. In a Roman city-residence the little court-yard back of the entrance was as mathematically exact in all its measurements as a diagram in Euclid. This controlling method, handed down through the Middle Ages, when introduced into France and England, worked sad havoc for a time amid the wooded knolls of the British Isles. That the simple laws of order and symmetry so long ruled alone, even to the exclusion of higher principles, is sufficient testimony that they are permanent elements, never to be overlooked in this art.

SECT. 2. THE GENERAL AIM OF GRANDEUR IN EXTENT AND PICTURESQUENESS IN GROUPING, CONSPIRING WITH ELEGANCE IN FORMS AND RICHNESS IN COLOR.

Kent had already called attention to this second aim in landscape-gardening when Lord Kames wrote: "Gardening, besides the emotions of beauty from regularity, order, proportion, color and utility, can raise emotions of grandeur, of sweetness, of gayety, of melancholy, of wildness and even of surprise and wonder." The attaining of true grandeur, beauty with massiveness or in wide extent, sought in architecture by M. Angelo and in sculpture by Phidias, belongs to the great Architect of nature in landscape. Landscape-gardening, taking advantage of his methods and his material in the range of wood and field, of hill and dale, may most fully secure this effect.

The "picturesque" requires the opposite of order in some portions of a work. Sir. Richard Morris makes the picturesque to consist in "unfinished" as opposed to "finished" forms. As Phidias made the very roughness of Minerva's brow give polish to that very feature when seen in the distance, so, as Ruskin contends, in a landscape-garden a rock that would be a blemish if the wild brush around it were removed, may, in a vista view, give a grace which no pruning could effect. Lord Kames suggests that though "nature in organized bodies, comprehended under one view, studies regularity," yet she "in her large works neglects these properties;" and hence in "embellishing a field . . . the artist ought to neglect them."

In the picturesque, however, the general outline of forms must be elegant and the colors rich. The skill requisite is so to group the finished and unfinished portions of the landscape, by pleasing juxtaposition of contrasted objects, as of a tangled copse and a shorn lawn, of an ivy-covered wall and a cleared grove, of a wild cascade and a neatly-walled lake, that the aspect of slovenly neglect do not prevail over that of elegant carelessness. So, too, whatever the clime, the colors of foliage and flowers, of buildings and fences, must possess in themselves a richness which shall not allow an unpleasant impression from a near view to mar in remembrance the pleasure of the distant prospect. Eve's work in Paradise was "to support" each flower of "gay carnation, purple, azure, gold," whose head would otherwise "hang drooping," and thus its richness be lost to view.

SECT. 3. THE SPECIAL EFFECTS OF ASSOCIATION; AS THE NOVEL OR VENERABLE, THE NATIVE OR FOREIGN, THE ENLIVENING OR DEPRESSING.

The power of association may be secured in landscape-gardening more fully than in any other art; especially the impressions of the novel and the venerable, of the native and the foreign.

Novelty may be attained both in new forms and new groupings. In the flower-garden every shower gives fuller shape and size and adds freshened tints; and autumn frosts paint vast panoramas with sober, yet gorgeous hues. Yet more, by new groupings of familiar plants and trees and new selections of rare flowers and shrubs, as well as in architectural and sculptural decorations and in animal accessories, variety may be attained. The Chinese are noted for the surprises introduced into their gardens; the gardens of Versailles have an excess of quaint devices in hedges and fountains; and the Hebrew Solomon had exotic plants and even apes and peacocks brought from India for his pleasure-gardens.

The counterpart of love for the novel is reverence for the venerable. A dilapidated wall, a broken column, a fragment of a statue, or even a dead tree covered with ivy, recalls days bygone. The fondness for the antique led the Romans to bear off obelisks from Egypt and statues from Greece to adorn their city and suburban villas; while the Chinese, showing the more the naturalness of this impulse from its rude development, introduce old trees artificially transplanted. Lord Kames, with a nice analysis, suggests that the Gothic is more appropriate than Grecian in gardening, because "the Gothic exhibits the triumph of time over strength, a melancholy but not unpleasant thought;" while "a Grecian ruin suggests rather the triumph of barbarity over taste, a gloomy and discouraging thought."

As the mingling of the new and venerable gives pleasing contrasts in time, so the blending of the native and foreign give a kindred contrast in place. Every maiden seeks some rare plant or bird; and the conservatory of exotics and the park of foreign animals are chief centres of attraction in every public garden. Some bold designer has suggested for the environs of the American Capital, an enclosure of some miles in area in which sections be planted, stocked and peopled by the trees, animals and men of the three continents of the Old World.

With power of moral adaptation the gardens on the Bosphorus decked with gay flowers and cheerful shrubbery, sparkling with glittering waters and enlivened by warbling birds, may give exhilaration; the quiet grove of Academus may woo to reflection; or the venerable olives of Gethsemane may dispose the soul to prayer. The church-yard, too, more worthy of study, may, with moss-covered stone and bramble-carpeted grave, make death seem gloomy and the tomb dreary; with gay flowers and lively sculpture, it may give the associations of holiday dissipation; or, again, with the drooping willow and dark clustering myrtle, it may awaken that equable impression which seems fittest at the tomb.

SECT. 4. THE SPECIAL EFFECTS OF MOTION, APPARENT OR REAL; IN UNDULATION OF SOIL, IN RUNNING WATER, IN WAVING FORMS AND SUSCEPTIBILITIES OF TREES, AND IN ANIMATE CREATURES.

In Grecian art the apparent motion of the beings that seemed to live in the marble and on the tablet was the distinguishing feature. In landscape motion may be both apparent and real. In land called "undulating," not only is the superficial extent increased, as by the flutes on columns, but the eye and the feet in moving over such a surface seem to feel the billowy movement of the sea.

In water there is real motion; the gentle ripple on the lake, the gliding slide of the running stream, the vase-shaped curve of the waterfall or fountain-jet, being chief charms in landscape since the days of primitive Eden. Even the indication of the presence of water, as the encircling shells around the basins in the little court-yards of the old Roman houses at Pompeii, awaken a peculiar delight.

The motion of plants has also its charm. The aspen's quiver in the calmest air, the rocking of the golden grain in the zephyr. the swaying of the elm's broad top and the floating, like streamers, of the willow-boughs in the gentle breeze, as well as the rocking of the maple and the oak before the storm, inspire the beholder.

Animate creatures give a double attraction. The lawn and the forest are the home of the browsing sheep and the gnawing squirrel; while the picketed deer and water fowl, and even the chained bear and caged eagle in themselves, and the associations of the place are the delight of a park.

SECT. 5. THE RARE RESORT TO FICTITIOUS EFFECTS; AS THE IMITATIVE, THE DECEPTIVE, THE GROTESQUE.

Hogarth dwells on intricacy as a fascination in art. The impulse which makes children fond of riddles and puzzles and youth of involved plots in romance, which stimulates the hunter and explorer in tracking intricate mountain-passes, led Milton to picture as a charm of Eden, the witchery of "crisped brooks," which "ran with mazy error under pendant shades."

In attempts by imitation to awaken pleasing deception, natural effects should seem to be produced by a natural cause. An artificial rock made of loose stones should be so covered with vines as to hide the junctures; a brick arched grotto should, by a mastic coating, be made to appear stone; and a fountain-jet should rather issue from the snout of a whale or elephant than from the mouth of a dolphin or the beak of a swan. Bronze lions or dogs chained at a gate, or even stuffed deer or birds half hidden among the foliage, are legitimate deceptions; though foliage cut into animal forms is illegitimate, since it is less even of a deception than of an imitation.

The garden is the legitimate field for the grotesque. The natural location of a grotto is a shaded hill-side; whence Milton introduced into the first garden of man, "umbrageous grots and caves." But, if nature has not furnished a hill-side, an artificial mound may serve as a grotto. As the reptile seeks the dark shade of the grotto for his burrow, the garden-grotto is the select repository for this class of sculpture. In the oak carving of a dark old lizard-haunted castle, however, such forms may be appropriate.

SECT. 6. STUDIES IN SCIENCE AND ART RELATING TO LANDSCAPE-GARDENING, AND REQUISITE TO THE MASTER IN THIS ART.

In gardening, as in the other fine arts, the science of his profession is essential to uniform success in the master; and to the mere student it is the main object of acquisition.

In geometry, whose name originated in the necessity of restoring field-bounds in Egypt every year after the Nile's overflow, familiarity with every variety of rectangular and curvilinear figure is essential to the landscape plotter. The principles of descriptive geometry and optics, also, as they relate to perspective, are essential for the study of effects in landscape in the distance. In useful and ornamental gardening agricultural chemistry as well as botany and vegetable physiology are requisite in the selection and training of plants. Of the wisest of men we are told that "he spake of trees, from the cedar that is in Lebanon even unto the hyssop that springeth out of the wall;" and the sweetest of Roman poets, the graceful and pensive Virgil, has in his Georgics and Bucolics shown the dignity as well as the extent of the science of plant-study and culture which the master in gardening may attain.

In art as well as in science the successful gardener must be an adept. To accomplish the effects sought in color and form, relation and motion, the principles of design, the analysis and æsthetic power of hues and tints, and a power in combining and grouping akin to composition in painting, must be attained.

CHAPTER II.

THE MATERIALS BY WHICH THE EFFECTS OF LANDSCAPE-GARDENING ARE SECURED.

The variety in material employed by sculptors and painters, the marble of Lebanon, Pentelicus and Carrara, and the ochres of India, of Egypt and Greece, found in three continents, are substantially one. The range of the landscape-gardener takes in every variety of inorganic material, as earth, stone and wood, and every class of organic creation as herb, shrub and tree, bird, reptile and quadruped.

In sculpture and architecture the entire form, and in painting the color, is to be the artist's work. In gardening part of the forms and all color are furnished in nature, and only their grouping belongs to the artist. The land and its undulations and covering of green are natural elements to be wrought by his skill into fit surroundings for an abode of man. The house to shelter him, the stalls for the beasts that serve, the fences and the out-houses that add defence, convenience and comfort to his domain, are artificial parts of the one whole. The securing of harmony in grounds and buildings, the happy combination of the natural with the artificial, makes the whole a composition worthy to be ranked as a high art.

SECT. 1. THE STRUCTURE OF THE SURFACE OF THE GROUND TO BE ADORNED; AS THE CONTROLLING NATURAL FEATURE IN LANDSCAPE-GARDENING.

The structure of the ground, whether a sandy plain, a meadow of dark mould, a rolling succession of gravelly hills, or a rocky mountain-side, is fixed by nature; and the cast of edifices to be erected and the choice of plants to be reared must be made dependent on this structure of surface as the leading feature. The eye of taste, indeed, may search for a spot presenting the greatest variety for the accomplishment of its ends; as the Romans followed up the Anio for miles to select sites fitted for their favorite villas. When selected, however, the surface of the ground must control the natural, and to a certain extent the artificial ornamentation of its face.

In a level country, carriage and foot-paths and especially field-bounds, demand straight lines; for though a serpentine avenue is allowable in a level garden, a curved field-bound would be unnatural. On the other hand, there is a habit in animal instinct, which thus becomes a law of nature, to seek a winding path over an eminence; the camel in a mountain path, the dray-horse on a steep avenue, the cattle browsing on a hill-side, making for themselves a serpentine path; guided by which instinct of the animal, the road-builder in a new region is led to the most accessible pass. The landscape-gardener wars with nature who lays out straight avenues on an undulating surface; as does the engineer who cuts a high road straight over an eminence even when to wind gracefully around its base would save labor and distance.

True taste again would make the outline of a lake in a deep valley not an unvarying ellipse, but in curves conformed to the foot of the hill-slopes around; and it would place a grotto in the steepest side, where rock, if not present, is indicated by the precipitous slope. Still following nature also, it would fringe the lake with willows, and sprinkle cedars on the rocky heights; for while the monarch of Lebanon may be transplanted to the Garden of Plants at Paris, and the palm may tower in Hyde Park at London, the cedar must be planted on a bleak, rocky hill-side and the palm in a sunny and sheltered nook.

SECT. 2. THE STYLE OF BUILDINGS TO BE ERECTED; AS THE LEADING ARTIFICIAL FEATURE IN LANDSCAPE-GARDENING.

As surface of ground is the controlling natural feature in landscape, so the style of architecture chosen is the leading artificial feature. This suggests, first, the circumstances which must influence choice in architectural style; second, the extent to which harmony requires adherence to one style.

The general design of private buildings is always the same; a mansion requiring servants' quarters, stables, barns and granary; also arbors and conservatories. From the mansion the other structures should take their type. The demands of surface require that a Swiss cottage should be nestled under a steep hill; that a square mansion with broad Chinese verandah, stand on an open field with a sunny exposure; and that Grecian colonnade, Italian villa and French château structures, be located on a surface slightly undulating. The necessities imposed by climate relate more to compactness of walls than to general structure. The requisites of material are that Grecian types be of light-colored, in fact, of white material, Egyptian of neutral gray, and Gothic of dark-colored stone; pure marble for Grecian, granite for Egyptian, and red sandstone for Gothic, being a rule of exacting taste.

While harmony with the grounds fixes the general style chosen, harmony in buildings as a whole suggests added principles. In general all buildings coming into one range of view should accord with each other in style. In a small private enclosure there is but one main view; but in extended grounds each range of hills, or shaded avenue, may have separate fields adapted to diverse architectural structures; as is admirably effected in the Villa Borghese, where the styles of Egypt, of Greece, and of later ages are reconstructed in different sections of the grounds. The chapel of a cemetery may be a Grecian temple standing on a gentle eminence or in an open field, or a Gothic cathedral amid a thick surrounding shade; while the tombs and monuments in each cluster or range should be of the same class, whether Egyptian or Roman, Grecian or Gothic.

SECT. 3. THE BOUNDING LIMITS OF GROUNDS; FENCES SUNKEN OR RAISED, DITCHED OR TERRACED; PALINGS OF WOOD OR OF IRON; WALLS OF BRICK OR OF STONE; AND HEDGES OF SHRUBBERY.

Fences designed for protection, chiefly from cattle, require adequate strength. Art demands that they be made to seem a natural rather than an artificial limit. The surface of the ground and the material furnished are controlling guides in the construction of fences.

In undulating fields fences winding through the depressions are hidden; on a hill-side an embankment wall with a low open fence leaves the view least obstructed; while on a level field a fence should be a tall hedge or an open paling of wood or iron. In utter violation of this principle, close high fences around private gardens give a prison-like confinement, disagreeable to the proprietor, annoying to the passer-by denied his just public enjoyment, and injurious to the plants themselves shut out from the cooling breeze.

The supply of material generally corresponds to the nature of surface; both harmonizing in the style of fences appropriate. Stone for embankment walls and terraces generally abounds in hilly, and wood in dry low grounds; while in marshy lands, as Egypt and Holland, willow-bordered ditches harmonize nature and art. In the limited enclosures of a cemetery, lightness united to strength commends open iron-work, either wire-netting, chains or foliated castings, as also small hedges.

SECT. 4. THE WALKS AND DRIVES; DEPENDENT AS TO DIRECTION AND CURVATURE UPON INEQUALITIES AND OBSTRUCTIONS OF GROUNDS, AND ON THE POSITION OF THE PRINCIPAL BUILDINGS.

In carriage-drives and foot-paths, designed to give access to grounds and buildings, art requires that varied and pleasing views be afforded; an end best secured by a curved avenue.

Before a mansion in an open level field, a smooth lawn from the highway to the end of the mansion, with a straight avenue of shade trees at one side, furnishes in separate features the richest possible variety. On grounds slightly sloping, a single uniform curve is most tasteful; while over an undulating surface a winding approach of gradual rise and sweep is most desirable. Foot-paths in open grounds, as a vegetable or flower-garden, naturally assume straight lines; while in a grove the zigzag course necessary to pass obstructions makes the serpentine the preferred line of a wooded path.

The question how far natural obstructions, such as rocks and old trees, deep dells and sharp acclivities, should be left undisturbed, long discussed in English gardening, turns on the decision, what are permanent and what accidental features. A stump as a mark of the unfinished work of the woodman is unsightly by a road-side; but a sweep of a few feet to save a noble tree awakens pleasure, since it is a preserved work of the Creator. A low ragged rock seems no sufficient obstacle to give turn to a carriage road; yet in a foot-path it is a legitimate occasion for a bend. In general the principle of nature, always that of beauty, will be sufficiently suggestive in the arranging of the drives and walks of a landscape.

SECT. 5. THE CONDUCT OF WATER, DEPENDENT ON SLOPE OF GROUNDS; AND ITS EMPLOY IN FOUNTAINS, RILLS AND POOLS.

Water in grounds is requisite for plants and domestic animals; and is desirable to give swimming space for water-fowl and a bathing place for animals and men. In the introduction and conduct of water in landscape, ruled as it is by the force of gravity, the slope of the ground is a controlling feature; the flow of a rill depending on declivity, and a lake being naturally located in a plain or meadow. A jet, though appropriate in a narrow court-yard, in extended grounds seems more natural in a valley or on a hill-side.

As a narrow enclosure offers little variety in the conduct of water, it requires special adornment of the fountain-jet and basin; as is illustrated in ancient Pompeii, where the basin of the fountain in the little court-yard of private houses is tastefully decorated with sea-shells and groups of miniature animals. In the larger gardens of ancient and modern times art has exhausted its skill in designs for the improvement of this feature.

SECT. 6. THE LOCATION OF TILLED LANDS AND USEFUL PLANTS; AS VEGETABLE-GARDENS, FRUIT-ORCHARDS, WHEAT-FIELDS, GRASS AND PASTURE-LANDS.

The field-beds, of which fences, roads and water-courses are but borders, are occupied by two classes of products: useful and ornamental plants. In all larger suburban retreats, utility is the main end; and to what an extent beauty may conspire with usefulness the ancient Egyptian and Roman, and the modern Chinese and English gardens are interesting testimonials.

Universal taste has suggested that a vegetable garden should be in the rear, not in front of a mansion; and if necessarily located so as to be seen in front, that it be shielded by a flower-border, a hedge or a row of flowering shrubs.

In grouping tilled land, hay-fields and pasturage, regard should be paid to their relative position. The early and short grains, as wheat, show to best advantage in front of the taller maize; and a hay-field, always green, appears best intervening between the high road or drive and the tilled lands. Orchards should be in the rear of tilled grounds and of a kitchen garden. In their position relatively to each other, in fruit as in ornamental trees, regard should be paid to forms, as the drooping peach and erect cherry; and also to color of foliage and blossoms. Low grounds in the rear of tilled grounds form appropriate pasturage; but an enclosed park for deer, or a lawn for sheep, is an attractive ornament of front grounds.

Convenience as well as beauty suggests a rectangular form for fields and beds, the plough necessarily moving in a straight line; while the ornamental portions as naturally take the curved line.

SECT. 7. THE GROUPING OF ORNAMENTAL PLANTS AND TREES; THE ADJUSTING OF FLOWER BORDERS AND SHRUBBERY; AND THE ARRANGEMENT OF GROVES, AVENUES AND CLUMPS OF TREES, ACCORDING TO CLASS, FORM, COLOR AND MOBILITY.

The classes of ornamental plants are trees, shrubs, flowering-stalks and grass-sward. The general form of flower-borders must conform to that of the drives and walk. In court-yards elaborate shapes as stars and varied ovals, may be introduced; but simple are preferable to complicated forms.

As to relative position, shrubs require, like trees, independent locations; either in lines along drives, or in clumps upon grass-plots. As in summer flowering plants will be the chief charm, and in winter evergreen shrubs, these should be so intermingled as to relieve each other. Along drives flowers should be between, not in front of shrubs, and shrubs between, yet slightly behind trees; but along foot-paths the reverse order should prevail, shrubs rising behind flower-beds, and trees back of them. Broad lawns between avenues should be dotted with clumps of shrubs. In general the arrangement should be such that larger shrubs and smaller plants shall be seen in vistas beyond each other.

As respects form, tall and tapering shrubs, as the arbor-vitæ, should be made to set off round-topped bushes as the box or holly; and dwarfed shrubs should be beneath the high boughs of the lilac or althea. The securing of harmony in color is a more difficult study. As in making up a bouquet the just gradation of colors according to the laws of contrast and complement, the shading of the lively into the sombre, and the relieving of the whole by a background of green, requires the skill of an artist, so does the grouping of the natural flowers in a landscape-garden.

Ornamental trees, the grand feature of public parks and private grounds, are designed for both shade and ornament. Without them the thoroughfares of villages and cities would be intolerable, while as ornaments, from their size they conspire to grandeur as well as beauty.

Groves are naturally formed of native forest growth and of one class of trees. As favorite resorts for a quiet ramble, or as gathering places for open-air discourse, poets have had in groves their sweetest dreams, and philosophers, as opposite as Plato and Epicurus, have found their shade minister alike to the most ideal of spiritual breathings, and to the grossest of sensual pleasures. Avenues required to line walks and highways admit trees of greater variety, since they are supposed to be transplants; yet being designed for shade they require chiefly trees with broad tops and thick foliage. Clumps are designed for ornament merely; and therefore admit every form and variety. Originally they are the natural forest growth, left simply to save labor on rocky ridges; they reach their rarest perfection when an extensive meadow, devoted to this end, grows for years under the eye and hand of a genuine amateur as an ever-improving gem of art.

In the grouping of clumps nice gradation of class, form, color and mobility, is called into exercise. The winter's stripping requires that the bare limbs of deciduous trees have as a relief the spruce, cedar and pine, green during winter; the corners of intersecting paths especially demanding such landmarks in the season of frost. The form of trees is an element of effective harmony or of expressive sentiment; the most enchanting effect being produced by a skillful succession in a vista of conical firs and spruces, of the oval maple and poplar, the acorn-shaped oak and chestnut, and the umbrella-topped willow and elm; while to the Mohammedan the tall, conical, sky-pointing cypress, and to the Christian, the drooping form of the weeping willow is a fit monitor at the grave. Color, too, adds a pleasing effect when at each step the vista changes from the dark bottle-green of the fir, through the varied shades of green and yellow, to the snow-white of the silver-leaved poplar. The most sublime effects of motion, too, may be achieved by the skillful grouping of the aspen, the willow and the elm.

SECT. 8. ARTIFICIAL ACCESSORIES; AS SCULPTURED FORMS; RUSTIC SEATS, ARBORS AND GROTTOES FOR REST; AND SWINGS, VEHICLES AND BOATS FOR MOTION.

Besides the buildings essential as abodes, arbors for occasional shelter may be made the gems of a landscape; while sculptured forms may decorate enclosures too small for architectural ornamentation.

The idea of the ancient Germans alluded to by Tacitus has peopled groves and rocky heights with rural deities; making the open air of the garden a chief field for sculpture. A large portion of the works of Grecian sculpture have been rescued from villas; colossal vases and rustic deities being the ornament of groves and fountains. Funereal monuments especially are companions of the green sod that covers the dead.

Among the smaller erections of gardens the simplest is the rustic seat under trees, the more conformed to nature in material and structure the more truly artistic; a moss-covered bank, a stone smoothly hewn, a lounge formed of knotty boughs and vine-branches, or an iron seat cast in imitation of foliated and intertwining boughs. In open ground a canopy as well as a seat is required; an extemporized booth made of boughs of trees; an open wooden frame covered with creeping vines; or a richly adorned Asiatic kiosk. For deeper seclusion from heat, the grotto has always been a resort; either natural cavities in a rocky hill-side, or rude masonry in a thicket.

In larger grounds a swing hung upon a strong oak or elm, pigmy carriages drawn by neatly harnessed goats, light row-boats after the pattern of the Turkish caique or Venetian gondola, have in every age and land been made accessories in pleasure-grounds.

SECT. 9. ANIMAL ACCESSORIES; SMALLER AND LARGER QUADRUPEDS WILD AND DOMESTIC; BIRDS FREE OR CAGED; FISH AND REPTILES.

The water, the air and the dry land were peopled long ere man appeared on earth; since which era they have always been needed companions.

The domestic animals of the farm, the horse and the cow, the sheep and the goat, made to feed upon the herbage unfitted for man, are a pleasure and pride to their possessor; while rare quadrupeds, such as the deer and elk, and the undomesticated hare and squirrel, are a delight in extended country grounds or in an open city square. Besides herbiferous animals, ranging free, chained or caged beasts of prey, as the native fox and bear, and the leopard and lion of other continents, are garden-denizens suggested by the demands of true art.

To quadrupeds will be added fowls. As the farmer prides himself upon his "stock," so does the farmer's wife on her "poultry." To the ordinary domestic fowls the rich landholder adds the peacock and the swan; and besides the pigeon, the swallow and the wren, coveted tenants of the humblest barn, the caged canary, mocking-bird and parrot, are favorite enliveners of the summer piazza; and the chained owl and eagle attractions in a public garden.

Even fish and reptiles have their place in the garden. The frogs of the ditch and the fish of the brooks give amusement to youth; the tortoise on the grass and the lizard on the wall give interest even to age; and from the sage Aristotle to the simplest maiden the tiny gold-fish in a glass and the luscious trout in the costly fish-pond will ever be favorite accessories in beautified grounds.

SECT. 10. CLIMATE AND SEASONS, BLEAK AND SUNNY EXPOSURES, AS INFLUENCING CHOICE OF PLANTS AND STYLE OF BUILDINGS.

In grounds specially guarded, the effect of climate and changing seasons may be controlled by conservatories and other shelters.

Seeking the ends of utility, however, the fruit-grower finds that the apple and the pear mature best in a northerly, the peach and the plum in a medium, the fig and orange under a more southerly sky; as also among the cereals, rye, wheat and rice have correspondent latitudes for healthful development. Among ornamental shrubs, the hawthorn, the privet, the arbor vitæ and the osage orange have each their appropriate latitudes; while in the gardens of Syria and Mexico, the cactus, which is a hothouse plant in the north, grows to gigantic size, and forms a strong and secure hedge. Among shade trees the stately elm falls a prey to insects in a southerly clime; while the fairest of the oaks, the willow or water-oak, never shows itself in a northern forest.

The alternation of seasons has a subordinate influence. A large class of trees, as well as of plants, seem made for every clime. In the choice of plants and trees for ornament, regard to season suggests that a cemetery hedge, visited alike in summer and winter, since death has "all seasons for its own," should be evergreen; while in all adorned grounds symmetry in foliage should be preserved by so interspersing winter's green that no portion may at any time look bare and barren. The rest, or sleeping time of plants should be regarded; that of the oak being the winter of the frigid and the summer of the torrid zone; while the corn is planted early and ripens late under a southern sky because of the long summer drought when its growth is arrested.

Yet more importance is to be attached to southern as opposed to northern exposure. The degree of heat which the earth receives from the sun depends mainly upon the perpendicularity and consequent directness with which its rays fall. Any child can test this by holding the back or more sensitive portion of his hand near a fire; turning the hand so that the rays of heat strike it now in perpendicular lines and now at an acute angle. For this reason southern summers are not warmer though longer than northern. The farmer may indefinitely prolong the growing season by planting his garden upon a sunny southern exposure; and the vintner on the Rhine secures an Italian clime almost up to Arctic regions.

Buildings in colder climates require more durable material and more compact structure; but suburban residences, designed for the summer only, naturally assume everywhere the light style of southern latitudes. Special regard, however, should be paid to exposure in the location of a mansion; a front due north and south, leaving one side perpetually without sunlight and the other blistered by its constant rays; while a house on a northern slope never can be healthful.

CHAPTER III.

ANCIENT AND ASIATIC STYLES OF LANDSCAPE-GARDENING.

WHILE gardening, beginning with the works of nature, is the art most conformed in its style to nature's method, the leading peculiarities of country and age, marking sculpture, architecture and painting, will be found to characterize this art. As the early home of mankind was in Asia, so primitive gardening was an Asiatic art; the people of that continent retaining this, as other arts, from the earliest period in its original rude stage of advancement.

The extreme antiquity of the art is exemplified in the Garden of Eden; its first and rudimentary stages in the Egyptian and Assyrian; its second stage of advance in the Syrian and Persian; its culminating influence in the Grecian and Roman; its lingering sway in the early Christian of Southern Europe, while its present type may be studied in modern Turkish and Chinese gardens.

SECT. 1. THE PRIMITIVE "GARDEN OF EDEN;" AS THE PERFECTION OF NATURE AND ART.

The sacred and traditional historic fact that man in primitive simplicity was made to occupy a garden as his happy abode is testimony to the attraction of this art. As to the fact, conspiring Grecian and Indian traditions are in striking confirmation of the Mosaic narrative. As to location the universal Asiatic tradition, alluded to alike in the Laws of Menu of India, the Zendavesta of Persia and the Koran of Arabia, agree with the Hebrew record in locating it at the headwaters of the Tigris and Euphrates, among the valleys of the Caucasus, still peopled by the noblest specimens of the human race.

The wide park-like extent of this primitive abode, its "delights," in broad watered valleys, in mountains filled with "every precious stone," its trees giving shade like the "cedar" and affording every variety of fruit, are pictured by Milton in fiction founded on reliable testimony. The statement that, with all its perfection derived from the Creator's hand, its lordly occupant was with his companion "to dress and keep it," has been in all ages and lands an index to a lofty aspiration in this climactic art.

SECT. 2. EGYPTIAN AND ASSYRIAN GARDENS; CONTROLLED IN THEIR FEATURES BY THE SAMENESS OF SURFACE AND RICHNESS OF SOIL BELONGING TO LEVEL RIVER BOTTOMS.

Numerous historical allusions, illustrated by the pictured representations on the walls of ancient tombs, and confirmed by modern customs, enable us with great accuracy to reconstruct the Egyptian garden of the age of the Pharaohs.

Moses alludes to Egyptian gardens as, "by the river-side," having "cedar-trees" and "gardens of herbs." The sculptures of the tombs picture gardens with rows of dark conical trees on the river bank; and their beds of flowers, clumps of trees, vineyards and fish-pools are geometrically squared. The palm, the fig, the pomegranate and the vine formed borders; all the processes of culturing and gathering are pictured on the tombs; while in fruit vases deposited with the dead, the fig, prune and various nuts are found preserved. Pools of water are interspersed; in which are growing the lotus and papyrus with their rich lily flowers. Arbors and shrines for deities also rise amid the green.

The Assyrian gardens were Egyptian in model; the banks of the Euphrates being level like those of the Nile. The ancient dramatic poem of Job describes them as traversed by streams, with rows of shade trees like the willow along the banks, and clumps of the olive, vine and the fragrant lign-aloes in rocky places; while Herodotus Diodorus and Layard illustrate these statements of the early Chaldean.

Diodorus and Strabo give the distinctive idea of both Assyrian and Egyptian gardens in picturing the hanging gardens built by the king of Babylon for his Median wife; who in the unvarying plains of Babylonia sighed for something like her native hills. Those gardens rose in terraces like a pyramid; having a base four hundred feet square and a perpendicular central height of three hundred and fifty-feet. The minute description of arches, of water tight terrace basins, and of latticed summer arbors indicates the perfection of this art as early as B. C. 600.

SECT. 3. SYRIAN AND PERSIAN GARDENS; ILLUSTRATED SPECIALLY AT JERUSALEM AND PERSEPOLIS; ALLOWING THE VARIETY OF FEATURES BELONGING TO A ROCKY HILL COUNTRY.

The hill country of Judea took the Persian model in its gardens. They were of two classes, the small suburban and the broad park in the country.

Solomon's gardens about Jerusalem bore sweet herbs, spices and nuts; they were fenced with hedges; among their flowers were the rose or narcissus, and the lily; among fruit trees the apple, the fig, the pomegranate, the date-palm, the pistachio nut, the grapevine and the olive; and they were watered by fountains, pouring refreshing streams. Pliny remarks: "Syria is most laboriously cultured for gardens; and thence the proverb among the Greeks, 'The many garden vegetables of the Syrians.'" Two gardens hallowed in Christ's life still retain their interest; Gethsemane, an enclosure of about an acre, shaded by aged olive trees, and the garden in which Jesus was crucified and buried, now covered by the Church of the Holy Sepulchre, three hundred feet long and two hundred feet wide.

The larger or park garden of Syria is illustrated by Solomon and Xenophon. Its designation "paradise," both in the Hebrew and Greek, is from the most ancient Japhetic tongue; it had groves and orchards, fountains and fish-pools, "garden houses" or summer palaces.

One, seven miles south of Jerusalem, noted for its massive pools still existing, was among the highlands still called "Mountain of Paradise;" and a second was in the valleys of Lebanon. To these, afterward alluded to by Strabo, Solomon brought exotic trees and foreign birds and animals from India. The type of these larger gardens Xenophon describes in Persia where the name Paradise originated. In one, mentioned in his Cyropædia, young Cyrus learned to hunt the stag and wild boar. In another, described in his Anabasis, "Cyrus had a palace and an extensive park full of wild beasts," in which he hunted to give himself and his horses exercise. Through the wildest of this park the river Meander runs. In a third, alluded to in his Hellenics, in addition to the hunting park there was "a river full of all sorts of fish, and plenty of birds for those fond of fowling."

SECT. 4. ANCIENT GRECIAN AND ROMAN GARDENS; CHARACTERIZED BY GEOMETRIC EXACTNESS OF OUTLINE AND ELEGANCE OF FORMS IN ADORNMENT.

Gardening as an art has to do with the real rather than the ideal; and no originating genius in Greece was devoted to it. The allusions of the Greek authors show that their ideas and methods were Asiatic, derived from Persia. Among practical Romans, however, gardening attained the characteristics of geometric exactness in outline and richness of ornamentation preserved in Southern Europe to this day.

The gardens of the Hesperides, merely alluded to by Hesiod and later Greek writers, called by Strabo "the islands of the blessed," in their very name from *espera*, evening, or "the cool of the day," as well as in the legends of the forbidden fruit, seem the re-echoing of the traditional voice, always appreciative in Grecian philosophy and art. The gardens of Alcinous, in the Island of Corfu, on the other hand, pictured by Homer, seem to be a real rather than an ideal creation; though their author was an Asiatic Greek. These were located in front of the palace of the prince; they contained four acres, surrounded by a hedge; and the plants were arranged in parterres, among whose beds jetted two fountains. Their chief charms were tall fruit trees, as the apple, pear, olive, fig, pomegranate and grape, which bloomed with perpetual foliage, buds, flowers and fruit.

The only garden noted in the era of Greek philosophy was that whose history is given by Pausanias. It was a lot of ground about three-fourths of a mile from Athens, given by Academus to the citizens for a gymnasium; which was unenclosed until Hipparchus, about B. C. 520, surrounded it with a wall. Cimon, the popular leader before Pericles, as Plutarch states, "first adorned the city with those elegant and noble places for exercise and disputation which a little after came to be so much admired. He planted the forum with plane trees; and, whereas the Academy was before a dry and unsightly plat, he brought water to it and sheltered it with groves, so that it abounded with neat avenues and shady walks." While, however, Plato planted his school in this garden, though in both his Republic and Laws he urges that for music, sculpture and architecture, government should make special provision, he has no suggestion as to gardens for public or private resort. Xenophon expressly says of the park constructed by himself in Elis, which had two streams flowing through it, lakes of fresh fish and shell-fish on the sea-shore, hunting-grounds for the boar, the antelope and the deer, pastures and stalls for horses, oxen, goats and swine, and above all, a beautiful little temple in it with a statue of cypress wood, that it was after the model of one at Ephesus. The casual mention that Dinocrates, Alexander's architect, proposed to carve Mount Athos into a bust of the monarch, making one hand to rest on a lower peak and in its hollow a lake, while the other stretched to an opposite peak and held a city upon its palm, was a suggestion of the degenerate age, when mere massiveness began to take the place of elaborate finish.

Among the Romans gardening became a high art; Cicero, the philosopher, and Vitruvius, the architect, devoting their time and money specially to it. The eminent popularity of the Georgics and Bucolics of Virgil, and of Pliny's Natural History, are a striking comment on this taste.

The Romans had the "villa rustica" or farm, and the "villa urbana," or suburban villa. The farm villa had three large shaded courts, one for the mansion, a second for laborers' quarters, and a third for stables. Two such villas, belonging to himself, Pliny the younger describes at length.

His Laurentine or winter villa, Pliny states, seventeen miles from Rome on the sea-coast, was reached by a sandy road, heavy for a carriage, "but easy and pleasant to those riding on horseback." The house was close built, had a semi-circular open porch; back of which was an enclosed portico, and back of this was the *atrium*, or central hall, radiating from which were the principal rooms, one of which looked out on the sea, another on a terrace, and another on the play-ground. The play-ground was a grass sward surrounded by a box-hedge without shade trees to admit the winter sun; within which was a garden surrounded by grape vines, fig and mulberry trees.

Pliny's summer villa, north of the Tiber, approached from Rome by a gradual rise, had a stiff soil with abundant water, and was cooled by breezes from the Apennines. The mansion fronted south, and had a wide portico; before it was the *xystus*, or court-yard, the *gestatio*, or play-ground, the *ambulatio*, or promenade, and the *hippodrome*, or circus for riding; behind which was the kitchen-garden.

The dining-room overlooked the hippodrome; before which was a spring-house shaded by four plane-trees, having a central fountain with a marble basin; over which was a sleeping berth with a frescoed ceiling. Adjoining was a bath-room having three basins, one of hot, another of cold, and a third of tepid water, heated by the sun. In the rear of the mansion, in a warm exposure, was the kitchen, with the vegetable garden adjoining; and on the north side was an open portico, under whose floor was a cool grotto.

The court-yard in front was enclosed by a box-hedge cut into the shapes of various animals, and around it was a promenade with a border of clipped evergreen. Beyond this were the gestatio and hippodrome, enclosed by a bank wall. The hippodrome had three rectilinear sides bordered by plane trees covered with ivy; between which were clumps of box, and back of these bay trees; "the plane trees blending their shade with the bays;" while the fourth side was semi-circular, bordered by tall, dark cypress, to "vary the prospect and cast a deeper gloom." The inner walks around the race course were bordered by rose bushes, to "correct in delightful contrast the coolness of the shade by the warmth of the sun."

Beyond the hippodrome was a succession of fields and meadows, which owed "as many beauties to nature as that within the wall to art." A broad avenue bordered by box, cut into the letters forming the name of the proprietor, led by lateral paths to several fields. The first was dotted with fruit trees interspersed with obelisks and statuary; the next, "suddenly in the midst of elegant regularity, surprised by the contrast of the negligent beauty of rural nature presented by a knot of dwarf plane trees." A pathway here, bordered by trees cut in fantastic shapes and festooned with the soft twining acanthus, led to an alcove of white marble, supported by four slender columns, shaded with vines, furnished with a seat, beneath which a fountain gushed up, with a basin in front having a broad brim and filled from the fountain; where Pliny says he often took a noonday repast, making the basin-rim his table, having his dishes in the shape of ships and water-fowl floating on the water, which cooled their contents. Fronting this alcove was a summer retreat of exquisitely carved marble, furnished with seats and jetting fountains with rills running around; having doors opening on one side into a green arborescent enclosure, and on another side into a small sleeping-room dark with overhanging vines.

Virgil gives extended lists of fruit and shade trees; with their adaptation to soil, climate and sunny exposures. He describes various hedges and garden accessories as statuary, fountains, grottoes and water-fowl. He urges the value of skill in grouping, "that the prospect may give delight to the mind;" and enumerates as horticultural associations, by which æsthetic and moral impressions are awakened, these: "the ash is fairest in the forest, the pine in gardens, the poplar by rivers, and the fir on lofty mountains;" "the poplar is most grateful to Hercules, the vine to Bacchus, to lovely Venus the myrtle, to Apollo his own laurel, while Phyllis loves even the hazels." He advises especially that whatever is undertaken in gardening be perfected; commending the maxim, "Admire a large farm; cultivate a small one."

Vitruvius, the architect, treats of grounds as subordinate to buildings; urging that health demands due light and heat for both man and beast, that a north front be avoided, and a south front for the kitchen and stable be always sought; that to granaries and storehouses the air have free admission; light and air being always chief requisites in everything about a villa.

The remains of ancient villas, now visited near Rome and Naples, still illustrate their structure; while the actual reconstruction of many of them in later times links Roman to mediæval gardening.

SECT. 5. GARDENS OF THE MIDDLE AGES; CHRISTIAN AND MOHAMMEDAN; ROMAN IN ARRANGEMENT, AND ASIATIC IN ADORNMENT.

The spirit of Christianity, adopting Roman methods with new associations in art, is thus presented by Eusebius in his Life of Constantine, written about A. D. 350, "Then might be seen fountains in the midst of the Forum graced with figures representing the Good Shepherd and Daniel with the lions, cast in brass, and resplendent with plates of gold." In the eighth century Charlemagne established gardens for improvement in horticulture, prescribing by a royal edict the plants that should be reared in them.

In the North, the life of feudal lords in strong-walled castles, and of learned monks in close-built convents, made the common castle and convent gardens perfect counterparts of the old Roman court-yards in city residences. In later times cardinals who had gathered large wealth lavished their treasures in the planting and adorning of gardens around Rome, arranged after the ancient model; the Cardinal Alphonso d'Este in the sixteenth century being a leader in this improvement.

The feudal castle had an exterior moat; whose banks were adorned with grass-sward, flowering plants, willows and other shade trees. The interior yard was laid off in small parterres and flower-beds. The remains of old Roman and more modern English castles yet show the former structure of their gardens.

Convent gardens, alike illustrated among the Copts of Egypt, the Greeks of Asia Minor, and in the monasteries of Italy, France, England and America, are permanent embodiments of the unvarying medieval type. Thus in the perfect desert, at Mt. Sinai, the garden of the Greek Convent is built in terraces on the western slope of the Sacred Mount, well watered from the mountain springs, and thickly strewn with fruit-trees, as the apple, pear, apricot, quince, fig, mulberry, pomegranate, the olive and also the grape; at its foot vegetable beds, flower borders and spicy shrubs mingle their odors and flavors; while the tall blank outer wall is relieved by towering cypresses and creeping ivy.

Sect. 6. Modern Chinese gardens; characterized by fondness for the diminutive in dimensions and the grotesque in forms.

Lord Kames says that gardens are "in China brought to greater perfection than in any known country." In skill devoted to productiveness this is true; while in artistic merit Chinese gardens rank with their architecture, sculpture and painting.

Necessarily divided among the swarming population into the minutest beds, which to save space are without fences, pushed as each little field is to the most luxuriant productiveness, the Chinaman's patches of rice and wheat, of beans and beets, are a pervading element of delightful green, filling the whole region around cities. Where wealth permits ornamentation, the Chinese excel in mere imitation, aiming at novelty and grotesqueness. The beds and banks of artificial lakes and rills are made to have gravelly or sandy bottoms, and to assume a serpentine and quiet flow, or to rush from cavern-mouths and to dash over precipices. Every rock and stump is left as a contrast to surrounding verdure; and islands in artificial lakes are completely rocky and barren, or clothed with an exuberance of flowering shrubs. Trees are skillfully combined according to shape and depth of green; and sometimes the effect of perspective vista views is attempted. The chief effort is at sudden transition, accompanied by a heaping of grotesque and pigmy forms in architecture and sculpture, such as miniature mills and boats, wooden quadrupeds, clay reptiles and canvas birds.

SECT. 7. MODERN TURKISH GARDENS; DISTINGUISHED BY LUXURIANCE IN NATURAL ADORNMENT AND VOLUPTUOUSNESS IN ARTIFICIAL ACCESSORIES.

In the Oriental or Turkish garden the natural features of beauty in plants, trees and waters, and in artificial accompaniments, are directly designed to minister to corporeal pleasures.

This voluptuous character is set forth in the Koran; the sacred authority in art as well as in morals. The prophet announces: "This is the description of Paradise; it is watered by rivers, its fruit is perpetual, and its shade ever green." In fuller visions the streams are pictured as flowing with milk, wine and clarified honey; the trees of dark green "loaded with fruit from top to bottom;" fountains jet with cooling showers; while "pavilions, with couches adorned with gold and precious stones," curtained with "fine silk interwoven with gold," are attended by "damsels having complexions like rubies and pearls, and large black eyes like pearls hidden in their shells, reposing on cushions of green and flowery carpets."

Alike on the low river banks of the Nile as at Shoobra, and on the highlands of the Bosphorus as in the "valleys of sweet waters" above Constantinople, the dream of the Arabian prophet as well as of the Persian poet is realized.

An extended green sward furnishes a natural seat for men and women reclining in Oriental ease; kiosks stand on terraced hillocks, or by the side of rills from the heights; the walks are few and irregular; the banks of mountain streams are simply cleared of undergrowth and the green sward trimmed; while at some points the stream is made to flow over marble beds to fill basins, and to jet from fountains.

CHAPTER IV.

MODERN EUROPEAN LANDSCAPE-GARDENING.

GARDENING has taken the type of other arts, especially of painting, in modern improvements; partaking in Italy of the bright aspect of nature, in France of the operatic artificial style, in Holland of homely cheerfulness; while in England it culminated in the picturesque style.

SECT. 1. ITALIAN LANDSCAPE-GARDENING; VILLA AND PALACE GARDENS, AS INFLUENCED BY CLIMATE, SURFACE OF COUNTRY, AND BY FONDNESS FOR ANCIENT FORMS AND ARCHITECTURAL ACCESSORIES.

The genius of Italy, balanced between reverence for the past and love of nature, has developed two tendencies in gardening. The controlling feature is artificial rather than natural adornment.

The gardens of Italy are the ornaments of villas and convents. The mild summer breezes from the sea favor the culture of juicy fruits; the shade trees have light green foliage to which the clear air imparts an amber tinge. The winter winds from the Apennines make the architectural and sculptural features, unrelieved to any great extent by evergreens, a needed attraction.

The area is usually surrounded by a high close wall of stone, capped with an ornamental parapet; similar walls divide and even subdivide the extended enclosure; between which are arranged colonnades and summer-houses and statuary under canopied roofs.

The numerous villas, such as the Albani and Borghese, which extend from Rome to the Apennine range, originated in the taste of cardinals resident at Rome after the era of revived art; who, gaining their position on account of superior intellectual and æsthetic culture, and having no families to share their large income, sought in art both gratification and honor. A leader in this revived art was the Cardinal Hippolito d'Este; who conceived the idea of reconstructing at Tivoli Hadrian's villa.

The villa Albani was designed originally to provide tasteful, open colonnades for treasures of exhumed statuary; a collection in which Winckelmann became so able a critic. The villa Borghese had as its aim the reconstruction of ancient architecture; the Egyptian with its varied types; the Grecian with its three orders; and the Roman with its circular ground-plot and exuberant ornament. The Madama is admirable for its terraces overlooking Rome; and the Dora for its extensive park. The D'Este and Braschi', reconstructions on the old Roman type, with their clipped hedges and squared fields, seem hardly in keeping with the wild luxuriance of the ilex and cypress; and the machinery of artificial waterworks, at Frascati employed as a power to work an immense organ, seems a child's device alongside of the grand cascades pouring from the cliffs overhanging the Anio.

The palace gardens of Caserta, thirteen miles north of Naples, planted in the middle of the eighteenth century by the first of the Spanish Bourbons, present an interesting contrast to the villa gardens about Rome; and prepare the way for the transition to French landscape-gardening. From the southern summer-house, called the Casino, the eye ranges over three miles of hill and vale, of grove and water-fall, to the palace on the north; and then stretches at least a mile southward to the limit in that direction. On one side is an English garden, fitted up by the romantic Queen Caroline; and on the other a dense forest which formed an ancient hunting-ground, still full of game. In front of the palace, meandering for miles in extent, skirted by lawns, flower-borders, groves and arbors, flows a stream brought from springs at the north through an aqueduct twenty-seven miles long, piercing two mountains in its course, and spanning valleys on arches of dizzy height, till within the grounds it is tortured into every conceivable form of fountain and cascade, and is made to fill broad basins supplied with fish of rare variety and quality.

SECT. 2. FRENCH LANDSCAPE-GARDENING; METROPOLITAN, SUBURBAN AND CHÂTEAU GARDENS; MODIFIED FROM THE ITALIAN BY A NATURALLY WOODED COUNTRY, AND BY NATIVE TASTE FOR LIVELY FORMS AND COLORS.

French gardens prior to the age of Louis XIV. belong to the the Middle Ages. The conception of the gardens of Versailles formed an era in the history of the art, not only in France but in Europe.

The public gardens of France are of three classes: the metropolitan, suburban and château gardens or parks. To the former class belong those of the Luxembourg and of the Tuileries; to the second the Bois de Boulogne and the old palace garden of St. Cloud; and to the third the old hunting park of Compiègne, and the grand works of Versailles.

The surface of the country in France, more gently undulating than that of Italy, allows a wider extent of view and greater variety of scenery. This feature invites the curved line in ground-plot and elevation, serpentine foot-paths and winding avenues, rugged rockeries covered with wild vines, and knolls tangled with undergrowth; a characteristic specially alluded to by Rapin, the early English rhymester on gardening.

A later feature of French gardening is the attempt to represent fable and allegory; too severely criticised by the opposite taste of Lord Kames. The attempt to represent in clipped clumps of box animals conversing together after the manner of Æsop is absurd, since neither in form, color or expression can there be even the shadow of an approximation to reality; and the sense of the ludicrous awakened by such an attempt is too strongly mixed with the conviction of failure not to be changed to contempt for the artist. When, moreover, as Lord Kames urges, lions and wolves, deer and lambs are breathing water from their nostrils, the device is disagreeable; as the modern conceït of urinating Cupids is objectionable in its moral as well as its æsthetic expression. The idea, however, of representing jets of water spouting from the nostril of a whale, or the proboscis of an elephant, or even from the trumpet of a bugler, or the bill of a swan, is not unnatural, though the latter cases are a mere surprise.

In the garden of the Luxembourg, level in surface, the structure is mechanical; since there is no natural feature to set off the square flower-beds and oval and serpentine box-borders. In the grounds of the Tuileries this feature is relieved by avenues of shade trees like the horse-chestnut, by groves of orange, by beds and borders of flowers and shrubs interspersed with statuary and fountains. The Champs Elysées, or Elysian Fields, a narrow drive of about a mile and a quarter long, with its central avenues of shade trees, its side parterres of flowers and shrubs, its circus and summer houses, terminated by the "Arc de Triomphe," unite the features of a park and garden. The Bois de Boulogne, an old royal forest of about two thousand acres lying along the Seine, one of whose lakes is three-quarters of a mile in length, though mainly level, has meadows, which by ditching, mounding and rock transportation, and by its winding avenues shaded by the oak, the beech and the pine, possess the picturesqueness of an English garden; while the allegorical idea and operatic execution of the main rock-work, including the grotto, cascade and fountains, are characteristic of French taste.

St. Cloud, for generations the type of the old chateau garden, in its location overlooking the Seine, in its aged trees, winding avenues and deep dells, contrasted with sunny knolls, is the embodiment of Kames' idea of true art in gardens, "nature itself adorned."

The forest of Compiègne, about sixty miles north-east of Paris, a hunting park before the days of William the Conqueror, fitted up with a summer residence by Louis IX., and a costly palace by Louis XIV., the favorite resting place of the war-worn Napoleon I. and of Napoleon III., contains over thirty-six thousand acres; its roads measure more than six hundred miles; and it is truly a forest, rather than a park.

In the palace and park gardens of Versailles, Louis XIV. attempted an extravagance of expenditure and an idea of leisurely seclusion from care for his subjects, which Asiatic despotism even cannot maintain. The halls of the palace, now ranges of picture galleries, are a mile in entire length. The grounds comprise the garden proper, the small park and the large park. In front of the palace gushes a small river, whose waters flow past marble basins in a central channel throughout the entire grounds; along whose course are varied classic devices wrought in bronze, as the peasants of Libya turned into frogs for denying water to thirsty Latona, and compelled for ever to spout torrents of water over her. The garden is occupied by an orangery, a conservatory and beds and parterres of flowers. The small park is twelve and the large park sixty miles in circuit.

SECT. 3. DUTCH LANDSCAPE-GARDENING; CONTROLLED BY LOWLAND SCENERY; CHARACTERIZED BY STRAIGHT LINES IN ROADS AND CANALS, IN FIELD-BOUNDS, BANK-TERRACES AND SHADED AVENUES.

The lowland scenery of the Netherlands, which gave to Dutch painting its low horizon, led to straight roads and canals giving form to field-bounds and garden-borders. As trees on lowlands are generally transplants, through their commerce with the Indies gardens among the Dutch became noted for exotics; especially for roots rich in nutriment and bearing flowers of rare beauty.

The public grounds of the Lowland cities are chiefly wide avenues with rows of trees serving as drives and promenades. At Amsterdam, Rotterdam and Hamburg the moats outside of the old walls, and the canals, are bordered with green sward and lines of trees; while at Utrecht, Frankfort, Leipsic and Vienna the foundations of the old walls form, like the Boulevards of Paris, broad carriage roads skirted by avenues of trees; a style introduced by William III. into England, and by the German princes into Russia.

In modern German and Russian cities the picturesque style of England has prevailed. Munich has a park four miles long, undulating and wooded, with winding drives and foot-paths; and at Berlin, while the old gardens are still laid out in rectangles, the new parks conform to the natural undulations of the soil. The grand park of Tsarkoe Selo, near St. Petersburg, has a surface beautifully diversified; it contains a Chinese village with a pagoda, a Turkish town with kiosks and a mosque, a Grecian city with temples and statues of classic grace, and an Egyptian temple with pyramids and obelisks; while in the mountain-sides are caves, in the forest hermitages, and on the plains monuments of civic and military glory.

SECT. 4. ENGLISH LANDSCAPE-GARDENING; CHARACTERIZED SPECIALLY BY LAWNS, PARKS AND ANIMAL COLLECTIONS; IN STYLE THE EARLY ROMAN, MODIFIED BY THE ANCIENT DUTCH, AND THEN SUPERSEDED BY THREE SUCCESSIVE NATIVE SCHOOLS, THE BALD OF KENT, THE PICTURESQUE OF PRICE AND THE GARDENESQUE OF REPTON.

The soil, climate and tastes of the people of Great Britain have made landscape-gardening the art of England; as sculpture was of

Greece, architecture of Rome, and painting of Italy. The surface of Great Britain is undulating, and the damp from the Gulf Stream covers it with a coat of the darkest green. The fondness of the British people for an out-door, stirring life has naturally led them to add beauty and grace to their out-door haunts.

The early English garden, derived from the Romans, was a little square court-yard, with beds of cramped proportions. An innovation was made upon this style by Charles II., in employing Le Notre, who laid out the grounds of Versailles for Louis XIV., to plant the parks of St. James and of Greenwich. The instructive utterance of the old style, resisting nature, appeared in the innocent inquiry of Lord Stafford, "What would have been the additional expense to make the banks of this piece of water straight?" The new style met a reaction under William III., Dutch in education both as to religion and art; as is illustrated in the Duke of Marlborough's estate called "Blenheim," whose rows of shade-trees were arranged in lines corresponding to the order of the regiments in Marlborough's line of battle. Under the house of Brunswick, gardening became pre-eminently an English art; and under George III., through the prevalence of Hogarth's ideas, so great was the opposite tendency that Sir William Chambers remarked: "If this mania be not checked, there will not be remaining three trees standing in a line throughout the kingdom." The principle that no line is beautiful except the curve, rejected projecting piazzas, terraces and enclosed court-yards, since these would break up the rounded outline of nature. The natural green sward, closely cut, skirted the foundations of the mansion; the carriage-way wandered by an easy gradation up to the mansion; and trees were left standing or cut without any regular order. This extreme was soon entitled the bald style; since it left the exterior of the mansion and the front lawn entirely bare. In the conflict of tastes numerous critical writers, as well as the poets Cowper, Shenstone and Mason, advocating the theory of Kent, threw around the art as a literal copying of nature the charm of poetic picturing which Virgil had attempted for the Romans.

As among landscape-painters, so among gardeners, there was a reaction against the extreme natural of Kent. The aim of the second style was a contrast between the finish of the mansion and its immediate surroundings and the untrimmed thickets upon its sides and in the background. It urged that on the front court-yard, and select spots in the wild grounds, the highest culture should be lavished; while the main portion of the landscape should be left in a state of nature more untouched than that of Kent. This style, called the "picturesque," gained the favor of critics and landscape painters; Lord Kames stating that in "the picturesque of Price gardening was brought to greater perfection than in any other known country of the world." It arrested the crusade against hoary trees *because* they had been planted in straight rows; it led philosophic minds, as Lord Kames in his "Gentleman Farmer" suggests, to "test proposed improvements in agriculture by rational principles."

A third method was suggested in the principle that sudden and violent contrasts between finished and unfinished grounds are unnatural; while a gradually diminished culture, complete in prominent and not slovenly in obscure parts, is the true law of nature, and therefore of art. This final style, that of Repton, recognized the fact that as a single human figure by Phidias or Apelles is more attractive than a confused group, so a single noble oak standing alone on the plain is an object more admired than a "clump that hides the monarch." His system would harmonize congruity in grouping and elegance in individual forms; his two principles being that "relative fitness" should be regarded, since gardening is a useful art, and, again, "comparative proportion," since it is a fine art. The leading idea that ornamental trees are *transplants* forbids the undergrowth of a clump; and equally demands that trees be at proportionate distances, and be contrasted and complementary in size, form and color. Suggesting the same law for shrubs and flowering plants, it required that exotics be brought in summer from conservatories and be planted in the open sunlight. This style, designated "gardenesque," because it gave the character of a garden alike to a small court-yard and to the broadest fields, has been greatly promoted by the progress of landscape-painting and by the yet greater advance made in agricultural science.

SECT. 5. AMERICAN LANDSCAPE-GARDENING; AFFORDING A FIELD FOR UNLIMITED VARIETY, AND REQUIRING A NATIVE THOUGH CHASTENED TASTE.

The New World has, in gardening, an advantage over the Old; since her artists have the combined methods of all Europe, while the field for their art is unmarred by former errors in workmanship.

In the American colonies on the seaboard English taste early prevailed. In Carolina the earlier English method has maintained its sway, the Battery of Charleston and the public grounds of Columbia illustrating this; while around Boston the later English methods are seen in Lyman's lawn, in Perkins' oak-groves, and in Cushing's flower and fruit-beds. From Louisiana the French style of Louis XIV. has extended along the Gulf of Florida, and up the Mississippi to Missouri; the immense box-hedges and clumps cut into vases and sofas and the initials of proprietors, being seen in the towns of Alabama and Georgia, and north to St. Louis.

The geological structure of the United States territory invites comprehensive methods of gardening. The mountain range cutting every Atlantic State gives to each the features of three zones, the steep peaks with the dark firs of the frigid, the undulating hills with the maple and apple of the higher temperate, and the level savannas with the willow-oak and fig of the lower temperate regions: while its undisturbed virgin growth, like marble fresh from the quarry, woos a worthy master. The able treatises of Kenrick in the Eastern, of Downing in the Middle, and of Kern in the Western States indicate the amount of intelligent native thought already devoted to this art.

BOOK VII.

THE DECORATIVE ARTS; ARTIFICIAL ACCESSORIES AND ORNAMENTS OF OBJECTS IN NATURE AND OF WORKS IN ART.

THE decorative arts, though confined to "decoration," as distinct from the forming of a principal object, are truly "arts;" since they require studied design and elaborate execution.

The objects legitimate for decoration are human beings and human implements. It is a perversion of art when lower animals, trees and plants are tricked with fantastic decorations. In objects employed by man the decorative are subsidiary to the higher arts, adding a frame to a painting, a pedestal to a statue, and capitals to columns; while in useful mechanism they add grace to strength.

The field of the decorative arts is as limitless as human wants. The pages of critical and descriptive authors like Pliny and Herodotus, of tourists ancient and modern, are filled with objects coming within this range. A concise classification of the principal wants of man which have called forth skill in this department, a reference to the principles of design employed in decoration, and a brief history of varied methods employed in different lands and ages, may aid in the grouping of such a mass of detail.

CHAPTER I.

THE FIELD OF DECORATIVE ART; COEXTENSIVE WITH HUMAN WANTS; AND VARIED ACCORDING TO MATERIAL EMPLOYED AND TASTE EXERCISED.

HUMAN wants have always called out inventive skill; and the measure of success attained in decoration has been in part dependent on the material employed, as of wood or stone, and of the implements at command, whether flint, bronze or steel. Designs in decoration have been drawn from three leading sources: animal and vegetable forms; geometric figures, apprehensions of reason, and ideas of the imagination, or pure spiritual devices. The first class are the earliest and simplest, as in the three orders of Egyptian capitals; while they are the foundation of the highest creations in ancient and modern art. Very early geometric figures became formative models; the Egyptians employing the rectangle and the trapezoid, the circle and the globe; the Greeks analyzing the ellipse, the parabola and the volute; while in later mosaic and heraldic devices, forms became as infinite as the combinations possible to be made with straight and curved lines. In the third field of design proper, the ideal, all nations have conspired to call the artist's work a creation.

SECT. 1. DRESS AND ORNAMENTS; THEIR CLASSES, MATERIAL AND MODES OF ELABORATION.

Form and color in dress, depending partly on material, partly on national customs, have from time immemorial been the recognized sphere of woman's taste and skill.

The first raiment was in form a short half skirt or pinafore, its color simple green, its material broad leaves; followed soon by "coats" or close-fitting tunics, of the "skins of animals." The monuments of Egypt, as well as present customs among all nations, show that the tunic, chemise, shirt or frock, all kindred in form, is the universal primitive dress for male and female. To this as a temporary covering the robe, mantle, shawl or cloak was added. The closer-fitting vest, boddice and jacket, and the trowsers or pantaloons, originated later in a northern clime. The head-dress, varying so greatly from fancy, is hardly susceptible of analysis or of historic tracing. The shoe, necessarily conformed more than any part of the dress to the form of the foot, has varied from the mere sandal to high-topped boots.

The simplest material employed in dress consisted of the vegetable and animal tissues still used by rude tribes. At an early day, however, the idea of spinning short animal and vegetable fibre, as wool, hair, hemp, cotton and afterward silk, came to displace the simpler fabrics. The advance of the art of spinning from the simple spindle, and of weaving from the two rough rods tied to posts now used in Africa, is a study worthy the ablest mind.

As to form, the true ideal of dress is that which sets off the person to the best advantage; and this, in the main, prevails in youth when its claims alone control. Comfort and health demand a flowing dress, especially for matrons. Homer pictures veils and skirts which "swept the ground;" and Herodotus, three centuries later, describes the progress of dress as that of the orders in columnar architecture, first the plain Dorian, then the matronly Ionian, and finally the maiden Corinthian.

The color of dress, originally that of its material, is very early made artificial; as is seen in the buffalo robes of the American Indian, and in the ancient Egyptian dyes, "red, blue, scarlet, crimson, and purple." The early tinctures gave the same hue to every part of woven fabrics. Dyeing, as Aristotle and Pliny indicate, became truly an art when by tinging, first with one, then with another color, as "purple on a dark rose," new tints of rare beauty were attained.

It was a new art when by the needle and loom threads of different dyes were interwoven, in which art Homer reveals surpassing perfection as attained, before Troy fell, by Trojan and Grecian matrons. Pliny recorded the stages of advance; first, the invention of spinning and weaving wool; then the Phrygian fine needle-work, the Pergamean interweaving of gold thread, and the Babylonian dyeing with parti-colors; and finally the Alexandrian interweaving of figures by colored thread distributed in the warp and web.

In addition to dress as a necessity, ornaments are sought; especially by females. In this department, pre-eminently in engraving on precious stones, decorative art approaches the fine arts.

The forehead is decked with wreaths of flowers in childhood; with a fringe of shells and feathers among savages; with the turban in Asia; and with the fillet and jewel droplets of the Greek maidens. Among rude tribes the nose, and in refined ages the ear, invite pendant ornaments; and in every land the necklace, an ancient royal badge and funereal decoration, is retained as a female and childhood ornament. The breast-plate or girdle, a favorite token of exchange between Grecian and Trojan heroes, still retains its character in the rosette as an official badge. For females, bracelets on the arms and rings on the fingers are still worthy ornaments. Even anklets, with which eastern damsels of old "made a tinkling as they went," retain their attraction.

As material, calcareous substances, shell, bone, horn, ivory and pearl have from the days of Solomon been preferred for ordinary ornaments. The metals, as silver and gold, and especially precious stones, are the most costly; valued even by princes.

SECT. 2. IMPLEMENTS OF BUSINESS, AND HOUSE UTENSILS, FURNITURE AND WALL DECORATIONS; THEIR USES, MATERIAL AND VARYING FORMS AND STYLES.

In hours of toil, implements for man's out-door and utensils for woman's in-door employ have been demanded, from the day when Cain tilled the soil and Abel slaughtered his lamb. An Arab's tent, an Indian's wigwam, an army bivouac, reveal how simple these may be.

The material of implements is controlled partly by necessity; the Egyptian finding a wooden plough adapted to a soft soil, but the Syrian being compelled to use an iron coulter. Civilization has converted the flint hatchet first into bronze then into steel. The implements of the farmer, carpenter, smith and potter have changed most in mere finish; while in utensils of glass, clay and porcelain art was early perfected.

The forms of implements have improved, while their material has remained unchanged. The modern farmer is eloquent over the *beauty* of his patented plough.

As the house is the resting-place from toil it needs appropriate funiture. The hall requires receptacles for out-door raiment; the saloon, convenient seats; the parlor, chairs and lounges for special guests; the dining-room, its seats and tables; the sleeping chamber, its beds, wardrobe and varied conveniences. The furniture of the humblest cottage is a study calling for the exercise of taste.

Asiatic taste luxuriates in this field. The sculpture of the oldest Egyptian tomb is a wonder in every variety of house furniture. Homer, too, tells of Agamemnon's "gilded throne," of Juno's "golden couch," of Helen's "loom" and of Hecuba's "odoriferous wardrobe." In this ancient art, color as well as form influenced ornamentation; the Asiatics setting off the graceful curves of ottomans by their rich blue and yellow housings: while the Greeks, as pictured by Homer and Virgil, allowed the land of luxury to rule in this her appropriate sphere. The same Asiatic richness is in modern times seen in the gorgeous divans of a Turkish saloon; while the taste of Europe has grown in exquisiteness of workmanship and chasteness of design.

Besides the furniture of a mansion, the doors and their casings, the windows with their sashes, the fire-place with its jambs and mantles, and indeed the entire face of the walls, require not only proportion but artistic decoration. Here architecture, sculpture and painting all meet to create decorative art.

Walls, made either of wood or plaster, have been decorated by carvings as in English oak, by painting as in Italian fresco, by needle-work as in ancient and modern tapestry.

Ceiling cornices may be moulded in stucco, and carved in wood; or, mere shading in paper or fresco may accomplish their effect. Heavy doors may be in oak or bronze; but delicate window-tracings must be partly in metal. Even balcony railings, anciently cumbersome, become light and graceful in modern castings.

SECT. 3. TRAVELING EQUIPAGE; TRAPPINGS OF ANIMALS AND STYLES OF VEHICLES.

Called from home by business or pleasure, traveling equipage is required for guiding and controling animals, and for the carriage of the rider; either the back of the animal, or a vehicle drawn behind him, serving this purpose.

The horse, favorite for his strength and swiftness, is managed by rude tribes without saddle or bridle; the Greeks had these so simple as to originate the fable of the centaurs; while the Persians, with Asiatic sumptuousness, loaded down their horses with trappings. The Asiatic uses the donkey, camel and elephant as well as the horse; showing a special taste in decking their halters, saddles and howdahs; and from the days of Abraham to Jesus, in Western Asia, a donkey or mule has been a princely riding beast.

In Egypt the chariot, not the saddle, was from early times employed. The Romans in their country, less hilly than Greece, adopted the chariot; covering not only Italy but Western Asia with paved carriage-roads for their narrow vehicles.

SECT. 4. BOOK ILLUSTRATIONS AND PICTURE BORDERS; THEIR DESIGN AND THE PRINCIPLE OF THEIR ADAPTATION.

Besides his physical needs man has intellectual wants; to meet which art addresses the eye.

While rude tribes from necessity used picture writing, Egyptian wise men employed it to conceal their meaning from the multitude. Under Christian civilization, pre-eminently, art has come to the aid of written speech.

Egyptian records and monuments show that the idea of an enlarged and ornamented initial letter was of early origin. In Christian history the "limning" or "*illuminating*" of the text in missals or liturgies containing prayers at *mass*, became a high art. From the crimson red employed, such works were called "rubrics." Retained in early German and English printing, ritualists still perpetuate it in religious literature.

In modern times the art of engraving fills the place of ancient limning; its tendency, not only in light literature but in solid science, being to exclude rather than aid true apprehension.

An æsthetic, distinct from the intellectual want, demands that the painter's canvas have a finished border and the statue a pedestal; and design in decorative art seeks an appropriate supply for this lack. The leading idea in a picture-frame is, that its slope inward seem a window or doorway through which the view is obtained. Its form and color should suit the tone of the general design. For landscape the rectangle as of a window half opened, and for portrait the oval are preferred because appropriate.

While the inner rim should be plain, the exterior may be adorned with geometric or floral decorations in imitation of wreaths. Gilt stucco gives richness to a picture by its reflected light. Special skill is required in mounting and hanging paintings in a gallery.

In statuary, regard should be had to the proportions of the pedestal and the color of the background. A statuette should always be elevated on a mantel or bracket, and a colossal statue on a broad pedestal of dark material; while a life-size statue should stand nearly on a level with the beholder. Statues in niches, as the Greeks learned, need, as in the open air, an azure background to give the best relief.

SECT. 5. INSIGNIA OF PERSONAL RANK AND OF NATIONALITY, WITH THEIR SYMBOLIC CHARACTER AND ELABORATE ADAPTATION; DEFENSIVE ARMOR AND OFFENSIVE WEAPONS.

The relations of civil society, calling for officers with authority to use force, require badges of rank and instruments of power. Insignia of rank are borne on the forehead and left breast and in the right hand, as the seats of intelligence, affection and power.

The first token of civil power is the sceptre; an emblem borne by Hebrew princes and Grecian chiefs; Ulysses' "rod" being distinguished from the *kērukeion*, or *caduceus*, borne by heralds, as Mercury; and also from the *skytalē*, or baton, of the Greek general. In Christian ages the crosier or shepherd's crook, an ecclesiastical badge, has been made to accompany the sceptre of civil and the baton of military authority; which is burlesqued in the tall horse-hair tufted poles of officials in Eastern Asia.

The second badge of rank is the crown; illustrated in the cap of Egyptian and Hebrew priests, and in the Persian *tiara*, which in its band furnished the type of the modern diadem, out of which has grown the triple crown of the Papal ecclesiastic.

The third badge, the star or rosette, is perhaps the "*latus clavus*" worn by Romans of consular rank; whence also originated the "banner" of feudal lords. The rosette on the left breast is now the only distinctive badge of Turkish officials.

Military insignia, more elaborate than civic, include standards, or national symbols, and ensigns, or party signals. These take the form of a banner stretched and supported at its centre, or of a flag floating free in the breeze. The term "colors" refers to the fact that for distinctness pure colors, as red, are chosen as a contrast to sky and earth. The Egyptian standards were feather-shaped; the Persians carried silk streamers; Themistocles' battle-flag was of scarlet; while the Romans, beginning with a wisp of straw on a spear, added the animal forms of the eagle, the wolf, the minotaur, the horse and the boar. The former of these, under the consul Marius, about B. C. 104, became the sole recognized symbol; beneath which hung the banner of square silk. To this was added the *vexillum* or swallow-tailed flag, as a cavalry ensign. Modern Christian civilization has retained the old military emblems.

With military ensigns are directly associated armor for defence and weapons for offence. The former includes the helmet, casque or cap for the head, the coat of mail or corselet for the body, greaves for the legs, sandals or boots for the feet, and the movable shield. Weapons of offence, as to the mode of wielding and the distance at which they are used, include three classes; those for bruising, as the club, whirling mace and sling-stone; for thrusting, as the knife, spear, dagger, bayonet, lance and arrow; and for slashing, as the axe and sword.

SECT. 6. RELIGIOUS VESSELS AND SYMBOLS; FESTAL DECORATIONS AND FUNEREAL MONUMENTS AND TABLETS.

Moral and religious cravings call for memorial symbols to be supplied by decorative art.

The two ideas of offering and of purification, aside from the conception of images of Deity which belongs to sculpture, embrace the fields of religious symbolism proper. The Greeks and Romans had their altars and vases; as the Hebrews had their altar, table and censer, and their font and vases; and as the Christian Church has its fonts and bowls for Baptism, and plates, ewers and chalices for the Sacred Supper.

To these the Hebrew and Christian systems add the peculiar provision for spiritual enlightenment embodied in the ark with its tables and books of the law; to which the Christian faith, more imperative than any other in its demands on decorative art, adds candelabras, the pulpit, book-stands and furnished pews.

Social and civil relations, founded in the moral nature, seek in religious festivities at once the recreation and refining of an associated community.

Festal decorations have taken the floral and the geometric or architectural types; the floral being borrowed directly from nature in the peasant's wreaths and garlands; the architectural agreeing with the measured and polished character of city and court life. The latter, scientific in principle, should always be the foundation of the former; as the arborescent of the Gothic never reaches its climax except when grounded upon the framework of the Grecian and Roman.

Tombs and their inscriptions speak of the end of human life. The true idea of burial is the grave; where "dust returns to dust;" over which a slab was laid or a headstone was reared. The idea of the soul's inseparable union to the body, originating the embalming of the body and sealed tombs, reached its Asiatic climax in the pyramids and rock-tombs of Egypt, and its degenerate Grecian extravagance in the *mausoleum* of Artemisia. The comprehensive spirit of Christianity adopts every species of funeral monument in its tablets; recording memories and sentiments speaking to the soul.

CHAPTER II.

ASIATIC DECORATIVE ART; RUDIMENTARY IN STYLE, DEFECTIVE IN FORM, EXCESSIVE IN ORNAMENT, BUT ELABORATE IN FINISH.

In decorative art Asiatics fall behind Europeans in conceptions of style, form and color, but are superior in the patient labor of the hand.

Sect. 1. The Indian as the permanent source, and the Egyptian as the ancient storehouse, of Asiatic decorative art.

From India in the earliest days came even to Egypt, as well to Syria and Phœnicia, and afterward to Greece and Rome, every form of luxury in decorative art; as now they come to modern Europe. As Herodotus and Pliny conceded to the Indians superiority in this department over the Greeks and Romans, so modern English residents agree that in silk and cotton weaving, wood and ivory ornamentation, Indian operatives show skill superior to that of Western Europe.

The long-hidden Egyptian tombs, rich in minute works of art, reveal a special religious idea presiding over the secular life of that people; well illustrated in their sacred symbols and utensils. The globe with wings, or beetle holding the ball containing its maturing eggs, with asps ready to devour its young when hatched, the sacred vases of fruit and water deposited for the dead, finely moulded and finished, indicate in their conception superior intellect, guiding gross superstition. Among other articles the Egyptian earthenware is second only to the Etruscan; while Egyptian glass is first in rank. The mosaic in the British Museum is inimitable by modern art; while the enameled obelisks in the Great Oasis, mentioned by Pliny, must have rivaled the Porcelain Tower at Nankin.

SECT. 2. CHINESE AND JAPANESE AS THE DEGENERATING STAGE, AND POLYNESIAN AND AMERICAN AS THE DEGRADED DECLINE OF ASIATIC DECORATIVE ART.

While inferior in some arts to the Indian, Chinese ornamental manufactures are in porcelain superior. This superiority depends partly on the fine material found in their mountains; the infusible portion, *kaolin* or clay, and the fusible, *petuntse* or silicon, furnishing their inimitable watery white porcelain, which is colored by metallic oxides. This art of China the Greeks knew and called it *keramicos;* but the Portuguese were the first to bring it to Europe. In all other respects Chinese art is a degeneracy; the exuberant fancy displayed in the endless variety of exported Chinese toys and notions indicating a lack in elevated sentiment. Japanese decoration excels the Chinese in both color and form. The method of giving adhesion to colors laid on metal, as that called japanning, seems peculiar to that people.

Every voyager to the Pacific isles adds to the treasures of Polynesian decorative art; while every wandering camp of American Indians has its venders of rude decorated workmanship. A careful comparison with the line of kindred art westward to China indicates a kindred taste; displaying itself in fondness for pure colors and fine texture in material. The northern tribes decorate buffalo hides and the southern the delicate buffalo pleura, with the same colors; while for carvings, ivory, coral or flint are chosen where each is found.

SECT. 3. HEBREW DECORATIVE ART; THE CENTRAL AND HALLOWED TYPE OF THE ASIATIC STYLE.

The glory of the Hebrews was not military prowess, nor civil dominion, but their possession of the "Oracles of God." All professed revelations, the Vedas, Zendavesta and Koran, have emanated from Asia; as false coin is issued nigh the source of the true. Both the Old and New Testament, have come to the world mainly from Hebrew pens.

Hebrew art excelled in religious emblems; their altar and candlestick becoming types for all ages. Not only the vessels of their worship, and their priestly vestments adorned with golden fringes presenting alternately a bell and a pomegranate, but even common utensils, were so hallowed that "Holiness to the Lord" was to be inscribed "on the bells of the horses." The Hebrew, therefore, has become for all subsequent ages, uninterrupted by progressing European civilization, the type of religious symbolism.

SECT. 4. ARABIAN, PHŒNICIAN, SYRIAN AND ASSYRIAN DECORATIVE ART; THE FIRST STAGE OF ADVANCE IN THE ASIATIC STYLE.

The Arabians, an intelligent and permanent Shemitic family, have possessed a high type of decorative art. This eminence is indicated in the designation Arabesque; a term applied to the tracery-work heaped upon the façades of Moorish palaces and mosques in the mediæval age, and given since to highly embossed work.

With the Assyrians, between India and Asia Minor, decoration was a chief aspiration in art; the pictures given by the Hebrew writers and by Herodotus and Pliny illustrating this characteristic; while the explorations of Layard have made it palpable in implements and utensils of every variety.

Phœnicia, with Tyre its capital, furnishing the purple dye celebrated among the Greeks and the glass lauded by Pliny, excelled in rich ornament; becoming so exuberant that not only men and women, but their riding camels, were decked with necklaces and jewelry.

Finally Syria, with its capital Damascus, lives in the works bearing its name; as *damask*, a silk fabric with embossed figures, *damassin*, a similar silk interwoven with threads of gold and silver, *damaskin*, a sword-blade of rare tempered steel, and *damaskeen*, the adorning of steel sword-blades and scabbards, knives, etc., with inlaid gold and silver thread. This inimitable workmanship forms a link never to be broken in the union of ancient Asiatic and modern European art. When, after the fall of the Roman Empire, Genoa and Venice were bringing not only the material but the arts of Arabia into Europe, one of the most fascinating episodes in Cennini's history of early Italian art is a description of his own enthusiasm in trying to copy the exquisite work on the scabbard of a Damascus scimetar; as Faraday's last triumph was the discovery of the composition of Arabian steel which formed its blade.

SECT. 5. PERSIAN AND GREEK COLONIAL DECORATIVE ART; THE MOST ADVANCED ASIATIC, AND THE CONNECTING LINK TO THE GRECIAN TYPE.

The connection of the Persians with both Southern Asia and with the Greeks, as indicated by Homer, Herodotus and Xenophon, is more intimate in ornamental than in the higher arts. The pyramidal tombs alike of Hector and Achilles, the sceptres both of Priam and Agamemnon, are links reaching from Egypt to Greece. The adoption by the Greeks of the chaste architectural trefoil of Persia, and their rejection of the high cap and necklaces peculiar also to the Egyptians, show that this intercommunication in art was only partial. The couch for reclining at meals, borrowed from Persia through Asiatic Greece, whose history is epitomized in the *klinē* of Matthew addressing Asiatics, in the *klinidion* of Luke appealing to Greeks, and in the *krabbaton* or Latin *grabbatum* of Mark writing for Roman readers, is a specimen of the tendency of luxury to pass from a lower to a higher civilization.

CHAPTER III.

EUROPEAN DECORATIVE ART; CONTROLLED BY THE ALTERNATING PROGRESS AND DECLINE OF SCIENCE AND ART, OF SOCIAL, INTELLECTUAL, MORAL AND RELIGIOUS IMPROVEMENT.

As the traditional reverence of the Asiatic for the past is specially manifest in dress, equipage, furniture, implements, utensils and personal ornaments, so is the European spirit aspiring to progress.

SECT. 1. GRECIAN AND ROMAN DECORATIVE ART; THE ONE EXACT IN FORM AND CHASTE IN FINISH; THE OTHER ELABORATE IN DETAIL AND PROFUSE IN ORNAMENT.

In higher art the Grecian artist showed three national characteristics: first, mathematical exactness in form, as in architectural ornamentation; second, simplicity in outline, as in the curve of their Etruscan vase unbroken by embossments; and third, elaborateness of finish. These characteristics made the Greeks in some respects eclectic; as when in sculpture the early Ionic style of female dress, with hair curled or frizzled and held by a jeweled fillet, and long robes, was harmonized with the later Dorian fashion of plain straight hair tied in a knot, and short skirts. The control of mathematical simplicity in Grecian decorative art is seen alike in the tripod as opposed to four-footed supports of chairs and tables, and in plain vases for holding the ashes of the dead.

The cumbersome and gorgeous detail which prevailed in Roman architecture pervaded Roman decorative art. The labor devoted by the Greek to polish, the Roman exhausted in embossed decorations.

The severe religious simplicity inculcated at Rome by Numa, abjuring images and leaving the Pantheon walls blank, gave to Roman art a permanent foundation of strength, to which luxury added a gorgeous exterior; as is seen in the relics of Pompeii. In dress Roman plainness preserved the *tunica* or frock-shirt, called *stola* for females, at first short and without sleeves, and the *toga* or sack-coat, known as *palla*, for women; while, however, the native fondness for ornament displayed itself in the rings universally worn by men. and in the profusion of jewelry decorating their women. Their variety in elaborate furniture and equipage forbids enumeration.

SECT. 2. EARLY CHRISTIAN DECORATIVE ART; MARKED ESPECIALLY BY SYMBOLS OF RELIGIOUS IDEAS PECULIAR TO THE NEW FAITH.

Diognetus, the teacher of Marcus Aurelius, about B. C. 140, wrote of the early Christians: "They are not distinguished from other men by their place of residence, their language or manners." In decorative art the early Christians were transformed in nothing but in religious symbols.

Didron, Münter and Lord Lindlay have illustrated the emblems wrought into early Christian decorative art. The representation of God the Father was a hand and arm stretched from a cloud. The Son was symbolized by the monogram X and ρ, from *Christos*, overlapping; by a cross, a lamb, a lamp, a vine, a rock and a pelican; and also by a fish, the Greek *Ichthus* being made up of the initials of *Iēsous*, *Christos*, *Theos*, *Uios*, *Soter*. The Holy

Spirit was figured by a dove bearing an olive branch; also by a candlestick with seven branches. The Trinity was pictured by three beams of light radiating from Christ's head; by a rainbow with three arches; by the thumb, fore and index fingers of Christ raised erect; or by the index finger straight and the thumb hooked, the index and ring finger crossed, and the little finger crooked, making together the letters I. C. and X. C., the first and last letters of *Iēsous Christos*. The four Evangelists were designated in general by four rivers; and in particular, Matthew by an angel, Mark by a lion, Luke by an ox, and John by an eagle. Among the apostles, Paul was indicated by a sword, and Peter by the keys. The three graces, Faith, Hope and Charity, were represented by the cross, anchor and heart; purity by a lily; incorruptibility by a rose; victory by a wreath of palm; and peace by an olive-branch. The sacrament of baptism was symbolized by water poured on the cross, and the Lord's Supper by wheat in the ear and grapes, or by a loaf of bread and a cup of wine.

SECT. 3. MEDIÆVAL DECORATIVE ART, ECCLESIASTIC AND SECULAR; ARTIFICIAL IN DESIGN AND LIMITLESS IN INVENTION.

After Constantine images took the place of symbols; God the Father was pictured as an old man; the Council of Trent, A. D. 692, ordered that images of Christ should be substituted for the symbol of the Lamb; and till the eighth century, masterpieces of design in mosaic and painting were produced. Then symbolism again became prominent; showing its character in emblems of apostolic and priestly offices, and in the dress of the head and person of the Virgin.

Architecture having assumed a distinct ecclesiastical type, called for decoration: the common designation, *kyriakē*, *kirche*, *kirk*, or *church*, indicating the prominence which the "Lord's" *house* had attained. The edifice, in ground-plot a cross, with the choir as its head, the transept as its cross-arms, and the nave as its body, had a narrow section of the nave at the entrance called *narthex* or oblong, fenced off for penitents. The choir was frescoed or hung with oil paintings and had niches for statuary; its floor had a raised platform or *bema*, with a front railing called *cancelli* or chancel; upon the *bema* was an altar, before which was the *cathedra* or bishop's chair, called from its sanctity, *hierateion*, from its seclusion *adyton*, and from its authority, *presbyterion;* and on one side was the pulpit for the preacher. The organ and choir gallery, at first behind the altar, was afterward moved to the side or transept, then to the front of the nave. On one side near the door or in a separate building in the rear was the baptistery; and in a tower, at first joined with, then separated from, the front, were the bells. Each of these portions of the edifice with its furniture became a field for elaborate ornament.

Doors, windows and pavements in churches, also were ornamented; the doorways with carvings in stone, often grotesque in style; the windows with stained glass, superior in execution though rude in design; and the pavements with mosaics after the Roman style. To this decoration the spirit of Christianity and of art alike agreed; the criticism of extreme reform showing its unphilosophic cast in the objection of Bernard to the pavement: "Those passing over them often spit in the mouth of an angel, or grind the face of some saint with their heels."

In dress the common people followed national customs; a few ascetics, pointing to John's camel-hair raiment, and insisting that Christians of patrician rank lay aside the toga; while the intelligent, like Tertullian, regarding Jesus' example, exclaimed: "We are no Hindoo fakirs!" In the dress of ecclesiastics excessive richness grew up; and the *tiara* of the Persian noble, the *stolē* or robe of the Roman Pontifex Maximus, the *ephod* of the Jewish high-priests, and the *ring* and *crosier* were adopted.

The civic and military decoration styled "heraldry" and "blazonry," from *herald* and *blasen*, to proclaim, designed to indicate the nationality, community and family of knights when completely cased in armor, though known in the age of Henry I. of England, was perfected as a system during and after the Crusades. The field or escutcheon, having a crest above, a scroll below and the colors at the sides, was divided into nine compartments. The three at the top and the three at the bottom were horizontal; the former being called the dexter, middle and sinister chiefs; the latter the dexter middle and sinister basis; while the three uniting them were perpendicular, called honor, fess and nombril points. Diagonal bands, called chief, pale, bend, bend sinister, fess, bar, chevron, cross and saltire, and also eight curved or bent lines, entitled the engraved, inverted, wavy, embattled, nebuly, raguly, indented and dancette, subdivided the field. Nine colors were introduced: *or* or gold, *gule* or red, *azure* or blue, *sable* or black, *vert* or green, *purpure* or purple, *tenny* or orange, *sanguine* or crimson, and *murrey* or brown-red. Finally, various figures, as crosses, shells, birds, beasts, dragons, stars, flowers, etc., called charges, were inserted.

SECT. 4. MODERN CHANGES IN MATERIAL AND HANDICRAFT; MODIFYING THE STYLE, AND DETERIORATING THE FINISH OF ORNAMENTAL WORK.

New species of material and new forms of the old have been introduced into decorative art; modifying its form and style. Cheap iron castings take the place of elaborately wrought bronze and nicely hewn marble. Modern Parian, as plastic as clay, rivals the finest porcelain. In coloring the *moiré antique*, giving by the action of acids on metallic plates rainbow hues in wavy lines, opens a new field of art.

While modern machinery gives exactness of form, the neglect of handicraft, because of this easier method, tends to a degeneracy in the execution of the carver and chiseler.

The aid of improved chemical agents makes easy the former severe toil of Cennini in *damaskeening;* but in porcelain and glass staining, experiment has not attained to the chemical law employed by the Asiatic.

SECT. 5. MODERN METHODS OF LOCOMOTION AND ENGINES OF WAR; VARYING THE FORM AND ADORNMENT OF VEHICLES AND OF VESSELS, AND REVOLUTIONIZING THE STYLES OF ARMOR AND WEAPONS.

In convenient adaptations for animal carriage the moderns have made improvements on ancient methods; though these should not be confounded with ornamentation. The use of steam has introduced on land and sea traveling mansions. The modern car invites paneled walls, carving and painting. Passenger-vessels, having their exterior marred by unsightly chimneys, demand a peculiar skill in securing external grace. The inner saloons, rivaling palace apartments, require tact in order to secure proportion; on which alone the excess of decoration assumes a worthy aspect.

In the conflicts of bordering nations the invention of gunpowder and modern projectiles has substituted for lustrous metal designed for defence, variegated woolens and silks; which in actual service are subdued into the sober blue and gray of close-fitting jackets, with a simple leaf, eagle or star on the shoulder to indicate rank.

Modern offensive weapons, cannon, guns and pistols, exposed to soot and smoke, at their first invention, and since as mere ornaments for princely hands, have been enriched with inlaid and embossed decoration; as is seen alike in the matchlock muskets of the Imaum of Muscat and in the richly embossed brass cannon of Louis XIV. Weapons for service require elaborate polish but no ornament.

SECT. 6. MODERN VIEWS OF POPULAR EQUALITY; SIMPLIFYING OFFICIAL INSIGNIA AND MULTIPLYING ILLUSTRATIVE METHODS OF IMPARTING KNOWLEDGE.

Ascetic and cynic philosophy in religion and politics may become extreme in demanding simplicity in dress and ornament appropriate to civil and religious offices. In the French Legislative Assembly, and in the Lower House of the English Parliament, the mediæval insignia are laid aside. In the American republic, no badge marks the highest executive and legislative officials; only the robe of the chief judicial officers being a memorial of the ancient insignia.

Military and naval official badges, however, remain in every land true to ancient ideas; as their office is unchanged by ameliorating civilization.

In childhood and among uncultured people the eye instructs the mind. Expanding reason, however, forms truer conceptions by its own efforts at comprehension; reaching the reality, where childhood stops at the image.

In a community where all are educated, the necessity for early application to industrial pursuits makes the mental training of most youth purely elementary. This necessitates the multiplying in school-rooms and in text-books of illustrations which address the eye. The pure mathematics must be illustrated by diagrams; but, in the applied mathematics the pupil should be trained to form his conceptions of mechanism independently of apparatus. In the fine arts the artist must learn to conceive with no model before the eye, and the critic may be hindered instead of aided by the imperfect drawings of the text-book. By the missal paintings of the Middle Ages, as well as by the engraved Scripture illustrations of modern times, the intellect is only aroused; its apprehension must be completed by its own effort. In history, natural, civil and religious, in science and in symbolism, secular and Christian, modern progress modifies, but does not supersede book illustrations.

SECT. 7. MODERN REFINEMENTS IN METAPHYSICAL AND THEOLOGICAL SCIENCE; ORIGINATING NEW DEVICES TO REPRESENT SPIRITUAL TRUTH AND FUTURE SPIRITUAL LIFE.

Intellectual progress, manifestly extending in every portion of Europe and reacting on Asia, is tending to unity in habits, customs and conveniences of life; as is seen in the assimilation of dress, of modes of locomotion and of military armament reaching from Constantinople to London. A kindred unity in metaphysical, moral and religious convictions is leading on from more refined forms of personal adornment and of civic insignia to more spiritual religious symbols and funereal memorials. In American society, where every form of European and even Asiatic and African prejudice and precedent, social, civil and ecclesiastical, are meeting, even churches and cemeteries indicate a tendency to unity in conception.

Much of man's devotion to art ever has shown and ever will show itself in funeral monuments; which speak of the deceased at once, in pleasant memory of his past, and in lively hope of his future. The Egyptian kings carried this sentiment at first to an extreme; building pyramidal abodes, as much more costly than their palaces as the body's rest in one was to be longer than in the other; while during all their history Egyptian royal tombs were as expensive as their temples. In its early history, German, English and American sculpture has been chiefly confined to funeral monuments; to which also it must be permanently devoted.

Unity, however, implies a whole made up of differing parts; for we do not speak of the unity of a rock, but of the unity of a tree or landscape. Unity, therefore, in science or art is true when it creates a whole of infinite variety.

In nothing more than in funereal monuments, which embody the sweetest memories of the past, the most exalted conceptions of imagination and the liveliest hopes of the future, has this unity in variety shown its pervading power.

The marked distinction between modern Christian and ancient Egyptian, Hebrew and even Grecian and Roman types for funeral monuments, is to be traced to the distinct philosophy of each as to the power and province of death. The spirit of the ancients was based on the idea that matter is eternal; in its nature possessed by indwelling evil; as uncreated beyond the power of the spiritual Ruler and Redeemer to transform and purify; and thence for ever shut up to the lament, which "says to corruption, 'Thou art my father,' and to the worm, 'Thou art my mother.'" The Egyptian and Hebrew, even till the burial of Jesus Christ, embalmed the body and sealed it in a tomb; while the Greek and Roman burned it to ashes and enclosed it in an urn.

The Christian idea is based on the fact of Christ's personal bodily purity and immortality; that matter, made from nothing by God's word, is not in itself evil, or controlled by its power, but that after death "both soul and body" may be redeemed. The spirit of this revelation has led Christians and even Mohammedans to deck the dead body with flowers and to inscribe on funereal monuments such devices as the dove bearing a rosebud to heaven, and the worm breaking the chrysalis and soaring with wings.

The consideration of funereal monuments under the Christian revelation is a fitting close to this treatise on the fine arts and their criticism. Monuments to the dead demand from all the arts, drawing, sculpture, architecture, landscape-gardening and decoration, their highest efforts. It is the field for art, last in order, speaking of man's final end; it is the most exalted, looking to his higher life; and it is exhaustless, drawing emblems from every field of nature, and from the philosophy and poetry of all ages and nations. Above all, it embodies the highest conceptions of the true, the beautiful, and the good this side the grave; and deriving its light from a purer world, it aspires to the perfect right in its home beyond the tomb.

ILLUSTRATIONS.

IN a concise and comprehensive text-book, covering the field of all the fine arts, it is impossible that any considerable attempt to furnish engraved illustrations should be expected. To obtain a thorough mastery in detail of each department the teacher and thorough student have three resources: first, works of art themselves gathered in chief cities; second, large and numerous engraved copies of such works collected in well-appointed libraries; and third, photographic views of the best existing works in sculpture, architecture and painting, now readily obtained either in personal tours in Europe or through the leading houses of our commercial cities.

In the department of drawing any teacher can furnish himself with elementary illustrated works, and especially with specimens of wood and copper-plate engravings, lithographs and photographs. In sculpture, stereoscopic views, with an ordinary stereoscopic instrument, should be employed; in painting, which forbids stereoscopic views, excellent photographs as well as engravings may be procured; while in architecture, collections of engravings and of both monocular and binocular photographs are requisite to a thorough student.

In the illustrations which follow three are designed to present important principles in perspective; while all the remainder are devoted to the most practically important art, that of architecture. In the latter the author has availed himself of drawings prepared for various works, chiefly English.

PLATE I.

Fig. 1.—A geometric figure, presenting two squares of equal surface, the one at twice the distance from the eye of the other; in which the lines of vision in both the horizontal and vertical planes are seen to diverge from the eye as a focus, the line subtending this angle and forming the third side of a triangle increasing in length in proportion to its distance from the eye. It is thus observed that one-fourth of the square nearest the eye hides from view the entire square at twice the distance; and in general, that the field of vision enlarges in the ratio of the square of the distance.

Fig. 2.—Lionardo's diagram; showing that by the sight of the two eyes more than half the contour of a ball comes within the field of vision, and that the entire surface of a wall behind the ball is distinctly in view; thus exhibiting the two principles of binocular perspective.

Fig. 3.—An optical illustration of the diminution both in breadth and heighth of a line of objects as they are removed farther from the eye; presenting a specimen of linear perspective.

PLATE I.

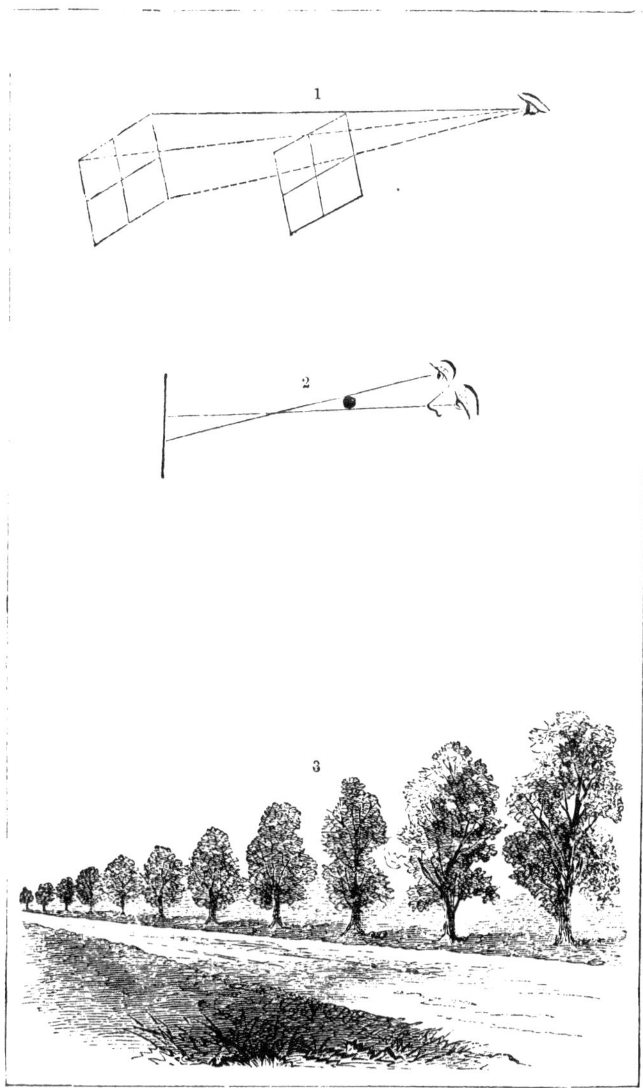

PLATE II.

Fig. 4.—The delicate or adorned order of Egyptian columns; having the open flower of the lotus as its capital, a slender shaft and an ornamented foot.

Fig. 5.—The medium, or Osiride Egyptian column; having as its capital a female face, with cows' ears and a hooded turban, above which rises the façade of a miniature temple as a cap to the head; with its shaft plain or sculptured, and its base straight and unadorned.

Fig. 6.—The robust order of Egyptian columns; having the lotus bud as its capital, the reeded and banded shaft in imitation of a bundle of lotus stalks, and the foliations of the tuber-root of the lotus as its base.

Fig. 7.—The true and false Egyptian cornice; the former having a curve forward only in the upper half of its elevation, which curve is swept by the radius of one-half the height of the cornice; the false having its curve from the base of the cornice, with its entire height as radius.

Fig. 8.—A section of the reeded and banded robust Egyptian column; illustrating the geometric precision of its fluting.

Fig. 9.—Model of a pylon preserved in front of the temple at Edfoo; about 100 feet high and 300 feet in breadth.

Fig. 10.—Interior of a public hall in India; the ceiling supported by tree-trunks, with branches at top, employed as sustaining columns.

Fig. 11.—Façade of the Temple of Dendera erected by the Romans; having Osiride columns; showing the flat roof; and adding a latticed-screen between the columns rising to about one-half their height.

PLATE II.

PLATE III.

Fig. 12.—Grecian Corinthian; its capital tall in proportion to its breadth, and having only foliations, or leaf ornaments, usually of the acanthus.

Fig. 13.—Grecian Ionic column; front view; showing the side curls, intervening fillet and jewel droplets; exhibiting also the base and taper of the shaft.

Fig. 14.—Grecian Doric column; the middle of the shaft cut out, showing the amount of its taper from bottom to top.

Fig. 15.—Front of a temple *in antis;* having two Ionic columns in a recess.

Fig. 16.—The log-cabin as the model of the Grecian temple, after the suggestion of Vitruvius; the end of the rafters grooved forming the triglyphs, and the spaces between called *metopes*, originally left open in the plain Doric temple.

Fig. 17.—Front of the Parthenon; showing the platform; the front Doric columns; the entablature; the gentle slope of the roof; and the tympanum with its recess filled with statuary.

PLATE III.

PLATE IV.

Fig. 18.—The outlet of the Cloaca Maxima, or great sewer of ancient Rome; the best preserved arch of the early Roman era.

Fig. 19.—Plan of the hemispheric Roman dome; showing the intersections and slope of the stones forming its double curvature.

Fig. 20.—Plan of the Roman arch; the faces of its stones lying in planes cutting the axis of the half-cylinder formed by its curve.

Fig. 21.—The Roman Ionic; more elaborate than the Grecian; at corners having a side front, the curl projecting diagonally between the two faces.

Fig. 22.—The Roman Doric; with capital more elaborate than the Grecian; having floral decorations.

Fig. 23.—The Tuscan column; the improved gate-post; the plainest of the Roman orders.

Fig. 24.—The Roman Composite order; with the curls of the Ionic and the foliations of the Corinthian united.

Fig. 25.—The Roman Corinthian; stouter than the Grecian; having also strong spines in the centre and a heavy curl of the leaves at the corners.

Fig. 26.—The Tomb of Absalom; cut from the solid rock east of Jerusalem under Herod the Great in the age of Augustus; a Roman mingling of Grecian and Asiatic styles; the base being Ionic and the upper part an Indian pagoda.

Fig. 27.—The Tomb of Zachariah; of the age also of Herod and Augustus, having an Ionic base and an Egyptian pyramid above.

Fig. 28.—The Temple of Vesta, still standing at Rome; a specimen of a circular edifice, with surrounding colonnade, and having a roof of tiles.

PLATE IV.

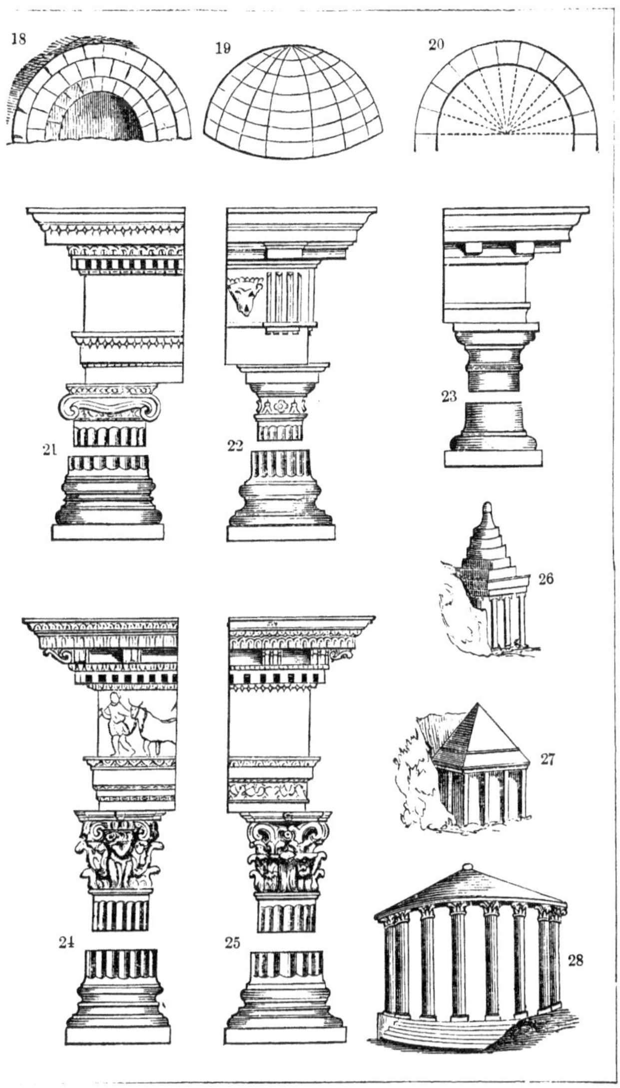

PLATE V.

Fig. 29.—The Coliseum at Rome; with elliptical groundplot; and having four orders of pilasters: the Doric, Ionic, Corinthian and Composite, in stages above each other on its exterior.

Fig. 30.—The Pantheon; its circular walls and hemispheric dome being among the oldest and best preserved works of the days of the Roman kings; the Grecian portico being built under the early emperors, and the two bell-towers added by Christian bishops.

Fig. 31.—Façade of the Basilica di San Spirito at Florence, Italy; showing the scroll-relief above the wings.

Fig. 32.—A section of a *basilica* church; showing its interior structure; the roofed centre being much higher than the wings.

PLATE V.

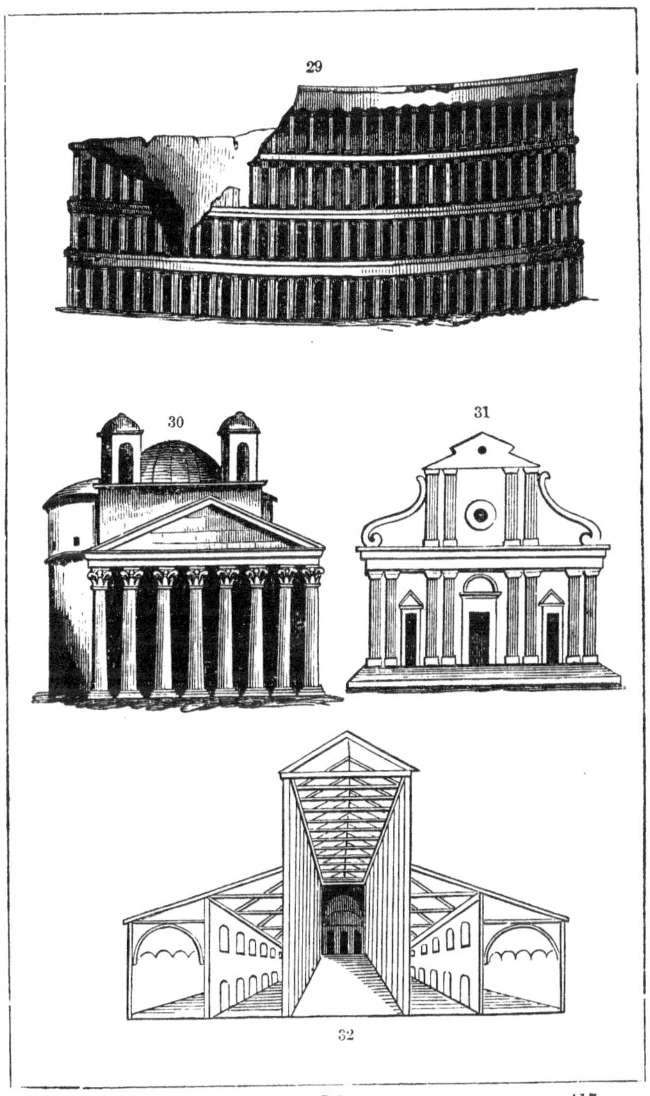

PLATE VI.

Fig. 33.—Section of the Byzantine church of St. Sophia at Constantinople; showing the interior supports of the dome.

Fig. 34.—Pitch of roofs as a fundamental element in architectural styles; the Egyptian without slope; the Grecian having but a few degrees of elevation; the Roman a right angle at the peak, inscribed in the semicircle of the Roman arch; the Gothic 60°, or less, at the apex.

Fig. 35.—The Mosque of Omar at Jerusalem; the groundplot of the Greek cross changed to an octagonal form; the dome Byzantine.

Fig. 36.—The elements of the Gothic arch, formed of two arcs of circles whose centres are at A and B; the line of its outward thrust lying in the direction of the chord C D, which subtends two-thirds of one of the two arcs, or one-third of both the arcs, forming the arch.

Fig. 37.—Line of pressure in the semi-circular Roman arch; its resultant lying in the direction C D of the chord B C of 60°, or of one-third of the semi-circle forming the arch; its lateral thrust requiring that the supporting wall slope outward in that line, or have a weight, strength or adhesion of material equivalent, as a counterpoise to that thrust.

PLATE VI.

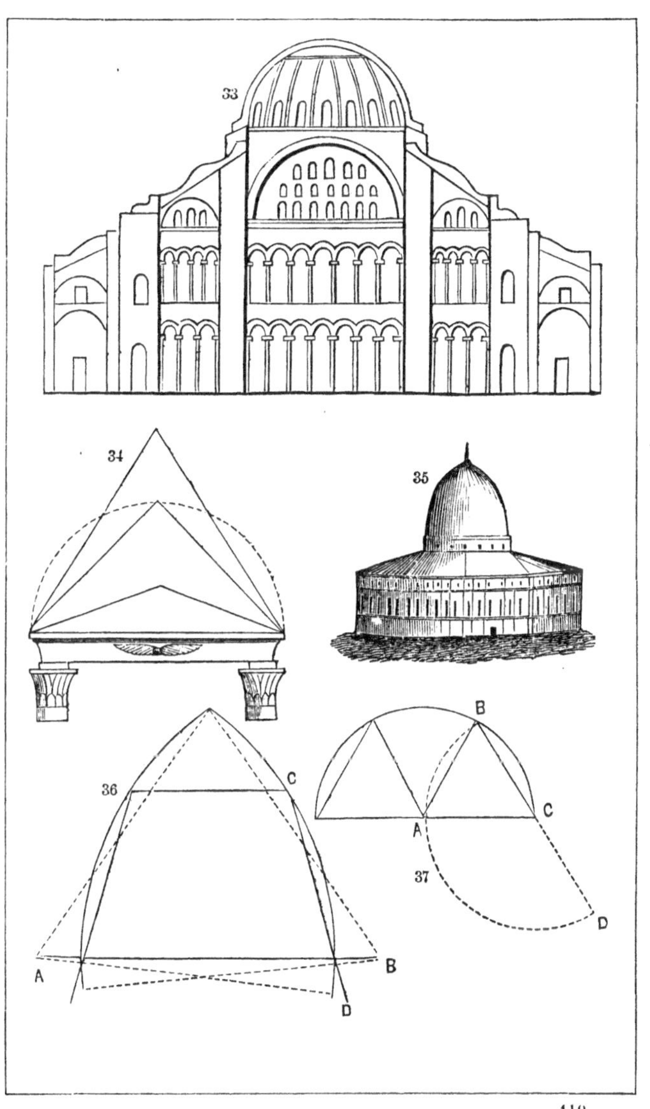

PLATE VII.

Fig. 38.—Crypt of Glasgow Cathedral; showing the junctures of the stones in the Gothic arch.

Fig. 39.—Arched ceiling of a tomb at Delhi, India; illustrating the perpetuated use of the Gothic arch among the Asiatics.

Fig. 40.—Arch covering an ancient sewer in Nimroud, or Nineveh; showing that the Gothic, as well as the circular arch, was known to the ancient Chaldeans and Brahmins.

Fig. 41.—Norman architecture; walls of finished stone, decorated Roman arches, and notched embattled parapet.

Fig. 42.—Saxon architecture; a wall of unhewn stone; with Roman arched windows and a plain parapet.

Fig. 43.—The perfected Gothic; the arcs forming the arch meeting at an angle of about 60°, with a roof of corresponding slant; surmounted by decorated pinnacles.

Fig. 44.—The early pointed Gothic; with three windows, usually united into one.

PLATE VII.

PLATE VIII.

Fig 45.—Façade of Westminster Hall, London; a chaste specimen of Tudor Gothic.

Fig. 46.—The florid Gothic; with arches having an obtuse angle at the apex; its windows capped with Tudor hoods; and its window tracery, parapet and pinnacles overloaded with elaborate carving.

Fig. 47.—Section of the Alhambra, a palace of the Moors at Grenada in Southern Spain; illustrating the excessive ornamentation of the Arabesque or florid Saracenic.

Fig. 48.—A Saracenic arch; re-entering like a horse-shoe in a doorway, window or corridor; mitre or acorn-shaped in a dome.

PLATE VIII.

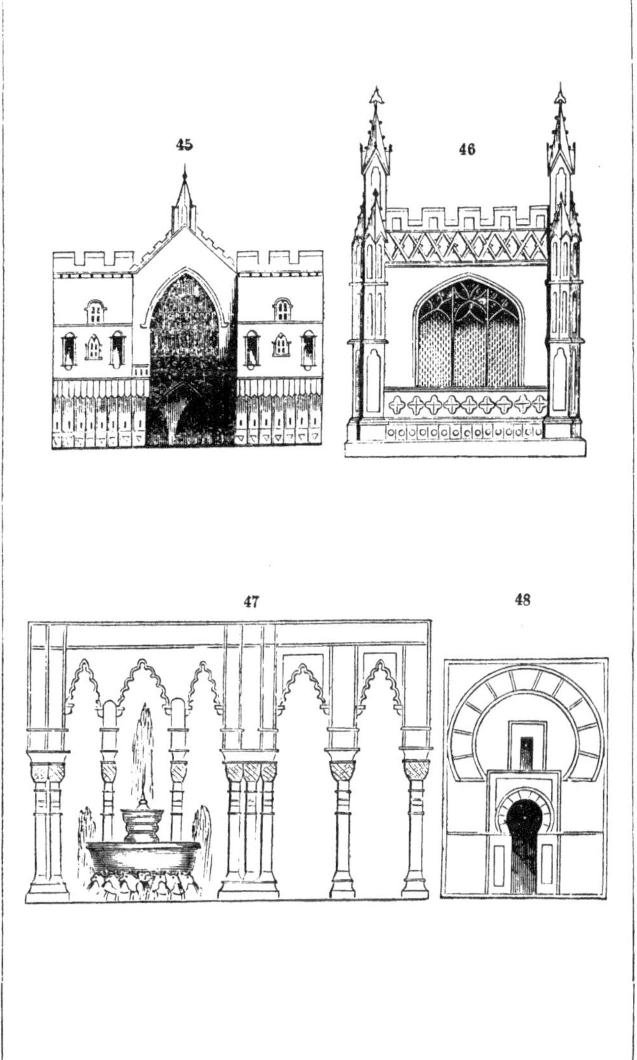

PLATE IX.

Fig. 49.—The elevation of the central portico, dome and lantern of the U. S. Capitol at Washington, D. C.; illustrating the revived Grecian; three stages of columns and one of pilasters rising above each other, all in pure Grecian Corinthian.

PLATE IX.

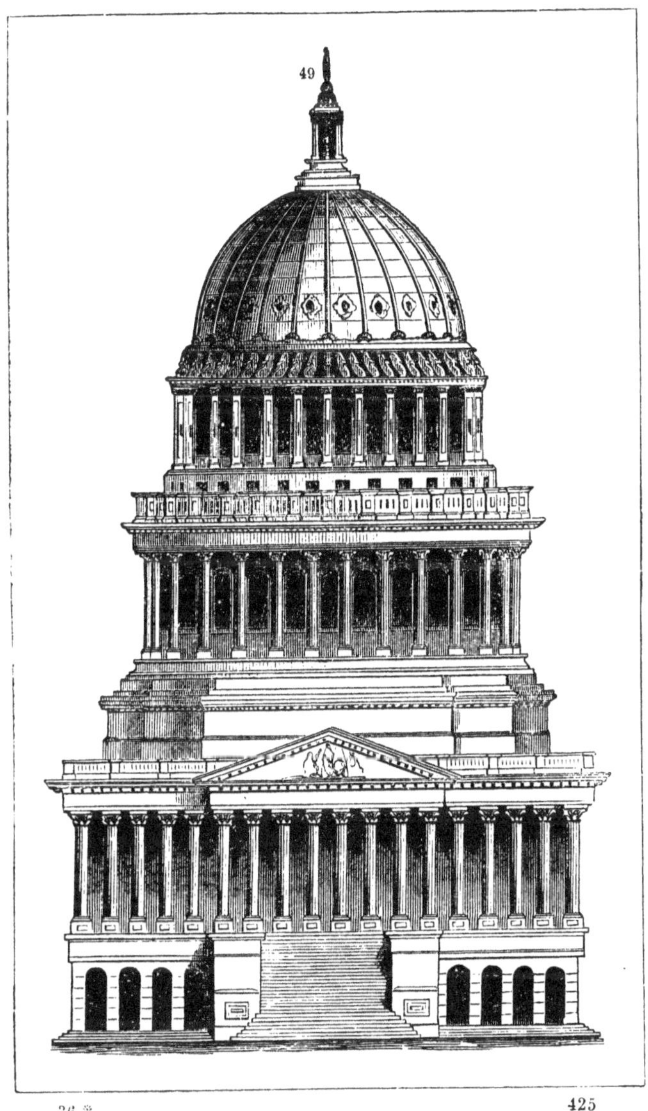

www.ingramcontent.com/pod-product-compliance
Lightning Source LLC
LaVergne TN
LVHW011148110826
845150LV00006B/1185